GREAT AMERICAN

★ ★ ★ ★

BRAND NAME
BAKING

PUBLICATIONS INTERNATIONAL, LTD.

ISBN: 1-56173-343-1

Library of Congress Catalog Card Number: 91-65677

Pictured on the front cover: Top row, left: Blueberry Orange Corn Muffins (page 18), Apple Nugget Muffins (page 23), Raspberry Apple Streusel Muffins (page 21), center: Sour Cherry Pie (page 178), right: Cheesecake Topped Brownies (page 226). Bottom row, left: New York Style Cheesecake (page 154), center: Cinnamon-Apricot Tart Oatmeal Cookies (page 78), Chocolate-Orange Chip Cookies (page 48), right: Chocolate Dream Torte (page 139).

Pictured on the back cover: Clockwise from top left: Ice Cream Cone Cakes (page 258), Star Christmas Tree Cookies (page 276), Chocolate and Cherry Braid (page 42).

Manufactured in the United States.

8 7 6 5 4 3 2

Contents

GUIDELINES FOR BAKING SUCCESS

There is nothing quite like the tantalizing aromas and luscious flavors of home-baked treats. These delightful recipes will help you discover, or rediscover, the many pleasures of baking.

From mile-high cakes to melt-in-your-mouth cookies, you can achieve baking success every time. The following guidelines will help you master all types of baking skills, including yeast breads and pie crusts. Each section focuses on a different baked treat and takes you from preparing to baking to storing. Even the most accomplished bakers will discover helpful tips to make their time in the kitchen easier and more enjoyable. Combine all this information with over 600 kitchen-tested recipes developed by your favorite brand name food companies, and you have an impressive collection of baking recipes to treasure for years to come.

GENERAL BAKING TIPS & TECHNIQUES

These tips and techniques lay the foundation of good baking skills because they apply to a wide variety of baking recipes.

• Read the entire recipe before beginning to make sure you have all the necessary ingredients and baking utensils.

• Remove butter, margarine and cream cheese from the refrigerator to soften, if necessary.

• Toast and chop nuts, pare and slice fruit, and melt chocolate before preparing the batter or dough.

• Measure all the ingredients accurately and assemble them in the order they are called for in the recipe.

• Use the pan size specified in the recipe. Prepare the pans according to the recipe directions.

• Adjust oven racks and preheat the oven. Check oven temperature for accuracy with an oven thermometer.

• Follow recipe directions and baking times exactly. Check for doneness using the test given in the recipe.

Measuring Ingredients

Dry Ingredients: Always use standardized measuring spoons and cups. Fill the correct measuring spoon or cup to overflowing and level it off with a metal spatula or knife.

When measuring flour, lightly spoon it into a measuring cup and then level it off. Do not tap or bang the measuring cup as this will pack the flour. If a recipe calls for "sifted flour," sift the flour before it is measured. If a recipe calls for "flour, sifted," measure the flour first and then sift it.

Liquid Ingredients: Use a standardized glass or plastic measuring cup with a pouring spout. Place the cup on a flat surface, fill to the desired mark and check the measurement at eye level.

When measuring sticky liquids such as honey and molasses, grease the measuring cup or spray it with vegetable cooking spray before adding the liquid to make their removal easier.

Beating Egg Whites

Separate eggs while they are cold because the yolk is firm and less likely to break. Let the whites sit out at room temperature for 30 minutes before beating in order to achieve their highest volume.

Make sure that the bowl and beaters you are using are clean and dry; any grease or yolk that is present will decrease the volume of the egg whites. For best results, use a copper, stainless steel or glass bowl (plastic bowls have an oily film, even after repeated washings).

Add a pinch of cream of tartar and salt to the egg whites after they have been beaten slightly and are foamy; this will prevent them from collapsing.

When a recipe calls for sugar, as for a meringue, add the sugar slowly to the egg whites, beating well after each addition. If the mixture feels grainy to the touch, continue beating before adding more. If the egg whites are to be folded into other ingredients, this should be done immediately after they are beaten.

Whipping Cream

Chill the beaters, bowl and cream for the best results. Beat the cream slowly, increasing speed as it thickens to prevent spattering. To sweeten the cream, add granulated or powdered sugar in small amounts while beating until you reach the desired sweetness. If possible, whip cream shortly before using to prevent separation. If whipped ahead of time, use a wire whisk to briefly remix, if necessary.

Folding Ingredients

Folding is a technique that combines two mixtures while retaining the air in the lighter mixture. Place about one-third of the lighter mixture (egg whites or whipped cream) on top of the heavier mixture. Using a rubber spatula, cut down through the center of the mixture, then sweep across the bottom of the bowl and up the side using a circular motion. Turn the bowl slightly and repeat until blended. Add the remaining airy mixture and continue folding until combined.

Melting Chocolate

Make sure the utensils used for melting are completely dry. Moisture makes the chocolate become stiff and grainy. If this happens, add ½ teaspoon shortening (not butter) for each ounce of chocolate and stir until smooth. Chocolate scorches easily, and once scorched cannot be used. Follow one of these three methods for successful melting.

Double Boiler: This is the safest method because it prevents scorching. Place the chocolate in the top of a double boiler or in a bowl over hot, not boiling, water; stir until smooth. (Make sure that the water remains just below a simmer and is one inch below the top pan.) Be careful that no steam or water gets into the chocolate.

Direct Heat: Place the chocolate in a heavy saucepan and melt over very low heat, stirring constantly. Remove the chocolate from the heat as soon as it is melted. Be sure to watch the chocolate carefully since it is easily scorched with this method.

Microwave Oven: Place an unwrapped 1-ounce square or 1 cup of chips in a small microwavable bowl. Microwave on High (100%) 1 to 1½ minutes, stirring after 1 minute. Stir the chocolate at 30-second intervals until smooth. Be sure to stir microwaved chocolate since it retains its original shape even when melted.

Toasting Nuts

Toasting nuts brings out their flavor and makes them crisp. Spread the nuts in a single layer on a rimmed baking sheet. Bake in a 325°F oven for 8 to 10 minutes or until golden. Shake the pan or stir the nuts occasionally during baking to ensure even toasting. The nuts will darken and become crisper as they cool. To toast a small amount of nuts, place them in a dry skillet over low heat. Stir constantly for 2 to 4 minutes, until the nuts darken slightly.

Toasting Coconut

Spread the flaked coconut in a thin layer on a rimmed baking sheet. Bake in a 325°F oven for 7 to 10 minutes. Shake the pan occasionally during baking to promote even browning and prevent burning.

Tinting Coconut

Dilute a few drops of food coloring with ½ teaspoon milk or water in a small bowl. Add 1 to 1⅓ cups flaked coconut and toss with a fork until evenly tinted.

QUICK BREADS

These breads are quick to make because they rely on quick-acting leavening agents such as baking soda, baking powder and eggs rather than yeast to make them rise. Quick breads include muffins, loaves, biscuits and scones.

Muffins

For most muffin recipes, combine the dry ingredients together first to evenly distribute the baking powder and/or baking soda. Next, combine the liquid ingredients and add them all at once to the dry ingredients. Stir just until the dry ingredients are moistened. The batter should be lumpy; the lumps will disappear during baking. Overbeating the batter will result in tunnels, peaked tops and a tough texture.

Standard size muffin pans have cups that are 2½ or 2¾ inches in diameter; giant muffin pans (often called Texas-size) have 4-inch diameter cups. Grease the cups or use paper baking liners and fill them ⅔ to ¾ full with batter. Pour water into any empty cups to prevent the pan from warping in the oven. Muffins are done when the center springs back when lightly touched and a wooden toothpick inserted into the center comes out clean and dry.

Remove muffins from their cups immediately after baking and cool them on a wire rack. They are best when served warm. Stored in an airtight plastic bag, muffins will stay fresh for several days. For longer storage, wrap and freeze. To reheat, wrap frozen muffins in foil and heat in a 350°F oven for 15 to 20 minutes. For best flavor, use frozen muffins within one month.

Quick Loaves

Some quick loaves are prepared the same way as muffins—the dry ingredients are quickly and lightly combined with the liquids to avoid overbeating. In some sweeter breads, the butter or shortening is creamed with the sugar and eggs, and then the dry ingredients are added. Pans are filled one-half to two-thirds full. The bread is done when it pulls away slightly from the sides of the pan and a wooden toothpick inserted into the center comes out clean and dry. Often a crack will form across the top of a quick loaf during baking; this is a perfectly normal occurrence.

Let the bread cool in the pan for about 10 minutes, then remove it to a wire rack. After the bread has cooled completely, it may be sliced. Wrap the loaves well and store at room temperature overnight to let the flavors develop. They will stay fresh for about one week. Well-wrapped loaves can be frozen for up to three months. Thaw the loaves unwrapped at room temperature. To reheat, cover loosely with foil and heat in a 350°F degree oven for about 10 minutes.

Biscuits and Scones

When preparing biscuits, cut the butter or shortening into the dry ingredients with a pastry blender or two knives until the mixture forms coarse crumbs. Blending the fat in any further produces mealy biscuits. Mix the dough gently and quickly to achieve light and tender results. Overworking the dough makes the biscuits tough. On a lightly floured surface, roll or pat out the dough to the desired thickness. Press a floured cutter straight down through the dough; twisting produces lopsided biscuits. For crusty biscuits, place them at least one inch apart on the baking sheet. For soft, fluffy biscuits, place them close together. Biscuits are best when served hot from the oven.

Scones are similar to biscuits, but the dough is richer due to the addition of cream and eggs. While the dough can be cut into any shape, scones are usually cut into wedges or triangles. They are traditionally served with butter, preserves and whipped cream.

YEAST BREADS

The wonderful flavors and aromas of homemade yeast breads far surpass the extra effort required to make them. Yeast is actually a live plant and requires a little more time and care to work its leavening magic. Yeast feeds on the sugar in the dough and produces carbon dioxide gas causing the dough to expand and rise. Yeast breads include traditional loaves, coffee cakes and dinner and sweet rolls.

Dissolving Yeast

Dissolve the yeast with a pinch of sugar in a warm liquid (105° to 115°F) such as milk or water. The warmth and sugar cause the yeast to grow and multiply. After about 5 minutes the yeast should start to foam and bubble. If it doesn't, start over as the yeast may no longer be active. It is best to use a thermometer to check the temperature of the liquid. If it is too hot, it will kill the yeast; if it is too cool, the yeast will not become activated. Also be sure to check the expiration date on the yeast packet; if it has expired the yeast may be inactive.

Some recipes call for mixing the yeast with other dry ingredients and then adding a very warm (120° to 130°F) liquid. This is simply another mixing method. The yeast will not be killed by the warmer liquid because it is mixed in with other ingredients.

Kneading

Although bread dough starts out soft and sticky, it becomes smooth and elastic when kneaded. The purpose of kneading is to develop the gluten, a protein present in flour. The gluten forms long elastic strands in the dough that trap carbon dioxide gas produced by the yeast. It is the trapped gas that causes the bread to rise.

To knead, shape the dough into a ball and place on a lightly floured surface. Fold the dough in half toward you, and using the heel of your hand, press it away from you. Give the dough a quarter turn and continue folding, pushing and turning. As you knead, it may be necessary to add more flour to prevent the dough from sticking to your hands and the work surface. (Sweet yeast doughs used in coffee cakes contain butter and eggs that make the dough even stickier.) After about 10 minutes the dough should become smooth, shiny and elastic with air bubbles or blisters appearing just below the surface.

Rising

Shape the kneaded dough into a ball and place in a lightly oiled bowl; turn the ball to coat the entire surface with oil. This prevents the bread from forming a crust that could hinder rising. Cover the bowl with a cloth towel and set it in a warm (80° to 85°F), draft-free place. A gas oven with the pilot light on, or an electric oven that has been heated for 1 minute and then turned off are good places. Let the dough rise until it has doubled in size, usually about 1 hour. One way to test if the dough has doubled is to press two fingertips about ½ inch into the dough; the indentations should remain when you remove your fingers.

Shaping and Second Rising

After the dough has doubled, punch it down with your fist. This removes large air bubbles, giving the bread a fine, even texture. Pull the edges of the dough to the center to form a ball. Shape the dough according to the recipe directions and place on a greased baking sheet or in a greased loaf pan. Cover the shaped loaves and let them rise again in a warm place until they have doubled in size, about 1 hour. (Do *not* use your fingertips to test if the loaf has doubled; judge this by appearance.)

Baking

Place the bread on the center rack of a preheated oven. The bread is done when it is golden brown, well-rounded, and sounds hollow when lightly tapped. For a crisp crust, place a pan of water in the bottom of the oven during baking, or brush the top of the loaf with water. For a softer crust, brush the loaves with softened butter immediately after baking.

Cooling and Storing

Immediately remove the bread from the pan or baking sheet and place it on a wire rack to cool. Once the bread has cooled completely, wrap it in plastic wrap or place in an airtight plastic bag. Store the bread at room temperature; placing it in the refrigerator actually causes it to become stale faster. If it is well wrapped, bread can be frozen for up to six months. Freeze coffee cakes before adding glazes or icings; frost them after thawing. Thaw unwrapped yeast breads at room temperature for 2 to 3 hours; or heat them partially unwrapped in a 375°F oven for 20 minutes.

COOKIES

The word cookie comes from the Dutch word, "koekje," meaning "little cake." The Dutch brought these little cakes to their first settlements in America, and they have been popular ever since. With so many flavors, shapes and sizes to choose from, cookies have definitely earned their place as America's favorite snack food.

Preparation Tips

Chill cookie dough before rolling or shaping it. This makes it much easier to handle. Remove only the amount of dough from the refrigerator that you will work with at one time. When making cut-out cookies, save any trimmings and re-roll them all at once to prevent the dough from becoming tough.

Cookies that are uniform in size and shape will finish baking at the same time. To easily shape drop cookies into a uniform size, use an ice cream scoop with a release bar. The bar usually has a number on it indicating the number of scoops that can be made from one quart of ice cream. The handiest size for cookies is a #80 or #90 scoop. This will yield about one rounded teaspoonful of dough for each cookie.

When baking brownies and bar cookies, always use the pan size called for in the recipe. Substituting a different pan will affect the texture. A smaller pan will give the bars a more cake-like texture and a larger pan will produce a flatter bar with a drier texture.

Baking

The best cookie sheets to use are those with little or no sides. They allow the heat to circulate easily during baking and achieve even browning. Another way to achieve even baking and browning is to place only one cookie sheet at a time in the center of the oven. If using more than one sheet at a time, or if your oven has uneven heat distribution, turn the cookie sheets halfway through the baking time.

When a recipe calls for greasing the cookie sheets, use shortening or a vegetable cooking spray for best results. Lining the cookie sheets with parchment paper is an alternative to greasing. It eliminates clean-up, bakes the cookies more evenly and allows them to cool right on the paper instead of on wire racks.

Allow cookie sheets to cool between batches; the dough will spread if placed on a hot cookie sheet.

Most cookies bake quickly and should be watched carefully to avoid overbaking. Check them at the minimum baking time, then watch carefully to make sure they don't burn. It is generally better to slightly underbake, rather than to overbake cookies.

Most cookies should be removed from cookie sheets immediately after baking and placed in a single layer on wire racks to cool. Fragile cookies may need to cool slightly on the cookie sheet before being moved. Always cool cookies completely before stacking and storing. Bar cookies may be cooled and stored right in the baking pan.

Storing

Unbaked cookie dough can be refrigerated for up to two weeks or frozen for up to six weeks. Rolls of dough should be sealed tightly in plastic wrap; other doughs should be stored in airtight containers. Label dough with baking information for convenience.

Store soft and crisp cookies separately at room temperature to prevent changes in texture and flavor. Keep soft cookies in airtight containers. If they begin to dry out, add a piece of apple or bread to the container to help them retain moisture. Store crisp cookies in containers with loose-fitting lids to prevent moisture buildup. If they become soggy, heat undecorated cookies in a 300°F oven for 3 to 5 minutes to restore crispness. Store cookies with sticky glazes, fragile decorations and icings in single layers between sheets of waxed paper.

As a rule, crisp cookies freeze better than soft, moist cookies. Brownies are an exception to this rule since they freeze extremely well. Freeze baked cookies in airtight containers or freezer bags for up to six months. Thaw unwrapped cookies and brownies at room temperature. Meringue-based cookies do *not* freeze well and chocolate-dipped cookies will discolor if frozen.

CAKES

Cakes are divided into two basic categories according to what makes them rise. Butter cakes rely primarily on baking powder or baking soda for height while sponge cakes depend on the air trapped in the eggs during beating. Tortes are multi-layered cakes with rich fillings and are often made with little or no flour. Some cake recipes specifically call for cake flour. Cake flour contains less protein than all-purpose flour and produces a more tender cake.

Butter Cakes

Butter cakes include pound cakes and yellow, white, spice and chocolate layer cakes. These cakes use butter, shortening or oil for moistness and richness and are leavened with baking powder and/or baking soda. Before mixing the batter, soften the butter so that it mixes easily with the sugar.

Sponge Cakes

These cakes achieve their high volume from beaten eggs rather than a leavening agent like baking powder. Sponge cakes do not contain butter, oil or shortening. Angel food cakes are the most popular and are literally fat-free since they use only egg whites, not yolks. Yellow sponge cakes are prepared with whole eggs. Chiffon cakes are also lightened with beaten eggs, but they are not true sponge cakes because they contain vegetable oil. When preparing sponge cakes, be sure to beat the eggs to the proper stage; do not over- or underbeat them. Handle the beaten eggs gently when folding the other ingredients into them or they will lose air and volume. (See Folding Ingredients on page 6.)

Preparing Pans

Always use the exact pan size called for in the recipe. If the pan is too large, the cake will not rise properly or brown evenly. If the pan is too small, the cake will sink in the middle and the texture will be coarse; the batter may also run over the top of the pan during baking.

For butter cakes, grease and flour the pans before mixing the cake batter so that the cake can be baked immediately. To grease and flour cake pans, use a paper towel, waxed paper or your fingers to apply a thin, even layer of shortening. Sprinkle flour into the greased pan; shake or tilt the pan to coat evenly with flour, then tap lightly to remove any excess. To line pans with paper, trace the bottom of the cake pan onto a piece of waxed or parchment paper and cut to fit. Grease the pan, but *do not* flour it. Press the paper onto the bottom of the greased pan.

Sponge cakes are usually baked in tube pans. The center tube helps the heat circulate during baking and also supports the delicate structure of the cake. *Do not* grease the pans for sponge cakes. The ungreased pan lets the batter cling to the sides as it rises.

Baking

Place the cake pan(s) in the center of a preheated oven. Oven racks may need to be set lower for cakes baked in tube pans. If two racks are used, arrange them so they divide the oven into thirds and then stagger the pans so they are not directly over each other. Avoid opening the oven door during the first half of the baking time. The oven temperature must remain constant in order for the cake to rise properly.

A butter cake is done when it begins to pull away from the sides of the pan, the top springs back when lightly touched and a cake tester or wooden toothpick inserted into the center comes out clean and dry. A sponge cake is done when it is delicately browned and the top springs back when lightly touched.

Cooling

After removing butter cakes from the oven, let them stand in their pans on wire racks for 10 minutes, or as the recipe directs. Run a knife around the edge of the cake to loosen it from the sides of the pan and invert it onto a wire rack. Remove the paper liner from the cake if one was used. Turn the cake top-side up onto a second rack to finish cooling.

Invert a sponge cake baked in a tube pan onto a funnel or bottle immediately after removing it from the oven. If it is cooled top side up, it will fall. Do not remove a sponge cake from the pan until it is completely cool.

Frosting

Make sure the cake is completely cool before frosting it. Brush off any loose crumbs from the cake's surface. To keep the cake plate clean, place small pieces of waxed paper under the edges of the cake; remove them after the cake has been frosted. For best results, use a flat metal spatula for applying frosting. You will achieve a more professional look if you first apply a thin layer of frosting on the cake as a base coat to help seal in any remaining crumbs.

Storing

Store one-layer cakes in their baking pan, tightly covered. Store two- or three-layer cakes in a cake-saver or under a large inverted bowl. If the cake has a fluffy or cooked frosting, insert a teaspoon handle under the edge of the cover to prevent an airtight seal and moisture buildup. Cakes with whipped cream frostings or cream fillings should be stored in the refrigerator. Unfrosted cakes can be frozen for up to four months if well wrapped in plastic. Thaw in their wrapping at room temperature. Frosted cakes should be frozen unwrapped until the frosting hardens, and then wrapped and sealed;

freeze for up to two months. To thaw, remove the wrapping and thaw at room temperature or in the refrigerator. Cakes with fruit or custard fillings do not freeze well as they become soggy when thawed.

Cheesecakes

Soften cream cheese before beginning the recipe. It will then combine easily with other ingredients and prevent lumps from forming in the batter. Beat cheesecake batter gently. Overbeating can cause the cheesecake to crack. Another common cause of cracks is overbaking. A simple doneness test is to gently shake the cheesecake—a 1-inch area in the center of the cheesecake should jiggle slightly. This area will firm during cooling. After baking, run a knife around the inside of the pan to loosen the edges of the crust. Let cool and then refrigerate for several hours before removing the rim of the pan. Cheesecakes can be stored in the refrigerator for up to one week, but for the best flavor, bring them to room temperature before serving. Cheesecakes are not recommended for freezing.

PIES AND TARTS

Making flaky tender pie crusts can now be as easy as—pie! These few simple guidelines for combining ingredients and handling dough will ensure perfect pastry every time. Be sure to see pages 166–167 in the Pies & Tarts chapter for step-by-step photos of preparing pastry and fluting decorative edges. Tarts are similar to single-crust pies and are baked in a fluted pan with shallow sides and a removable bottom.

Preparing Pastry

For tender, flaky pie crusts, follow these two basic rules: 1) keep the ingredients cold and 2) handle the dough as little as possible. Tough crusts are the result of overdeveloping gluten, a protein present in flour. Following these rules helps prevent the development of gluten.

If you use butter in your pastry dough, it must be chilled. If the butter is soft, it cannot distribute evenly throughout the flour. Vegetable shortening and lard, although soft at room temperature, do not need to be chilled. Also make sure that the liquid you add is cold. The cold liquid keeps the fat solid.

Blend the flour and salt together, then cut the fat in quickly with a pastry blender, two knives or your fingertips until the fat particles are about the size of peas. Add cold water gradually, 1 tablespoon at a time, stirring lightly with a fork.

Add just enough water so that the mixture holds together with slight pressure and can be gathered into a ball. Too little water produces a dry, crumbly pastry that will not hold together, and too much water makes the dough sticky and develops the gluten. Avoid overworking the dough or the pastry will be tough. Wrap the ball of dough in plastic wrap and refrigerate it for at least 1 hour. Chilling the dough makes it easier to handle and helps prevent shrinkage during baking.

Rolling

Place the chilled dough on a lightly floured surface and flatten it into a 1/2-inch-thick circle. Roll the dough with a floured rolling pin, pressing out from the center to the edge using quick, short strokes. Continue rolling until the dough is 1/8 inch thick and 2 inches larger than the inverted pie pan.

Loosely fold the dough into quarters and place the point of the folded dough into the center of the pie pan. Gently unfold the dough and ease it into the pan; do not stretch the dough or it will shrink during baking. For a single-crust pie, trim the dough and flute the edge.

Baking

Single-Crust Pies: Some single-crust pies, like custard pies, are baked in an unbaked pastry shell. Others require the shell to be prebaked so that it does not become soggy. If the pastry shell is to be baked "blind" (without the filling), prick the dough all over with a fork. Line the pastry with aluminum foil, waxed paper or parchment paper and spread dried beans or peas, or pie weights over the bottom. Weighing down the pastry prevents it from puffing and losing its shape during baking. (The dried beans are not edible after baking, but you can reuse them for blind baking.) The pastry can be fully or partially baked in this manner. Cool completely before adding the filling.

Double-Crust Pies: These pies are made by placing the filling (usually fruit) between two unbaked layers of pastry. Spoon the filling into the pastry shell and brush the rim of the shell with water. Roll out the top crust and place it over the filling. Press the pastry edges together to seal, then trim and flute. Cut a few slits or vents in the top crust to allow steam to escape. Before baking a double-crust pie, try glazing the top crust with milk or cream to promote browning. Brushing it with beaten egg will add color and shine; sprinkling it with granulated sugar will add a little sparkle.

If the top crust or edges of the pie shell are browning too quickly, cover the pie loosely with aluminum foil and continue baking.

Storing

Meringue-topped pies are best when served the day they are made; refrigerate any leftovers. Refrigerate custard or cream pies immediately after cooling. Fruit pies can be covered and stored at room temperature overnight; refrigerate them for longer storage.

To freeze unbaked pies, do not cut steam vents in the top crust. Cover the top with an inverted paper plate for extra protection and package in freezer bags or freezer wrap. To bake, do not thaw. Cut slits in the top crust and allow an

additional 15 to 20 minutes of baking time. Baked pies can also be cooled and frozen. To serve, let the pie thaw at room temperature for 2 hours, then heat until warm. Pies with cream or custard fillings and meringue toppings are not recommended for freezing.

Unbaked pie dough can be frozen in bulk for later use. Simply flatten the dough into circles and stack them in a freezer bag with waxed paper separating each layer. Freeze prepared pastry shells in pie pans with waxed paper between the shells. Bulk pie dough must be thawed before using while pastry shells should be baked frozen.

DESSERTS

Bread puddings and custards, cream puffs and fruit cobblers—desserts cover a wide range of sweets. Although many are long-time favorites, some of the techniques used may be new to you. These desserts can be better than you remember with only a quick review of some helpful tips.

Cobblers and Crisps

Always use the size dish called for in the recipe to allow room for the filling to bubble during baking. These desserts taste best when served warm. Ice cream or whipped cream are wonderful topping additions.

Bread Puddings

Always use the type of bread called for in the recipe. Substituting a different bread can affect the amount of liquid that is absorbed. The pudding is done when a knife inserted in the center comes out clean.

Store leftover cobblers, crisps and bread puddings in the refrigerator for up to two days. Reheat them, covered, in a 350°F oven until warm.

Baked Custards and Puddings

When preparing baked custards and puddings, beat the eggs just until blended. Do not beat until foamy to avoid bubbles on the baked surface.

Baking the custards and puddings in a hot water bath is an important step. The bath provides a constant, steady heat source, ensuring even, slow cooking. To test for doneness, insert a knife near the edge of the cup. If the blade comes out clean, it is done and should be removed from the water bath immediately in order to stop the cooking process. If overcooked or cooked without a hot water bath, the custard or pudding will become rubbery. Once cooled, store covered in the refrigerator and serve within two to three days.

Cream Puffs

Fill cream puffs no sooner than 1 hour before serving, or they will become soggy. The filling can be made ahead of time and refrigerated until ready to use.

To fill cream puffs, cut a small hole in one end and fill using a pastry bag. Or, slice the top off, spoon the filling in and replace the top. Dust the filled cream puffs with powdered sugar or glaze with an icing.

WEIGHTS AND MEASURES

Dash = less than 1/8 teaspoon

1/2 tablespoon = 1 1/2 teaspoons

1 tablespoon = 3 teaspoons

2 tablespoons = 1/8 cup

1/4 cup = 4 tablespoons

1/3 cup = 5 tablespoons plus 1 teaspoon

1/2 cup = 8 tablespoons

3/4 cup = 12 tablespoons

1 cup = 16 tablespoons

1/2 pint = 1 cup or 8 fluid ounces

1 pint = 2 cups or 16 fluid ounces

1 quart = 4 cups or 2 pints or 32 fluid ounces

1 gallon = 16 cups or 4 quarts

1 pound = 16 ounces

EQUIVALENTS

Almonds, blanched, slivered	4 oz. = 1 cup
Apples	1 medium = 1 cup sliced
Bananas	1 medium, mashed = $1/3$ cup
Coconut, flaked	$3^1/2$ oz. = $1^1/3$ cups
Cranberries	12 oz. = 3 cups

Flour
   White or all-purpose   1 lb. = $3^1/2$ to 4 cups
   Whole-wheat   1 lb. = $3^3/4$ to 4 cups

Lemon	1 medium = 1 to 3 tablespoons juice and 2 to 3 teaspoons grated rind
Oranges	1 medium = 6 to 8 tablespoons juice and 2 to 3 tablespoons grated rind
Peaches	1 lb. or 4 medium = 2 cups sliced
Pears	1 lb. or 4 medium = 2 cups sliced
Pecans, shelled	1 lb. = 4 cups halved or $3^1/2$ to 4 cups chopped
Strawberries, fresh	1 quart = $3^1/2$ to 4 cups sliced

Sugar
   Granulated   1 lb. = $2^1/2$ cups
   Brown, packed   1 lb. = $2^1/4$ cups
   Confectioners' or powdered   1 lb. = $3^3/4$ to 4 cups, unsifted

Walnuts, chopped	$4^1/2$ oz. = 1 cup
Whipping cream	1 cup = 2 cups whipped

SUBSTITUTION LIST

If You Don't Have:	Use:
1 teaspoon baking powder	¼ teaspoon baking soda + ½ teaspoon cream of tartar
½ cup firmly packed brown sugar	½ cup granulated sugar mixed with 2 tablespoons molasses
1 cup buttermilk	1 tablespoon lemon juice or vinegar plus milk to equal 1 cup (Stir; let mixture stand 5 minutes.)
1 ounce (1 square) unsweetened baking chocolate	3 tablespoons unsweetened cocoa + 1 tablespoon shortening
3 ounces (3 squares) semi-sweet baking chocolate	3 ounces (½ cup) semi-sweet chocolate morsels
½ cup corn syrup	½ cup granulated sugar + 2 tablespoons liquid
1 tablespoon cornstarch	2 tablespoons all-purpose flour *or* 4 teaspoons quick-cooking tapioca
1 cup sweetened whipped cream	4½ oz. frozen whipped topping, thawed
1 cup heavy cream (for baking, not whipping)	¾ cup whole milk plus ¼ cup butter
1 whole egg	2 egg yolks + 1 tablespoon water
1 cup cake flour	1 cup *minus* 2 tablespoons all-purpose flour
1 cup honey	1¼ cups granulated sugar + ¼ cup water
1 teaspoon freshly grated orange or lemon peel	½ teaspoon dried peel
1 teaspoon apple or pumpkin pie spice	Combine: ½ teaspoon cinnamon, ¼ teaspoon nutmeg and ⅛ teaspoon *each* allspice and cardamom
1 package active dry yeast	1 cake compressed yeast

SOLUTIONS TO COMMON BAKING PROBLEMS

Problems:	Solutions:
QUICK BREADS	
Tough, tunnels, peaked tops	Avoid overstirring; batter should be lumpy.
Raisins or other dried fruit sink	Toss fruit lightly with flour before adding to batter.
YEAST BREADS	
Bread is heavy and compact	Liquid used to dissolve yeast may have been too hot or too cold; check temperature with thermometer.
	Too much flour was added during kneading; do not exceed maximum amount called for in recipe.
Bread is crumbly	Dough has risen too much. Let rise just until double for first rising; until nearly double for second rising.
Bread has large holes	Press or punch air bubbles out of dough thoroughly before shaping.
COOKIES	
Uneven browning	Bake on one oven rack at a time; use cookie sheets with no sides.
Cookies spread too much	Allow cookie sheets to cool between batches before reusing. If dough is too soft, chill slightly before baking. Avoid overgreasing cookie sheets.
Cut-out cookies are tough	Save dough scraps to reroll all at once; handle dough as little as possible. Use just enough flour on board to prevent sticking.
CAKES & CHEESECAKES	
Cake falls in middle	Avoid overbeating—too much air is incorporated into batter. Avoid opening oven door before cake sets.
Cake peaks in center	Oven temperature may be too high and cake will rise too quickly; use oven thermometer to check for accuracy.
Cake is dry	Avoid overbeating egg whites.
	Avoid overbaking. Check for doneness at minimum baking time.
Cheesecake cracks	Avoid overbeating; too much air is incorporated into batter causing cheesecake to rise up, then fall and crack.
	Loosen rim of pan exactly as recipe directs to prevent cheesecake pulling away from sides and cracking.
PIE CRUSTS	
Pastry is crumbly	Add more water, 1 teaspoon at a time, stirring lightly.
Pastry is tough	Avoid overworking dough; mix just until evenly moistened.
Crust shrinks excessively	Roll pastry from the center outward; roll to an even thickness.
	Avoid stretching pastry when transferring to pie plate.

BREADS & COFFEE CAKES

Home-baked breads scent your kitchen with enticing aromas. Whip up a batch of golden fruit-filled breakfast muffins, or try your hand at baking a crusty loaf for sandwiches. Buttery coffee cakes and gooey sweet rolls make brunches extra special. And super-easy quick loaves are perfect for snacking or alongside soups and salads. (For additional bread and coffee cake recipes, see the Jump-Start Baking and Festive Holiday Baking chapters.)

Homestyle Blueberry Muffins

> 1 (8 oz.) pkg. PHILADELPHIA BRAND® Cream Cheese, softened
> 1/4 cup sugar
> 1 egg yolk
> 1 teaspoon vanilla
> 1 (23.5 oz.) pkg. bakery style blueberry muffin mix
> 3/4 cup water
> 1 egg
> 1 teaspoon grated lemon peel
> 1 teaspoon cinnamon

- Preheat oven to 400°F.
- Beat cream cheese, sugar, egg yolk and vanilla in small mixing bowl at medium speed with electric mixer until well blended.
- Rinse and drain blueberries. Stir together muffin mix, water, egg and lemon peel in large bowl (mixture will be lumpy). Fold in blueberries.
- Pour muffin batter into well-greased medium-sized muffin pan. Spoon cream cheese mixture over batter; sprinkle with combined topping mix and cinnamon.
- Bake 18 to 22 minutes or until lightly browned. Cool 5 minutes. Loosen muffins from rim of pan; cool before removing from pan.

Makes 1 dozen muffins

Prep time: 20 minutes
Cooking time: 22 minutes

Blueberry Orange Corn Muffins

> 1/3 cup margarine or butter, softened
> 1/2 cup sugar
> 2 to 3 teaspoons grated orange peel
> 3/4 cup MOTT'S® Regular Apple Sauce
> 1 egg
> 1 cup all-purpose flour
> 1/2 cup cornmeal
> 1/2 teaspoon baking powder
> 1/2 teaspoon baking soda
> 1/4 teaspoon salt
> 1 cup fresh blueberries

Preheat oven to 375°F. Grease bottoms only of 12 muffin cups or line with paper baking cups. In large bowl, beat margarine and sugar until fluffy. Add orange peel, apple sauce and egg; blend well. Stir in flour, cornmeal, baking powder, baking soda and salt. Blend just until dry ingredients are moistened. Gently stir in blueberries. Fill prepared muffin cups 2/3 full. Bake 20 to 25 minutes or until toothpick inserted in center comes out clean. Cool 5 minutes; remove from pan. Serve warm.

Makes 12 muffins

Top to bottom: Homestyle Blueberry Muffins, Caramel Pecan Sticky Buns (page 40)

Blueberry Yogurt Muffins

**2 cups QUAKER® Oat Bran
    Hot Cereal, uncooked
¹/₄ cup firmly packed brown
    sugar
2 teaspoons baking powder
1 carton (8 oz.) plain low fat
    yogurt
2 egg whites, slightly beaten
¹/₄ cup skim milk
¹/₄ cup honey
2 tablespoons vegetable oil
1 teaspoon grated lemon
    peel
¹/₂ cup fresh or frozen
    blueberries**

Preheat oven to 425°F. Line 12 medium muffin cups with paper baking cups. Combine oat bran, brown sugar and baking powder. Add combined yogurt, egg whites, skim milk, honey, oil and lemon peel, mixing just until moistened. Fold in blueberries. Fill muffin cups almost full. Bake 18 to 20 minutes or until golden brown.

Makes 12 muffins

Two Tone Muffins

**2 cups all-purpose flour
¹/₂ cup sugar
1 tablespoon baking powder
1 teaspoon salt
³/₄ cup toasted chopped
    almonds
³/₄ cup orange juice
¹/₃ cup almond or vegetable
    oil
1 egg, beaten
¹/₄ cup unsweetened cocoa
1 teaspoon grated orange
    peel**

Preheat oven to 400°F. Paper-line 12 (2¹/₂-inch) muffin cups. In large bowl, combine flour, sugar, baking powder and salt. Stir in almonds, reserving some for garnish. In small bowl, combine orange juice, oil and egg. Stir into flour mixture just until moistened. Transfer ¹/₂ of the batter into another small bowl;

stir in cocoa and set aside. Stir orange peel into remaining batter.

Carefully spoon orange batter into one side of each cup. Fill other side with cocoa batter. Sprinkle reserved almonds over tops. Bake 20 minutes or until wooden pick inserted in center comes out clean. Remove from pan. Serve warm.

Makes 12 muffins

*Favorite recipe from **Almond Board of California***

Walnut Streusel Muffins

**3 cups all-purpose flour
1¹/₂ cups packed brown sugar
³/₄ cup butter or margarine
1 cup chopped DIAMOND®
    Walnuts
2 teaspoons baking powder
1 teaspoon *each* ground
    nutmeg and ginger
¹/₂ teaspoon *each* baking soda
    and salt
1 cup buttermilk or sour milk
2 eggs, beaten**

Preheat oven to 350°F. In medium bowl, combine 2 cups of the flour and the sugar; cut in butter to form fine crumbs. In small bowl, combine ³/₄ cup of the crumbs and ¹/₄ cup of the walnuts; set aside. Into remaining crumb mixture, stir in remaining 1 cup flour, the baking powder, spices, soda, salt and remaining ³/₄ cup walnuts. In another small bowl, combine buttermilk and eggs; stir into dry ingredients just to moisten. Spoon into 18 greased or paper-lined 2³/₄-inch muffin cups, filling about ²/₃ full. Top each with a generous spoonful of reserved crumb-nut mixture. Bake 20 to 25 minutes or until springy to the touch. Cool in pans 10 minutes. Loosen and remove from pans. Serve warm.

Makes 1¹/₂ dozen muffins

Streusel Raspberry Muffins

**Pecan Streusel Topping
    (recipe follows)
1¹/₂ cups all-purpose flour
¹/₂ cup sugar
2 teaspoons baking powder
¹/₂ cup milk
¹/₂ cup butter or margarine,
    melted
1 egg, beaten
1 cup fresh or individually
    frozen, whole unsugared
    raspberries**

Preheat oven to 375°F. Grease or paper-line 12 (2¹/₂-inch) muffin cups. Prepare Pecan Streusel Topping; set aside.

In large bowl, combine flour, sugar and baking powder. In small bowl, combine milk, butter and egg until blended. Stir into flour mixture just until moistened. Spoon ¹/₂ of the batter into muffin cups. Divide raspberries among cups, then top with remaining batter. Sprinkle Pecan Streusel Topping over tops. Bake 25 to 30 minutes or until golden and wooden pick inserted in center comes out clean. Remove from pan.

Makes 12 muffins

PECAN STREUSEL TOPPING: In small bowl, combine ¹/₄ cup *each* chopped pecans, packed brown sugar and all-purpose flour. Add 2 tablespoons melted butter or margarine, stirring until mixture resembles moist crumbs.

Streusel Raspberry Muffins

Raspberry Apple Streusel Muffins

Batter:
   2 cups all-purpose flour
   1/2 cup sugar
   2 teaspoons baking powder
   1/2 teaspoon baking soda
   1/2 teaspoon salt
   1 cup MOTT'S® Regular or Natural Apple Sauce
   1/2 cup vegetable oil
   1 teaspoon grated lemon peel
   2 eggs
   1 cup fresh or frozen raspberries
Topping:
   1/3 cup sugar
   1/4 cup flour
   2 tablespoons margarine or butter

Preheat oven to 400°F. Grease bottoms only of 12 muffin cups or line with paper baking cups. For batter, in large bowl, combine flour, sugar, baking powder, baking soda and salt; mix well. In small bowl, combine apple sauce, oil, lemon peel and eggs; blend well. Add to dry ingredients; stir just until moistened. Carefully fold in raspberries. Fill prepared muffin cups 3/4 full. In small bowl, combine all topping ingredients. Sprinkle over batter.

Bake 18 to 20 minutes or until light brown and toothpick inserted in center comes out clean. Cool 5 minutes; remove from pan. Serve warm.

Makes 12 muffins

Clockwise from top: Apple Nugget Muffins (page 23), Raspberry Apple Streusel Muffins, Blueberry Orange Corn Muffins (page 18)

Morning Muffins

   2 3/4 cups QUAKER® Crunchy Bran Cereal, finely crushed to 1 cup
   1 1/2 cups all-purpose flour
   1/3 cup packed brown sugar
   4 teaspoons baking powder
   1 teaspoon ground cinnamon
   1 cup chopped pitted prunes
   1 1/4 cups 2% low-fat milk
   1/3 cup vegetable oil
   1 egg

Preheat oven to 400°F. Grease or paper-line 12 (2 1/2-inch) muffin cups. In large bowl, combine cereal, flour, brown sugar, baking powder and cinnamon. Stir in prunes. In small bowl, combine milk, oil and egg. Add to flour mixture, stirring just until moistened. Fill muffin cups almost full. Bake 25 minutes or until wooden pick inserted in center comes out clean. Cool in pan on wire rack 5 minutes. Remove from pan. Cool on wire rack.   *Makes 12 muffins*

Orange Coconut Muffins

   3/4 cup all-purpose flour
   3/4 cup whole wheat flour
   2/3 cup toasted wheat germ
   1/2 cup sugar
   1/2 cup coconut
   1 1/2 teaspoons baking soda
   1/2 teaspoon salt
   1 cup dairy sour cream
   2 eggs
   1 can (11 ounces) mandarin oranges, drained
   1/2 cup chopped nuts

Preheat oven to 400°F. In large bowl, combine flours, wheat germ, sugar, coconut, baking soda and salt. In small bowl, blend sour cream, eggs and oranges. Stir into flour mixture just until moistened. Fold in nuts. Spoon into buttered 2 1/2-inch muffin cups, filling 3/4 full. Bake 18 to 20 minutes or until wooden pick inserted in center comes out clean. Remove from pan. Cool on wire rack.

Makes about 12 muffins

*Favorite recipe from **Wisconsin Milk Marketing Board** © 1991*

Double Oat Muffins

Double Oat Muffins

**2 cups QUAKER® Oat Bran
Hot Cereal, uncooked
1/3 cup firmly packed brown
sugar
1/4 cup all-purpose flour
2 teaspoons baking powder
1/4 teaspoon salt (optional)
1/4 teaspoon nutmeg (optional)
1 cup skim milk
2 egg whites, slightly beaten
3 tablespoons vegetable oil
1 1/2 teaspoons vanilla
1/4 cup QUAKER® Oats (quick
or old fashioned,
uncooked)
1 tablespoon firmly packed
brown sugar**

Preheat oven to 400°F. Line 12
medium muffin cups with paper
baking cups. Combine oat bran,
1/3 cup brown sugar, flour, baking
powder, salt and nutmeg. Add
combined milk, egg whites, oil
and vanilla, mixing just until
moistened. Fill muffin cups
almost full. Combine oats and
remaining 1 tablespoon brown
sugar; sprinkle evenly over
batter. Bake 20 to 22 minutes or
until golden brown.

Makes 12 muffins

Microwave Directions: Line 6
microwaveable muffin cups with
double paper baking cups.
Prepare batter as above. Fill
muffin cups almost full.
Combine oats and remaining 1
tablespoon brown sugar; sprinkle
evenly over batter. Microwave at
HIGH 2 minutes 30 seconds to 3
minutes or until wooden pick
inserted in center comes out
clean. Remove from pan; cool 5
minutes before serving. Line
muffin cups with additional
double paper baking cups.
Repeat procedure with
remaining batter.

Apple Nugget Muffins

½ cup margarine or butter, softened
½ cup firmly packed brown sugar
1½ cups MOTT'S® Natural Apple Sauce
¼ cup milk
1 teaspoon vanilla
2 eggs
1½ cups all-purpose flour
½ cup whole wheat flour
1 teaspoon baking powder
1 teaspoon baking soda
¼ teaspoon salt
1 cup chopped walnuts
1 cup grated apple
½ cup raisins

Preheat oven to 375°F. Grease bottoms only of 12 muffin cups or line with paper baking cups. In large bowl, beat margarine and brown sugar until fluffy. Add apple sauce, milk, vanilla and eggs; blend well. Stir in all-purpose flour, whole wheat flour, baking powder, baking soda and salt. Blend just until dry ingredients are moistened; stir in walnuts, apple and raisins. Fill prepared muffin cups.
Bake 20 to 25 minutes or until toothpick inserted in center comes out clean. Cool 5 minutes; remove from pan.
Makes 12 muffins

Apple Cheddar Muffins

1 egg, lightly beaten
½ cup milk
¼ cup vegetable oil
1 cup applesauce
¼ cup sugar
1½ cups flour
2 teaspoons baking powder
½ teaspoon salt
½ teaspoon ground cinnamon
½ cup (2 oz.) SARGENTO® Shredded Mild or Sharp Cheddar Cheese

Preheat oven to 400°F. In large bowl, combine egg, milk, oil, applesauce and sugar. In small bowl, sift flour, baking powder, salt and cinnamon together. Add dry ingredients with Cheddar cheese to liquid mixture, stirring just until moistened. (Batter will be lumpy; do not overmix.)
Spoon batter evenly into 12 greased muffin cups, filling each cup more than ⅔ full. Bake 20 minutes or until golden brown. Cool in pan 5 minutes. Loosen and remove from pan; cool completely on wire rack.
Makes 12 muffins

Banana Scotch Muffins

1 ripe, large DOLE® Banana, peeled
1 egg, beaten
½ cup sugar
¼ cup milk
¼ cup vegetable oil
1 teaspoon vanilla
1 cup all-purpose flour
1 cup quick-cooking rolled oats, uncooked
1 teaspoon baking powder
½ teaspoon baking soda
½ teaspoon salt
½ cup butterscotch chips

Preheat oven to 400°F. Puree banana in blender (⅔ cup). In medium bowl, combine pureed banana, egg, sugar, milk, oil and vanilla. In large bowl, combine flour, oats, baking powder, baking soda and salt. Stir banana mixture into dry ingredients with butterscotch chips until just blended. Spoon into well-greased 2½-inch muffin cups. Bake 12 to 15 minutes. Remove from pan.
Makes 12 muffins

Banana Poppy Seed Muffins

2 ripe, medium DOLE® Bananas, peeled
1 egg
¾ cup sugar
¼ cup vegetable oil
2 teaspoons grated DOLE® orange peel
2 cups all-purpose flour
1½ tablespoons poppy seeds
2 teaspoons baking powder
½ teaspoon salt
Citrus Glaze (recipe follows)

Preheat oven to 375°F. Puree bananas in blender (1 cup). In medium bowl, mix bananas, egg, sugar, oil and orange peel until well blended. In large bowl, combine flour, poppy seeds, baking powder and salt. Stir banana mixture into flour mixture until evenly moistened. Spoon batter into greased 2½-inch muffin cups. Bake 20 minutes or until wooden pick inserted in center comes out clean. Remove from pan; cool on wire rack. Top with Citrus Glaze while warm.   *Makes 12 muffins*
CITRUS GLAZE: In medium bowl, combine 1¼ cups powdered sugar, ¼ cup orange juice, 1 teaspoon grated DOLE® orange peel and 1 teaspoon vanilla until smooth.

Banana Poppy Seed Muffins

Apricot-Pecan Muffins

    2 cups flour
2½ teaspoons baking powder
    1 teaspoon ground cinnamon
½ teaspoon salt
⅓ to ½ cup packed brown
    sugar
¾ cup chopped, California
    dried apricots
½ cup chopped pecans
    1 egg, slightly beaten
½ cup milk
½ cup apricot nectar
¼ cup vegetable oil

Preheat oven to 400°F. Grease or paper-line 12 (2½-inch) muffin cups. In large bowl, sift together flour, baking powder, cinnamon and salt. Stir in brown sugar, apricots and nuts; set aside.

Mix together egg, milk, apricot nectar and oil; add to apricot-flour mixture, stirring with spoon just until combined. Batter will be lumpy; do not overmix.

Spoon batter into muffin cups, filling about ⅔ full. Bake 20 minutes or until golden brown. Serve warm.

Makes 12 muffins

*Favorite recipe from **California Apricot Advisory Board***

Apricot-Pecan Muffins

Chocolate & Peanut Butter Muffins

1½ cups all-purpose flour
    1 cup (half of 11½-oz. pkg.)
    NESTLÉ® Toll House®
    Milk Chocolate Morsels
⅓ cup sugar
    1 tablespoon baking powder
¼ teaspoon salt
¾ cup milk
½ cup peanut butter
⅓ cup vegetable oil
    1 egg

Preheat oven to 400°F. Grease or paper-line 12 muffin cups. In large bowl, combine flour, milk chocolate morsels, sugar, baking powder and salt. In small bowl, combine milk, peanut butter, oil and egg; stir into flour mixture just until dry ingredients are moistened. Spoon mixture into prepared muffin cups, filling each ¾ full.

Bake 20 minutes or until wooden toothpick inserted into center comes out clean. Cool 5 minutes; remove from cups. Serve warm or cool completely.

Makes 12 muffins

Cheddar Almond Muffins

Topping:
    2 tablespoons butter, melted
    1 teaspoon Worcestershire
    sauce
½ teaspoon garlic salt
⅓ cup chopped blanched
    slivered almonds
Muffins:
    2 cups sifted all-purpose
    flour
¼ cup sugar
    1 tablespoon baking powder
    1 teaspoon salt
¾ cup (3 oz.) shredded
    Wisconsin Cheddar
    cheese
    1 egg
    1 cup milk
    3 tablespoons butter, melted

To make Topping: In bowl, blend together butter, Worcestershire sauce and garlic salt. Stir in almonds; reserve.

To make Muffins: Preheat oven to 400°F. In large bowl, sift together flour, sugar, baking powder and salt. Stir in cheese. In small bowl, beat together egg and milk; stir in butter. Add to dry ingredients and stir just until dry ingredients are moistened, about 25 strokes. Fill buttered muffin cups about ⅔ full.

Sprinkle about 1 teaspoon of the reserved almond mixture over each muffin, pressing almonds into batter slightly. Bake 20 to 25 minutes or until golden brown. *Makes 12 muffins*

Parmesan Almond Muffins:
Make muffins following above directions, except substitute ½ cup grated Parmesan cheese for the Cheddar cheese.

*Favorite recipe from **Wisconsin Milk Marketing Board** © 1991*

Favorite Corn Muffins

1 cup all-purpose flour
¾ cup cornmeal
¼ cup wheat bran cereal
2 teaspoons baking powder
1½ teaspoons salt
½ teaspoon baking soda
1 cup dairy sour cream
2 eggs
¼ cup honey
¼ cup butter, melted

Preheat oven to 425°F. In large bowl, combine flour, cornmeal, bran, baking powder, salt and baking soda. In medium bowl, beat sour cream, eggs, honey and butter until blended. Add to flour mixture, stirring just until moistened. Spoon batter into generously buttered 2½-inch muffin cups. Bake 15 to 20 minutes or until wooden pick inserted in center comes out clean. Cool in pan on wire rack 5 minutes. Remove from pan. Serve warm.   *Makes 12 muffins*

Favorite recipe from **Wisconsin Milk Marketing Board** ©*1991*

Ranch Muffins

¾ cup solid vegetable
    shortening
¼ cup sugar
2 eggs, beaten
1⅔ cups all-purpose flour
1 cup quick-cooking oats,
    uncooked
1½ teaspoons baking powder
1 teaspoon baking soda
1 package (.4 ounce)
    HIDDEN VALLEY
    RANCH® Buttermilk
    Recipe Original Ranch®
    Salad Dressing Mix
½ cup chopped walnuts or
    pecans
1½ cups buttermilk

Preheat oven to 350°F. In large bowl, combine shortening and sugar. Add eggs; mix well and set aside. In medium bowl, stir together flour, oats, baking powder, baking soda, salad

Bacon-Cheese Muffins

dressing mix and nuts. Add dry ingredients alternately with buttermilk to egg mixture. Stir until just combined. Spoon batter into greased or paper-lined muffin pans, filling each cup two-thirds full. Bake until toothpick inserted in center comes out clean, 15 to 20 minutes.   *Makes 12 muffins*

Bacon-Cheese Muffins

½ pound bacon (10 to
    12 slices)
    Vegetable oil
1 egg, beaten
¾ cup milk
1¾ cups all-purpose flour
¼ cup sugar
1 tablespoon baking powder
1 cup (4 ounces) shredded
    Wisconsin Cheddar
    cheese
½ cup crunchy nugget-like
    cereal

Preheat oven to 400°F. In large skillet, cook bacon over medium-high heat until crisp. Drain, reserving drippings. If necessary, add oil to drippings to measure ⅓ cup. In small bowl, combine dripping mixture, egg and milk; set aside. Crumble bacon; set aside.

In large bowl, combine flour, sugar and baking powder. Make well in center. Add dripping-egg mixture all at once to flour mixture, stirring just until moistened. Batter should be lumpy. Fold in bacon, cheese and cereal. Spoon into greased or paper-lined 2½-inch muffin cups, filling about ¾ full. Bake 15 to 20 minutes or until golden. Remove from pan. Cool on wire rack.   *Makes 12 muffins*

Favorite recipe from **Wisconsin Milk Marketing Board** ©*1991*

Cheddar Cheese Biscuits

**2 cups all-purpose flour
1 tablespoon baking powder
½ teaspoon salt
¼ cup shortening
1 beaten egg
¾ cup milk
½ cup shredded sharp
    Wisconsin Cheddar
    cheese (2 ounces)
1 tablespoon butter, melted
    Poppy seeds**

Preheat oven to 450°F. In medium bowl stir together flour, baking powder and salt. Cut in shortening until mixture resembles coarse crumbs. Make well in center. In small bowl combine egg and milk; add all at once to dry ingredients. Add cheese. Stir just until dough clings together.

Knead gently on lightly floured surface 10 to 12 times. Roll or pat dough to ½-inch thickness. Cut with floured 2½-inch biscuit cutter; dip cutter in flour between cuts. Place biscuits on ungreased baking sheet. Brush tops with melted butter; sprinkle with poppy seeds. Bake 10 to 12 minutes or until golden.

Makes 10 biscuits

Preparation time: 20 minutes

*Favorite recipe from **Wisconsin Milk Marketing Board** ©1991*

Country Biscuits

**2 cups all-purpose flour
1 tablespoon baking powder
1 teaspoon salt
⅓ cup CRISCO® Shortening
¾ cup milk**

1. Preheat oven to 425°F. Combine flour, baking powder and salt in medium bowl. Cut in CRISCO® using pastry blender or two knives to form coarse crumbs. Add milk. Mix with fork until particles are moistened and

Country Biscuits

cling together. Form dough into ball.

2. Transfer dough to lightly floured surface. Knead gently 8 to 10 times. Roll dough ½ inch thick. Cut with floured 2-inch round cutter. Place on ungreased baking sheet.

3. Bake 12 to 14 minutes or until golden.

Makes 12 to 16 biscuits

Cheddar Cheese Popovers

**4 tablespoons butter
1⅓ cups all-purpose flour
¼ teaspoon dry mustard
⅔ cup water
⅔ cup milk
4 eggs
½ cup (2 ounces) shredded
    Wisconsin Mild Cheddar
    cheese**

Preheat oven to 375°F. Place eight 6-ounce custard cups on baking sheet. Measure 1½ teaspoons butter into each cup. Combine flour and dry mustard in large bowl. Gradually stir in water and milk until blended. Beat in eggs, one at a time, until mixture is smooth. Fold in cheese. Place baking sheet with

custard cups in oven 3 to 5 minutes until butter melts and custard cups are hot. Fill cups ½ to ⅔ full with batter. Bake 45 minutes. Do not open oven until end of baking time. Remove popovers from custard cups; serve immediately.

Makes 8 popovers

*Favorite recipe from **Wisconsin Milk Marketing Board** ©1991*

Apricot Scones

**1½ cups flour
1 cup oat bran
2 tablespoons sugar
1 tablespoon baking powder
½ teaspoon salt
½ cup margarine
1 egg, beaten
3 tablespoons low-fat milk
1 can (17 ounces) California
    apricot halves, drained
    and chopped**

Preheat oven to 400°F. In large bowl, combine flour, oat bran, sugar, baking powder and salt. Cut margarine into flour mixture until mixture resembles fine crumbs. Add egg, milk and canned apricots; stir just until dough leaves side of bowl.

Divide dough in half; turn onto floured surface. Sprinkle surface of dough with additional flour. Roll or pat dough into 6-inch circle, 1 inch thick. Repeat with remaining dough. Cut each circle with floured knife into six wedges. Place on ungreased cookie sheet. Bake 12 minutes or until golden brown.

Makes 12 scones

*Favorite recipe from **California Apricot Advisory Board***

Apple Cheddar Nut Scones

- 1½ **cups all-purpose flour**
- ½ **teaspoon baking powder**
- ½ **teaspoon baking soda**
- ¼ **teaspoon salt**
- ¼ **cup margarine or butter**
- 8 **oz. (2 cups) shredded Cheddar cheese**
- ¼ **cup unsalted sunflower nuts**
- ½ **cup MOTT'S® Regular Apple Sauce**

Preheat oven to 400°F. In medium bowl, combine flour, baking powder, baking soda and salt. Using pastry blender or fork, cut in margarine until mixture is crumbly. Stir in cheese and nuts. Add apple sauce; stir just until moistened.

On floured surface, knead dough gently 5 or 6 times. Place on ungreased cookie sheet; press into 8-inch circle, about ½ inch thick. Cut into wedges; separate slightly. Bake 12 to 16 minutes or until lightly browned. Serve warm.   *Makes 8 to 12 servings*

Apple Cheddar Nut Scones

Pineapple Orange Walnut Bread

- 1 **cup walnut pieces**
- 2 **cups flour**
- 1 **teaspoon baking powder**
- 1 **teaspoon baking soda**
- ¼ **teaspoon salt**
- ¾ **cup sugar**
- ¼ **cup margarine**
- 1 **egg**
- ¼ **cup orange juice**
- 1 **tablespoon grated orange peel**
- 1 **can (8¼ oz.) DOLE® Crushed Pineapple**
- 1 **cup DOLE® Raisins**

Preheat oven to 350°F. In food processor or blender, process walnuts until finely ground. In small bowl, combine nuts with flour, baking powder, baking soda and salt. In large bowl, beat sugar with margarine until fluffy.

Add egg, juice and peel; beat well. Beat in ⅓ flour mixture until blended. Beat in half the undrained pineapple. Repeat, ending with flour. Stir in raisins. Pour into greased 9×5-inch loaf pan. Bake 65 to 70 minutes or until cake tester inserted in center comes out clean. Cool in pan 10 minutes. Turn onto wire rack to finish cooling.

Makes 1 loaf

Cocoa Banana Nut Bread

- 2 **extra-ripe, medium DOLE® Bananas, peeled and cut into chunks**
- 1½ **cups all-purpose flour**
- 1⅓ **cups sugar**
- 6 **tablespoons unsweetened cocoa**
- 1 **teaspoon baking soda**
- ½ **teaspoon salt**
- ¼ **teaspoon baking powder**
- 2 **eggs**
- ½ **cup vegetable oil**
- ⅓ **cup chopped nuts**

Preheat oven to 350°F. Puree bananas in food processor or blender (1 cup puree). In large mixing bowl, combine flour, sugar, cocoa, baking soda, salt and baking powder. Add eggs, oil and bananas; mix just until dry ingredients are moistened. Stir in nuts. Pour batter into greased 9×5-inch loaf pan.

Bake 55 to 60 minutes or until wooden toothpick inserted in center comes out clean. Cool in pan 10 minutes. Remove from pan. Cool completely before slicing. (Loaf may be stored in refrigerator, well wrapped, for up to 1 week.)   *Makes 1 loaf*

Cocoa Banana Nut Muffins: Follow recipe, omitting nuts in batter. Spoon scant ½ cup batter into 10 greased 6-oz. custard cups or muffin cups. Top each muffin with 1 teaspoon chopped nuts. Bake 20 to 22 minutes or until wooden toothpick inserted in center comes out clean. Serve warm.   *Makes 10 muffins*

Piña Colada Bread

    2¹/₂ cups flour
    ¹/₂ cup sugar
     2 teaspoons baking powder
    ¹/₂ teaspoon baking soda
    ¹/₂ teaspoon salt
     2 eggs
    ¹/₂ cup KARO® Light Corn
        Syrup
    ¹/₃ cup MAZOLA® Corn Oil
    ¹/₄ cup rum
     1 can (8 ounces) crushed
        pineapple in
        unsweetened juice,
        undrained
     1 cup flaked coconut

Preheat oven to 350°F. Grease and flour 9×5×3-inch loaf pan. In medium bowl combine flour, sugar, baking powder, baking soda and salt. In large bowl with mixer at medium speed, beat eggs, corn syrup, corn oil and rum until blended. Gradually stir in flour mixture just until moistened. Stir in pineapple and coconut. Pour into prepared pan. Bake 60 to 65 minutes or until wooden toothpick inserted into center comes out clean. Cool in pan 10 minutes. Remove from pan; cool on wire rack.

Makes 1 loaf or 12 servings

Prep time: 15 minutes
Cooking time: 65 minutes, plus cooling

Peanut Butter Bread

     2 cups flour
    ¹/₂ cup sugar
     2 teaspoons baking powder
    ¹/₂ teaspoon baking soda
    ¹/₂ teaspoon salt
     1 cup SKIPPY® Super
        Chunk® or Creamy
        Peanut Butter
    ¹/₂ cup KARO® Light or Dark
        Corn Syrup
     2 eggs
     1 cup milk

Preheat oven to 350°F. Grease and flour 9×5×3-inch loaf pan. In medium bowl combine flour, sugar, baking powder, baking soda and salt. In large bowl with mixer at medium speed, beat peanut butter and corn syrup until smooth. Beat in eggs 1 at a time. Gradually beat in milk. Stir in flour mixture just until moistened. Pour into prepared pan. Bake 50 to 55 minutes or until wooden toothpick inserted into center comes out clean. Cool in pan 10 minutes. Remove from pan; cool on wire rack.

Makes 1 loaf or 12 servings

Prep time: 15 minutes
Bake time: 55 minutes, plus cooling

Blueberry Oat Bread

     2 cups flour
     1 cup uncooked quick or old-
        fashioned oats
     1 tablespoon baking powder
     1 teaspoon salt
    ¹/₂ teaspoon baking soda
    ¹/₂ teaspoon cinnamon
     2 eggs
     1 cup milk
    ¹/₂ cup sugar
    ¹/₃ cup KARO® Light Corn
        Syrup
    ¹/₄ cup MAZOLA® Corn Oil
    1¹/₂ cups fresh or frozen
        blueberries*

Preheat oven to 350°F. Grease and flour 9×5×3-inch loaf pan. In large bowl combine flour, oats, baking powder, salt, baking soda and cinnamon. In small bowl combine eggs, milk, sugar, corn syrup and corn oil until blended; set aside. Toss blueberries in flour mixture. Stir in egg mixture until well blended. Pour batter into prepared pan.

*If using frozen blueberries, do not thaw before adding to flour mixture.

Bake 60 to 70 minutes or until wooden toothpick inserted into center comes out clean. Cool in pan 10 minutes. Remove from pan; cool on wire rack.

Makes 1 loaf or 12 servings

Prep time: 15 minutes
Bake time: 70 minutes, plus cooling

Streusel Lemon Bread

     1 cup finely chopped pecans
    ¹/₂ cup firmly packed light
        brown sugar
    ¹/₂ teaspoon ground nutmeg
        or cinnamon
     2 cups unsifted flour
     1 teaspoon baking powder
    ¹/₂ teaspoon baking soda
    1¹/₄ cups granulated sugar
    ¹/₂ cup margarine or butter,
        softened
     3 eggs
    ¹/₂ cup REALEMON® Lemon
        Juice from Concentrate
    ¹/₂ cup BORDEN® or MEADOW
        GOLD® Milk

Preheat oven to 350°F. In small bowl, combine nuts, brown sugar and nutmeg. Combine flour, baking powder and baking soda. In large mixer bowl, beat sugar and margarine until fluffy. Add eggs; beat well. Gradually beat in REALEMON® brand. Stir in milk alternately with flour mixture until well blended. Spoon half the batter into greased and floured 9×5-inch loaf pan. Reserving ³/₄ cup nut topping, sprinkle remainder over batter. Spread with remaining batter; sprinkle with reserved topping.

Bake 60 to 70 minutes or until wooden toothpick inserted near center comes out clean. Cool 15 minutes; remove from pan. Cool completely. Store tightly wrapped.   *Makes 1 loaf*

Prep time: 15 minutes
Baking time: 60 minutes

Clockwise from top: Blueberry Oat Bread, Peanut Butter Bread, Piña Colada Bread

Irish Soda Bacon Bread

Irish Soda Bacon Bread

4 cups all-purpose flour
3 tablespoons sugar
1½ tablespoons low sodium baking powder
1 teaspoon baking soda
6 tablespoons unsalted margarine or butter, cold
1 cup golden raisins
6 slices ARMOUR® Lower Salt Bacon, cooked crisp and crumbled
2 eggs
1½ cups buttermilk

Preheat oven to 375°F. Combine flour, sugar, baking powder and soda in large bowl; cut in margarine until mixture resembles coarse crumbs. Stir in raisins and bacon. Beat eggs slightly in small bowl; remove and reserve 1 tablespoon egg. Add buttermilk and remaining eggs to flour mixture; stir to make soft dough. Turn out onto lightly floured surface; knead about 1 to 2 minutes, or until smooth.

Shape dough into round loaf. Spray round 2-quart casserole dish with nonstick cooking spray; place dough in dish. With floured knife, cut a 4-inch cross about ¼ inch deep on top of loaf. Brush loaf with reserved egg. Bake 55 to 65 minutes, or until toothpick inserted into center comes out clean. (Cover loaf with foil during last 30 minutes of baking to prevent overbrowning.) Cool on wire rack 10 minutes; remove from dish. Serve with light cream cheese or honey butter, if desired.

Makes 1 loaf

Golden Apple Wheat Loaf

1½ cups chopped Golden
    Delicious apples
1 cup packed brown sugar
1 teaspoon baking soda
1 tablespoon vegetable oil
1 cup boiling water
2 eggs, slightly beaten
1½ cups all-purpose flour
1 cup whole wheat flour
2½ teaspoons baking powder
1 teaspoon salt
1 cup chopped walnuts

Preheat oven to 350°F. Combine apples, brown sugar, baking soda and oil in large bowl. Add boiling water; mix well. Let mixture cool. Beat in eggs. In small bowl, combine all-purpose flour, whole wheat flour, baking powder and salt. Add to apple mixture; blend well. Fold in walnuts. Turn into greased 9×5×3-inch loaf pan. Bake 1 hour or until wooden toothpick inserted near center comes out clean. *Makes 1 loaf*

Favorite recipe from **Washington Apple Commission**

Banana Oat Bread

1¼ cups unsifted flour
¾ cup quick-cooking oats
½ cup firmly packed light
    brown sugar
1 teaspoon baking powder
1 teaspoon baking soda
½ teaspoon plus ⅛ teaspoon
    ground cinnamon
½ teaspoon salt
2 eggs, beaten
1 cup mashed ripe bananas
    (2 medium)
½ cup plus 2 tablespoons
    CARY'S® VERMONT
    MAPLE ORCHARDS or
    MACDONALD'S Pure
    Maple Syrup
3 tablespoons vegetable oil
2 tablespoons granulated
    sugar

Preheat oven to 350°F. In large bowl, combine flour, oats, brown sugar, baking powder, baking soda, ½ teaspoon cinnamon and salt. In small bowl, combine eggs, bananas, ½ cup pure maple syrup and oil. Stir into flour mixture just until moistened. Turn into greased 9×5-inch loaf pan.
Bake 45 to 50 minutes or until wooden toothpick inserted near center comes out clean. Cool 10 minutes; remove from pan. Brush top with remaining 2 tablespoons pure maple syrup. Combine granulated sugar and remaining ⅛ teaspoon cinnamon; sprinkle over top. *Makes 1 loaf*

Prep time: 15 minutes
Baking time: 45 minutes

Pumpkin Cheese Bread

2½ cups sugar
1 (8 oz.) pkg. PHILADELPHIA
    BRAND® Cream Cheese,
    softened
½ cup PARKAY® Margarine
4 eggs
1 (16 oz.) can pumpkin
3½ cups flour
2 teaspoons baking soda
1 teaspoon salt
1 teaspoon cinnamon
½ teaspoon CALUMET®
    Baking Powder
¼ teaspoon ground cloves
1 cup chopped nuts
    Icing

• Preheat oven to 350°F.
• Beat sugar, cream cheese and margarine in large mixing bowl at medium speed with electric mixer until well blended.
• Add eggs, one at a time, mixing well after each addition. Blend in pumpkin.
• Add combined dry ingredients, mixing just until moistened. Fold in nuts. Pour into two greased and floured 9×5-inch loaf pans.
• Bake 1 hour or until wooden pick inserted in center comes out clean. Cool 5 minutes; remove from pans. Drizzle with Icing.

Garnish with pecan halves and red maraschino cherry halves, if desired. *Makes 2 loaves*

Icing

2 cups powdered sugar
3 tablespoons milk

• Stir ingredients together in small bowl until smooth.

Prep time: 20 minutes
Cooking time: 1 hour plus cooling

Strawberry Bread

1 cup unsweetened
    individually quick frozen
    strawberries
1 teaspoon sugar
1⅔ cups all-purpose flour
1 cup sugar
1 teaspoon cinnamon
½ teaspoon baking soda
½ teaspoon salt
2 eggs, slightly beaten
⅔ cup CRISCO® Oil
¾ teaspoon vanilla
¼ teaspoon strawberry
    extract* (optional)

1. Preheat oven to 350°F. Grease and flour 9×5×3-inch loaf pan.
2. Combine strawberries and 1 teaspoon sugar in small bowl. Thaw strawberries completely. Drain and discard liquid. Cut each berry into fourths.
3. Combine flour, 1 cup sugar, cinnamon, baking soda and salt in medium bowl. Mix well.
4. Combine eggs and CRISCO® Oil in small bowl. Add vanilla, strawberry extract and strawberries; mix well. Add to flour mixture. Stir until well moistened. Spread in pan.
5. Bake 40 to 50 minutes or until wooden toothpick inserted in center comes out clean. Cool 20 minutes in pan. Remove from pan to cooling rack. Cool completely before slicing.
Makes 1 loaf
*Increase vanilla to 1 teaspoon if strawberry extract is omitted.

Chocolate Peanut Butter Bread

2 cups all-purpose flour
1 (4¹/₈-ounce) package
      ROYAL® Instant
      Chocolate Pudding & Pie
      Filling*
2 teaspoons baking powder
1³/₄ cups buttermilk
1 teaspoon baking soda
1 cup chunky peanut butter
¹/₃ cup firmly packed light
      brown sugar
2 eggs
2 tablespoons miniature
      semisweet chocolate
      chips
      Confectioners' sugar, for
      garnish

Preheat oven to 350°F. In small bowl, combine flour, pudding mix and baking powder; set aside.

In large bowl, with electric mixer at low speed, combine buttermilk and baking soda. Blend in peanut butter, brown sugar and eggs. Stir in dry ingredients and chocolate chips just until moistened. (Dough will be stiff.) Spoon into greased 9×5×3-inch loaf pan.

Bake 70 to 75 minutes or until knife inserted in center comes out clean. Cool in pan on wire rack for 10 minutes. Remove from pan; cool completely on wire rack. Sprinkle with confectioners' sugar if desired.
Makes 1 loaf

*1 (4-serving size) package ROYAL® Instant Butterscotch or Vanilla Pudding & Pie Filling may be substituted.

Date-Nut Bread

2¹/₂ cups sifted all-purpose
      flour
1¹/₄ teaspoons ARM &
      HAMMER® Pure Baking
      Soda
1 teaspoon salt
1 cup chopped dates
2 eggs
5 tablespoons white vinegar
³/₄ cup milk
¹/₂ cup firmly packed light
      brown sugar
¹/₄ cup vegetable shortening,
      melted
³/₄ cup chopped nuts

Preheat oven to 350°F. Sift together flour, baking soda and salt into large bowl. Stir in chopped dates. In separate bowl, beat eggs; add vinegar and milk. Stir in brown sugar. Add melted shortening. Pour egg mixture into flour mixture all at once. Stir only until all flour is moistened; add nuts and mix lightly.

Turn into greased 9×5-inch loaf pan. Bake 1 hour or until wooden toothpick inserted in center comes out clean. Remove from pan; cool several hours or overnight before slicing.
Makes 1 loaf

California Walnut Bread

2 cups all-purpose flour
²/₃ cup sugar
2¹/₄ teaspoons baking powder
³/₄ teaspoon salt
1 egg
1 cup milk
3 tablespoons vegetable oil
³/₄ teaspoon vanilla
1 cup chopped DIAMOND®
      Walnuts
      Chopped DIAMOND®
      Walnuts (optional)

To prepare Basic Loaf: Preheat oven to 350°F. In medium bowl, sift flour with sugar, baking powder and salt. In small bowl, beat egg; add milk, oil and vanilla. Stir into dry mixture, mixing just until flour is moistened. Stir in 1 cup chopped walnuts. Turn into well-greased 8×4-inch loaf pan. If desired, sprinkle with additional chopped walnuts. Bake 1 hour or until wooden toothpick inserted in center comes out clean. Cool in pan 10 minutes. Remove from pan and cool completely on wire rack.
Makes 1 loaf

Walnut Orange Ring: Make basic loaf, using ¹/₂ cup *each* milk and orange juice in place of 1 cup milk and substituting 1 teaspoon grated orange peel for the vanilla. Turn into greased and floured 8-inch springform pan with tube. If desired, sprinkle with additional chopped walnuts. Bake as directed for basic loaf. While slightly warm, glaze ring. To make glaze, in small bowl, combine ¹/₃ cup sifted powdered sugar, 1 teaspoon grated orange peel and 2 teaspoons orange juice, stirring until smooth.
Makes 1 ring

Apple Muffins: Preheat oven to 400°F. Make basic loaf, reducing milk to ²/₃ cup and adding ³/₄ cup coarsely grated pared apple, 1 teaspoon grated lemon peel and ¹/₄ teaspoon ground cinnamon. Spoon into 12 greased 2¹/₂-inch muffin cups. Bake 20 to 25 minutes or until lightly browned.
Makes 1 dozen muffins

Walnut Cranberry Bread: Make basic loaf, adding 1 cup whole or halved fresh cranberries and 1 tablespoon grated orange peel. Bake as directed for basic loaf.
Makes 1 loaf

Walnut Banana Bread: Make basic loaf, omitting milk and vanilla and adding 1 additional beaten egg and 1 cup mashed ripe banana. Bake as directed for basic loaf.
Makes 1 loaf

Chocolate Peanut Butter Bread

Clockwise from top left: Healthy Pecan Bread (page 36), Banana Pecan Braid, 60-Minute Oatmeal Nut Loaf, Cheddar 'n Pecan Swirls

Banana Pecan Braid

6 cups all-purpose flour, divided
1/2 cup plus 2 tablespoons sugar
1 cup pecan halves, chopped
1 teaspoon salt
2 pkgs. FLEISCHMANN'S® RapidRise Yeast
1/3 cup undiluted evaporated milk
1/3 cup water
1/3 cup margarine or butter
2 eggs, at room temperature
1 cup mashed banana
2 tablespoons margarine or butter, melted
1 teaspoon ground cinnamon

Set aside 1 cup flour. In large bowl, mix remaining 5 cups flour, 1/2 cup sugar, pecans, salt and yeast. In saucepan over low heat, heat evaporated milk, water and 1/3 cup margarine until very warm (125° to 130°F); stir into dry mixture. Mix in eggs, banana and enough reserved flour to make soft dough. On lightly floured surface, knead until smooth and elastic, about 8 to 10 minutes. Cover, let rest 10 minutes.

Divide dough into 6 equal pieces; shape each piece into a 15-inch rope. Braid 3 ropes together for each loaf; seal ends. Place on greased baking sheets. Cover; let rise in warm (80° to 85°F) draft-free place until doubled in size, about 1 hour.

Preheat oven to 375°F. Brush loaves with melted margarine. Combine 2 tablespoons sugar and cinnamon; sprinkle over loaves. Bake 30 to 35 minutes or until golden brown. Remove from pans; cool on wire racks.

Makes 2 loaves

Favorite recipe from **National Pecan Marketing Council**

60-Minute Oatmeal Nut Loaf

3¼ cups all-purpose flour, divided
1 cup rolled oats, uncooked
1/2 cup pecan pieces
2 teaspoons grated orange peel
1/2 teaspoon salt
1 pkg. FLEISCHMANN'S® RapidRise Yeast
1 cup milk
1/4 cup water
2 tablespoons honey
1 tablespoon margarine or butter
1 egg, beaten
1/2 cup powdered sugar
1 to 1½ teaspoons milk Pecan halves

Set aside 1 cup flour. In large
bowl, mix remaining 2¼ cups
flour, oats, pecan pieces, orange
peel, salt and yeast. In saucepan,
over low heat, heat 1 cup milk,
water, honey and margarine
until very warm (125° to 130°F);
stir into dry mixture. Mix in
only enough reserved flour to
make soft dough. On lightly
floured surface, knead 4 minutes.
Roll dough into 13×9-inch
rectangle. Roll up from short side
as for jelly roll; seal seam and
ends. Place on greased baking
sheet; flatten slightly to form
oval. Cover; let rise in warm (80°
to 85°F) draft-free place 20
minutes.

Preheat oven to 375°F. Make 3
diagonal slashes on top of loaf;
brush with beaten egg. Bake 20
to 25 minutes or until golden
brown. Remove from baking
sheet; cool on wire rack. In small
bowl, mix powdered sugar and 1
teaspoon milk. Add additional
milk, if necessary, to make glaze
desired consistency. Drizzle glaze
over loaf; garnish with pecan
halves.   *Makes 1 loaf*

*Favorite recipe from **National Pecan Marketing Council***

Crusty Oval Rolls

Crusty Oval Rolls

  1 package active dry yeast
1⅓ cups warm water (105° to
      115°F)
  1 tablespoon honey
  1 tablespoon shortening,
      melted, cooled
  1 teaspoon salt
3¼ to 4 cups bread flour
  ¼ cup cold water
  1 teaspoon cornstarch

In large bowl, combine yeast and
warm water; stir to dissolve
yeast. Stir in honey, shortening,
salt and 2½ cups of the flour;
beat until very elastic. Stir in
enough of the remaining flour to
make dough easy to handle.
Turn out onto floured surface.
Knead 15 minutes or until
dough is smooth and elastic,
adding as much remaining flour
as needed to prevent sticking.
Shape dough into ball. Place in
large, greased bowl; turn dough
once to grease surface. Cover
with towel; let rise in warm
place (80° to 85°F) until
doubled, about 1 hour.

Punch dough down; knead
briefly on floured surface. Cover;
let rest 10 minutes. Divide
dough into 10 equal pieces;
shape each piece into ball.
Starting at center and working
toward opposite ends, roll each
ball on floured surface with
palms of hands into tapered oval.
Place, evenly spaced, on 2
greased baking sheets. Cover; let
rise in warm place until almost
doubled, about 25 minutes.
Preheat oven to 375°F. In small
saucepan, combine cold water
and cornstarch. Bring to a boil
over high heat, stirring
constantly. Boil until thickened
and clear, about 2 minutes; cool
slightly. Brush risen rolls with
warm cornstarch mixture. Slash
each roll lengthwise with razor
blade or sharp knife, cutting ½
inch from each end and about
½ inch deep. Bake 30 to 35
minutes or until rolls are golden
brown and sound hollow when
tapped. Remove to wire racks
to cool.   *Makes 10 rolls*

Cheddar 'n Pecan Swirls

¾ cup chopped onion
  3 tablespoons margarine,
      softened, divided
  3 cups all-purpose flour,
      divided
  1 tablespoon sugar
½ teaspoon salt
  1 pkg. FLEISCHMANN'S®
      RapidRise Yeast
¾ cup water
¼ cup milk
  1 cup (4 oz.) shredded
      Cheddar cheese
½ cup pecan halves, chopped
      Paprika

In medium skillet over medium
heat, cook onion in 2 tablespoons
margarine until tender; set
aside.

Set aside 1 cup flour. In large
bowl, mix remaining 2 cups
flour, sugar, salt and yeast. In
saucepan, over low heat, heat
water, milk and remaining 1
tablespoon margarine until very
warm (125° to 130°F); stir into
dry mixture. Mix in only enough
reserved flour to make soft
dough. On lightly floured
surface, knead 4 minutes.
Roll dough into 14×8-inch
rectangle. Spread onion mixture
evenly over dough; sprinkle with
cheese and pecans. Roll up from
long side as for jelly roll; seal
seam. Cut roll into 12 equal
pieces. Arrange cut-side up in
greased 8-inch round cake pan;
cover. Let rise in warm (80° to
85°F) draft-free place 20 minutes.
Preheat oven to 375°F. Sprinkle
rolls with paprika. Bake 25 to 30
minutes or until golden brown.
Remove from pan; cool slightly
on wire rack. Serve warm.
      Makes 1 dozen

*Favorite recipe from **National Pecan Marketing Council***

Touch of Honey Bread

Touch of Honey Bread

2¹/₂ to 3 cups all-purpose flour
1 cup QUAKER® Oat Bran
Hot Cereal, uncooked
1 pkg. quick-rise yeast
¹/₂ teaspoon salt
1¹/₄ cups water
2 tablespoons honey
2 tablespoons margarine

In large mixer bowl, combine 1 cup flour, oat bran, yeast and salt. Heat water, honey and margarine until very warm (120° to 130°F). Add to dry ingredients; beat at low speed of electric mixer until moistened. Increase speed to medium; continue beating 3 minutes. Stir in enough remaining flour to form a stiff dough.

Lightly spray another large bowl with vegetable oil cooking spray or oil lightly. Turn dough out onto lightly floured surface.

Knead 8 to 10 minutes or until dough is smooth and elastic. Place into prepared bowl, turning once to coat surface of dough. Cover; let rise in warm place (80° to 85°F) 30 minutes or until doubled in size.

Lightly spray 8×4-inch loaf pan with vegetable oil cooking spray or oil lightly. Punch down dough. Roll into 15×7-inch rectangle. Starting at narrow end, roll up dough tightly. Pinch ends and seam to seal; place seam-side down in prepared pan. Cover; let rise in warm place 30 minutes or until doubled in size.

Preheat oven to 375°F. Bake 35 to 40 minutes or until golden brown. Remove from pan; cool on wire rack at least 1 hour before slicing. Serve as sandwich bread, toasted or spread with jelly, jam or fruit preserves.

Makes 16 slices

Healthy Pecan Bread

5 cups all-purpose flour,
divided
2 cups whole wheat flour
¹/₂ cup wheat germ
1 cup pecan halves, chopped
2 teaspoons salt
2 pkgs. FLEISCHMANN'S®
RapidRise Yeast
1 cup water
1 cup plain yogurt
¹/₃ cup honey
¹/₄ cup margarine or butter
2 eggs, at room temperature

Set aside 1 cup all-purpose flour. In large bowl, mix remaining 4 cups all-purpose flour, whole wheat flour, wheat germ, pecans, salt and yeast. In saucepan, over low heat, heat water, yogurt, honey and margarine until very warm (125° to 130°F); stir into dry mixture. Mix in eggs and only enough reserved flour to make soft dough. On lightly floured surface, knead until smooth and elastic, about 8 to 10 minutes. Cover; let rest 10 minutes.

Divide dough in half; shape each half into smooth ball. Place in two greased 8-inch round cake pans. Cover; let rise in warm (80° to 85°F) draft-free place until doubled in size, about 1 hour and 15 minutes.

Preheat oven to 375°F. Bake 35 to 40 minutes or until golden brown. Remove from pans; cool on wire racks.

Makes 2 loaves

*Favorite recipe from **National Pecan Marketing Council***

Savory Bubble Cheese Bread

6 to 7 cups flour, divided
2 tablespoons sugar
4 teaspoons instant minced onion
2 teaspoons salt
2 packages active dry yeast
½ teaspoon caraway seeds
1¾ cups milk
½ cup water
3 tablespoons butter or margarine
1 teaspoon TABASCO® Pepper Sauce
2 cups (8 ounces) shredded sharp Cheddar cheese, divided
1 egg, lightly beaten

In large bowl of electric mixer combine 2½ cups flour, sugar, onion, salt, yeast and caraway seeds. In small saucepan combine milk, water and butter. Heat milk mixture until very warm (120°F to 130°F); stir in TABASCO® pepper sauce.

With mixer at medium speed gradually add milk mixture to dry ingredients; beat 2 minutes. Add 1 cup flour. Beat at high speed 2 minutes. With wooden spoon stir in 1½ cups cheese and enough flour to make a stiff dough. Turn dough out onto lightly floured surface. Knead 8 to 10 minutes or until dough is smooth and elastic, adding as much remaining flour as needed to prevent sticking. Place in large greased bowl and invert dough to bring greased side up. Cover with towel; let rise in warm place (80° to 85°F) 1 hour or until doubled in bulk.

Punch dough down. Divide into 16 equal pieces; shape each piece into a ball. Place ½ the balls in well-greased 10-inch tube pan. Sprinkle with remaining ½ cup cheese. Arrange remaining balls on top. Cover with towel; let rise in warm place 45 minutes or until doubled in bulk.

Preheat oven to 375°F. Brush bread with egg. Bake 40 to 50 minutes or until golden brown. Remove loaf from pan. Cool completely on wire rack.

Makes 1 loaf

Pepper-Cheese Bread

5½ to 6 cups all-purpose flour
2 packages active dry yeast
1 cup milk
⅔ cup butter, cut up
1 tablespoon sugar
1 to 2 teaspoons coarse black pepper
1 teaspoon salt
4 eggs
2 cups (8 ounces) shredded sharp Wisconsin Cheddar cheese
1¼ cups unseasoned mashed potatoes

In large mixer bowl combine 2 *cups* flour and yeast. In small saucepan combine milk, butter, sugar, pepper, and salt. Cook and stir until warm (115° to 120°F) and butter is almost melted. Add to flour mixture. Add eggs. Beat on low speed for 30 seconds, scraping sides of bowl. Beat on high speed for 3 minutes. Stir in Cheddar cheese, potatoes, and as much remaining flour as can be mixed in with a spoon.

Turn out onto a lightly floured surface. Knead 6 to 8 minutes or until dough is smooth and elastic, adding as much remaining flour as needed to make a moderately stiff dough. Shape into a ball. Place in greased bowl; turn once to grease surface. Cover; let rise in warm place (80° to 85°F) until double (about 1 hour).

Punch down dough; turn out onto lightly floured surface. Divide into 6 pieces. Cover; let rest 10 minutes. Roll each piece into 16-inch-long rope. On greased baking sheet braid 3 ropes together. Repeat on second greased baking sheet with remaining ropes. Cover; let rise in warm place until nearly doubled (about 30 minutes).

Preheat oven to 375°F. Bake 35 to 40 minutes or until golden brown, covering with foil during end of baking. Remove from pans; cool. *Makes 2 braids*

Favorite recipe from **Wisconsin Milk Marketing Board** © *1991*

Pepper-Cheese Bread

Cottage Dill Bread

2 packages active dry yeast
2 teaspoons sugar
¹/₂ cup warm water (105° to
   115°F)
2 cups Cottage cheese
2 tablespoons minced onion
2 tablespoons dill weed
2 tablespoons sugar
2 teaspoons salt
1 teaspoon baking powder
2 eggs, beaten
3¹/₂ to 4¹/₂ cups all-purpose
   flour

Dissolve yeast and 2 teaspoons sugar in warm water. Mix together Cottage cheese, onion, dill weed, 2 tablespoons sugar, salt, baking powder and eggs in large bowl. Beat in yeast mixture and 1 cup flour until smooth. Stir in enough remaining flour to make a stiff dough.

Turn dough onto lightly floured surface. Knead dough 8 to 10 minutes, adding as much remaining flour as needed to prevent sticking. When dough is smooth and elastic, place in large greased bowl. Turn over once, cover with plastic wrap and let rise in a warm place (80° to 85°F) until double, about 1 hour.

Punch down dough and knead a few times on a lightly floured surface. Divide and shape into 2 loaves. Place in 2 well-buttered 9×5-inch loaf pans and let rise, covered, 30 minutes.

Preheat oven to 350°F. Bake 30 minutes or until golden brown. Remove from pans and cool on rack.   *Makes 2 loaves*

Favorite recipe from **Wisconsin Milk Marketing Board** © *1991*

Apple Cinnamon Rolls

Sally Lunn Bread

1 package active dry yeast
¹/₄ cup warm water (105° to
   115°F)
³/₄ cup milk
¹/₄ cup sugar
¹/₄ cup butter or margarine
1 teaspoon grated orange
   peel
1 teaspoon salt
1 cup Florida orange juice
2 eggs, beaten
6 cups sifted all-purpose
   flour
2 Florida oranges, sliced

In small bowl, dissolve yeast in warm water; set aside. In medium saucepan, scald milk; add sugar, butter, orange peel and salt. Stir until sugar dissolves and butter melts. Cool.

In large bowl, combine milk mixture, yeast, orange juice, eggs and flour. Beat until smooth (dough will be very soft).

Turn into a greased Bundt® pan or 10-inch tube pan. Let rise in warm place (80° to 85°F), covered, until doubled in bulk, about 1 hour.

Preheat oven to 400°F. Bake 15 minutes. *Reduce oven temperature to 350°F and bake*

15 to 20 minutes longer, or until bread is browned. Cool in pan 5 minutes; turn out on wire rack and cool completely.

Garnish serving platter with orange slices cut in half.
       Makes one loaf

Favorite recipe from **Florida Department of Citrus**

Apple Cinnamon Rolls

Dough:
3 to 3³/₄ cups all-purpose
   flour
¹/₄ cup granulated sugar
¹/₂ teaspoon salt
1 pkg. active dry yeast
1 cup MOTT'S® Natural
   Apple Sauce
¹/₄ cup margarine or butter
1 egg
Filling:
¹/₄ cup margarine or butter,
   softened
³/₄ cup MOTT'S® Natural,
   Cinnamon, or Chunky
   Apple Sauce
¹/₄ cup firmly packed brown
   sugar
¹/₄ cup chopped nuts
1¹/₂ teaspoons cinnamon

For dough, in small bowl, combine 1 cup flour, granulated sugar, salt and yeast; blend well. In small saucepan, heat 1 cup apple sauce and ¼ cup margarine until very warm (120° to 130°F). Add warm liquid and egg to flour mixture. Blend at low speed until moistened; beat 2 minutes at medium speed. Stir in 1¾ to 2 cups flour to form a stiff dough.

On floured surface, knead in ¼ to ¾ cup flour until dough is smooth and elastic, about 5 to 10 minutes. Place in greased bowl; cover loosely with plastic wrap or cloth towel. Let rise in warm place (80° to 85°F) until light and doubled in volume, about 30 minutes.

Grease 13×9-inch pan. On lightly floured surface, roll dough into 15×12-inch rectangle. For filling, spread ¼ cup margarine evenly over dough. In small bowl, combine ¾ cup apple sauce, brown sugar, nuts and cinnamon; spread evenly over margarine. Starting with 12-inch side, roll up tightly, pressing edges to seal. Cut into 12 (1-inch) slices; place cut-side down in prepared pan. Cover with plastic wrap; refrigerate overnight.

When ready to bake, uncover rolls; let stand at room temperature 30 minutes. Preheat oven to 375°F. Bake 25 to 35 minutes or until golden brown. Cool 5 minutes; remove from pan. If desired, drizzle with powdered sugar glaze.

Makes 12 rolls

Chocolate-Caramel Pecan Rolls

Rolls:
 4¼ to 4¾ cups all-purpose flour, divided
 1 pkg. active dry yeast
 1 cup milk
 ⅓ cup granulated sugar
 10 tablespoons (1¼ sticks) butter, divided
 ½ teaspoon salt
 2 eggs
One 6-oz. pkg. (1 cup) NESTLÉ® Toll House® Semi-Sweet Chocolate Morsels, divided

Caramel Sauce:
 ⅔ cup firmly packed brown sugar
 ¼ cup (½ stick) butter
 2 tablespoons corn syrup
 ⅔ cup pecans, coarsely chopped

Rolls: In large mixer bowl, combine 2 cups flour and yeast. In small saucepan, combine milk, granulated sugar, 6 tablespoons butter and salt. Cook over medium heat just until very warm (120° to 130°F), stirring occasionally. Gradually beat milk mixture into flour mixture. Add eggs; beat at low speed 30 seconds, scraping sides of bowl constantly. Beat 3 minutes on high speed. With spoon, stir in enough remaining flour to make soft dough. Turn dough onto lightly floured surface. Knead 6 to 8 minutes until dough is smooth and elastic.

Place dough in lightly greased bowl; turn over to grease surface. Cover with cloth towel; let rise in warm place (75° to 80°F) until double in bulk, about 1 hour. Punch down; divide dough in half. Cover; let rest 10 minutes.

Melt ⅔ cup semi-sweet chocolate morsels and 2 tablespoons butter, stirring until smooth; set aside.

Caramel Sauce: In small saucepan, combine brown sugar, butter and corn syrup. Cook over medium heat, stirring, until butter is melted.

Divide Caramel Sauce evenly between two 9-inch round baking pans. Sprinkle with pecans; set aside. On lightly floured surface, roll half of dough into 12×8-inch rectangle. Spread half of chocolate mixture over dough. Roll up jelly-roll style, beginning from long side. Moisten edge with water; pinch to seal seam well. Slice into 12 pieces. Arrange rolls cut-side down in 1 prepared pan. Repeat with remaining dough and chocolate mixture. Cover; let rise in warm place until nearly double in bulk, about 20 minutes.

Preheat oven to 375°F. Bake 18 to 20 minutes. Immediately invert onto serving plate. In small heavy-gauge saucepan, melt remaining ⅓ cup semi-sweet chocolate morsels and 2 tablespoons butter, stirring until smooth. Drizzle over warm rolls. Serve warm.   *Makes 24 rolls*

Chocolate-Caramel Pecan Rolls

Caramel Pecan Sticky Buns

    1 (8 oz.) pkg. PHILADELPHIA
       BRAND® Cream Cheese,
       cubed
    ³/₄ cup cold water
    1 (16 oz.) pkg. hot roll mix
    1 egg
    ¹/₃ cup granulated sugar
    1 teaspoon cinnamon
    ³/₄ cup packed brown sugar
    ¹/₂ cup light corn syrup
    ¹/₄ cup PARKAY® Margarine,
       melted
    1 cup pecan halves

• Stir together 6 ounces cream cheese and water in small saucepan. Cook over low heat until mixture reaches 115° to 120°F, stirring occasionally.

• Stir together hot roll mix and yeast packet in large bowl. Add cream cheese mixture and egg, mixing until dough pulls away from sides of bowl.

• Knead dough on lightly floured surface 5 minutes or until smooth and elastic. Cover; let rise in warm place 20 minutes.

• Beat remaining cream cheese, granulated sugar and cinnamon in small mixing bowl at medium speed with electric mixer until well blended.

• Roll out dough to 18×12-inch rectangle; spread cream cheese mixture over dough to within 1 inch from outer edges of dough.

• Roll up from long end, sealing edges. Cut into twenty-four ³/₄-inch slices.

• Stir together remaining ingredients in small bowl. Spoon 2 teaspoonfuls mixture into bottom of greased medium-sized muffin pans.

• Place dough, cut side up, in cups. Cover; let rise in warm place 30 minutes.

• Preheat oven to 350°F. Bake 20 to 25 minutes or until golden brown. Invert onto serving platter immediately.

Makes 2 dozen buns

Prep time: 30 minutes plus rising
Cooking time: 25 minutes

Apple-Cheese Coffee Cake

    2 packages active dry yeast
    ¹/₂ cup warm water (105° to
       115°F)
    1¹/₄ cups buttermilk
    2 eggs
    5¹/₂ to 6 cups all-purpose flour,
       divided
    ¹/₂ cup butter
    ¹/₂ cup sugar
    2 teaspoons baking powder
    2 teaspoons salt
    2 cans (21 ounces each)
       apple pie filling (ready-
       to-use)
    2 cups (8 oz.) shredded
       Wisconsin Cheddar
       cheese, divided

In large mixer bowl, dissolve yeast in warm water. Add buttermilk, eggs, 2¹/₂ cups flour, butter, sugar, baking powder and salt. Blend ¹/₂ minute on low speed, scraping bowl constantly. Beat 2 minutes on medium speed, scraping bowl occasionally. Stir in enough remaining flour to make soft, slightly sticky dough that is easy to handle. Turn onto well-floured board; knead 5 minutes. Let rest 5 minutes.

Preheat oven to 350°F. Divide dough into 3 equal parts. Roll one part into a 10×15-inch rectangle; transfer to buttered baking sheet. Spread ²/₃ of a can of pie filling lengthwise down center of rectangle in 3-inch wide strip. Sprinkle ¹/₃ of cheese on top of pie filling. With scissors make 2-inch-deep cuts along 15-inch sides of dough at 1-inch intervals. Fold top and bottom ends of rectangle over pie filling. Pull up and overlap cut strips of dough alternately, one from each side, over pie filling to create a braided appearance. Repeat with remaining dough, filling and cheese. Let rise in warm place (80° to 85°F) until

double, about 1 hour. Bake about 25 minutes or until golden brown.

Frost with your favorite icing and sprinkle with almonds if desired.

Makes 3 braided coffee cakes

*Favorite recipe from **Wisconsin Milk Marketing Board** © 1991*

Peanut Butter and Jam Swirl Coffee Cake

    ¹/₂ cup milk
    ¹/₃ cup packed brown sugar
    ¹/₂ teaspoon salt
    1 package active dry yeast
    ¹/₄ cup warm water (105° to
       115°F)
    1¹/₂ to 2¹/₂ cups all-purpose
       flour, divided
    ¹/₄ cup peanut butter
    1 egg
    ¹/₃ cup raspberry or
       strawberry jam

In small saucepan over medium heat, scald milk. In medium heatproof bowl, combine sugar and salt. Add hot milk; stir to dissolve sugar. Cool until warm (105° to 115°F). Add yeast to water; stir to dissolve yeast. Add 1 cup flour and peanut butter to milk mixture; beat until smooth. Stir in yeast mixture and egg; beat well. Stir in enough remaining flour to make thick batter; beat well. Cover with waxed paper; let rise in warm place (80° to 85°F) until bubbly and doubled, about 1 hour.

Stir down batter. Spread in well-greased 9-inch round pan. With floured fingers, press spiral-shaped indentation in top of batter, starting at center and working toward outside. Fill indentation with jam. Cover; let rise in warm place until doubled, about 45 minutes.

Preheat oven to 350°F. Bake 30 to 35 minutes or until golden brown. Remove to wire rack to cool. *Makes 1 coffee cake*

*Favorite recipe from **Oklahoma Peanut Commission***

Orange Raisin Bread

1 cup dark raisins
1 cup Florida orange juice
1 package active dry yeast
¼ cup warm water (105° to 115°F)
2 large eggs, beaten
⅓ cup butter or margarine, melted
⅓ cup firmly packed brown sugar
2 teaspoons grated orange peel
1 teaspoon salt
½ teaspoon ground cinnamon
5 to 6 cups all-purpose flour

In small bowl, soak raisins in orange juice 1 hour. In large bowl, combine yeast and warm water; stir until yeast is dissolved. Add raisin and orange juice mixture, eggs, butter, brown sugar, orange peel, salt and cinnamon. Beat in enough flour to make soft dough.

Turn out onto lightly floured surface. Knead 5 minutes or until dough is smooth and elastic, adding as much flour as necessary to prevent sticking. Place dough in large greased bowl; turn dough once to grease surface. Cover with towel; let rise in warm place (80° to 85°F) about 1 hour or until doubled in bulk. Punch down dough and turn out on lightly floured board. Knead about 5 minutes, until smooth. Shape into loaf to fit greased 9×5-inch loaf pan. Cover; let rise in warm place about 50 minutes or until doubled in bulk.

Preheat oven to 350°F. Bake 55 to 60 minutes or until golden. Cool in pan 5 minutes; remove from pan and cool completely on wire rack.   *Makes 1 loaf*

Favorite recipe from **Florida Department of Citrus**

Chocolate Chip Brioche

1 pkg. active dry yeast
⅓ cup warm water (105° to 115°F)
2 tablespoons sugar
3 to 3¼ cups all-purpose flour, divided
6 tablespoons (¾ stick) butter
⅓ cup heavy or whipping cream
½ teaspoon salt
2 eggs
1 cup (half of 12-oz. pkg.) NESTLÉ® Toll House® Semi-Sweet Chocolate Mini Morsels
1 egg, beaten

Grease 8×3-inch fluted brioche mold or round casserole. In small bowl, dissolve yeast in warm water; stir in sugar and ¼ cup flour. Cover; let stand in warm place (75° to 80°F) 10 minutes or until mixture bubbles. In small saucepan, combine butter and heavy cream. Cook, stirring constantly, over medium heat until very warm (120° to 130°F).

In large mixer bowl, combine 1 cup flour and salt. Add yeast mixture, cream mixture and eggs; beat at low speed until smooth, then at high speed for 3 minutes. With spoon, stir in enough remaining flour to make soft dough. Turn dough onto lightly floured surface. Knead about 5 minutes or until smooth and elastic. Knead in mini morsels.

Reserve about ⅙ of dough. Shape larger portion of dough into smooth ball; place in prepared mold. Cut small slit in top of dough. For "topknot," shape reserved dough into 2- or 3-inch cone. Tuck long portion of cone into slit in top of dough; pat gently to shape evenly. Cover with cloth towel; let rise in warm place until double in bulk, about 1 hour.

Preheat oven to 350°F. Brush brioche with beaten egg. Bake 40 to 45 minutes until loaf sounds hollow when tapped with fingertips. Remove from mold; cool slightly. Serve warm or cool completely.

Makes 8 to 10 servings

Chocolate Chip Brioche

Chocolate and Cherry Braid

Bread:
2¼ to 2¾ cups all-purpose
    flour, divided
2 pkgs. active dry yeast
⅔ cup milk
¼ cup granulated sugar
2 tablespoons (¼ stick)
    butter
½ teaspoon salt
1 egg
One 6-oz. pkg. (1 cup) NESTLÉ®
    Toll House® Semi-Sweet
    Chocolate Morsels
½ cup maraschino cherries,
    halved and patted dry
1 egg yolk, beaten

Glaze:
½ cup sifted confectioners'
    sugar
¼ teaspoon vanilla extract
    Milk
    Candied cherries, halved

Bread: Grease large cookie sheet. In large mixer bowl, combine 1 cup flour and yeast. In small saucepan, combine milk, granulated sugar, butter and salt. Cook, stirring constantly, over medium heat until very warm (120° to 130°F). Gradually beat milk mixture into flour mixture until smooth. Add egg; beat 2 minutes at high speed. With spoon, stir in semi-sweet chocolate morsels, maraschino cherries and enough remaining flour to make a soft dough. Turn dough onto lightly floured surface. Knead 6 to 8 minutes until dough is smooth and elastic.

Divide dough into thirds. Cover with cloth towel; let rest 10 minutes. Roll each third into 18-inch rope. Braid ropes loosely, beginning in middle and working toward ends. Press ends to seal and tuck under. Place on prepared cookie sheet. Cover; let rise in warm place (75° to 80°F) until double in bulk, about 1 hour.

Preheat oven to 350°F. Brush bread with beaten egg yolk. Bake 30 to 35 minutes until

Chocolate and Cherry Braid

bread sounds hollow when tapped. Remove from cookie sheet; cool.

Glaze: In small bowl, combine confectioners' sugar, vanilla extract and enough milk (about 2 teaspoons) to make glaze of drizzling consistency. Drizzle over braid; garnish with candied cherries. *Makes 1 loaf*

Cardamom-Boysenberry Braids

1 package plus 1 teaspoon
    active dry yeast
¼ cup warm water (105° to
    115°F)
3 eggs
½ cup (1 stick) butter, melted
    and cooled
½ cup dairy sour cream
½ cup honey
2 teaspoons ground
    cardamom
1½ teaspoons salt
1 teaspoon vanilla
4½ to 5 cups all-purpose flour,
    divided
1 cup boysenberry preserves
3 tablespoons light corn
    syrup
1 tablespoon boiling water
¼ cup sliced almonds
2 teaspoons sugar

Dissolve yeast in warm water. In large bowl, beat eggs. Add butter, dairy sour cream, honey, cardamom, salt and vanilla. Stir until well blended. Stir in dissolved yeast and 1½ cups of the flour; beat until smooth. Mix in enough remaining flour to make soft dough. Turn dough onto lightly floured surface. Knead 8 to 10 minutes or until dough is smooth and elastic, adding as much remaining flour as needed to prevent sticking. Place in buttered bowl and turn buttered side up. Cover bowl with plastic wrap. Let dough rise in warm place (80° to 85°F) until doubled, about 1½ hours.

Punch down dough; divide in half. Roll half the dough on lightly floured surface into 12×9-inch rectangle; transfer to buttered baking sheet. Spread half the boysenberry preserves lengthwise down center of rectangle in 4-inch-wide strip. Make 2½-inch-deep cuts along 12-inch sides of dough at 1-inch intervals. Fold strips from alternating sides over filling at an angle, creating braided pattern. Repeat with remaining dough and boysenberry preserves. Loosely cover braids; let rise in warm place until doubled, about 1 hour.

Preheat oven to 350°F. Combine corn syrup and water; lightly brush over tops of braids. Sprinkle with almonds, then sugar, dividing evenly. Bake 20 to 25 minutes or until golden brown. Cool completely on wire racks before serving.
Makes 2 braids

*Favorite recipe from **Wisconsin Milk Marketing Board** © 1991*

Cream Cheese Swirl Coffee Cake

Lemon Cheese Coffeecake

Cake
- 1 package DUNCAN HINES® Moist Deluxe Lemon Supreme Cake Mix, divided
- 2 eggs
- 1 cup all-purpose flour
- 1 package active dry yeast
- ²/₃ cup warm water (105° to 115°F)

Filling
- 2 packages (8 ounces each) cream cheese, softened
- 2 eggs
- ¼ cup sugar
- 1 tablespoon all-purpose flour
- 1 tablespoon milk

Topping
- ¼ cup plus 2 tablespoons butter or margarine, softened

Glaze
- 1 cup confectioners' sugar
- 1 tablespoon corn syrup
- 1 tablespoon water

1. Preheat oven to 350°F. Grease 13×9×2-inch pan.

2. For Cake, combine 1½ cups cake mix, 2 eggs, 1 cup flour, yeast and ²/₃ cup warm water in large bowl. Beat at medium speed with electric mixer for 2 minutes. Spread batter in pan.

3. For Filling, combine cream cheese, 2 eggs, sugar, 1 tablespoon flour and milk in small bowl. Beat at low speed with electric mixer until blended. Spoon filling over cake batter, spreading to pan edge.

4. For Topping, mix remaining cake mix and butter until crumbly. Sprinkle over cheese filling. Bake 40 to 45 minutes or until golden brown.

5. For Glaze, combine confectioners' sugar, corn syrup and 1 tablespoon water in small bowl until smooth. Drizzle over hot coffeecake.

Makes 16 to 20 servings

Cream Cheese Swirl Coffee Cake

- 2 (3-ounce) packages cream cheese, softened
- 2 tablespoons confectioners' sugar
- 2 tablespoons REALEMON® Lemon Juice from Concentrate
- 2 cups unsifted flour
- 1 teaspoon baking powder
- 1 teaspoon baking soda
- ¼ teaspoon salt
- 1 cup granulated sugar
- ½ cup margarine or butter, softened
- 3 eggs
- 1 teaspoon vanilla extract
- 1 (8-ounce) container BORDEN® or MEADOW GOLD® Sour Cream Cinnamon-Nut Topping

Preheat oven to 350°F. In small bowl, beat cheese, confectioners' sugar and REALEMON® brand until smooth; set aside. Stir together flour, baking powder, baking soda and salt; set aside. In large mixer bowl, beat granulated sugar and margarine until fluffy. Add eggs and vanilla; mix well. Add dry ingredients alternately with sour cream; mix well. Pour half of batter into greased and floured 10-inch tube pan. Spoon cheese mixture on top of batter to within ½ inch of pan edge. Spoon remaining batter over filling, spreading to pan edge. Sprinkle with Cinnamon-Nut Topping. Bake 40 to 45 minutes or until wooden toothpick inserted near center comes out clean. Cool 10 minutes; remove from pan. Serve warm.

Makes one 10-inch cake

CINNAMON-NUT TOPPING: Combine ¼ cup finely chopped nuts, 2 tablespoons granulated sugar and ½ teaspoon ground cinnamon.

Chocolate Chip Streusel Coffeecake

½ cup packed brown sugar
½ cup flour
¼ cup PARKAY® Margarine
¼ cup chopped walnuts
1 cup mini semi-sweet chocolate pieces
1 (8 oz.) pkg. PHILADELPHIA BRAND® Cream Cheese, softened
1½ cups granulated sugar
¾ cup PARKAY® Margarine, softened
3 eggs, beaten
¾ teaspoon vanilla
2½ cups flour
1½ teaspoons CALUMET® Baking Powder
¾ teaspoon baking soda
¼ teaspoon salt
¾ cup milk

• Preheat oven to 350°F.
• Stir together brown sugar and flour in mixing bowl; cut in ¼ cup margarine until mixture resembles coarse crumbs. Stir in walnuts and chocolate pieces.
• Beat cream cheese, granulated sugar and ¾ cup margarine in large mixing bowl at medium speed with electric mixer until well blended. Blend in eggs and vanilla.
• Add combined dry ingredients alternately with milk, mixing well after each addition.
• Spoon batter into greased and floured 13×9-inch baking pan. Sprinkle with crumb mixture.
• Bake 50 minutes or until wooden pick inserted in center comes out clean.
                    Makes 12 to 16 servings

Prep time: 20 minutes
Cooking time: 50 minutes

Variation: Substitute loose bottom 10-inch tube pan for 13×9-inch baking pan. Bake at 350°F, 1 hour or until wooden pick inserted in center comes out clean. Cool 10 minutes; remove tube insert from outer pan. Cool thoroughly before removing cake from tube insert.

Apple Peach Puff Pancake

Chocolate Streusel 'n Spice Coffeecake

1 package (10 to 13 ounces) fruit, cinnamon, spice or bran muffin mix
½ cup HERSHEY'S® Semi-Sweet Chocolate Chips
¾ cup powdered sugar
½ cup chopped nuts
¼ cup HERSHEY'S® Cocoa
3 tablespoons butter or margarine, melted

Preheat oven to 350°F. Grease *bottom only* of 9-inch square baking pan. Prepare muffin mix as directed for coffeecake; stir in chocolate chips. Pour batter into prepared pan. In small bowl, stir together powdered sugar, nuts and cocoa; with fork, stir in butter until crumbly. Sprinkle over batter.
Bake 25 to 30 minutes or until wooden pick inserted in center comes out clean. Cool in pan on wire rack.   *Makes 9 servings*

Apple Peach Puff Pancake

Batter:
3 eggs
½ cup milk
1 tablespoon granulated sugar
¼ teaspoon salt
½ cup all-purpose flour
2 tablespoons margarine or butter

Topping:
1 cup MOTT'S® Chunky Apple Sauce
1 cup sliced fresh or frozen peaches
½ teaspoon cinnamon
Powdered sugar

Preheat oven to 425°F. For batter, in large bowl, beat eggs. Add milk, granulated sugar and salt. Gradually add flour, beating until well blended. Place margarine in 10-inch ovenproof skillet. Melt in oven just until margarine sizzles, about 2 minutes. Remove skillet from oven; tilt to coat bottom with melted margarine. Immediately pour batter into hot skillet. Bake 15 to 20 minutes or until puffed and dark golden brown. For topping, in small saucepan, combine apple sauce, peaches and cinnamon. Heat over low heat until hot. Pour over pancake. Sprinkle with powdered sugar. Serve immediately.

Makes 4 servings

German Pancake with Bacon

1 cup all-purpose flour
3/4 teaspoon low sodium baking powder
1 cup skim milk
6 eggs, slightly beaten
2 teaspoons vegetable oil
8 slices ARMOUR® Lower Salt Bacon, cooked crisp
3 cups frozen or fresh mixed fruit, thawed if frozen

Preheat oven to 425°F. Combine flour and baking powder in large bowl. Stir in milk and eggs. Brush oil on bottom and side of 10-inch ovenproof skillet. Pour batter all at once into skillet. Arrange bacon spoke-fashion on batter. Bake, uncovered, about 20 to 25 minutes, or until pancake is puffed and golden brown. Top with fruit; cut into wedges. Serve immediately.

Makes 4 servings

Plum Wonderful Coffee Cake

1/4 cup butter or margarine, softened
3/4 cup sugar
1 egg
1/4 teaspoon almond extract
2 cups flour
2 1/2 teaspoons baking powder
1/2 teaspoon salt
3/4 cup milk
1/2 cup chopped toasted almonds
Almond Sour Cream Topping (recipe follows)
6 fresh firm California plums, pitted and sliced (1 pound)
Additional sugar

Preheat oven to 375°F. In large bowl cream butter and sugar; beat in egg and almond extract. In small bowl combine flour, baking powder and salt. Add to egg mixture alternately with milk, beating well after each addition. Stir in almonds. Spoon batter into greased 9×3-inch springform pan.

Bake 30 minutes. Meanwhile prepare Almond Sour Cream Topping. Remove cake from oven; spoon topping evenly over cake. Arrange plum slices on top. Sprinkle with additional sugar. Return to oven and bake 10 minutes. Cool on wire rack 30 minutes. Loosen side with knife; remove side of pan. Cool completely before serving.

Makes 8 to 10 servings

ALMOND SOUR CREAM TOPPING: In small bowl mix together 1 cup sour cream, 1 egg, 1 tablespoon sugar and 1/8 teaspoon almond extract.

Favorite recipe from California Tree Fruit Agreement

German Pancake with Bacon

Blueberry Coffee Cake

Hearty Whole-Grain Coffee Cake

Topping:
    ²/₃ cup QUAKER® Oats (Quick or Old Fashioned), uncooked
    ²/₃ cup packed brown sugar
    ½ cup chopped nuts
    ¼ cup butter or margarine, melted
    ½ teaspoon ground cinnamon

Coffee Cake:
    2 cups biscuit baking mix
    ²/₃ cup milk
    ½ cup QUAKER® Oats (Quick or Old Fashioned), uncooked
    1 egg
    2 tablespoons packed brown sugar
    ½ teaspoon ground cinnamon

To prepare Topping: In medium bowl, combine all topping ingredients; mix well.

To prepare Coffee Cake: Preheat oven to 375°F. In large bowl, combine all coffee cake ingredients; mix just until dry ingredients are moistened. Do not overmix. Spread half the batter in 8-inch square pan; sprinkle half the topping over batter. Repeat layers. Bake 35 to 40 minutes or until wooden toothpick inserted into center comes out clean. Cool slightly in pan on wire rack; serve warm.

Makes 1 coffee cake

Blueberry Coffee Cake

Crust
    1 package DUNCAN HINES® Moist Deluxe Yellow Cake Mix
    ½ cup butter or margarine, softened
    2 eggs, beaten
    ⅓ cup milk
    1 teaspoon vanilla extract

Filling
    3 cups fresh blueberries
    ²/₃ cup sugar
    2 tablespoons all-purpose flour
    ⅛ teaspoon cinnamon

Topping
    2 cups fresh blueberries
    1 cup orange marmalade
    1 teaspoon lemon juice

1. Preheat oven to 375°F. Grease and flour 13×9×2-inch pan. For Crust, combine cake mix and butter in large bowl. Cut butter into cake mix using pastry blender or two knives until coarse crumbs form. Add eggs, milk and vanilla extract. Stir with fork until smooth. Spread batter in bottom and 1 inch up sides of pan.

2. For Filling, sprinkle 3 cups blueberries over crust. Combine sugar, flour and cinnamon. Sprinkle over blueberries. Bake 40 to 50 minutes or until golden.

3. For Topping, sprinkle 2 cups blueberries over warm cake. Heat marmalade and lemon juice in small saucepan. Spoon over blueberries. Cool slightly. Cut into 3-inch squares.

Makes 12 servings

Tip: Serve warm or at room temperature. Top with whipped cream or ice cream, if desired.

Ladder Coffee Cakes

    ½ cup butter, softened
    ½ cup dairy sour cream
    1 cup all-purpose flour
    1 cup canned cherry pie filling
    ¼ cup chopped walnuts (optional)
    ½ cup sifted powdered sugar
    2 teaspoons milk

In large bowl, cream butter. Add sour cream; beat until fluffy. Add flour; mix well. Cover; refrigerate until firm, about 1 hour.

Preheat oven to 350°F. Divide dough in half. Roll out dough, half at a time, on lightly floured surface into 10×8-inch rectangle; place on greased baking sheet. Spread half the pie filling lengthwise down center third of rectangle; if desired, sprinkle half the walnuts over pie filling. Make 2½-inch-deep cuts along 10-inch sides of dough at 1-inch intervals. Fold strips over filling, pinching into narrow points at center. Repeat with remaining dough, filling and nuts. Bake 30 minutes or until golden. Remove to wire racks to cool. If desired, sprinkle additional chopped walnuts on top. In small bowl, combine sugar and milk; drizzle over cakes.

Makes 2 coffee cakes

Favorite recipe from **Wisconsin Milk Marketing Board** © 1991

Cinnamon Coffee Cake

½ **cup butter or margarine, softened**
1⅓ **cups sugar, divided**
2 **eggs**
½ **pint (8 ounces) sour cream**
1 **teaspoon vanilla extract**
2 **cups all-purpose flour**
1 **teaspoon baking powder**
1 **teaspoon baking soda**
½ **cup chopped pecans or walnuts, toasted**
2 **teaspoons ground cinnamon**
½ **cup raisins**

Preheat oven to 350°F. In large bowl, with electric mixer, beat butter with 1 cup sugar for 3 minutes or until light and fluffy. Beat in eggs, sour cream and vanilla; set aside.

In small bowl, combine flour, baking powder and baking soda. Add dry ingredients to egg mixture and beat 2 minutes.

In small bowl, combine remaining ⅓ cup sugar, pecans and cinnamon. Spread ½ of the batter into greased 9-inch tube pan. Evenly sprinkle with raisins and ½ of the pecan

mixture. Spread remaining batter into pan, then sprinkle with remaining pecan mixture. Bake 45 minutes or until toothpick inserted in center of cake comes out clean.

Makes about 8 servings

Favorite recipe from **Thomas J. Lipton Company**

Banana Spice Cake

2 **extra-ripe medium DOLE® Bananas, peeled and cut into chunks**
½ **cup brown sugar, packed**
1 **teaspoon ground cinnamon**
¼ **teaspoon ground nutmeg**
½ **cup margarine, divided**
¾ **cup chopped walnuts**
1 **cup all-purpose flour**
1 **cup whole wheat flour**
1 **teaspoon baking powder**
1 **teaspoon baking soda**
1 **teaspoon salt**
½ **cup granulated sugar**
3 **eggs**
1 **teaspoon vanilla extract**
1 **cup DOLE® Raisins**

Preheat oven to 350°F. Puree bananas in food processor or blender (1 cup puree). For topping, combine brown sugar, cinnamon and nutmeg in small bowl. Cut in ¼ cup margarine until mixture resembles coarse crumbs. Stir in walnuts; set aside. In separate bowl combine flours, baking powder, baking soda and salt.

In large bowl, beat remaining ¼ cup margarine with granulated sugar until light and fluffy. Beat in eggs and vanilla. Beat in flour mixture alternately with pureed bananas, ending with flour mixture. Stir in raisins. Spread half of batter in greased and floured 10-inch tube pan. Sprinkle with half of topping. Repeat with remaining batter and topping.

Bake 45 to 50 minutes or until wooden pick inserted in center comes out clean. Cool in pan 10 minutes. Remove from pan; cool.

Makes 12 servings

Orange Wake Up Cake

Cake
1 **package DUNCAN HINES® Moist Deluxe Yellow Cake Mix**
3 **egg whites**
1¼ **cups water**
⅓ **cup PURITAN® Oil**
1 **tablespoon grated orange peel**
Topping
½ **cup chopped pecans**
⅓ **cup firmly packed brown sugar**
¼ **cup fine graham cracker crumbs**
2 **tablespoons margarine, melted**
1 **tablespoon grated orange peel**
1½ **teaspoons ground cinnamon**
Glaze
1 **cup confectioners sugar**
2 **tablespoons CITRUS HILL® Orange Juice**

1. Preheat oven to 375°F. Grease and flour two 9-inch round cake pans.
2. For cake, combine cake mix, egg whites, water and oil in large bowl. Beat at medium speed with electric mixer for 2 minutes. Fold in 1 tablespoon orange peel. Pour into pans.
3. For topping, combine chopped pecans, brown sugar, graham cracker crumbs, melted margarine, 1 tablespoon orange peel and cinnamon in medium bowl. Stir until well mixed. Sprinkle over batter in pans.
4. Bake at 375°F for 25 to 30 minutes or until wooden toothpick inserted in center comes out clean.
5. For glaze, combine confectioners sugar and orange juice in small bowl; mix until smooth. Immediately pour glaze over baked layers. Serve warm or at room temperature.

Makes 12 to 16 servings

Tip: Recipe makes 2 cakes. If you like, serve one immediately and freeze the other for a quick coffeecake at a later time.

COOKIES

Warm-from-the-oven cookies and a tall glass of cold milk—kids of all ages find this combination irresistible! Whether you like cookies that are crispy or chewy, iced or spiced, here are dozens of scrumptious ways to fill your cookie jar, lunch box and tea-time tray. (For additional cookie recipes, see the Jump-Start Baking, Especially for Kids and Festive Holiday Baking chapters.)

Original Toll House® Chocolate Chip Cookies

2¼ cups all-purpose flour
1 teaspoon baking soda
1 teaspoon salt
1 cup (2 sticks) butter, softened
¾ cup granulated sugar
¾ cup firmly packed brown sugar
1 teaspoon vanilla extract
2 eggs
One 12-oz. pkg. (2 cups) NESTLÉ® Toll House® Semi-Sweet Chocolate Morsels
1 cup nuts, chopped

Preheat oven to 375°F. In small bowl, combine flour, baking soda and salt; set aside.

In large mixer bowl, beat butter, granulated sugar, brown sugar and vanilla extract until creamy. Beat in eggs. Gradually beat in flour mixture. Stir in semi-sweet chocolate morsels and nuts. Drop dough by rounded measuring tablespoonfuls onto ungreased cookie sheets.

Bake 9 to 11 minutes until edges are golden brown. Let stand on cookie sheets 2 minutes. Remove to wire racks to cool completely.

Makes about 5 dozen cookies

Toll House® Pan Cookies:
Preheat oven to 375°F. Spread dough in greased 15½×10½×1-inch baking pan. Bake 20 to 25 minutes. Cool completely. Cut into 2-inch squares.

Makes about 35 squares

Chocolate-Orange Chip Cookies

½ cup BUTTER FLAVOR CRISCO®
1¼ cups firmly packed brown sugar
2 squares (1 ounce each) unsweetened chocolate, melted and cooled
1 egg
2 tablespoons orange juice concentrate
2 tablespoons grated orange peel
1 teaspoon vanilla
1½ cups all-purpose flour
¾ teaspoon baking soda
¼ teaspoon salt
1 cup semi-sweet chocolate chips
½ cup blanched slivered almonds

1. Preheat oven to 375°F. Combine BUTTER FLAVOR CRISCO®, brown sugar and melted chocolate in large bowl. Beat at medium speed of electric mixer until well blended. Beat in egg, concentrate, peel and vanilla.

2. Combine flour, baking soda and salt. Mix into creamed mixture at low speed until well blended. Stir in chocolate chips and nuts.

3. Drop tablespoonfuls of dough 2 inches apart onto ungreased cookie sheet.

4. Bake 7 to 9 minutes, or until set. Cool 2 minutes on cookie sheet. Remove to cooling rack.

Makes about 3½ dozen cookies

Original Toll House® Chocolate Chip Cookies

Ivory Chip Strawberry Fudge Drops

²/₃ cup **BUTTER FLAVOR CRISCO®**
1 cup sugar
1 egg
½ teaspoon strawberry extract
½ cup buttermilk*
6 tablespoons pureed frozen sweetened strawberries
1³/₄ cups all-purpose flour
6 tablespoons unsweetened cocoa powder
³/₄ teaspoon baking soda
½ teaspoon salt
1½ cups white chocolate baking chips

1. Preheat oven to 350°F. Grease cookie sheet with BUTTER FLAVOR CRISCO®.
2. Combine BUTTER FLAVOR CRISCO®, sugar, egg and strawberry extract in large bowl. Beat at medium speed of electric mixer until well blended. Beat in buttermilk and strawberry puree.
3. Combine flour, cocoa, baking soda and salt. Mix into creamed mixture at low speed of electric mixer until blended. Stir in white chocolate chips.
4. Drop rounded tablespoonfuls of dough 2 inches apart onto cookie sheet.
5. Bake 11 to 12 minutes, or until tops spring back when pressed lightly. Remove immediately to cooling rack.

Makes about 2½ dozen cookies

*You may substitute 1½ teaspoons lemon juice or vinegar plus enough milk to make ½ cup for the buttermilk. Stir. Wait 5 minutes before using.

Ivory Chip Strawberry Fudge Drops

Chocolate Chips Cookies with Macadamia Nuts

²/₃ cup butter or margarine, softened
½ cup packed light brown sugar
½ cup granulated sugar
1 teaspoon vanilla extract
1 egg
1 cup all-purpose flour
¹/₃ cup HERSHEY'S® Cocoa
½ teaspoon baking soda
½ teaspoon salt
2 cups (12-ounce package) HERSHEY'S® Semi-Sweet Chocolate Chips
1 jar (3½ ounces) macadamia nuts, coarsely chopped (about ³/₄ cup)

In large mixer bowl, beat butter, brown sugar, granulated sugar and vanilla until creamy. Add egg; blend well. Stir together flour, cocoa, baking soda and salt; gradually add to butter mixture, blending well. Stir in chocolate chips and nuts. Cover; refrigerate 1 to 2 hours.
Preheat oven to 350°F. Using ice cream scoop or ¼ cup measuring cup, drop dough onto very lightly greased cookie sheet; flatten slightly. Bake 10 to 12 minutes. (Do not overbake; cookies will be soft. They will puff during baking; flatten upon cooling.) Cool slightly; remove from cookie sheet to wire rack. Cool completely.
Makes about 12 (3½-inch) cookies

Whole-Wheat Toll House® Chocolate Chip Cookies

2 cups whole-wheat flour
1 teaspoon baking soda
½ teaspoon salt
1 cup (2 sticks) regular margarine, softened
³/₄ cup granulated sugar
³/₄ cup firmly packed brown sugar
1 teaspoon vanilla extract
2 eggs
One 12-oz. pkg. (2 cups) NESTLÉ® Toll House® Semi-Sweet Chocolate Morsels
1 cup quick oats, uncooked
1 cup raisins

Preheat oven to 375°F. In small bowl, combine flour, baking soda and salt; set aside.

In large mixer bowl, beat margarine, granulated sugar, brown sugar and vanilla extract until creamy. Beat in eggs. Gradually beat in flour mixture. Stir in semi-sweet chocolate morsels, oats and raisins. Drop by slightly rounded measuring tablespoonfuls onto ungreased cookie sheets.

Bake 10 to 12 minutes until edges are lightly browned. Let stand on cookie sheets 2 minutes. Remove from cookie sheets; cool completely on wire racks.

Makes about 5 dozen cookies

Note: Cookies made with whole-wheat flour are darker in color than Original Toll House® Chocolate Chip Cookies.

Chewy Cherry Chocolate Chip Cookies

- ½ cup BUTTER FLAVOR CRISCO®
- ½ cup firmly packed brown sugar
- ½ cup granulated sugar
- ½ cup dairy sour cream
- 1 egg
- 1 tablespoon maraschino cherry juice
- ¾ teaspoon vanilla
- 1¼ cups all-purpose flour
- ½ teaspoon baking soda
- ¼ teaspoon salt
- 1 cup semi-sweet chocolate chips
- ½ cup chopped pecans
- ¼ cup well-drained chopped maraschino cherries

1. Preheat oven to 375°F. Combine BUTTER FLAVOR CRISCO®, brown sugar and granulated sugar in large bowl. Beat at medium speed of electric mixer until well blended. Beat in sour cream, egg, cherry juice and vanilla.

2. Combine flour, baking soda and salt. Mix into creamed mixture at low speed until well blended. Stir in chocolate chips, nuts and cherries.

3. Drop rounded tablespoonfuls of dough 2 inches apart onto ungreased cookie sheet.

4. Bake 10 to 12 minutes, or until set. Cool 2 minutes on cookie sheet. Remove to cooling rack.

Makes about 3 dozen cookies

White Chocolate Biggies

- 1½ cups butter or margarine, softened
- 1 cup granulated sugar
- ¾ cup packed light brown sugar
- 2 teaspoons vanilla
- 2 eggs
- 2½ cups all-purpose flour
- ⅔ cup unsweetened cocoa
- 1 teaspoon baking soda
- ½ teaspoon salt
- 1 package (10 ounces) large white chocolate chips
- ¾ cup pecan halves, coarsely chopped
- ½ cup golden raisins

Preheat oven to 350°F. Lightly grease cookie sheets or line with parchment paper. Cream butter, sugars, vanilla and eggs in large bowl until light. Combine flour, cocoa, baking soda and salt in medium bowl; blend into creamed mixture until smooth. Stir in white chocolate chips, pecans and raisins.

Scoop out about ⅓ cupful of dough for each cookie. Place on prepared cookie sheets, spacing about 4 inches apart. Press each cookie to flatten slightly.

Bake 12 to 14 minutes or until firm in center. Cool 5 minutes on cookie sheet, then remove to wire racks to cool completely.

Makes about 2 dozen cookies

"Buttery" Chocolate Chip Cookies

- 1 cup BUTTER FLAVOR CRISCO®
- 1 cup firmly packed brown sugar
- 2 eggs
- 1 teaspoon vanilla
- 2 cups all-purpose flour
- ½ teaspoon salt
- 1½ cups semi-sweet chocolate chips
- ¾ cup coarsely chopped dried apricots
- ¾ cup coarsely chopped toasted almonds

1. Preheat oven to 350°F. Combine BUTTER FLAVOR CRISCO®, brown sugar, eggs and vanilla in large bowl. Beat at medium speed of electric mixer until well blended.

2. Combine flour and salt. Mix into creamed mixture at low speed until well blended. Stir in chocolate chips, apricots and nuts.

3. Drop tablespoonfuls of dough 2 inches apart onto ungreased cookie sheet.

4. Bake 10 minutes, or until lightly browned. Cool 2 minutes on cookie sheet. Remove to cooling rack.

Makes about 5 dozen cookies

White Chocolate Biggies, Peanut Butter Jumbos (page 61)

Mocha Chips 'n' Bits, Malted Dream Drops

Mocha Chips 'n' Bits

- **1 cup BUTTER FLAVOR CRISCO®**
- **¾ cup granulated sugar**
- **½ cup firmly packed brown sugar**
- **2 tablespoons milk**
- **1 tablespoon instant coffee**
- **1 teaspoon vanilla**
- **2 eggs**
- **2⅓ cups all-purpose flour**
- **1½ tablespoons unsweetened cocoa powder**
- **1 teaspoon baking soda**
- **½ teaspoon salt**
- **1 cup coarsely chopped pecans**
- **1 cup milk chocolate big chips**
- **¾ cup raisins**
- **¾ cup flake coconut**

1. Preheat oven to 375°F. Combine BUTTER FLAVOR CRISCO®, granulated sugar, brown sugar, milk, instant coffee and vanilla in large bowl. Beat at medium speed of electric mixer until well blended. Beat in eggs.

2. Combine flour, cocoa, baking soda and salt. Mix into creamed mixture at low speed until just blended. Stir in nuts, milk chocolate chips, raisins and coconut. Drop rounded tablespoonfuls of dough 2 inches apart onto ungreased cookie sheet.

3. Bake 10 to 12 minutes. Cool 2 minutes on cookie sheet. Remove to cooling rack.

Makes about 3½ dozen cookies

Malted Dream Drops

- **½ cup BUTTER FLAVOR CRISCO®**
- **1 cup firmly packed brown sugar**
- **1 egg**
- **1 teaspoon vanilla**
- **½ cup evaporated milk**
- **1¼ cups all-purpose flour**
- **1 cup chocolate malted milk granules**
- **1 teaspoon baking powder**
- **¼ teaspoon salt**
- **1 cup semi-sweet chocolate chips**
- **1 cup coarsely chopped walnuts**

1. Combine BUTTER FLAVOR CRISCO® and brown sugar in large bowl. Beat at medium speed of electric mixer until well blended. Beat in egg and vanilla. Add milk; beat until smooth.

2. Combine flour, malted milk granules, baking powder and salt. Mix into creamed mixture at low speed until just blended. Stir in chocolate chips and nuts. Cover and refrigerate at least 1 hour.

3. Preheat oven to 350°F. Grease cookie sheet with BUTTER FLAVOR CRISCO®. Drop rounded teaspoonfuls of dough 2 inches apart onto cookie sheet.

4. Bake 10 to 12 minutes or until set. Cool 1 minute on cookie sheet. Remove to cooling rack.

Makes about 4 dozen cookies

Simply Delicious Minty Cookies

- **1 cup BUTTER FLAVOR CRISCO®**
- **1 package (8 ounces) cream cheese, softened**
- **¾ cup granulated sugar**
- **½ cup firmly packed brown sugar**
- **1 teaspoon vanilla**
- **2 cups all-purpose flour**
- **1¾ cups mint chocolate chips**

1. Preheat oven to 350°F. Combine BUTTER FLAVOR CRISCO®, cream cheese, granulated sugar, brown sugar and vanilla in large bowl. Beat at medium speed of electric mixer until well blended.

2. Mix flour into creamed mixture at low speed until just blended. Stir in mint chocolate chips. Drop rounded teaspoonfuls of dough 2 inches apart onto ungreased cookie sheet.

3. Bake 8 minutes, or until lightly browned. Cool 2 minutes on cookie sheet. Remove to cooling rack.

Makes about 5 dozen cookies

Chocolate Hazelnut Cookies

- **1¼ cups all-purpose flour**
- **½ teaspoon baking soda**
- **¼ teaspoon salt**
- **½ cup (1 stick) butter, softened**
- **½ cup firmly packed brown sugar**
- **¼ cup granulated sugar**
- **1 egg**
- **1 teaspoon vanilla extract**
- **One 10-oz. pkg. (1½ cups) NESTLÉ® Toll House® Treasures® Semi-Sweet Chocolate Deluxe Baking Pieces**
- **1 cup hazelnuts, chopped**

Preheat oven to 375°F. In small bowl, combine flour, baking soda and salt; set aside.

In large mixer bowl, beat butter, brown sugar and granulated sugar until creamy. Beat in egg and vanilla extract. Gradually beat in flour mixture. Stir in Treasures® semi-sweet chocolate deluxe baking pieces and hazelnuts. Drop by rounded measuring tablespoonfuls onto ungreased cookie sheets.

Bake 12 to 15 minutes until edges are lightly browned. Let stand on cookie sheets 2 minutes. Remove from cookie sheets; cool on wire racks.

Makes about 2 dozen cookies

Confetti Chocolate Chip Cookies

¾ cup **BUTTER FLAVOR CRISCO®**
1¼ cups firmly packed brown sugar
2 tablespoons milk
1 tablespoon vanilla
1 egg
1¾ cups all-purpose flour
1 teaspoon salt
¾ teaspoon baking soda
1 cup coarsely chopped walnuts
½ cup semi-sweet chocolate chunks
½ cup white chocolate baking pieces
½ cup milk chocolate chips

1. Preheat oven to 375°F. Combine BUTTER FLAVOR CRISCO®, brown sugar, milk and vanilla in large mixing bowl at medium speed of electric mixer until well blended. Beat in egg.

2. Combine flour, salt and baking soda. Beat into creamed mixture at low speed until blended.

3. Stir in walnuts, chocolate chunks, white chocolate baking pieces and milk chocolate chips. Drop two level measuring tablespoons of dough into mound for each cookie. Place 3 inches apart on ungreased cookie sheet.

4. Bake 8 to 9 minutes. (Cookies will appear moist; do not overbake.) Cool 2 minutes on cookie sheet; they will finish baking at this time. Remove to wire rack; cool completely.

Makes about 2 dozen cookies

Preparation time: 20 minutes
Bake time: 8 to 9 minutes

Double Chocolate Drops

Double Chocolate Drops

1⅓ cups **BUTTER FLAVOR CRISCO®**
1 cup granulated sugar
⅔ cup firmly packed brown sugar
3 tablespoons milk
1 tablespoon vanilla
2 eggs
2¼ cups all-purpose flour
⅔ cup unsweetened cocoa
1 teaspoon baking soda
1 teaspoon salt
1½ cups broken walnut or pecan pieces
1 cup semi-sweet chocolate chips

1. Preheat oven to 350°F. Cream BUTTER FLAVOR CRISCO®, granulated sugar, brown sugar, milk and vanilla in large bowl at medium speed of electric mixer until well blended. Add eggs one at a time. Beat well after each addition.

2. Combine flour, cocoa, baking soda and salt. Mix into creamed mixture. Stir in nuts and chips. Drop 2 level measuring tablespoonfuls of dough into mound for each cookie. Place 2 inches apart on ungreased cookie sheet.

3. Bake 9 to 11 minutes. Cool 2 minutes on cookie sheet. Remove to cooling rack.

Makes 2 to 2½ dozen cookies

Preparation time: 20 minutes
Bake time: 9 to 11 minutes

Hershey's® More Chips Chocolate Chip Cookies

1½ cups butter, softened
1 cup granulated sugar
1 cup packed light brown
    sugar
3 eggs
2 teaspoons vanilla extract
3⅓ cups all-purpose flour
1½ teaspoons baking soda
¾ teaspoon salt
4 cups (24-ounce package)
    HERSHEY'S® Semi-Sweet
    Chocolate Chips

Preheat oven to 375°F. In large mixer bowl, beat butter, granulated sugar and brown sugar until creamy. Add eggs and vanilla; beat until light and fluffy. Stir together flour, baking soda and salt; gradually beat into butter mixture. Stir in chocolate chips. Drop by rounded teaspoonfuls onto ungreased cookie sheet.

Bake 8 to 10 minutes or until lightly browned. Cool slightly; remove from cookie sheet to wire rack. Cool completely.

Makes about 7½ dozen cookies

Chocolate Oatmeal Chippers

1¼ cups all-purpose flour
½ cup NESTLÉ® Cocoa
1 teaspoon baking soda
½ teaspoon salt
1 cup (2 sticks) butter or
    margarine, softened
1 cup firmly packed brown
    sugar
½ cup granulated sugar
1 teaspoon vanilla extract
2 eggs
One 11½-oz. pkg. (2 cups)
    NESTLÉ® Toll House®
    Milk Chocolate Morsels
2 cups quick or old-
    fashioned oats,
    uncooked
1 cup walnuts, chopped

Preheat oven to 350°F. In small bowl, combine flour, cocoa, baking soda and salt; set aside. In large mixer bowl, beat butter, brown sugar, granulated sugar and vanilla extract until creamy. Add eggs, 1 at a time, beating well after each addition. Gradually beat in flour mixture. Stir in milk chocolate morsels, oats and walnuts. Drop by slightly rounded measuring tablespoonfuls onto ungreased cookie sheets.

Bake 9 to 10 minutes until edges are firm. Let stand on cookie sheets 2 minutes. Remove from cookie sheets; cool on wire racks.

Makes about 4 dozen cookies

Chocolate Oatmeal Pan Cookies:
Preheat oven to 350°F. Grease 15½)(10½)(1 inch baking pan Prepare dough as directed. Spread in prepared pan. Bake 25 to 30 minutes. Cool completely. Cut into 2-inch squares.

Makes about 3 dozen squares

Chocolate Oatmeal Chippers

Island Treasure Cookies

1⅔ cups all-purpose flour
¾ teaspoon baking powder
½ teaspoon baking soda
½ teaspoon salt
14 tablespoons (1¾ sticks)
    butter, softened
¾ cup firmly packed brown
    sugar
⅓ cup granulated sugar
1 teaspoon vanilla extract
1 egg
One 10-oz. pkg. (1½ cups)
    NESTLÉ® Toll House®
    Treasures® Milk
    Chocolate Deluxe Baking
    Pieces
¾ cup shredded coconut,
    toasted if desired
¾ cup macadamia nuts or
    walnuts, chopped

Preheat oven to 375°F. In small bowl, combine flour, baking powder, baking soda and salt; set aside.

In large mixer bowl, beat butter, brown sugar, granulated sugar and vanilla extract until creamy. Beat in egg. Gradually beat in flour mixture. Stir in Treasures® milk chocolate deluxe baking pieces, coconut and nuts. Drop by slightly rounded measuring tablespoonfuls onto ungreased cookie sheets.

Bake 10 to 12 minutes until edges are lightly browned. Let stand on cookie sheets 2 minutes. Remove from cookie sheets; cool completely on wire racks.

Makes about 2 dozen cookies

Tracy's Pizza-Pan Cookies

Tracy's Pizza-Pan Cookies

1 cup butter or margarine, softened
³/₄ cup granulated sugar
³/₄ cup packed brown sugar
1 package (8 ounces) cream cheese, softened
1 teaspoon vanilla
2 eggs
2¹/₄ cups all-purpose flour
1 teaspoon baking soda
¹/₄ teaspoon salt
1 package (12 ounces) semisweet chocolate chips
1 cup chopped pecans

Preheat oven to 375°F. Lightly grease two 12-inch pizza pans Cream butter, sugars, cream cheese and vanilla in large bowl. Add eggs; beat until light. Combine flour, baking soda and salt in small bowl. Add to creamed mixture; blend well. Stir in chocolate chips and nuts. Divide dough in half; press each half evenly into a prepared pan. Bake 20 to 25 minutes or until lightly browned around edges. Cool completely in pans on wire racks. To serve, cut into slim wedges or break into pieces.

Makes two 12-inch cookies

Oatmeal Chocolate Chip Cookies

1 can (20 oz.) DOLE® Crushed Pineapple in Syrup*
1¹/₂ cups brown sugar, packed
1 cup margarine, softened
1 egg
¹/₄ teaspoon almond extract
4 cups rolled oats, uncooked
2 cups flour
1 teaspoon baking powder
1 teaspoon salt
1 teaspoon ground cinnamon
¹/₂ teaspoon ground nutmeg
1 pkg. (12 oz.) semisweet chocolate chips
³/₄ cup DOLE® Slivered Almonds, toasted
2 cups flaked coconut

Preheat oven to 350°F. Grease cookie sheets. Drain pineapple well, reserving ¹/₂ cup syrup. In large bowl, cream brown sugar and margarine until light and fluffy. Beat in egg. Beat in pineapple, reserved syrup and almond extract. In small bowl, combine oats, flour, baking powder, salt, cinnamon and nutmeg. Add to creamed mixture; beat until blended. Stir in chocolate chips, almonds and coconut.

Drop by heaping tablespoonfuls onto cookie sheets. Flatten cookies slightly with back of spoon. Bake 20 to 25 minutes or until golden. Cool on wire racks.

Makes about 5 dozen cookies

*May use pineapple packed in juice if desired.

Giant Chocolate Oatmeal Cookies

1 cup shortening
1³/₄ cups packed light brown sugar
3 eggs
2 teaspoons vanilla extract
1¹/₃ cups all-purpose flour
¹/₂ cup HERSHEY'S® Cocoa
2 teaspoons baking soda
¹/₄ teaspoon salt
¹/₂ cup water
1 cup flaked coconut
1 cup raisins
1 cup REESE'S® Peanut Butter Chips
3 cups quick-cooking rolled oats
Additional REESE'S® Peanut Butter Chips and coconut (optional)

In large mixer bowl, beat shortening, brown sugar, eggs and vanilla until light and fluffy. Stir together flour, cocoa, baking soda and salt; add alternately with water to shortening mixture. Stir in coconut, raisins, peanut butter chips and oats, blending well. Cover; refrigerate 2 hours.

Preheat oven to 350°F. Using a ¹/₄-cup ice cream scoop or measuring cup, drop dough about 4 inches apart onto lightly greased cookie sheet. Sprinkle additional chips and coconut on top, if desired.

Bake 10 to 12 minutes or until set (do not overbake). Cool slightly; remove from cookie sheet to wire rack. Cool completely.

Makes about 36 (3-inch) cookies

Pudding Chip Cookies

1 cup PARKAY® Magarine, softened
³/₄ cup firmly packed light brown sugar
¹/₄ cup granulated sugar
1 package (4-serving size) JELL-O® Instant Pudding and Pie Filling, Butter Pecan, Butterscotch, Chocolate, Milk Chocolate, Chocolate Fudge, French Vanilla or Vanilla Flavor
1 teaspoon vanilla
2 eggs
2¹/₄ cups all-purpose flour
1 teaspoon baking soda
1 package (12 ounces) BAKER'S® Semi-Sweet Real Chocolate Chips
1 cup chopped nuts (optional)

Preheat oven to 375°F. Beat margarine, sugars, pudding mix and vanilla in large bowl until smooth and creamy. Beat in eggs. Gradually add flour and baking soda. Stir in chips and nuts. (Dough will be stiff.) Drop by teaspoonfuls 2 inches apart onto ungreased cookie sheets. Bake 8 to 10 minutes or until lightly browned. Remove; cool on wire racks.

Makes about 7 dozen cookies

Prep time: 30 minutes
Baking time: 30 minutes

Chocolate Chip Cinnamon Crinkles

- ½ cup butter or margarine, softened
- ½ cup packed brown sugar
- ¼ cup plus 2 tablespoons granulated sugar
- 1 teaspoon vanilla
- 1 egg
- 1 teaspoon cream of tartar
- ½ teaspoon baking soda
- ⅛ teaspoon salt
- 1⅓ cups all-purpose flour
- 1 cup (6 ounces) semisweet chocolate chips
- 2 teaspoons unsweetened cocoa
- 1 teaspoon ground cinnamon

Preheat oven to 400°F. Line cookie sheets with parchment paper or leave ungreased. Cream butter, brown sugar, the ¼ cup granulated sugar, vanilla and egg in large bowl until light and fluffy. Beat in cream of tartar, baking soda and salt. Add flour; mix until dough is blended and stiff. Stir in chocolate chips.

Combine the 2 tablespoons granulated sugar, cocoa and cinnamon in small bowl. Shape rounded teaspoonfuls of dough into balls about 1¼ inches in diameter. Roll balls in cinnamon mixture until coated on all sides. Place 2 inches apart on cookie sheets.

Bake 8 to 10 minutes or until firm. Do not overbake. Remove to wire racks to cool.

Makes about 3½ dozen cookies

Prized Peanut Butter Crunch Cookies

- 1 cup BUTTER FLAVOR CRISCO®
- 2 cups firmly packed brown sugar
- 1 cup JIF® Extra Crunchy Peanut Butter
- 4 egg whites, slightly beaten
- 1 teaspoon vanilla
- 2 cups all-purpose flour
- 1 teaspoon baking soda
- ½ teaspoon baking powder
- 2 cups crisp rice cereal
- 1½ cups chopped peanuts
- 1 cup quick oats (not instant or old fashioned), uncooked
- 1 cup flake coconut

1. Preheat oven to 350°F. Combine BUTTER FLAVOR CRISCO®, brown sugar and JIF® Extra Crunchy Peanut Butter in large bowl. Beat at medium speed of electric mixer until blended. Beat in egg whites and vanilla.

2. Combine flour, baking soda and baking powder. Mix into creamed mixture at low speed until just blended. Stir in, one at a time, rice cereal, nuts, oats and coconut with spoon.

3. Drop rounded measuring tablespoonfuls of dough 2 inches apart onto ungreased cookie sheet.

4. Bake 8 to 10 minutes or until set. Remove immediately to cooling rack.

Makes about 4 dozen cookies

Prized Peanut Butter Crunch Cookies

Chewy Choco-Peanut Pudgies

Cookies
- ½ cup **BUTTER FLAVOR CRISCO®**
- 1¼ cups firmly packed brown sugar
- ¾ cup **JIF® Creamy Peanut Butter**
- 1 tablespoon light corn syrup
- 1 egg
- 1 tablespoon milk
- 1 teaspoon vanilla
- 1½ cups all-purpose flour
- ½ teaspoon baking soda
- ½ teaspoon salt
- 1½ cups coarsely chopped unsalted peanuts (raw or dry roasted)
- ½ cup granulated sugar

Frosting
- ½ teaspoon **BUTTER FLAVOR CRISCO®**
- ½ cup semi-sweet chocolate chips
- ½ teaspoon granulated sugar

1. Preheat oven to 375°F. Grease cookie sheet with BUTTER FLAVOR CRISCO®.

2. For Cookies, combine BUTTER FLAVOR CRISCO®, brown sugar, JIF® Creamy Peanut Butter and corn syrup in large bowl. Beat at medium speed of electric mixer until well blended. Beat in egg, milk and vanilla.

3. Combine flour, baking soda and salt. Mix into creamed mixture at low speed until just blended. Stir in nuts.

4. Form dough into 1¼-inch balls. Roll in granulated sugar. Place 2 inches apart on cookie sheet.

5. Bake 8 to 9 minutes, or until set. Cool 2 minutes on cookie sheet. Remove to cooling rack.

6. For Frosting, combine BUTTER FLAVOR CRISCO®, chocolate chips and granulated sugar in microwave-safe

Peanut Butter Kisses

measuring cup. Microwave at 50% (MEDIUM). Stir after 1 minute. Repeat until smooth (or melt on rangetop in small saucepan on very low heat). Generously drizzle over cooled cookies.

Makes about 4 dozen cookies

Peanut Butter Kisses

- 1 cup **BUTTER FLAVOR CRISCO®**
- 1 cup **JIF® Creamy Peanut Butter**
- 1 cup firmly packed brown sugar
- 1 cup granulated sugar
- 2 eggs
- ¼ cup milk
- 2 teaspoons vanilla
- 3¼ cups all-purpose flour
- 2 teaspoons baking soda
- 1 teaspoon salt
  Granulated sugar for rolling
- 72 to 90 milk chocolate kisses or stars, unwrapped

1. Preheat oven to 375°F. Combine BUTTER FLAVOR CRISCO®, JIF® Creamy Peanut Butter, brown sugar and 1 cup granulated sugar in large bowl. Beat at medium speed of electric mixer until well blended. Beat in eggs, milk and vanilla.

2. Combine flour, baking soda and salt. Mix into creamed mixture at low speed until just blended. (Dough will be stiff.)

3. Form dough into 1-inch balls. Roll in granulated sugar. Place 2 inches apart on ungreased cookie sheet.

4. Bake 8 minutes. Press milk chocolate kiss into center of each cookie. Return to oven. Bake 3 minutes. Cool 2 minutes on cookie sheet. Remove to cooling rack.

Makes 6 to 7½ dozen cookies

Jam-Filled Peanut Butter Kisses: Omit milk chocolate kisses. Prepare recipe as directed for steps 1 through 3. Bake 8 minutes. Press handle of wooden spoon gently into center of each cookie. Return to oven. Bake 3 minutes. Finish as directed. Fill cooled cookies with favorite jam.

Peanut Butter Secrets

Chocolate Thumbprints

Cookies
 ½ cup BUTTER FLAVOR CRISCO®
 ½ cup granulated sugar
 1 tablespoon milk
 ½ teaspoon vanilla
 1 egg yolk
 1 square (1 ounce) unsweetened chocolate, melted and cooled
 1 cup all-purpose flour
 ¼ teaspoon salt
 ⅓ cup semi-sweet miniature chocolate chips

Peanut Butter Cream Filling
 2 tablespoons BUTTER FLAVOR CRISCO®
 ⅓ cup JIF® Creamy Peanut Butter
 1 cup confectioners' sugar
 2 tablespoons milk
 ½ teaspoon vanilla

1. Preheat oven to 350°F. Grease cookie sheet with BUTTER FLAVOR CRISCO®.

2. For Cookies, combine BUTTER FLAVOR CRISCO®, granulated sugar, milk, vanilla and egg yolk in large bowl. Beat at medium speed of electric mixer until well blended. Add melted chocolate. Mix well.

3. Combine flour and salt. Add to chocolate mixture. Mix until blended. Stir in chocolate chips. Form dough into 1-inch balls. Place 2 inches apart on cookie sheet. Press thumb gently in center of each cookie.

4. Bake 8 minutes. Press centers again after baking. Cool completely on wire rack.

5. For Peanut Butter Cream Filling, combine BUTTER FLAVOR CRISCO® and JIF® Creamy Peanut Butter in medium bowl. Stir with spoon until blended. Add confectioners' sugar; stir well. Add milk and vanilla; stir until smooth. Fill cooled thumbprint cookies with filling.

Makes about 2½ dozen cookies

Preparation time: 25 minutes
Bake time: 8 minutes

Peanut Butter Secrets

Cookies
 1 cup BUTTER FLAVOR CRISCO®
 ¾ cup firmly packed brown sugar
 ½ cup granulated sugar
 ½ cup JIF® Creamy Peanut Butter
 1 egg
 1 teaspoon vanilla
 2 cups all-purpose flour
 1 teaspoon baking soda
 ½ teaspoon salt
 40 to 45 chocolate-covered miniature peanut butter cups, unwrapped

Glaze
 1 teaspoon BUTTER FLAVOR CRISCO®
 1 cup semi-sweet chocolate chips
 2 tablespoons JIF® Creamy Peanut Butter

1. Preheat oven to 375°F. Grease cookie sheet with BUTTER FLAVOR CRISCO®.

2. For Cookies, combine BUTTER FLAVOR CRISCO®, brown sugar, granulated sugar and JIF® Creamy Peanut Butter in large bowl. Beat at medium speed of electric mixer until well blended. Beat in egg and vanilla.

3. Combine flour, baking soda and salt. Mix into creamed mixture at low speed until just blended.

4. Form rounded teaspoonfuls of dough around each peanut butter cup. Enclose entirely. Place 2 inches apart on cookie sheet.

5. Bake 8 to 10 minutes or until cookies are just browned. Remove immediately to cooling rack.

6. For Glaze, combine BUTTER FLAVOR CRISCO®, chocolate chips and JIF® Creamy Peanut Butter in microwave-safe cup. Microwave at 50% (MEDIUM). Stir after 1 minute. Repeat until smooth (or melt on rangetop in small saucepan on very low heat). Dip cookie tops in glaze.

Makes about 3½ dozen cookies

Peanut Butter Jumbos

½ cup butter or margarine,
      softened
1 cup packed brown sugar
1 cup granulated sugar
1½ cups peanut butter
3 eggs
2 teaspoons baking soda
1 teaspoon vanilla
4½ cups uncooked rolled oats
1 cup (6 ounces) semisweet
      chocolate chips
1 cup candy-coated
      chocolate pieces

Preheat oven to 350°F. Lightly grease cookie sheets or line with parchment paper.

Cream butter, sugars, peanut butter and eggs in large bowl until light. Blend in baking soda, vanilla and oats until well mixed. Stir in chocolate chips and candy pieces.

Scoop out about ⅓ cupful of dough for each cookie. Place on prepared cookie sheets, spacing about 4 inches apart. Press each cookie to flatten slightly. Bake 15 to 20 minutes or until firm in center. Remove to wire racks to cool.

Makes about 1½ dozen cookies

Peanut Butter Cookies

½ cup BUTTER FLAVOR
      CRISCO®
1 cup JIF® Creamy Peanut
      Butter
¾ cup granulated sugar
½ cup firmly packed brown
      sugar
1 tablespoon milk
1 teaspoon vanilla
1 egg
1¼ cups all-purpose flour
¾ teaspoon baking soda
½ teaspoon baking powder
¼ teaspoon salt

1. Preheat oven to 375°F. Combine BUTTER FLAVOR CRISCO®, JIF® Creamy Peanut Butter, granulated sugar, brown sugar, milk and vanilla in large bowl. Beat at medium speed of electric mixer until well blended. Beat in egg.
2. Combine flour, baking soda, baking powder and salt. Mix into creamed mixture. Drop rounded tablespoonfuls of dough 2 inches apart onto ungreased cookie sheet. Flatten in crisscross pattern with fork dipped in flour.
3. Bake 8 to 10 minutes. Cool 2 minutes on cookie sheet. Remove to cooling rack.

Makes about 2 dozen cookies

Preparation time: 20 minutes
Bake time: 8 to 10 minutes

Peanut Butter Perfection

1 cup BUTTER FLAVOR
      CRISCO®
1 cup JIF® Extra Crunchy
      Peanut Butter
1 cup firmly packed brown
      sugar
1 cup granulated sugar
3 eggs
2 teaspoons milk
1 teaspoon vanilla
3½ cups all-purpose flour
1 teaspoon baking soda
½ teaspoon salt
¾ cup peanut butter chips

1. Preheat oven to 375°F. Grease cookie sheet with BUTTER FLAVOR CRISCO®.
2. Combine BUTTER FLAVOR CRISCO®, JIF® Extra Crunchy Peanut Butter, brown sugar and granulated sugar in large bowl. Beat at medium speed of electric mixer until well blended. Beat in eggs, milk and vanilla.
3. Combine flour, baking soda and salt. Mix into creamed mixture at low speed until just blended. Stir in peanut butter chips.

4. Form dough into 1-inch balls. Place 2 inches apart on cookie sheet. Make crisscross pattern on dough with floured fork.
5. Bake 9 to 11 minutes or until lightly browned. Cool 1 minute on cookie sheet. Remove to cooling rack.

Makes about 6 dozen cookies

Peanut Butter Sunshine Cookies

½ cup BUTTER FLAVOR
      CRISCO®
¾ cup JIF® Extra Crunchy
      Peanut Butter
1 cup sugar
½ cup orange marmalade
2 eggs
1 teaspoon vanilla
2 cups all-purpose flour
1 tablespoon baking powder
½ teaspoon salt
1 cup butterscotch-flavored
      chips

1. Preheat oven to 350°F. Grease cookie sheet with BUTTER FLAVOR CRISCO®.
2. Combine BUTTER FLAVOR CRISCO®, JIF® Extra Crunchy Peanut Butter and sugar in large bowl. Beat at medium speed of electric mixer until well blended. Beat in marmalade, eggs and vanilla.
3. Combine flour, baking powder and salt. Mix into creamed mixture at low speed until just blended. Stir in butterscotch chips.
4. Drop rounded teaspoonfuls of dough 2 inches apart onto cookie sheet.
5. Bake 10 to 12 minutes or until lightly browned. Cool 2 minutes on cookie sheet. Remove to cooling rack.

Makes about 4 dozen cookies

Crispie Coconut Refrigerator Cookies

1 cup BUTTER FLAVOR
    CRISCO®
1 cup sugar
2 tablespoons milk
1 egg
2¼ cups all-purpose flour
½ teaspoon salt
½ teaspoon baking soda
3 cups flake coconut,
    divided
1 egg yolk
1 tablespoon milk
70 pecan halves (about 1¼
    cups)

1. Cream BUTTER FLAVOR CRISCO®, sugar and 2 tablespoons milk in large bowl at medium speed of electric mixer until well blended. Beat in egg. Combine flour, salt and baking soda. Add to creamed mixture. Add 2 cups coconut. Mix until well blended.

2. Divide dough in half. Form each half into a roll 1½ inches in diameter. Cut 2 pieces waxed paper 18 inches long. Sprinkle ½ cup coconut on each piece. Roll dough in coconut. Roll up in waxed paper. Refrigerate several hours or overnight.

3. Preheat oven to 325°F. Grease cookie sheet with BUTTER FLAVOR CRISCO®. Cut dough with sharp knife into ¼-inch slices. Place 2 inches apart on cookie sheet. Combine egg yolk and 1 tablespoon milk. Stir well. Brush on cookie slices. Top each slice with pecan half. Bake 12 minutes. Remove to cooling rack.

Makes about 6 dozen cookies

Hint: Cookie rolls can be frozen for up to three months.

Preparation time: 20 minutes
Chill time: 2 hours or overnight
Bake time: 12 minutes

Pineapple Carrot Cookies

2 cans (8 ounces each)
    DOLE® Crushed
    Pineapple in Juice
¾ cup margarine, softened
½ cup brown sugar, packed
½ cup granulated sugar
1 egg
1 teaspoon vanilla extract
1 cup shredded DOLE®
    Carrots
1 cup chopped walnuts
1 cup DOLE® Raisins
1½ cups flour
1 teaspoon ground cinnamon
½ teaspoon ground ginger
½ teaspoon baking powder
¼ teaspoon salt

Preheat oven to 375°F. Drain pineapple well. In large mixer bowl, beat margarine and sugars until light and fluffy. Beat in egg and vanilla. Beat in pineapple, carrots, nuts and raisins. In medium bowl, combine remaining ingredients; beat into pineapple mixture until well blended.

Drop heaping tablespoons of batter 2 inches apart onto greased cookie sheets. Flatten tops with spoon. Bake 15 to 20 minutes or until golden.

Makes about 3 dozen cookies

Pineapple Carrot Cookies

Hawaiian Oatmeal Cookies

¾ cup BUTTER FLAVOR
    CRISCO®
1 cup firmly packed brown
    sugar
1 egg
¼ cup plus 2 tablespoons
    orange marmalade
½ teaspoon vanilla
1½ cups all-purpose flour
½ teaspoon baking powder
½ teaspoon baking soda
¼ teaspoon salt
2 cups quick oats (not
    instant or old fashioned),
    uncooked
½ cup well drained, crushed
    pineapple
½ cup flake coconut

1. Preheat oven to 350°F. Grease cookie sheet with BUTTER FLAVOR CRISCO®.

2. Combine BUTTER FLAVOR CRISCO®, brown sugar, egg, orange marmalade and vanilla in large bowl. Beat at medium speed of electric mixer until well blended.

3. Combine flour, baking powder, baking soda and salt. Mix into creamed mixture at low speed until well blended. Stir in oats, pineapple and coconut with spoon. Drop rounded tablespoons of dough 2 inches apart onto cookie sheet.

4. Bake 10 to 12 minutes, or until edges are lightly browned and cookie is still soft. Cool 2 minutes on cookie sheet. Remove to cooling rack.

Makes about 3 dozen cookies

Coconut Macaroons

2 (7-ounce) packages *flaked* coconut (5⅓ cups)
1 (14-ounce) can EAGLE® Brand Sweetened Condensed Milk (NOT evaporated milk)
2 teaspoons vanilla extract
1½ teaspoons almond extract

Preheat oven to 350°F. In large bowl, combine coconut, sweetened condensed milk and extracts; mix well. Drop by rounded teaspoonfuls onto aluminum-foil-lined and *generously greased* cookie sheets; garnish as desired.

Bake 8 to 10 minutes or until lightly browned around edges. *Immediately* remove from cookie sheets (macaroons will stick if allowed to cool). Store loosely covered at room temperature.

Makes about 4 dozen cookies

Chocolate: Omit almond extract. Add 4 (1-ounce) squares unsweetened chocolate, melted. Proceed as above.

Chocolate Chip: Omit almond extract. Add 1 cup mini chocolate chips. Proceed as above.

Cherry Nut: Omit almond extract. Add 1 cup chopped nuts and 2 tablespoons maraschino cherry syrup. Before baking, press maraschino cherry half into center of each macaroon.

Rum Raisin: Omit almond extract. Add 1 cup raisins and 1 teaspoon rum flavoring. Proceed as above.

Almond Brickle: Add ½ cup almond brickle chips. Proceed as above. Bake 10 to 12 minutes. Cool 3 minutes; remove from cookie sheets.

Maple Walnut: Omit almond extract. Add ½ cup finely chopped walnuts and ½ teaspoon maple flavoring. Proceed as above.

Nutty Oat: Omit almond extract. Add 1 cup oats and 1 cup chopped nuts. Proceed as above.

Coconut Macaroons

Double Chocolate Banana Cookies

Double Chocolate Banana Cookies

3 to 4 extra-ripe, medium DOLE® Bananas, peeled and cut into chunks
2 cups rolled oats, uncooked
2 cups sugar
1³/₄ cups flour
¹/₂ cup unsweetened cocoa powder
1 teaspoon baking soda
¹/₂ teaspoon salt
2 eggs, slightly beaten
1¹/₄ cups margarine, melted
1 cup DOLE® Chopped Natural Almonds, toasted
1 to 2 cups semisweet chocolate chips

In food processor or blender, process bananas until pureed (2 cups). In large bowl, combine oats, sugar, flour, cocoa, baking soda and salt until well mixed.

Stir in pureed bananas, eggs and margarine until blended. Stir in nuts and chocolate chips. Refrigerate dough 1 hour or until mixture becomes partially firm (dough runs during baking if too soft).

Preheat oven to 350°F. Drop dough by ¹/₄ cupfuls onto greased cookie sheet. Flatten slightly with spatula into 2¹/₂- to 3-inch circles. Bake 15 to 17 minutes. Remove to wire rack to cool.

Makes about 2¹/₂ dozen cookies

Macaroon Kiss Cookies

¹/₃ cup butter or maragarine, softened
1 package (3 ounces) cream cheese, softened
³/₄ cup sugar
1 egg yolk
2 teaspoons almond extract
2 teaspoons orange juice
1¹/₄ cups all-purpose flour
2 teaspoons baking powder
¹/₄ teaspoon salt
5 cups (14-ounce package) flaked coconut, divided
54 HERSHEY'S® KISSES Chocolates (9-ounce package), unwrapped

In large mixer bowl, beat together butter, cream cheese and sugar. Add egg yolk, almond extract and orange juice; beat well. Stir together flour, baking powder and salt; gradually add to butter mixture. Stir in 3 cups coconut. Cover tightly; refrigerate 1 hour or until firm enough to handle.

Preheat oven to 350°F. Shape dough into 1-inch balls; roll in remaining 2 cups coconut. Place on ungreased cookie sheet. Bake 10 to 12 minutes or until lightly browned. Remove from oven; immediately press KISS on top of each cookie. Cool 1 minute. Carefully remove from cookie sheet; cool completely on wire rack.

Makes about 4¹/₂ dozen cookies

Marvelous Macaroons

1 can (8 ounces) DOLE® Crushed Pineapple in Juice
1 can (14 ounces) sweetened condensed milk
1 package (7 ounces) flaked coconut
¹/₂ cup margarine, melted
³/₄ cup DOLE® Chopped Natural Almonds, toasted
Grated peel from 1 DOLE® Lemon
¹/₄ teaspoon almond extract
1 cup flour
1 teaspoon baking powder

Preheat oven to 350°F. Drain pineapple well, pressing out excess juice with back of spoon. In large bowl, combine pineapple, condensed milk, coconut, margarine, nuts, lemon peel and extract. In small bowl, combine flour and baking powder. Beat into pineapple mixture until blended.

Drop heaping tablespoons of batter 1 inch apart onto greased cookie sheets. Bake 13 to 15 minutes or until lightly browned. Cool on wire rack. Store in covered container in refrigerator.

Makes about 3¹/₂ dozen cookies

Banana Drop Cookies

2 ripe, medium DOLE® Bananas, peeled and cut into chunks
1 cup margarine, softened
1 cup granulated sugar
¹/₂ cup packed brown sugar
2 eggs
1 teaspoon vanilla
2 cups all-purpose flour
1 teaspoon baking soda
1 teaspoon ground cinnamon (optional)
¹/₂ teaspoon salt
1 cup peanut butter chips
1 cup chopped walnuts
1 cup DOLE® raisins

Preheat oven to 375°F. In food processor or blender, process bananas until pureed (1 cup). In large bowl, cream margarine and sugars. Beat in pureed bananas, eggs and vanilla. In small bowl, combine flour, baking soda, cinnamon and salt. Gradually beat flour mixture into banana mixture. Fold in chips, nuts and raisins.

Drop batter by tablespoonfuls 2 inches apart onto greased cookie sheets. Bake 12 minutes or until golden brown. Remove to wire racks to cool.

Makes about 4 dozen cookies

San Francisco Cookies

2 extra-ripe, medium DOLE®
    Bananas, peeled and cut
    into chunks
2 cups granola
1½ cups flour
1 cup brown sugar, packed
1 teaspoon baking powder
1 teaspoon ground cinnamon
2 eggs
½ cup margarine, melted
¼ cup vegetable oil
1 cup chocolate chips

Preheat oven to 350°F. In food processor or blender, process bananas until pureed (1 cup). Combine granola, flour, brown sugar, baking powder and cinnamon in large mixing bowl. Beat in pureed bananas, eggs, margarine and oil. Fold in chocolate chips.

Drop dough by ¼ cupfuls onto greased cookie sheets. Spread dough into 2½- to 3-inch circles. Bake 16 minutes. Remove to wire racks to cool.

Makes about 16 cookies

Double Chocolate Pretzels

1 cup unsalted butter,
    softened
1 cup powdered sugar, sifted
½ teaspoon salt
1½ eggs*
1 teaspoon vanilla
2¾ cups all-purpose flour
½ cup unsweetened cocoa
¼ teaspoon baking powder
1 package (12 ounces)
    semisweet chocolate
    chips
¼ cup shortening

In large bowl, beat butter, powdered sugar and salt until light and fluffy. Beat in eggs and vanilla until smooth. In medium bowl, combine flour, cocoa and baking powder. Using rubber spatula, gradually fold flour mixture into butter mixture. Divide dough into quarters. Wrap each portion; refrigerate until firm, about 1½ hours.

Preheat oven to 350°F. Working with one quarter of dough at a time, roll scant tablespoonfuls of dough into 6×¼-inch ropes. Form each rope into pretzel shape. Place 1½ inches apart on parchment-paper-lined cookie sheets. Bake 10 to 12 minutes or until firm to the touch; do not overbake. Let cookies cool 5 minutes before removing them from cookie sheets to wire racks; cool completely.

In top of double boiler, melt chips and shortening over simmering water; stir to blend thoroughly. To dip cookies, gently push into chocolate mixture to coat. Lift out and shake to remove excess chocolate. Pull flat side of cookie across edge of pan to smooth bottom. Place cookies on waxed paper; let stand until chocolate is set.

Makes about 5 dozen cookies

*To measure ½ egg, lightly beat 1 egg in glass measuring cup; remove half for use in recipe.

Butter Pecan Crisps

1 cup unsalted butter,
    softened
¾ cup granulated sugar
¾ cup packed brown sugar
½ teaspoon salt
2 eggs
1 teaspoon vanilla
1½ cups finely ground
    pecans
2½ cups sifted all-purpose
    flour
1 teaspoon baking soda
30 pecan halves
4 squares (1 ounce each)
    semisweet chocolate
1 tablespoon shortening

Preheat oven to 375°F. In large bowl, beat butter, sugars and salt until light and fluffy. Add eggs, 1 at a time, beating well after each addition. Beat in vanilla and ground pecans. In small bowl, combine flour and baking soda. Gradually stir flour mixture into butter mixture.

Spoon dough into large pastry bag fitted with ⅜-inch round tip; fill bag halfway. Shake down dough to remove air bubbles. Hold bag perpendicular to and about ½ inch above parchment-paper-lined cookie sheets. Pipe dough into 1¼ inch balls, spacing 3 inches apart. Cut each pecan half lengthwise into 2 slivers. Press 1 sliver in center of each dough ball.

Bake 9 to 12 minutes or until lightly browned. Let cookies cool 5 minutes before removing them from cookie sheets to wire racks; cool completely.

In small, heavy saucepan over low heat, melt chocolate and shortening; stir to blend. Drizzle chocolate mixture over cookies. Let stand until chocolate is set.

Makes about 4 dozen cookies

Cut-Out Sugar Cookies

2/3 cup **BUTTER FLAVOR**
   CRISCO®
3/4 cup sugar
1 tablespoon plus
   1 teaspoon milk
1 teaspoon vanilla
1 egg
2 cups all-purpose flour
1½ teaspoons baking powder
¼ teaspoon salt

1. Combine BUTTER FLAVOR CRISCO®, sugar, milk and vanilla in large bowl. Beat at medium speed of electric mixer until well blended. Beat in egg.

2. Combine flour, baking powder and salt. Mix into creamed mixture at low speed until well blended. Cover and refrigerate several hours or overnight.

3. Preheat oven to 375°F. Roll out dough, half at a time, to about ⅛-inch thickness on floured surface. Cut out with cookie cutters. Place 2 inches apart on ungreased cookie sheet. Sprinkle with colored sugars and decors or leave plain and frost when cooled. Bake 7 to 9 minutes, or until set. Remove immediately to wire racks.

   Makes about 3 dozen cookies

Lemon or Orange Cut-Out Sugar Cookies: Add 1 teaspoon grated lemon or orange peel and 1 teaspoon lemon or orange extract to dough in Step 1.

CREAMY VANILLA FROSTING: Combine ½ cup BUTTER FLAVOR CRISCO®, 1 pound (4 cups) powdered sugar, ⅓ cup milk and 1 teaspoon vanilla in medium bowl. Beat at low speed of electric mixer until well blended. Scrape bowl. Beat at high speed for 2 minutes, or until smooth and creamy. One or two drops food color can be used to tint each cup of frosting, if desired. Frost cooled cookies. This frosting works well in decorating tube.

Lemon or Orange Creamy Frosting: Omit milk. Add ⅓ cup lemon or orange juice. Add 1 teaspoon orange peel with orange juice.

CHOCOLATE FROSTING: Place ⅓ cup BUTTER FLAVOR CRISCO® in medium microwave-safe bowl. Cover with waxed paper. Microwave at 100% (HIGH) until melted (or melt on rangetop in small saucepan on low heat). Add ¾ cup unsweetened cocoa powder and ¼ teaspoon salt. Beat at low speed of electric mixer until blended. Add ½ cup milk and 2 teaspoons vanilla. Beat at low speed. Add 1 pound (4 cups) powdered sugar, 1 cup at a time. Beat at low speed after each addition until smooth and creamy. Add more sugar to thicken or milk to thin for good spreading consistency.

Chocolate Dipped: Combine 1 cup semi-sweet chocolate chips and 1 teaspoon BUTTER FLAVOR CRISCO® in microwave-safe measuring cup. Microwave at 50% (MEDIUM). Stir after 1 minute. Repeat until smooth (or melt on rangetop in small saucepan on very low heat). Dip one end of cooled cookie halfway up in chocolate. Place on waxed paper until chocolate is firm.

Chocolate Nut: Dip cookie in melted chocolate as directed. Sprinkle with finely chopped nuts before chocolate hardens.

Drop Sugar Cookies

2½ cups sifted all-purpose
   flour
¾ teaspoon salt
½ teaspoon ARM & HAMMER®
   Pure Baking Soda
½ cup butter or margarine
½ cup vegetable shortening
1 cup sugar
1 teaspoon vanilla extract
1 egg
2 tablespoons milk

Preheat oven to 400°F. Sift together flour, salt and baking soda. Set aside. Using an electric mixer, cream together butter and shortening in large bowl; add sugar gradually and continue beating until light and fluffy. Beat in vanilla and egg. Add flour mixture and beat until smooth; blend in milk.

Drop dough by teaspoonfuls about 3 inches apart onto greased cookie sheets. Flatten with bottom of glass that has been dipped in sugar. Bake 12 minutes or until edges are lightly browned. Cool on wire racks.

   Makes about 5½ dozen cookies

Chocolate Drop Sugar Cookies

2/3 cup butter or margarine,
   softened
1 cup sugar
1 egg
1½ teaspoons vanilla extract
1½ cups all-purpose flour
½ cup HERSHEY'S® Cocoa
½ teaspoon baking soda
¼ teaspoon salt
⅓ cup buttermilk or sour
   milk*
Additional sugar

Preheat oven to 350°F. In large mixer bowl, beat butter and sugar until creamy. Add egg and vanilla; blend well. Stir together flour, cocoa, baking soda and salt; add alternately with buttermilk to butter mixture.

Using ice cream scoop or ¼ cup measuring cup, drop dough onto ungreased cookie sheets about 2 inches apart; sprinkle tops lightly with sugar.

Bake 13 to 15 minutes or until cookie springs back when touched lightly in center. Cool slightly; remove from cookie sheets to wire racks. Cool completely.

   Makes about 1 dozen cookies

***To sour milk:** Use 1 teaspoon white vinegar plus milk to equal ⅓ cup.

Cut-Out Sugar Cookies

Cream Cheese Cutout Cookies

        1 cup butter, softened
        1 package (8 ounces) cream
           cheese, softened
    1¹/₂ cups sugar
        1 egg
        1 teaspoon vanilla
      ¹/₂ teaspoon almond extract
    3¹/₂ cups all-purpose flour
        1 teaspoon baking powder
           Almond Frosting (recipe
              follows)
           Assorted candies for
              decoration (optional)

In large bowl, beat butter and cream cheese until well combined. Add sugar; beat until fluffy. Add egg, vanilla and almond extract; beat well. In small bowl, combine flour and baking powder. Add dry ingredients to cream cheese mixture; beat until well mixed. Divide dough in half. Wrap each portion; refrigerate until easy to handle, about 1¹/₂ hours.

Preheat oven to 375°F. Roll out dough, half at a time, ¹/₈ inch thick on lightly floured surface. Cut out with cookie cutters. Place 2 inches apart on ungreased cookie sheets. Bake 8 to 10 minutes or until edges are lightly browned. Remove to wire racks to cool completely. Decorate cookies as desired with Almond Frosting and candies.

Makes about 7 dozen cookies

ALMOND FROSTING: In small bowl, beat 2 cups sifted powdered sugar, 2 tablespoons softened butter and ¹/₄ teaspoon almond extract until smooth. For piping consistency, beat in 4 to 5 teaspoons milk. For spreading consistency, add a little more milk. If desired, tint with food coloring.

*Favorite recipe from **Wisconsin Milk Marketing Board** © 1991*

Melting Moments

      ¹/₂ cup butter or margarine,
           softened
      ¹/₃ cup sugar
        1 egg yolk
      ¹/₄ teaspoon vanilla
        1 cup all-purpose flour
        4 squares (1 ounce each)
           semisweet chocolate
        1 tablespoon shortening
           Orange Butter Cream
           (recipe follows)

In medium bowl, beat butter, sugar, egg yolk and vanilla until fluffy. Add flour; beat until well mixed. Wrap dough; refrigerate until firm, 1 hour.

Preheat oven to 375°F. Drop dough by level teaspoonfuls 2 inches apart onto ungreased cookie sheets or pipe through pastry bag fitted with large closed star tip. Bake 8 to 10 minutes or until lightly browned. Let cookies cool 1 minute before removing them from cookie sheets to wire racks; cool completely.

In small, heavy saucepan over low heat, melt chocolate and shortening; stir to blend. Dip half of each cookie in melted chocolate mixture. Place on waxed paper; let stand until chocolate sets. Prepare Orange Butter Cream. Place slightly rounded ¹/₂ teaspoon of butter cream filling on flat side of half the cookies. Top with remaining cookies, flat side down, forming sandwiches.

Makes about 24 sandwich cookies

ORANGE BUTTER CREAM: In small bowl, mix ¹/₂ cup powdered sugar, 2 tablespoons softened butter, 1¹/₂ teaspoons orange juice and ¹/₂ teaspoon grated orange peel. Stir until smooth.

Almond Buttons

        2 cups BLUE DIAMOND®
           Blanched Whole
           Almonds, toasted,
           divided
        2 cups flour
      ³/₄ cup powdered sugar
      ¹/₄ teaspoon salt
        1 cup plus 1¹/₂ tablespoons
           butter, softened, divided
        1 teaspoon vanilla
      ¹/₄ teaspoon almond extract
        3 ounces semisweet
           chocolate

Preheat oven to 350°F. Finely grind 1 cup almonds in food processor or blender. Transfer to large bowl. Add flour, sugar and salt. Thoroughly work in 1 cup butter, vanilla and almond extract by hand until a soft dough forms. Dough should not crumble. Chill. Shape into ¹/₂-inch balls. Place on ungreased cookie sheet; indent center of each cookie with finger. Bake 15 minutes or until very lightly browned. Cool on wire rack.

Place chocolate and remaining 1¹/₂ tablespoons butter in double boiler; stir over simmering water until smooth. With spoon drizzle *small* amount of chocolate into center of each cookie. Top each with one of remaining almonds.

Makes about 8 dozen cookies

Brandy Lace Cookies

      ¹/₄ cup sugar
      ¹/₄ cup MAZOLA® Margarine
      ¹/₄ cup KARO® Light or Dark
           Corn Syrup
      ¹/₂ cup flour
      ¹/₄ cup very finely chopped
           pecans or walnuts
        2 tablespoons brandy
           Melted white and/or
           semisweet chocolate
           (optional)

Preheat oven to 350°F. Lightly grease and flour cookie sheets. In small saucepan combine sugar, margarine and corn syrup.

Top to bottom: Brandy Lace Cookies, Kentucky Bourbon Pecan Tarts

Preheat oven to 350°F. Prepare Cream Cheese Pastry. Divide dough in half; set aside 1 half. On floured surface roll out pastry to ⅛-inch thickness. *If necessary, add small amount of flour to keep pastry from sticking.* Cut into 12 (2¼-inch) rounds. Press evenly into bottoms and up sides of 1¾-inch muffin pan cups. Repeat with remaining pastry. Refrigerate.

In medium bowl beat eggs slightly. Stir in granulated sugar, corn syrup, bourbon, margarine and vanilla until well blended. Spoon 1 heaping teaspoon pecans into each pastry-lined cup; top with 1 tablespoon corn syrup mixture.

Bake 20 to 25 minutes or until lightly browned and wooden toothpick inserted into center comes out clean. Cool in pans 5 minutes. Remove; cool completely on wire rack. If desired, sprinkle tarts with confectioners sugar.

Makes about 2 dozen tarts

Cream Cheese Pastry

    1 cup flour
    ¾ teaspoon baking powder
      Pinch salt
    ¾ cup MAZOLA® Margarine,
      softened
    1 package (3 ounces) cream
      cheese, softened
    2 teaspoons sugar

In small bowl combine flour, baking powder and salt. In large bowl mix margarine, cream cheese and sugar until well combined. Stir in flour mixture until well blended. Press firmly into ball with hands.

Prep time: 45 minutes
Bake time: 25 minutes, plus cooling

Bring to boil over medium heat, stirring constantly. Remove from heat. Stir in flour, pecans and brandy. Drop 12 evenly spaced half teaspoonfuls of batter onto prepared cookie sheets.

Bake 6 minutes or until golden. Cool 1 to 2 minutes or until cookies can be lifted but are still warm and pliable; remove with spatula. Curl around handle of wooden spoon; slide off when crisp. If cookies harden before curling, return to oven to soften. If desired, drizzle with melted chocolate.

Makes 4 to 5 dozen cookies

Prep time: 30 minutes
Bake time: 6 minutes, plus curling and cooling

Kentucky Bourbon Pecan Tarts

      Cream Cheese Pastry
      (recipe follows)
    2 eggs
    ½ cup granulated sugar
    ½ cup KARO® Light or Dark
      Corn Syrup
    2 tablespoons bourbon
    1 tablespoon MAZOLA®
      Margarine, melted
    ½ teaspoon vanilla
    1 cup chopped pecans
      Confectioners sugar
      (optional)

Petite Macaroon Cups

1 cup margarine or butter, softened
2 (3-ounce) packages cream cheese, softened
2 cups unsifted flour
1 (14-ounce) can EAGLE® Brand Sweetened Condensed Milk (NOT evaporated milk)
2 eggs, beaten
1½ teaspoons vanilla extract
½ teaspoon almond extract
1 (3½-ounce) can flaked coconut (1⅓ cups)

In large mixer bowl, beat margarine and cream cheese until fluffy; stir in flour. Cover; chill 1 hour.

Preheat oven to 375°F. Divide dough into quarters. On floured surface, shape 1 quarter into smooth ball. Divide into 12 balls. Place each ball in 1¾-inch muffin cup; press evenly on bottom and up side of each cup. Repeat with remaining dough. In medium bowl, combine sweetened condensed milk, eggs and extracts; mix well. Stir in coconut. Fill muffin cups ¾ full. Bake 16 to 18 minutes or until lightly browned. Cool in pans; remove. Store loosely covered at room temperature.

Makes about 4 dozen cookies

Chocolate Tassies

Pastry
2 cups all-purpose flour
2 packages (3 ounces each) cream cheese, cold, cut into chunks
1 cup butter or margarine, cold, cut into chunks
Filling
2 tablespoons butter or margarine
2 squares (1 ounce each) unsweetened chocolate
1½ cups packed brown sugar
2 teaspoons vanilla
2 eggs, beaten
Dash salt
1½ cups chopped pecans

To prepare Pastry: Place flour in large bowl. Cut in cream cheese and butter. Continue to mix until dough can be shaped into a ball. Wrap dough in plastic wrap; refrigerate 1 hour. Shape dough into 1-inch balls. Press each ball into ungreased miniature (1¾-inch) muffin pan cup, covering bottom and side of cup with dough. Preheat oven to 350°F.

To prepare Filling: Melt butter and chocolate in medium-sized heavy saucepan over low heat. Remove from heat. Blend in sugar, vanilla, eggs and salt; beat until thick. Stir in pecans. Spoon about 1 teaspoon filling into each unbaked pastry shell. Bake 20 to 25 minutes or until lightly browned and filling is set. Cool in pans on wire racks. Remove from pans; store in airtight containers.

Makes about 5 dozen cookies

Almond Fudge Cups

Pastry
¾ cup butter or margarine, softened
⅓ cup sugar
2 cups all-purpose flour
1 tablespoon almond- or fruit-flavored liqueur *or* water
1 teaspoon vanilla
Filling
1 cup (6 ounces) semisweet chocolate chips
¾ cup blanched almonds
2 eggs
½ cup sugar
Dash salt

To prepare Pastry: Lightly grease 3 dozen miniature (1¾-inch) muffin pan cups or small tart shells. Cream butter and sugar in large bowl until blended. Add flour, liqueur and vanilla; stir to make moist crumbs. Divide crumbs evenly among muffin cups; press to cover bottoms and sides of cups completely. Preheat oven to 350°F.

To prepare Filling: Place chocolate chips and almonds in food processor or blender. Process until finely ground. Beat eggs in medium bowl until thick; stir in sugar and salt. Blend in chocolate mixture. Spoon filling into unbaked pastry shells. Bake 20 minutes or until filling is set. Cool in pans on wire racks. Store in airtight containers.

Makes about 3 dozen cookies

Gingersnaps

1 cup packed brown sugar
¾ cup unsalted butter, softened
¼ teaspoon salt
1 egg
¼ cup light molasses
1 tablespoon ground ginger
2 teaspoons baking soda
1 teaspoon ground cinnamon
½ teaspoon ground cloves
2¼ cups all-purpose flour
⅓ to ½ cup granulated sugar
½ cup powdered sugar, sifted
1 to 1½ teaspoons strong brewed coffee, cooled
¼ teaspoon lemon juice

In large bowl, beat brown sugar, butter and salt until light and fluffy. Beat in egg. Gradually add molasses; mix well. Add ginger, baking soda, cinnamon and cloves. Beat until blended. Using rubber spatula, gradually fold in flour. (Dough will be soft and sticky.) Divide dough into quarters. Wrap each portion; refrigerate until firm, about 1½ hours.

Preheat oven to 350°F. Shape slightly rounded tablespoonfuls of dough into balls. Roll balls in granulated sugar to coat generously. Place 4 inches apart on greased cookie sheets. Bake about 10 minutes or until centers of cookies feel slightly firm. Let cookies cool 5 minutes before removing them from cookie sheets to wire racks; cool completely.

In small bowl, mix powdered sugar, 1 teaspoon of the coffee and lemon juice; stir until smooth. Stir in as much of remaining coffee as needed to make stiff icing for piping. Fit pastry bag with small round tip. Pipe icing on cookies forming spiral design. Let stand until icing is firm.

Makes about 4 dozen cookies

Spiced Apple-Raisin Cookies

**³/₄ cup butter, softened
 1 cup packed brown sugar
 1 egg
 1 teaspoon vanilla
 1½ cups all-purpose flour
 1 teaspoon baking powder
 ½ teaspoon baking soda
 ½ teaspoon salt
 ½ teaspoon ground cinnamon
 ½ teaspoon ground nutmeg
 1½ cups quick-cooking oats, uncooked
 1 cup finely chopped unpeeled apple
 ½ cup raisins
 ½ cup chopped nuts**

Preheat oven to 350°F. In large bowl, cream butter. Gradually add brown sugar; beat until light and fluffy. Beat in egg and vanilla. In small bowl, combine flour, baking powder, baking soda, salt and spices. Gradually add flour mixture to creamed mixture, blend well. Stir in oats, apple, raisins and nuts.

Drop rounded teaspoonfuls of dough 2 inches apart onto lightly buttered cookie sheets. Bake 10 to 12 minutes or until lightly browned. Remove to wire racks to cool completely.

Makes about 5 dozen cookies

*Favorite recipe from **American Dairy Association***

Maple Raisin Cookies

**Cookies
 2¼ cups all-purpose flour
 1 cup granulated sugar
 ³/₄ cup LAND O LAKES®
     Butter, softened
 ³/₄ cup applesauce
 1 egg
 1 teaspoon pumpkin pie spice
 ½ teaspoon baking soda
 ½ teaspoon salt
 1 cup raisins
 ½ cup chopped walnuts
Frosting
 4 cups powdered sugar
 ½ cup LAND O LAKES®
     Butter, softened
 3 to 4 tablespoons milk
 ½ teaspoon maple extract
 Raisins**

Preheat oven to 375°F. For Cookies, in large mixer bowl, combine flour, granulated sugar, butter, applesauce, egg, pumpkin pie spice, baking soda and salt. Beat at low speed, scraping bowl often, until well mixed, 2 to 3 minutes. Stir in raisins and nuts. Drop rounded teaspoonfuls of dough 2 inches apart onto greased cookie sheets. Bake for 10 to 12 minutes, or until lightly browned. Remove immediately; cool completely on wire racks.

For Frosting, in small mixer bowl, combine powdered sugar, butter, milk and maple extract. Beat at medium speed, scraping bowl often, until light and fluffy, 3 to 4 minutes. Spread over cooled cookies. Place 2 raisins in center of each cookie.

Makes about 3 dozen cookies

Maple Raisin Cookies

Top to bottom: Ginger Snap Oats, Mom's Best Oatmeal Cookies (page 75)

Old-Fashioned Molasses Cookies

**4 cups sifted all-purpose
  flour
2 teaspoons ARM & HAMMER®
  Pure Baking Soda
1½ teaspoons ground ginger
½ teaspoon ground cinnamon
⅛ teaspoon salt
1½ cups molasses
½ cup lard, melted
¼ cup butter or margarine,
  melted
⅓ cup boiling water**

Sift together flour, baking soda, spices and salt. Combine molasses, lard, butter and water in large bowl. Add dry ingredients to liquid mixture and blend well. Cover and chill several hours or overnight. Preheat oven to 350°F. Turn dough onto well-floured board. Using floured rolling pin, roll to ¼-inch thickness. Cut out with 3½-inch floured cookie cutter. Sprinkle with sugar and place on ungreased cookie sheets. Bake 12 minutes. Cool on wire racks.

Makes about 3 dozen cookies

Ginger Snap Oats

**¾ cup BUTTER FLAVOR
  CRISCO®
1 cup firmly packed brown
  sugar
½ cup granulated sugar
½ cup molasses
2 teaspoons vinegar
2 eggs
1¼ cups all-purpose flour
1 tablespoon ginger
1½ teaspoons baking soda
½ teaspoon cinnamon
¼ teaspoon ground cloves
2¾ cups quick oats (not
  instant or old fashioned),
  uncooked
1½ cups raisins**

1. Preheat oven to 350°F. Grease cookie sheet with BUTTER FLAVOR CRISCO®.
2. Combine BUTTER FLAVOR CRISCO®, brown sugar, granulated sugar, molasses, vinegar and eggs in large bowl. Beat at medium speed of electric mixer until well blended.
3. Combine flour, ginger, baking soda, cinnamon and cloves. Mix into creamed mixture at low speed until blended. Stir in oats and raisins. Drop rounded teaspoonfuls of dough 2 inches apart onto cookie sheet.
4. Bake 11 to 14 minutes. Cool 2 minutes on cookie sheet. Remove to cooling rack.

Makes about 5 dozen cookies

Lemon Butter Cookies

**2 cups all-purpose flour
½ teaspoon baking soda
1 cup BLUE BONNET®
  Margarine, softened
1 cup sugar
1 teaspoon vanilla extract
1 teaspoon grated lemon
  peel
1 egg
  Sugar**

Preheat oven to 375°F. In small bowl, combine flour and baking soda; set aside.

In medium bowl, with electric mixer at medium speed, beat margarine, sugar, vanilla and lemon peel just until blended. Beat in egg until light and fluffy. Gradually blend in flour mixture. Drop dough by rounded teaspoonfuls, 2 inches apart, onto ungreased cookie sheets. Grease bottom of small glass; dip in sugar. Press on dough to flatten slightly. Repeat for each cookie. Bake 8 to 10 minutes. Remove from cookie sheets; cool on wire racks. Store in airtight container.

Makes about 4½ dozen cookies

Lemon Nut Cookies

**1½ cups all-purpose flour
¾ teaspoon baking soda
½ teaspoon salt
¾ cup (1½ sticks) butter,
  softened
½ cup firmly packed brown
  sugar
¼ cup granulated sugar
1 egg
1 tablespoon lemon juice
One 10-oz. pkg. (1½ cups)
  NESTLÉ® Toll House®
  Treasures® Premier White
  Deluxe Baking Pieces
1 cup cashews or walnuts,
  coarsely chopped
1 teaspoon grated lemon
  rind**

Preheat oven to 375°F. In small bowl, combine flour, baking soda and salt; set aside.

In large mixer bowl, beat butter, brown sugar and granulated sugar until creamy. Beat in egg and lemon juice. Gradually beat in flour mixture. Stir in Treasures® Premier White deluxe baking pieces, nuts and lemon rind. Drop dough by heaping measuring tablespoonfuls onto ungreased cookie sheets.

Bake 7 to 10 minutes until edges are lightly browned. Let stand on cookie sheets 2 minutes. Remove from cookie sheets; cool on wire racks.

Makes about 2½ dozen cookies

Lemony Spritz Sticks

**1 cup butter or margarine,
   softened
1 cup confectioners' sugar
¼ cup REALEMON® Lemon
   Juice from Concentrate
2½ cups unsifted flour
¼ teaspoon salt
   Fudgy Chocolate Glaze
   Finely chopped nuts**

Preheat oven to 375°F. In large
mixer bowl, beat butter and
sugar until fluffy. Add
REALEMON® brand; beat well.
Stir in flour and salt; mix well.
Place dough in cookie press with
star-shaped plate. Press dough
into 3-inch strips onto greased
cookie sheets.

Bake 5 to 6 minutes or until
lightly browned on ends. Cool 1
to 2 minutes; remove from cookie
sheets. Cool completely. Dip ends
of cookies in Fudgy Chocolate
Glaze, then nuts.

Makes about 8½ dozen cookies

Tip: When using electric cookie
gun, use decorator tip. Press
dough into 3×½-inch strips onto
greased cookie sheets. Bake 8 to
10 minutes or until lightly
browned on ends.

FUDGY CHOCOLATE GLAZE: In
small saucepan, melt 3 ounces
sweet cooking chocolate and
2 tablespoons margarine or
butter.

Makes about ⅓ cup glaze

Lemony Spritz Sticks

Almond Tea Cookies

**1 cup BUTTER FLAVOR
   CRISCO®
2 tablespoons milk
1 teaspoon almond extract
½ cup granulated sugar
1⅔ cups all-purpose flour
⅔ cup chopped slivered
   almonds
¼ teaspoon salt
   Confectioners' sugar**

1. Preheat oven to 350°F. Cream
BUTTER FLAVOR CRISCO®,
milk and almond extract in large
bowl at medium speed of electric
mixer until well blended. Beat in
granulated sugar.
2. Combine flour, almonds and
salt. Mix into creamed mixture.
Shape dough into balls using one
level measuring tablespoon for
each. Place 2 inches apart on
ungreased cookie sheet.
3. Bake 10 to 12 minutes.
(Cookies will not brown. Do not
overbake.) Remove to cooling
rack.
4. Roll slightly warm cookie in
confectioners' sugar. Roll in
sugar again when cookies are
cool.

Makes about 3 dozen cookies

Preparation time: 15 minutes
Bake time: 10 to 12 minutes

Black Walnut Refrigerator Cookies

**3 cups all-purpose flour
1 cup firmly packed brown
   sugar
1 cup LAND O LAKES®
   Butter, softened
2 eggs
1 teaspoon baking soda
1 teaspoon cream of tartar
¼ teaspoon salt
1 teaspoon vanilla
1 cup chopped black walnuts**

In large mixer bowl, combine
flour, sugar, butter, eggs, baking
soda, cream of tartar, salt and
vanilla. Beat at low speed,
scraping bowl often, until well
mixed, 3 to 4 minutes. Stir in
nuts. Divide dough into halves.
Shape each half into a 12×2-inch
roll. Wrap in waxed paper;
refrigerate until firm, at least
2 hours.

Preheat oven to 350°F. Cut rolls
into ¼-inch slices. Place 1 inch
apart on ungreased cookie
sheets. Bake for 9 to 12 minutes,
or until lightly browned. Remove
immediately to wire racks to
cool.

Makes about 8 dozen cookies

Little Raisin Logs

**1 cup butter or margarine,
   softened
⅓ cup sugar
2 teaspoons brandy
   (optional)
2 teaspoons vanilla
½ teaspoon salt
1 cup SUN-MAID® Raisins,
   finely chopped
1 cup DIAMOND® Walnuts,
   finely chopped
2 cups all-purpose flour
1 package (6 ounces) real
   semisweet chocolate
   pieces
3 tablespoons vegetable
   shortening**

Preheat oven to 325°F. In large
bowl, cream butter and sugar.
Beat in brandy, vanilla and salt.
Stir in raisins, walnuts and flour.
Pinch off dough and roll with
hands on lightly floured board
into logs about ½ inch in
diameter and 2½ inches long.

Bake on ungreased cookie sheet
15 to 20 minutes. Cookies do not
brown. Remove to wire rack to
cool.

Meanwhile, in top of double
boiler, melt chocolate and
shortening over simmering
water, blending thoroughly.
When cookies have cooled, dip
one end into melted chocolate.
Place on wire rack to set.

Makes about 6 dozen cookies

Jam-Up Oatmeal Cookies

1 cup BUTTER FLAVOR CRISCO®
1½ cups firmly packed brown sugar
2 eggs
2 teaspoons almond extract
2 cups all-purpose flour
1 teaspoon baking powder
1 teaspoon salt
½ teaspoon baking soda
2½ cups quick oats (not instant or old fashioned), uncooked
1 cup finely chopped pecans
1 jar (12 ounces) strawberry jam
Sugar for sprinkling

1. Combine BUTTER FLAVOR CRISCO® and brown sugar in large bowl. Beat at medium speed of electric mixer until well blended. Beat in eggs and almond extract.

2. Combine flour, baking powder, salt and baking soda. Mix into creamed mixture at low speed until just blended. Stir in oats and chopped nuts with spoon. Cover and refrigerate at least 1 hour.

3. Preheat oven to 350°F. Grease cookie sheet with BUTTER FLAVOR CRISCO®. Roll out dough, half at a time, to about ¼-inch thickness on floured surface. Cut out with 2½-inch round cookie cutter. Place 1 teaspoonful of jam in center of half of the rounds. Top with remaining rounds. Press edges to seal. Prick centers; sprinkle with sugar. Place 1 inch apart on cookie sheet.

4. Bake 12 to 15 minutes, or until lightly browned. Cool 2 minutes on cookie sheet. Remove to cooling rack.

Makes about 2 dozen cookies

Jam-Up Oatmeal Cookies

Mom's Best Oatmeal Cookies

1 cup BUTTER FLAVOR CRISCO®
1½ cups firmly packed brown sugar
2 eggs
2 teaspoons vanilla
1½ cups all-purpose flour
1 teaspoon salt
1 teaspoon baking powder
1 teaspoon cinnamon
¼ teaspoon baking soda
2 cups quick oats (not instant or old fashioned), uncooked
1 cup chopped pecans
⅔ cup sesame seeds
⅔ cup flake coconut

1. Preheat oven to 350°F. Combine BUTTER FLAVOR CRISCO® and brown sugar in large bowl. Beat at medium speed of electric mixer until well blended. Beat in eggs and vanilla.

2. Combine flour, salt, baking powder, cinnamon and baking soda. Mix into creamed mixture at low speed until blended. Stir in, one at a time, oats, nuts, sesame seeds and coconut with spoon. Drop dough by rounded tablespoonfuls 2 inches apart onto ungreased cookie sheet.

3. Bake 10 minutes, or until lightly browned. Remove immediately to cooling rack.

Makes about 6 dozen cookies

Oatmeal Scotchies

Oatmeal Scotchies

1¼ cups all-purpose flour
1 teaspoon baking soda
½ teaspoon salt
½ teaspoon cinnamon
1 cup (2 sticks) butter, softened
¾ cup granulated sugar
¾ cup firmly packed brown sugar
2 eggs
1 teaspoon vanilla extract *or* grated rind of 1 orange
3 cups quick or old-fashioned oats, uncooked
One 12-oz. pkg. (2 cups) NESTLÉ® Toll House® Butterscotch Flavored Morsels

Preheat oven to 375°F. In small bowl, combine flour, baking soda, salt and cinnamon; set aside.

In large mixer bowl, beat butter, granulated sugar, brown sugar, eggs and vanilla extract until creamy. Gradually beat in flour mixture. Stir in oats and butterscotch morsels. Drop by measuring tablespoonfuls onto ungreased cookie sheets.

Bake 7 to 8 minutes for chewy cookies or 9 to 10 minutes for crisp cookies. Let stand on cookie sheets 2 minutes. Remove from cookie sheets; cool on wire racks.

Makes about 4 dozen cookies

Oatmeal Scotchie Pan Cookies:

Preheat oven to 375°F. Spread dough in greased 15½ x 10½ x 1-inch baking pan. Bake 18 to 22 minutes until very lightly browned. Cool completely. Cut into 2-inch squares.

Makes about 3 dozen squares

Old-Fashioned Oatmeal Cookies

¾ cup BUTTER FLAVOR CRISCO®
1¼ cups firmly packed brown sugar
1 egg
⅓ cup milk
1½ teaspoons vanilla
3 cups quick-cooking oats (not instant or old fashioned), uncooked
1 cup all-purpose flour
½ teaspoon baking soda
½ teaspoon salt
¼ teaspoon cinnamon
1 cup raisins
1 cup broken walnut pieces

1 Preheat oven to 375°F. Grease cookie sheet with BUTTER FLAVOR CRISCO®.

2. Cream BUTTER FLAVOR CRISCO®, brown sugar, egg, milk and vanilla in large bowl at medium speed of electric mixer until well blended.

3. Combine oats, flour, baking soda, salt and cinnamon. Mix into creamed mixture. Stir in raisins and nuts. Drop rounded tablespoonfuls of dough 2 inches apart onto cookie sheet.

4. Bake 10 to 12 minutes. Cool on cookie sheet 2 minutes. Remove to cooling rack.

Makes about 2½ dozen cookies

Preparation time: 20 minutes
Bake time: 10 to 20 minutes

German Chocolate Oatmeal Cookies

¾ cup BUTTER FLAVOR CRISCO®
1 cup firmly packed dark brown sugar
½ cup granulated sugar
2 eggs
2 packages (4 ounces each) German chocolate, melted and cooled
1 tablespoon water
1¼ cups all-purpose flour
½ teaspoon baking soda
½ teaspoon salt
3 cups quick oats (not instant or old fashioned), uncooked
1 cup coarsely chopped pecans
1 cup flake coconut

1. Preheat oven to 375°F. Grease cookie sheet with BUTTER FLAVOR CRISCO®.

2. Combine BUTTER FLAVOR CRISCO®, brown sugar, granulated sugar, eggs, chocolate and water in large bowl. Beat at medium speed of electric mixer until well blended.

3. Combine flour, baking soda and salt. Mix into creamed mixture at low speed until blended. Stir in oats, nuts and coconut with spoon.

4. Drop rounded tablespoonfuls of dough 2 inches apart onto cookie sheet.

5. Bake 10 minutes, or until bottoms are browned, but tops are slightly soft. Cool 3 minutes on cookie sheet. Remove to cooling rack.

Makes about 4 dozen cookies

Oatmeal Lemon-Cheese Cookies

1 cup BUTTER FLAVOR CRISCO®
1 package (3 ounces) cream cheese, softened
1¼ cups sugar
1 egg, separated
1 teaspoon lemon extract
2 teaspoons grated lemon peel
1¼ cups all-purpose flour
1¼ cups quick oats (not instant or old fashioned), uncooked
½ teaspoon salt
1 egg
Sugar for sprinkling
½ cup sliced almonds

1. Preheat oven to 350°F. Combine BUTTER FLAVOR CRISCO®, cream cheese and 1¼ cups sugar in large bowl. Beat at medium speed of electric mixer until well blended. Beat in egg yolk, lemon extract and lemon peel.

2. Combine flour, oats and salt. Stir into creamed mixture with spoon until blended.

3. Drop rounded teaspoonfuls of dough 2 inches apart onto ungreased cookie sheet. Beat whole egg with egg white. Brush over tops of cookies. Sprinkle lightly with sugar. Press almond slices lightly on top.

4. Bake 10 to 12 minutes, or until edges are lightly browned. Cool 2 minutes on cookie sheet. Remove to cooling rack.

Makes about 6 dozen cookies

Cinnamon-Apricot Tart Oatmeal Cookies

½ cup water
1 package (8 ounces) dried apricot halves, diced
1 cup BUTTER FLAVOR CRISCO®
1 cup firmly packed brown sugar
¼ cup granulated sugar
1 egg
2 teaspoons vanilla
1½ cups all-purpose flour
2 teaspoons cinnamon
1 teaspoon baking soda
1 teaspoon salt
1 cup plus 2 tablespoons chopped pecans
3 cups quick oats (not instant or old-fashioned), uncooked

1. Place ½ cup water in small saucepan. Heat to boiling. Place diced apricots in strainer over boiling water. Reduce heat to warm. Cover; steam for 15 minutes. Cool. Reserve liquid.

2. Preheat oven to 375°F. Grease cookie sheet with BUTTER FLAVOR CRISCO®. Combine BUTTER FLAVOR CRISCO®, brown sugar, granulated sugar, egg and vanilla in large bowl. Beat at medium speed of electric mixer until well blended.

3. Combine flour, cinnamon, baking soda and salt. Mix into creamed mixture at low speed until just blended. Stir in nuts, apricots and reserved liquid from apricots. Stir in oats with spoon. Drop dough by rounded tablespoonfuls 2 inches apart onto cookie sheet.

4. Bake 10 to 11 minutes. Cool 2 minutes on cookie sheet. Remove to cooling rack.

Makes 3½ to 4 dozen cookies

Santa Fe Sun Crisps

½ cup BUTTER FLAVOR CRISCO®
1 cup firmly packed brown sugar
½ cup granulated sugar
1 egg
1 tablespoon water
1 cup all-purpose flour
½ teaspoon baking powder
½ teaspoon baking soda
⅛ teaspoon ground red pepper or to taste
2 cups quick oats (not instant or old fashioned), uncooked
½ cup (about) shelled sunflower seeds

1. Preheat oven to 375°F. Combine BUTTER FLAVOR CRISCO®, brown sugar and granulated sugar in large bowl. Beat at medium speed of electric mixer until well blended. Beat in egg and water.

2. Combine flour, baking powder, baking soda and red pepper. Mix into creamed mixture at low speed until just blended. Stir in oats with spoon.

3. Form rounded teaspoonfuls dough into balls. Roll dough in sunflower seeds. Place 2 inches apart on ungreased cookie sheet.

4. Bake 7 to 8 minutes or until golden brown. Cool 2 minutes on cookie sheet. Remove to cooling rack.

Makes about 3 dozen cookies

Top to bottom: Chocolate-Orange Chip Cookies (page 48), Cinnamon-Apricot Tart Oatmeal Cookies

Left to right: Double Chocolate Pecan Cookies, Double Chocolate Cherry Cookies

Double Chocolate Cherry Cookies

1¼ **cups margarine or butter, softened**
1¾ **cups sugar**
2 **eggs**
1 **tablespoon vanilla extract**
3½ **cups unsifted flour**
¾ **cup unsweetened cocoa**
½ **teaspoon baking powder**
½ **teaspoon baking soda**
¼ **teaspoon salt**
2 **(6-ounce) jars maraschino cherries, well drained and halved (about 60 cherries)**
1 **(6-ounce) package semi-sweet chocolate chips (1 cup)**
1 **(14-ounce) can EAGLE® Brand Sweetened Condensed Milk (NOT evaporated milk)**

Preheat oven to 350°F. In large mixer bowl, beat margarine and sugar until fluffy; add eggs and vanilla. Mix well. Combine dry ingredients; stir into margarine mixture (dough will be stiff). Shape into 1-inch balls. Place 1 inch apart on ungreased cookie sheets. Press cherry half into center of each cookie. Bake 8 to 10 minutes. Cool.

In heavy saucepan, over medium heat, melt chips with sweetened condensed milk; cook until mixture thickens, about 3 minutes. Frost each cookie, covering cherry. Store loosely covered at room temperature.

Makes about 10 dozen cookies

Double Chocolate Pecan Cookies: Prepare cookies as above, omitting cherries. Flatten. Bake and frost as directed. Garnish each cookie with a pecan half.

Chocolate-Frosted Marshmallow Cookies

Cookies
½ **cup butter or margarine**
2 **squares (1 ounce each) unsweetened chocolate**
1 **egg**
1 **cup packed brown sugar**
1 **teaspoon vanilla**
½ **teaspoon baking soda**
1½ **cups all-purpose flour**
½ **cup milk**
1 **package (16 ounces) large marshmallows, halved crosswise**

Fudge Frosting
1½ **squares (1½ ounces) unsweetened chocolate**
¼ **cup butter or margarine**
1½ **cups powdered sugar**
1 **egg white***
1 **teaspoon vanilla**

To prepare Cookies: Preheat oven to 350°F. Lightly grease cookie sheets or line with parchment paper. Melt butter and chocolate in small heavy saucepan over low heat; stir to blend. Remove from heat; cool. Beat egg, brown sugar, vanilla and baking soda in large bowl until light and fluffy. Blend in chocolate mixture and flour until smooth. Slowly beat in milk to make light, cake-batter-like dough. Drop dough by teaspoonfuls 2 inches apart onto prepared cookie sheets.

Bake 10 to 12 minutes or until firm in center. Immediately place halved marshmallow, cut side down, onto each baked cookie. Return to oven 1 minute or just until marshmallow is warm enough to stick to cookie. Remove to wire racks to cool.

To prepare Frosting: Melt chocolate and butter in small heavy saucepan over low heat; stir to blend. Beat in powdered sugar. Beat in egg white and vanilla, adding a little water, if necessary, to make smooth, slightly soft frosting. Spoon over cookies to cover marshmallows.

Makes about 5 dozen cookies

*Use clean, uncracked egg.

Choco-Caramel Delights

**1/2 cup butter or margarine,
 softened
2/3 cup sugar
1 egg, separated
2 tablespoons milk
1 teaspoon vanilla extract
1 cup all-purpose flour
1/3 cup HERSHEY'S® Cocoa
1/4 teaspoon salt
1 cup finely chopped pecans
 Caramel Filling (recipe
 follows)
1/2 cup HERSHEY'S® Semi-
 Sweet Chocolate Chips
 or Premium Semi-Sweet
 Chocolate Chunks
1 teaspoon shortening**

In small mixer bowl, beat butter, sugar, egg yolk, milk and vanilla until blended. Stir together flour, cocoa and salt; blend into butter mixture. Refrigerate dough at least 1 hour or until firm enough to handle.

Preheat oven to 350°F. Beat egg white slightly. Shape dough into 1-inch balls. Dip each ball into egg white; roll in pecans to coat. Place on lightly greased cookie sheet. Press thumb gently in center of each ball. Bake 10 to 12 minutes or until set. While cookies are baking, prepare Caramel Filling. Remove cookies from oven; press center of each cookie again with thumb to make indentation. Immediately spoon about 1/2 teaspoon Caramel Filling in center of each cookie. Carefully remove from cookie sheet; cool on wire rack.

In small microwave-safe bowl, place chocolate chips and shortening. Microwave at HIGH (100%) 1 minute or until softened; stir. Allow to stand several minutes to finish melting; stir until smooth. Place

waxed paper under wire rack with cookies. Drizzle chocolate mixture over top of cookies.
Makes about 2 dozen cookies
CARAMEL FILLING: Combine 14 unwrapped light caramels and 3 tablespoons whipping cream in small saucepan. Cook over low heat, stirring frequently, until caramels are melted and mixture is smooth.

Sour Cream Chocolate Cookies

**2 eggs
1 cup granulated sugar
1 cup packed light brown
 sugar
1 teaspoon vanilla extract
1 cup dairy sour cream
1/2 cup butter, melted
1/2 cup shortening, melted
2 1/2 cups all-purpose flour
1 cup HERSHEY'S® Cocoa
1 teaspoon baking powder
1/2 teaspoon baking soda
1 cup chopped walnuts**

Preheat oven to 325°F. Grease cookie sheets. In large mixer bowl, beat eggs, granulated sugar, brown sugar and vanilla; blend in sour cream, butter and shortening. Stir together flour, cocoa, baking powder and baking soda; add to sugar mixture. Stir in walnuts. Drop dough by tablespoonfuls onto cookie sheets. Bake 10 to 12 minutes or just until set. Cool slightly; remove from cookie sheets. Cool completely on wire racks.
Makes about 4 dozen cookies

Cocoa Sandies

**1 cup butter, softened
1 1/4 cups confectioners' sugar
1 1/2 teaspoons vanilla extract
1/2 cup HERSHEY'S® Cocoa
1 3/4 cups all-purpose flour
 Quick Cocoa Glaze (recipe
 follows)**

Preheat oven to 300°F. In large mixer bowl beat butter, sugar and vanilla until creamy. Add cocoa; blend well. Gradually add flour, blending until smooth. On lightly floured surface or between 2 pieces of waxed paper roll dough to about 1/2-inch thickness. Cut dough into heart or star shapes with 2 1/2-inch cookie cutters. (Scraps can be gathered and rerolled.) Place on ungreased cookie sheet.

Bake 20 minutes or just until firm. Cool slightly; remove from cookie sheet to wire rack. Cool completely. Dip about half of each cookie into Quick Cocoa Glaze. Place on wire rack until glaze is set.
Makes about 2 dozen cookies

Quick Cocoa Glaze

**3 tablespoons butter or
 margarine
1/3 cup HERSHEY'S® Cocoa
1/4 cup water
1 teaspoon vanilla extract
1 1/2 cups confectioners' sugar**

In small saucepan over low heat melt butter. Stir in cocoa and water. Cook over low heat, stirring constantly, until mixture thickens; do not boil. Remove from heat; stir in vanilla. Gradually add confectioners' sugar, stirring with wire whisk until smooth. Add additional water, 1 teaspoon at a time, if needed for desired consistency.

Cinnamon-Chocolate Cutouts

2 squares (1 ounce each) unsweetened chocolate
1/2 cup butter or margarine, softened
1 cup granulated sugar
1 egg
1 teaspoon vanilla
3 cups all-purpose flour
2 teaspoons ground cinnamon
1/2 teaspoon baking soda
1/4 teaspoon salt
1/2 cup sour cream
Decorator Icing (recipe follows)

Melt chocolate in top of double boiler over hot, not boiling, water. Remove from heat; cool. Cream butter, melted chocolate, granulated sugar, egg and vanilla in large bowl until light. Combine flour, cinnamon, baking soda and salt in small bowl. Stir into creamed mixture with sour cream until smooth. Cover; refrigerate at least 30 minutes.

Preheat oven to 400°F. Lightly grease cookie sheets or line with parchment paper. Roll out dough, one-fourth at a time, 1/4 inch thick on lightly floured surface. Cut out with cookie cutters. Place 2 inches apart on prepared cookie sheets. Bake 10 minutes or until lightly browned, but not dark. Remove to wire racks to cool.

Prepare Decorator Icing. Spoon into pastry bag fitted with small tip or small heavy-duty plastic bag. (If using plastic bag, close securely. With scissors, snip off small corner from one side of bag.) Decorate cookies with icing.

Makes about 6 dozen cookies

Decorator Icing

1 egg white*
3 1/2 cups powdered sugar
1 teaspoon almond or lemon extract
2 to 3 tablespoons water

Beat egg white in large bowl until frothy. Gradually beat in powdered sugar until blended. Add almond extract and enough water to moisten. Beat until smooth and glossy.

*Use clean, uncracked egg.

Orange & Chocolate Ribbon Cookies

1 cup butter or margarine, softened
1/2 cup sugar
3 egg yolks
2 teaspoons grated orange zest
1 teaspoon orange extract
2 1/4 cups all-purpose flour, divided
3 tablespoons unsweetened cocoa
1 teaspoon vanilla
1 teaspoon chocolate extract

Cream butter, sugar and egg yolks in large bowl until light and fluffy. Remove half of the mixture; place in another bowl. Add orange zest, orange extract and 1 1/4 cups of the flour to half of the mixture; mix until blended and smooth. Shape into ball. Add cocoa, vanilla and chocolate extract to second half of the mixture; beat until smooth. Stir in remaining 1 cup flour; mix until blended and smooth. Shape into ball. Cover doughs; refrigerate 10 minutes. Roll out each dough separately on lightly floured surface to 12×4-inch rectangle. Pat edges of dough to straighten; use rolling pin to level off thickness. Place one dough on top of the other. Using sharp knife, make lengthwise cut through center of doughs. Lift half of dough onto other to make long, 4-layer strip of dough. With hands, press dough strips together. Wrap in plastic wrap; refrigerate at least

1 hour or up to 3 days. (For longer storage, freeze up to 6 weeks.)

Preheat oven to 350°F. Lightly grease cookie sheets or line with parchment paper. Cut dough crosswise into 1/4-inch-thick slices; place 2 inches apart on prepared cookie sheets. Bake 10 to 12 minutes or until very lightly browned. Remove to wire racks to cool.

Makes about 5 dozen cookies

Old-Fashioned Chocolate Cookies

1 cup all-purpose flour
1/2 teaspoon baking powder
1/2 teaspoon baking soda
1/2 teaspoon salt
1 foil-wrapped bar (2 oz.) NESTLÉ® Unsweetened Chocolate Baking Bar
1/2 cup (1 stick) butter, softened
1/2 cup granulated sugar
1/2 cup firmly packed brown sugar
1 egg
1/2 cup quick or old-fashioned oats, uncooked
1/2 cup shredded coconut

Preheat oven to 350°F. In small bowl, combine flour, baking powder, baking soda and salt; set aside. Melt unsweetened chocolate baking bar; set aside.

In large mixer bowl, beat butter, granulated sugar, brown sugar and egg until creamy. Blend in melted chocolate. Stir in flour mixture, oats and coconut. Drop dough by slightly rounded measuring tablespoonfuls onto ungreased cookie sheets.

Bake 8 to 10 minutes until edges are set; centers may appear moist. Let stand on cookie sheets 2 minutes. Remove from cookie sheets; cool completely on wire racks.

Makes about 2 dozen cookies

Cinnamon-Chocolate Cutouts, Orange & Chocolate Ribbon Cookies,
Chocolate-Mint Sandwiches (page 84)

Chocolate-Mint Sandwiches

2 squares (1 ounce each) unsweetened chocolate
½ cup butter or margarine, softened
1 cup packed light brown sugar
1 teaspoon vanilla
1 egg
⅛ teaspoon baking soda
2 cups all-purpose flour
Creamy Mint Filling (recipe follows)

Melt chocolate in top of double boiler over hot, not boiling, water. Remove from heat; cool. Cream butter and brown sugar in large bowl. Beat in vanilla, egg, melted chocolate and baking soda until light and fluffy. Stir in flour to make a stiff dough. Divide dough into 4 parts. Shape each part into a roll, about 1½ inches in diameter. Wrap in plastic wrap; refrigerate at least 1 hour or up to 2 weeks. (For longer storage, freeze up to 6 weeks.)

Preheat oven to 375°F. Line cookie sheets with parchment paper or leave ungreased. Cut rolls into ⅛-inch-thick slices; place 2 inches apart on cookie sheets. Bake 6 to 7 minutes or until firm. Remove to wire racks to cool. Prepare Creamy Mint Filling. Spread filling on bottoms of half the cookies. Top with remaining cookies, bottom sides down, forming sandwiches.

Makes about 36 sandwich cookies

Creamy Mint Filling

2 tablespoons butter or margarine, softened
1½ cups powdered sugar
3 to 4 tablespoons light cream or half-and-half
¼ teaspoon peppermint extract
Few drops green food coloring

Cream butter with powdered sugar and cream in small bowl until smooth and blended. Stir in peppermint extract and food coloring, blending well.

Chocolate Mint Snow-Top Cookies

1½ cups all-purpose flour
1½ teaspoons baking powder
¼ teaspoon salt
One 10-oz. pkg. (1½ cups) NESTLÉ® Toll House® Mint Flavored Semi-Sweet Chocolate Morsels, divided
1 cup granulated sugar
6 tablespoons (¾ stick) butter, softened
1½ teaspoons vanilla extract
2 eggs
Confectioners' sugar

In small bowl, combine flour, baking powder and salt; set aside. Melt 1 cup mint chocolate morsels; set aside.

In large mixer bowl, beat granulated sugar and butter until creamy. Beat in melted chocolate and vanilla extract. Beat in eggs. Gradually beat in flour mixture. Stir in remaining ½ cup mint chocolate morsels. Wrap dough in plastic wrap; freeze until firm, about 20 minutes.

Preheat oven to 350°F. Shape dough into 1-inch balls; coat with confectioners' sugar. Place on ungreased cookie sheets.

Bake 10 to 12 minutes until tops appear cracked. Let stand on cookie sheets 5 minutes. Remove to wire racks to cool completely.

Makes about 3 dozen cookies

Chocolate Mint Snow-Top Cookies

COOKIES

Mocha Pecan Pinwheels

1 square (1 ounce)
   unsweetened chocolate
½ cup (1 stick) butter or
   margarine, softened
¾ cup packed brown sugar
1 egg
1 teaspoon vanilla
¼ teaspoon baking soda
1¾ cups all-purpose flour
½ cup chopped pecans
1 teaspoon instant espresso
   coffee powder

Melt chocolate in small bowl over hot water. Stir until smooth. Cream butter, brown sugar, egg, vanilla and baking soda in large bowl, blending well. Stir in flour to make stiff dough. Remove half of dough; place in another bowl. Blend pecans and coffee powder into half of dough. Stir melted chocolate into remaining dough. Cover doughs; refrigerate 30 minutes.

Roll out light-colored dough to 15×8-inch rectangle between 2 sheets of plastic wrap. Roll chocolate dough out to same dimensions between 2 more sheets of plastic wrap. Remove top sheets of plastic wrap. Invert light-colored dough on top of chocolate dough; remove plastic wrap. Roll up firmly, jelly-roll fashion, starting with long side. Wrap in plastic; freeze. (Dough can be frozen up to 6 weeks.)

Preheat oven to 350°F. Line cookie sheets with parchment paper or leave ungreased. Cut frozen dough into ¼-inch-thick slices; place 2 inches apart on cookie sheets. Bake 9 to 12 minutes or until set. Remove to wire racks to cool.

Makes about 5 dozen cookies

Cocoa Shortbread

2 cups all-purpose flour
½ cup NESTLÉ® Cocoa
1 cup (2 sticks) butter,
   softened
1 cup sifted confectioners'
   sugar
1½ teaspoons vanilla extract

Preheat oven to 300°F. In small bowl, combine flour and cocoa; set aside.

In large mixer bowl, beat butter, confectioners' sugar and vanilla extract until creamy. Gradually blend in flour mixture. On lightly floured board, roll dough ½ inch thick; cut into 2×1-inch strips. With fork, pierce surface. Place on ungreased cookie sheets.

Bake 20 minutes or just until firm. Let stand on cookie sheets 2 minutes. Remove from cookie sheets; cool completely on wire racks.

Makes about 2 dozen cookies

Pinwheel Cookies

½ cup BUTTER FLAVOR
   CRISCO®
⅓ cup plus 1 tablespoon
   butter, softened and
   divided
2 egg yolks
½ teaspoon vanilla extract
1 package DUNCAN HINES®
   Moist Deluxe Fudge
   Marble Cake Mix

1. Combine BUTTER FLAVOR CRISCO®, ⅓ cup butter, egg yolks and vanilla extract in large bowl. Mix at low speed of electric mixer until blended. Set aside cocoa packet. Gradually add cake mix. Blend well.

2. Divide dough in half. Add cocoa packet and remaining 1 tablespoon butter to half the dough. Knead until well blended and chocolate colored.

3. Roll out yellow dough between two pieces of waxed paper into 18×12×⅛-inch rectangle. Repeat for chocolate dough. Remove top pieces of waxed paper from chocolate and yellow doughs. Lay yellow dough directly on top of chocolate dough. Remove remaining layers of waxed paper. Roll up dough, jelly roll fashion, beginning at wide side. Wrap in waxed paper; refrigerate 2 hours.

4. Preheat oven to 350°F. Grease cookie sheets. Cut dough into ⅛-inch slices. Bake 9 to 11 minutes or until lightly browned. Cool 5 minutes on cookie sheets. Remove to wire racks to cool.

Makes about 3½ dozen cookies

Tip: You can use DUNCAN HINES® White Cake Mix in place of Fudge Marble Cake Mix. Divide dough as above; color one portion of dough with red or green food coloring.

Chocolate Refrigerator Cookies

1⅔ cups all-purpose flour
⅓ cup NESTLÉ® Cocoa
½ teaspoon baking powder
½ teaspoon cinnamon
¾ cup sugar
½ cup (1 stick) margarine,
   softened
1 tablespoon skim milk
1 egg
¾ cup ground walnuts

In small bowl, combine flour, cocoa, baking powder and cinnamon; set aside.

In large mixer bowl, beat sugar and margarine until creamy. Beat in milk and egg. Gradually beat in flour mixture. Stir in walnuts. On waxed paper, shape dough into 1½-inch diameter log; roll in waxed paper. Refrigerate 2 to 3 hours or overnight.

Preheat oven to 350°F. Cut log into ¼-inch thick slices. Place on ungreased cookie sheets. Bake 10 minutes. Let stand on cookie sheets 2 minutes. Remove from cookie sheets; cool completely on wire racks.

Makes about 4 dozen cookies

BROWNIES & BARS

No time to bake dozens of cookies? Satisfy your sweet tooth with a batch of blissful brownies or bar cookies. Simply mix the batter, spread in a pan, bake—and enjoy! What could be easier? From sinfully rich brownies to fruit and nut studded bars, these quick-to-fix sweets are sure to become all-time family favorites. (For additional brownie and bar recipes, see the Jump-Start Baking, Especially for Kids and Festive Holiday Baking chapters.)

Almond Cheesecake Brownies

- **4 squares (1 ounce each) semisweet chocolate**
- **5 tablespoons butter or margarine, divided**
- **1 package (3 ounces) cream cheese, softened**
- **1 cup granulated sugar, divided**
- **3 eggs, divided**
- **½ cup plus 1 tablespoon all-purpose flour**
- **1½ teaspoons vanilla, divided**
- **½ teaspoon baking powder**
- **¼ teaspoon salt**
- **½ teaspoon almond extract**
- **½ cup chopped or slivered almonds**
- **Almond Glaze (recipe follows)**

Preheat oven to 350°F. Butter 8-inch square pan. Melt chocolate and 3 tablespoons of the butter in small heavy saucepan over low heat; set aside. Mix cream cheese with remaining 2 tablespoons butter in small bowl. Slowly add ¼ cup of the granulated sugar, blending well. Add 1 egg, the 1 tablespoon flour and ½ teaspoon of the vanilla; set aside. Beat remaining 2 eggs and ¾ cup granulated sugar in large bowl until light. Add the baking powder, salt and remaining ½ cup flour. Blend in chocolate mixture, remaining 1 teaspoon vanilla and the almond extract. Stir in almonds.

Spread half the chocolate mixture in prepared pan. Cover with cream cheese mixture, then spoon remaining chocolate mixture over top. Swirl with knife or spatula to create a marbled effect.

Bake 30 to 35 minutes or until set in center. Do not overbake. Meanwhile, prepare Almond Glaze. Cool brownies 5 minutes, then spread glaze evenly over top. Cool completely in pan on wire rack. Cut into 2-inch squares.   *Makes 16 brownies*

Almond Glaze

- **½ cup semisweet chocolate chips**
- **2 tablespoons butter or margarine**
- **3 tablespoons milk**
- **¼ teaspoon almond extract**
- **1 cup powdered sugar**

Combine chocolate chips, butter, milk and almond extract in small heavy saucepan. Stir over low heat until chocolate is melted. Add powdered sugar; beat until glossy and easy to spread.

Clockwise from left: Almond Cheesecake Brownies, Chocolate Dream Bars (page 109), Chocolate-Mint Brownies (page 88)

Chocolate-Mint Brownies

- **¹/₂ cup butter or margarine**
- **2 squares (1 ounce each) unsweetened chocolate**
- **2 eggs**
- **1 cup packed light brown sugar**
- **¹/₂ cup all-purpose flour**
- **1 teaspoon vanilla**
- **Mint Frosting (recipe follows)**
- **Chocolate Glaze (recipe follows)**

Preheat oven to 350°F. Grease and flour 8-inch square pan. Melt butter and chocolate in small heavy saucepan over low heat; stir until blended. Remove from heat; cool. Beat eggs in medium bowl until light. Add brown sugar, beating well. Blend in chocolate mixture. Stir in flour and vanilla. Spread batter evenly in prepared pan.

Bake 30 minutes or until firm in center. Cool in pan on wire rack. Prepare Mint Frosting. Spread over the top; refrigerate until firm. Prepare Chocolate Glaze. Drizzle over frosting; refrigerate until firm. Cut into 2-inch squares.   *Makes 16 brownies*

Mint Frosting

- **1¹/₂ cups powdered sugar**
- **2 to 3 tablespoons light cream or milk**
- **1 tablespoon butter or margarine, softened**
- **¹/₂ teaspoon peppermint extract**
- **1 to 2 drops green food coloring**

Blend powdered sugar, 2 tablespoons of the cream and the butter in small bowl until smooth. Add more cream, if necessary, to make frosting of spreading consistency. Blend in peppermint extract and enough green food coloring to make a pale mint-green color.

Chocolate Glaze

- **¹/₂ cup semisweet chocolate chips**
- **2 tablespoons butter or margarine**

Place chocolate chips and butter in small bowl over hot water. Stir until melted and smooth.

Chocolate Almond Brownies

- **1¹/₄ cups unsifted flour**
- **2 tablespoons sugar**
- **¹/₂ cup cold margarine or butter**
- **1 cup chopped almonds, toasted**
- **1 (14-ounce) can EAGLE® Brand Sweetened Condensed Milk (NOT evaporated milk)**
- **¹/₄ cup unsweetened cocoa**
- **1 egg**
- **2 tablespoons amaretto liqueur *or* 1 teaspoon almond extract**
- **¹/₂ teaspoon baking powder**
- **6 (1¹/₄-ounce) white candy bars with almonds, broken into small pieces**

Preheat oven to 350°F. In medium bowl, combine *1 cup* flour and sugar; cut in margarine until crumbly. Add *¹/₄ cup* nuts. Press in bottom of ungreased 9-inch round or square baking pan. Bake 15 minutes. In large mixer bowl, beat sweetened condensed milk, remaining *¹/₄ cup* flour, cocoa, egg, amaretto and baking powder until smooth. Stir in candy pieces and *¹/₂ cup* nuts. Spread over prepared crust. Top with remaining *¹/₄ cup* nuts. Bake 30 minutes or until center is set. Cool. Cut into wedges or squares. Store tightly covered at room temperature.
          Makes about 16 brownies

Prep time: 20 minutes
Baking time: 45 minutes

Ultimate Chocolate Brownies

Ultimate Chocolate Brownies

- **³/₄ cup HERSHEY'S® Cocoa**
- **¹/₂ teaspoon baking soda**
- **²/₃ cup butter or margarine, melted and divided**
- **¹/₂ cup boiling water**
- **2 cups sugar**
- **2 eggs**
- **1¹/₃ cups all-purpose flour**
- **1 teaspoon vanilla extract**
- **¹/₄ teaspoon salt**
- **1 cup HERSHEY'S® Semi-Sweet Chocolate Chips**
- **One-Bowl Buttercream Frosting (page 144)**

Preheat oven to 350°F. Grease 13×9×2-inch baking pan or two 8-inch square baking pans.

In large bowl, stir together cocoa and baking soda; blend in ¹/₃ cup butter. Add boiling water; stir until mixture thickens. Stir in sugar, eggs and remaining ¹/₃ cup butter; mix until smooth.

Add flour, vanilla and salt; mix until well blended. Stir in chocolate chips. Pour batter into prepared pan.

Bake 35 to 40 minutes for rectangular pan and 30 to 35 minutes for square pans or until brownies begin to pull away from sides of pan. Cool completely in pan on wire rack. Frost with One-Bowl Buttercream Frosting. Sprinkle with additional chips if desired. Cut into squares.

Makes about 36 brownies

Butterscotch Brownies

2 cups all-purpose flour
2 teaspoons baking powder
1/2 teaspoon salt
One 12-oz. pkg. (2 cups)
 NESTLÉ® Toll House® Butterscotch Flavored Morsels
1/2 cup (1 stick) butter
1 cup firmly packed brown sugar
4 eggs
1 teaspoon vanilla extract
1 cup nuts, chopped

Preheat oven to 350°F. Grease 15½×10½×1-inch baking pan. In small bowl, combine flour, baking powder and salt; set aside.

Melt butterscotch morsels and butter, stirring until smooth. Transfer to large mixer bowl. Stir in brown sugar; cool 5 minutes. Beat in eggs and vanilla extract. Blend in flour mixture. Stir in nuts. Spread in pan.

Bake for 20 minutes. Cool completely in pan on wire rack. Cut into 2-inch squares.

Makes 35 brownies

Blonde Brickle Brownies

1⅓ cups flour
1/2 teaspoon baking powder
1/4 teaspoon salt
2 eggs
1/2 cup granulated sugar
1/2 cup packed brown sugar
1/3 cup butter or margarine, melted
1 teaspoon vanilla extract
1/4 teaspoon almond extract
1 package (6 ounces) BITS 'O BRICKLE®, divided
1/2 cup chopped pecans (optional)

Preheat oven to 350°F. Grease 8-inch square pan.

Mix flour with baking powder and salt; set aside. In large bowl, beat eggs well. Gradually beat in granulated sugar and brown sugar until thick and creamy. Add melted butter, vanilla and almond extracts; mix well. Gently stir in flour mixture until moistened. Fold in ⅔ cup BITS 'O BRICKLE® and nuts. Pour into prepared pan.

Bake 30 minutes. Remove from oven; immediately sprinkle remaining BITS 'O BRICKLE® over top. Cool completely in pan on wire rack. Cut into squares.

Makes about 16 brownies

Blonde Brickle Brownies

Marbled Peanut-Butter Brownies

Marbled Peanut-Butter Brownies

- ½ cup butter or margarine, softened
- ¼ cup peanut butter
- 1 cup packed light brown sugar
- ½ cup granulated sugar
- 3 eggs
- 1 teaspoon vanilla
- 2 cups all-purpose flour
- 2 teaspoons baking powder
- ⅛ teaspoon salt
- 1 cup chocolate-flavored syrup
- ½ cup coarsely chopped salted mixed nuts

Preheat oven to 350°F. Lightly grease 13×9 inch pan. Cream butter and peanut butter in large bowl until blended; stir in sugars. Beat in eggs, one at a time, until batter is light. Blend in vanilla. Combine flour, baking powder and salt in small bowl. Stir into creamed mixture. Spread half the batter evenly in prepared pan. Spread syrup over top. Spoon remaining batter over syrup. Swirl with knife or spatula to create marbled effect. Sprinkle chopped nuts over top. Bake 35 to 40 minutes or until lightly browned. Cool completely in pan on wire rack. Cut into 2-inch squares.
Makes about 2 dozen brownies

Mocha Fudge Brownies

- 3 squares (1 ounce each) semisweet chocolate
- ½ cup butter or margarine, softened
- ¾ cup sugar
- 2 eggs
- 2 teaspoons instant espresso coffee powder
- 1 teaspoon vanilla
- ½ cup all-purpose flour
- ½ cup chopped toasted almonds
- 1 cup (6 ounces) milk chocolate chips, divided

Preheat oven to 350°F. Butter 8-inch square pan. Melt semisweet chocolate in top of double boiler over hot, not boiling, water. Remove from heat; cool. Cream butter and sugar in medium bowl. Beat in eggs until light and fluffy. Add melted chocolate, coffee powder and vanilla. Blend in flour, almonds and ½ cup of the chocolate chips. Spread batter evenly in prepared pan. Bake 25 minutes or just until firm in center. Remove from oven; sprinkle remaining ½ cup chocolate chips over the top. Let stand a few minutes until chips melt, then spread evenly over brownies. Cool completely in pan on wire rack. Cut into 2-inch squares.   *Makes 16 brownies*

Rocky Road Fudge Brownies

Bars
- ½ cup LAND O LAKES® Butter
- 2 squares (1 ounce each) unsweetened chocolate
- 2 eggs
- 1 cup sugar
- ⅔ cup all-purpose flour
- ¼ teaspoon salt
- 1 teaspoon vanilla

Topping
- ½ cup chopped salted peanuts
- ½ cup butterscotch chips
- 1 cup miniature marshmallows
- ¼ cup chocolate ice cream topping

Preheat oven to 350°F. Grease 9-inch square baking pan. For Bars, in heavy, small saucepan, combine butter and chocolate. Cook, stirring constantly, over medium heat, until melted, 3 to 5 minutes; set aside. In small mixer bowl, beat eggs at medium speed until light and fluffy, 2 to 3 minutes. Gradually beat in cooled chocolate mixture, sugar, flour, salt and vanilla, scraping bowl often, until well mixed, 1 to 2 minutes. Spread into prepared pan. Bake 20 to 25 minutes, or until brownies begin to pull away from sides of pan. For Topping, sprinkle nuts, butterscotch chips and marshmallows over hot brownies. Drizzle with ice cream topping. Continue baking for 12 to 18 minutes, or until lightly browned. Cool completely in pan on wire rack. Cut into bars.
Makes about 2 dozen brownies

Double Fudge Saucepan Brownies

- ½ cup sugar
- 2 tablespoons butter or margarine
- 2 tablespoons water
- 2 cups (12-ounce package) HERSHEY'S® Semi-Sweet Chocolate Chips, divided
- 2 eggs, slightly beaten
- 1 teaspoon vanilla extract
- ⅔ cup all-purpose flour
- ¼ teaspoon baking soda
- ¼ teaspoon salt
- ½ cup chopped nuts (optional)

Preheat oven to 325°F. Grease 9-inch square baking pan.

In medium saucepan over low heat, cook sugar, butter and water, stirring constantly, until mixture comes to a boil. Remove from heat; immediately add 1 cup chocolate chips, stirring until melted. Stir in eggs and vanilla until blended. Stir together flour, baking soda and salt; stir into chocolate mixture. Stir in remaining 1 cup chips and nuts, if desired. Pour batter into prepared pan.

Bake 25 to 30 minutes or until brownies begin to pull away from sides of pan. Cool completely in pan on wire rack; cut into squares.
Makes about 1½ dozen brownies

One-Bowl Homemade Brownies

One-Bowl Homemade Brownies

**4 squares (1 ounce each)
  BAKER'S® Unsweetened
  Chocolate**
**³⁄₄ cup (1½ sticks) margarine
  or butter**
2 cups sugar
3 eggs
1 teaspoon vanilla
1 cup all-purpose flour
**1 cup coarsely chopped nuts
  (optional)**

Microwave* chocolate and margarine in large microwavable bowl at HIGH 2 minutes or *until margarine is melted.* STIR UNTIL CHOCOLATE IS COMPLETELY MELTED.

Stir sugar into melted chocolate until well blended. Stir in eggs and vanilla until completely mixed. Mix in flour until well blended. Stir in nuts. Spread in greased 13×9-inch pan.

Bake at 350°F for 35 to 40 minutes or until wooden toothpick inserted in center comes out almost clean. (DO NOT OVERBAKE.) Cool completely in pan on wire rack; cut into squares.

Makes about 24 brownies

Range Top: Melt chocolate and margarine in 3-quart saucepan over very low heat; stir constantly until just melted. Remove from heat; continue as above.

Cakelike Brownies: Stir in ½ cup milk with eggs and vanilla. Increase flour to 1½ cups.

Double Chocolate Brownies: Add 1 cup BAKER'S® Real Semi-Sweet Chocolate Chips with the nuts.

Extra Thick Brownies: Bake in 9-inch square pan for 50 minutes.

Rocky Road Brownies: Prepare Brownies as directed. Bake 35 minutes. Immediately sprinkle 2 cups KRAFT® Miniature Marshmallows, 1 cup BAKER'S® Real Semi-Sweet Chocolate Chips and 1 cup coarsely chopped nuts over brownies. Continue baking 3 to 5 minutes until topping begins to melt together. Cool.

German Sweet Chocolate Cream Cheese Brownies

**1 package (4 oz.) BAKER'S®
  GERMAN'S® Sweet
  Chocolate**
¼ cup (½ stick) margarine
1 cup sugar
3 eggs
1 teaspoon vanilla
½ cup all-purpose flour
½ cup chopped nuts
**3 ounces PHILADELPHIA
  BRAND® Cream Cheese,
  softened**
**1 tablespoon all-purpose
  flour**

Microwave* chocolate and margarine in large microwavable bowl at HIGH 2 minutes *or until margarine is melted.* STIR UNTIL CHOCOLATE IS COMPLETELY MELTED.

Stir ³⁄₄ cup of the sugar into melted chocolate. Stir in 2 of the eggs and vanilla until completely mixed. Mix in ½ cup flour until well blended. Stir in nuts. Spread in greased 8-inch square pan.

Mix cream cheese, remaining ¼ cup sugar, remaining egg and 1 tablespoon flour in small bowl until smooth. Spoon over brownie mixture; swirl with knife to marbleize.

Bake at 350°F for 35 minutes or until wooden toothpick inserted in center comes out almost clean. (DO NOT OVERBAKE.) Cool completely in pan on wire rack; cut into squares.

Makes about 16 brownies

Range Top: Melt chocolate and margarine in 2-quart saucepan over very low heat; stir constantly until just melted. Remove from heat; continue as above.

Painted Desert Brownies

3 cups RICE CHEX® Brand Cereal, crushed to 1 cup
1 cup all-purpose flour
³/₄ cup sugar
¹/₂ teaspoon baking powder
¹/₂ cup margarine or butter, melted
4 teaspoons instant coffee, dissolved in 2 teaspoons boiling water, divided
1 package (21.5 oz.) chocolate brownie mix, plus ingredients to prepare mix
8 ounces cream cheese, softened
1 egg, beaten
¹/₄ cup powdered sugar

Preheat oven to 350°F. In large bowl combine cereal, flour, sugar and baking powder. Add margarine and 1 teaspoon coffee mixture, stirring until well combined. Press evenly and firmly into ungreased 13×9×2-inch baking pan. Bake 10 minutes.

Meanwhile prepare brownie mix according to package directions but do not bake; set aside. In medium bowl beat cream cheese, egg, powdered sugar and remaining 1 teaspoon coffee mixture until well combined. Pour reserved brownie mixture over hot crust. Pour cream cheese mixture in several places over brownie mixture. Swirl cream cheese mixture into brownie mixture with knife. Bake 30 to 35 minutes or until set. Cool completely in pan on wire rack. Cut into squares.

Makes about 40 brownies

Painted Desert Brownies

Triple Layer Brownies

2 cups sugar
2 cups all-purpose flour
²/₃ cup HERSHEY'S® Cocoa
1 teaspoon baking powder
¹/₂ teaspoon salt
³/₄ cup butter or margarine
4 eggs
2 teaspoons vanilla extract
2 cups miniature marshmallows
1²/₃ cups (10-ounce package) REESE'S® Peanut Butter Chips
2 tablespoons shortening
3 cups crisp rice cereal

Preheat oven to 350°F. Grease 13×9×2-inch baking pan.

In large bowl stir together sugar, flour, cocoa, baking powder and salt. With pastry blender cut in butter until mixture resembles coarse crumbs; set aside. In another large bowl lightly beat eggs and vanilla. Add dry mixture to egg mixture; beat until ingredients are well blended. Spoon batter into prepared pan.

Bake 25 minutes. Remove from oven. Sprinkle marshmallows evenly over brownies, covering entire surface. Return to oven. Bake additional 5 minutes. Remove from oven. Cool in pan for 10 minutes.

Combine peanut butter chips and shortening in top of double boiler over hot (not boiling) water. Stir until melted. Add rice cereal; stir until thoroughly coated. Immediately spread over top of marshmallows. Cool completely in pan on wire rack. Cut into squares.

Makes about 32 brownies

Raspberry Fudge Brownies

Raspberry Fudge Brownies

½ cup butter or margarine
3 squares (1 ounce each) bittersweet chocolate*
2 eggs
1 cup sugar
1 teaspoon vanilla
¾ cup all-purpose flour
¼ teaspoon baking powder
Dash salt
½ cup sliced or slivered almonds
½ cup raspberry preserves
1 cup (6 ounces) milk chocolate chips

Preheat oven to 350°F. Butter and flour 8-inch square pan. Melt butter and bittersweet chocolate in small heavy saucepan over low heat. Remove from heat; cool. Beat eggs, sugar and vanilla in large bowl until light. Beat in chocolate mixture. Stir in flour, baking powder and salt until just blended. Spread ¾ of batter in prepared pan; sprinkle almonds over top.

Bake 10 minutes. Remove from oven; spread preserves over almonds. Carefully spoon remaining batter over preserves, smoothing top. Bake 25 to 30 minutes or just until top feels firm.

Remove from oven; sprinkle chocolate chips over top. Let stand a few minutes until chips melt, then spread evenly over brownies. Cool completely in pan on wire rack. When chocolate is set, cut into 2-inch squares.

Makes 16 brownies

*Bittersweet chocolate is available in specialty food stores. One square unsweetened chocolate plus two squares semisweet chocolate may be substituted.

Fudgy Brownie Bars

1¼ cups unsifted flour
¼ cup sugar
½ cup cold margarine or butter
1 (14-ounce) can EAGLE® Brand Sweetened Condensed Milk (NOT evaporated milk)
¼ cup unsweetened cocoa
1 egg
1 teaspoon vanilla extract
½ teaspoon baking powder
1 (8-ounce) bar milk chocolate candy, broken into small pieces
¾ cup chopped nuts
Confectioners' sugar, optional

Preheat oven to 350°F. In medium bowl, combine *1 cup* flour and sugar; cut in margarine until crumbly. Press in bottom of 13×9-inch baking pan. Bake 15 minutes. In large mixer bowl, beat sweetened condensed milk, cocoa, egg, remaining *¼ cup* flour, vanilla and baking powder. Stir in chocolate pieces and nuts. Spread over prepared crust.

Bake 20 minutes or until center is set. Cool completely in pan on wire rack. Sprinkle with confectioners' sugar if desired. Store loosely covered at room temperature.

Makes 24 to 36 brownies

Chocolate White Treasure Brownies

1 cup all-purpose flour
¼ teaspoon baking soda
¼ teaspoon salt
¾ cup sugar
⅓ cup (5⅓ tablespoons) butter
2 tablespoons water
One 6-oz. pkg. (1 cup) NESTLÉ® Toll House® Semi-Sweet Chocolate Morsels *or* 3 foil-wrapped bars (6 oz.) NESTLÉ® Semi-Sweet Chocolate Baking Bars
1 teaspoon vanilla extract
2 eggs
One 10-oz. pkg. (1½ cups) NESTLÉ® Toll House® Treasures® Premier White Deluxe Baking Pieces

Preheat oven to 325°F. Grease 9-inch square baking pan. In small bowl, combine flour, baking soda and salt; set aside.

In small saucepan over medium heat, combine sugar, butter and water. *Bring just to a boil;* remove from heat. Add semi-sweet chocolate morsels *or* semi-sweet chocolate baking bars and vanilla extract, stirring until smooth.

Transfer to large mixer bowl. Add eggs, one at a time, beating well after each addition. Gradually blend in flour mixture. Stir in Treasures® Premier White deluxe baking pieces. Spread in prepared pan.

Bake 30 to 35 minutes until center is just set. Cool completely in pan on wire rack. Cut into 2¼-inch squares.

Makes 16 brownies

White Chocolate & Almond Brownies

**12 ounces white chocolate,
  broken into pieces
1 cup unsalted butter
3 eggs
³/₄ cup all-purpose flour
1 teaspoon vanilla
¹/₂ cup slivered almonds**

Preheat oven to 325°F. Grease and flour 9-inch square pan. Melt chocolate and butter in large saucepan over low heat, stirring constantly. (Do not be concerned if the white chocolate separates.) Remove from heat when chocolate is just melted. With electric mixer, beat in eggs until mixture is smooth. Beat in flour and vanilla. Spread batter evenly in prepared pan. Sprinkle almonds evenly over top.

Bake 30 to 35 minutes or just until set in center. Cool completely in pan on wire rack. Cut into 2-inch squares.

Makes about 16 brownies

Left to right: Brownie Fudge, White Chocolate & Almond Brownies

Brownie Fudge

**4 squares (1 ounce each)
  unsweetened chocolate
1 cup butter or margarine
2 cups sugar
4 eggs
1 cup all-purpose flour
1 cup chopped walnuts
2 teaspoons vanilla
  Fudge Topping (recipe
  follows)**

Preheat oven to 350°F. Butter 13×9-inch pan. Melt chocolate and butter in small heavy saucepan over low heat, stirring until completely melted; cool. Beat sugar and eggs in large bowl until light and fluffy. Gradually whisk chocolate mixture into egg mixture. Stir in flour, walnuts and vanilla. Spread evenly in prepared pan.

Bake 25 to 35 minutes or just until set. Do not overbake. Meanwhile, prepare Fudge Topping. Remove brownies from oven. Immediately pour topping evenly over hot brownies. Cool in pan on wire rack. Place in freezer until firm. Cut into 1-inch squares.

Makes about 9 dozen brownies

Fudge Topping

**4¹/₂ cups sugar
¹/₃ cup butter or margarine
1 can (12 ounces) evaporated
  milk
1 jar (7 ounces) marshmallow
  creme
1 package (12 ounces)
  semisweet chocolate
  chips
1 package (12 ounces) milk
  chocolate chips
2 teaspoons vanilla
2 cups walnuts, coarsely
  chopped**

Combine sugar, butter and milk in large saucepan. Bring to a boil over medium heat; boil 5 minutes, stirring constantly. Remove from heat; add remaining ingredients *except* walnuts. Beat until smooth. Stir in walnuts.

Apple Sauce Brownies

1 cup firmly packed brown
     sugar
½ cup margarine or butter,
     softened
2 eggs
1 cup MOTT'S® Regular or
     Cinnamon Apple Sauce
1 teaspoon vanilla
1 cup all-purpose flour
¼ cup unsweetened cocoa
1 teaspoon cinnamon
½ teaspoon baking powder
½ teaspoon baking soda
¼ teaspoon salt
½ cup chopped nuts
     Powdered sugar
     Unsweetened cocoa
¼ teaspoon cinnamon

Preheat oven to 350°F. Grease 9-inch square pan. In large bowl, combine brown sugar, margarine and eggs; mix well. Stir in apple sauce and vanilla; blend thoroughly. Stir in flour, ¼ cup cocoa, 1 teaspoon cinnamon, baking powder, baking soda and salt; mix well. Stir in nuts. Pour batter into prepared pan.

Bake 25 to 35 minutes or until toothpick inserted in center comes out clean. Cool in pan on wire rack. Just before serving, use foil strips to make design with powdered sugar, cocoa and ¼ teaspoon cinnamon. Cut into bars.   *Makes 16 servings*

Apple Sauce Brownies

Honey Brownies

⅓ cup butter or margarine,
     softened
½ cup sugar
⅓ cup honey
2 teaspoons vanilla extract
2 eggs
½ cup all-purpose flour
⅓ cup HERSHEY'S® Cocoa
½ teaspoon salt
⅔ cup chopped nuts
     Creamy Brownie Frosting
     (recipe follows)

Preheat oven to 350°F. Grease 9-inch square baking pan.

In small mixer bowl, beat butter and sugar; blend in honey and vanilla. Add eggs; beat well. Stir together flour, cocoa and salt; gradually add to butter mixture. Stir in nuts. Spread batter into prepared pan.

Bake 25 to 30 minutes or until brownies begin to pull away from sides of pan. Cool completely in pan on wire rack; frost with Creamy Brownie Frosting, if desired. Cut into squares.
        Makes about 16 brownies

Creamy Brownie Frosting

3 tablespoons butter or
     margarine, softened
3 tablespoons HERSHEY'S®
     Cocoa
1 tablespoon light corn
     syrup or honey
½ teaspoon vanilla extract
1 cup powdered sugar
1 to 2 tablespoons milk

In small bowl, beat butter, cocoa, corn syrup and vanilla. Add powdered sugar and milk; beat to spreading consistency.
        Makes about 1 cup frosting

Moist & Minty Brownies

1¼ cups all-purpose flour
½ teaspoon baking soda
¼ teaspoon salt
¾ cup sugar
½ cup (1 stick) butter
2 tablespoons water
One 10-oz. pkg. (1½ cups)
     NESTLÉ® Toll House®
     Mint Flavored Semi-
     Sweet Chocolate
     Morsels, divided
1 teaspoon vanilla extract
2 eggs

Preheat oven to 350°F. Grease 9-inch square baking pan. In small bowl, combine flour, baking soda and salt; set aside.

In small saucepan, combine sugar, butter and water. *Bring just to a boil;* remove from heat. Stir in 1 cup mint chocolate morsels and vanilla extract until smooth. Transfer to large mixer bowl. Add eggs, 1 at a time, beating well after each addition. Stir in flour mixture and remaining ½ cup mint chocolate morsels. Spread in pan. Bake 25 to 35 minutes, just until center is set. Cool completely in pan on wire rack. Cut into 2¼-inch squares.   *Makes 16 brownies*

Pecan Caramel Brownies

50 caramel candy cubes
2 tablespoons milk
1½ cups granulated sugar
1 cup butter or margarine, melted
4 eggs
2 teaspoons vanilla
1 cup all-purpose flour
⅔ cup unsweetened cocoa
½ teaspoon baking powder
¼ teaspoon salt
1 cup (6 ounces) semisweet chocolate chips
⅓ cup pecan halves
Cocoa Icing (recipe follows)

Preheat oven to 350°F. Butter 13×9-inch pan.

Unwrap caramels; melt with milk in small heavy saucepan over medium to low heat, stirring until caramels melt completely. Keep warm. Combine granulated sugar, butter, eggs, vanilla, flour, cocoa, baking powder and salt in large bowl. Beat with mixer at medium speed until smooth. Spread half of batter in prepared pan.

Bake 15 minutes. Carefully remove from oven; sprinkle with chocolate chips. Drizzle melted caramel mixture over chips, covering evenly. Spoon remaining batter over all. Return to oven; bake 20 minutes longer. Do not overbake.

Meanwhile, toast pecan halves in another pan in same oven 3 to 5 minutes. Prepare Cocoa Icing. Pour over warm brownies; arrange toasted pecans on top. Cool completely in pan on wire rack. Cut into 2-inch squares.

Makes about 2 dozen brownies

Cocoa Icing

2 tablespoons butter or margarine
2 tablespoons unsweetened cocoa
2 tablespoons milk
Dash salt
1 cup powdered sugar
1 teaspoon vanilla

Combine butter, cocoa, milk and salt in small heavy saucepan. Bring to a boil over medium heat, stirring constantly. Remove from heat; add powdered sugar and beat until smooth. Stir in vanilla.

Toffee-Bran Bars

¾ cup all-purpose flour
¾ cup NABISCO® 100% Bran
1¼ cups firmly packed light brown sugar
½ cup BLUE BONNET® Margarine, melted
2 eggs, slightly beaten
1 teaspoon DAVIS® Baking Powder
1 teaspoon vanilla extract
1 cup semisweet chocolate chips
½ cup flaked coconut, toasted
⅓ cup chopped walnuts

Preheat oven to 350°F. In small bowl, combine flour, ½ cup bran, ½ cup brown sugar and margarine. Press on bottom of 13×9×2-inch baking pan. Bake 10 minutes. Set aside.

In medium bowl, with electric mixer at high speed, beat remaining ¼ cup bran, ¾ cup brown sugar, eggs, baking powder and vanilla until thick and foamy. Spread over prepared crust. Bake for 25 minutes more or until set. Remove pan from oven. Sprinkle with chocolate chips; let stand for 5 minutes. Spread softened chocolate evenly over baked layer. Immediately sprinkle coconut and walnuts in alternating diagonal strips over chocolate. Cool completely in pan on wire rack. Cut into 24 (3×1½-inch) bars. Store in airtight container.

Makes 2 dozen bars

Chewy Bar Cookies

½ cup BLUE BONNET® Margarine, softened
1 cup firmly packed light brown sugar
2 eggs
3 (1¼-ounce) packages Mix 'n Eat CREAM OF WHEAT® Cereal Apple 'n Cinnamon Flavor
⅔ cup all-purpose flour
2 teaspoons baking powder
1 cup finely chopped walnuts

Preheat oven to 350°F. In large bowl, with electric mixer at medium speed, beat margarine and brown sugar until creamy. Beat in eggs until light and fluffy. Stir in cereal, flour and baking powder. Mix in walnuts. Spread batter in greased 15½×10½×1-inch baking pan. Bake 20 to 25 minutes or until golden brown. Cool completely in pan on wire rack. Cut into bars.

Makes about 4 dozen bars

Granola Bars

3 cups quick-cooking oats, uncooked
1 cup peanuts
1 cup raisins
1 cup sunflower meats
1½ teaspoons ground cinnamon
1 (14-ounce) can EAGLE® Brand Sweetened Condensed Milk (NOT evaporated milk)
½ cup margarine or butter, melted

Preheat oven to 325°F. Line 15×10-inch baking pan with aluminum foil; grease. In large bowl, combine all ingredients; mix well. Press evenly into prepared pan. Bake 25 to 30 minutes or until golden brown. Cool slightly; remove from pan and peel off foil. Cut into bars. Store loosely covered at room temperature.

Makes 36 to 48 bars

Toffee-Bran Bars, Chewy Bar Cookies

Top to bottom: Double Peanut-Choco Bars, Chocolate Mint Bars, Layered Lemon Crumb Bars

Double Peanut-Choco Bars

- 1 (18¼- or 18½-ounce) package white cake mix
- ½ cup plus ⅓ cup peanut butter
- 1 egg
- 1 (14-ounce) can EAGLE® Brand Sweetened Condensed Milk (NOT evaporated milk)
- 1 (6-ounce) package semi-sweet chocolate chips
- ¾ cup Spanish peanuts

Preheat oven to 350°F (325°F for glass dish). In large mixer bowl, combine cake mix, ½ cup peanut butter and egg; beat on low speed until crumbly. Press firmly on bottom of greased 13×9-inch baking pan. In medium bowl, combine sweetened condensed milk and remaining ⅓ cup peanut butter; mix well. Spread evenly over prepared crust. Top with chips and peanuts.

Bake 30 to 35 minutes or until lightly browned. Cool. Cut into bars. Store loosely covered at room temperature.

Makes 36 bars

Layered Lemon Crumb Bars

- 1 (14-ounce) can EAGLE® Brand Sweetened Condensed Milk (NOT evaporated milk)
- ½ cup REALEMON® Lemon Juice from Concentrate
- 1 teaspoon grated lemon rind
- ⅔ cup margarine or butter, softened
- 1 cup firmly packed light brown sugar
- 1½ cups unsifted flour
- 1 cup quick-cooking oats, uncooked
- 1 teaspoon baking powder
- ½ teaspoon salt
- ½ teaspoon ground cinnamon
- ½ teaspoon ground nutmeg

Preheat oven to 350°F (325°F for glass dish). In small bowl, combine sweetened condensed milk, REALEMON® brand and rind; set aside. In large mixer bowl, beat margarine and brown sugar until fluffy; add flour, oats, baking powder and salt. Mix until crumbly. Press half the oat mixture in bottom of lightly greased 13×9-inch baking pan. Top with lemon mixture. Stir spices into remaining crumb mixture; sprinkle evenly over lemon layer. Bake 20 to 25 minutes or until lightly browned. Cool. Chill. Cut into bars. Store covered in refrigerator.

Makes 24 to 36 bars

Chocolate Mint Bars

- 1 (6-ounce) package semi-sweet chocolate chips (1 cup)
- 1 (14-ounce) can EAGLE® Brand Sweetened Condensed Milk (NOT evaporated milk)
- ¾ cup plus 2 tablespoons margarine or butter
- ½ teaspoon peppermint extract
- 1¼ cups firmly packed light brown sugar
- 1 egg
- 1½ cups unsifted flour
- 1½ cups quick-cooking oats, uncooked
- ¾ cup chopped nuts
- ⅓ cup crushed hard peppermint candy, optional

Preheat oven to 350°F. In heavy saucepan, over low heat, melt chips with sweetened condensed milk and *2 tablespoons* margarine; remove from heat. Add extract; set aside. In large mixer bowl, beat remaining *¾ cup* margarine and brown sugar until fluffy; beat in egg. Add flour and oats; mix well. With floured hands, press two-thirds oat mixture in bottom of greased 15×10-inch baking pan; spread evenly with chocolate mixture. Add nuts to remaining oat mixture; crumble evenly over chocolate. Sprinkle with peppermint candy if desired. Bake 15 to 18 minutes or until edges are lightly browned. Cool. Cut into bars. Store loosely covered at room temperature.

Makes 36 to 48 bars

Choco-Coconut Layer Bars

- 1/3 cup margarine or butter, melted
- 3/4 cup unsifted flour
- 1/2 cup sugar
- 2 tablespoons unsweetened cocoa
- 1 egg
- 1 (14-ounce) can EAGLE® Brand Sweetened Condensed Milk (NOT evaporated milk)
- 1 (3 1/2-ounce) can flaked coconut (1 1/3 cups)
  Flavor Variations*
- 1 (6-ounce) package semi-sweet chocolate chips (1 cup)

Preheat oven to 350°F (325°F for glass dish). In medium bowl, combine margarine, flour, sugar, cocoa and egg; mix well. Spread evenly into lightly greased 9-inch square baking pan. In small bowl, combine 3/4 cup sweetened condensed milk, coconut and desired flavor variation; spread over chocolate layer. Bake 20 minutes or until lightly browned around the edges. In heavy saucepan, over low heat, melt chips with remaining sweetened condensed milk. Remove from heat; spread evenly over coconut layer. Cool. Chill. Cut into bars. Store loosely covered at room temperature.

Makes about 24 bars

*Flavor Variations:

Almond: Add 1 cup chopped slivered almonds and 1/2 teaspoon almond extract.

Mint: Add 1/2 teaspoon peppermint extract and 4 drops green food coloring if desired.

Cherry: Add 2 (6-ounce) jars maraschino cherries, chopped and well drained on paper towels.

Choco-Coconut Layer Bars

Crunchy Peanut Brickle Bars

- 2 cups quick-cooking oats, uncooked
- 1 1/2 cups unsifted flour
- 1 cup chopped dry-roasted peanuts
- 1 cup firmly packed brown sugar
- 1 teaspoon baking soda
- 1/2 teaspoon salt
- 1 cup margarine or butter, melted
- 1 (14-ounce) can EAGLE® Brand Sweetened Condensed Milk (NOT evaporated milk)
- 1/2 cup peanut butter
- 1 (6-ounce) package almond brickle chips, *or* 6 (1 3/8-ounce) milk chocolate-covered English toffee candy bars, cut into small pieces

Preheat oven to 375°F. In large bowl, combine oats, flour, peanuts, brown sugar, baking soda and salt; stir in margarine until crumbly. Reserving 1 1/2 cups crumb mixture, press remainder in bottom of greased 15×10-inch jelly-roll pan. Bake 12 minutes. Meanwhile, in small mixer bowl, beat sweetened condensed milk with peanut butter until smooth; spread evenly over prepared crust to within 1/4 inch of edge. In medium bowl, combine reserved crumb mixture and brickle chips. Sprinkle evenly over peanut butter mixture; press down firmly. Bake 20 minutes or until golden brown. Cool. Cut into bars. Store loosely covered at room temperature.

Makes 36 to 48 bars

Prep time: 20 minutes
Baking time: 32 minutes

Fudgy Chocolate Cookie Bars

1 3/4 cups unsifted flour
3/4 cup confectioners' sugar
1/4 cup unsweetened cocoa
1 cup cold margarine or butter
1 (12-ounce) package semi-sweet chocolate chips
1 (14-ounce) can EAGLE® Brand Sweetened Condensed Milk (NOT evaporated milk)
1 teaspoon vanilla extract
1 cup chopped nuts

Preheat oven to 350°F. In medium bowl, combine flour, sugar and cocoa; cut in margarine until crumbly (mixture will be dry). Press firmly in bottom of 13×9-inch baking pan. Bake 15 minutes. Meanwhile, in medium saucepan, over medium heat, melt *1 cup* chips with sweetened condensed milk and vanilla. Pour evenly over prepared crust; top with nuts and remaining *1 cup* chips; press down firmly. Bake 20 minutes or until set. Cool. Chill if desired. Cut into bars. Store tightly covered.
Makes 24 to 36 bars

Prep time: 20 minutes
Baking time: 35 minutes

Fudgy Chocolate Cookie Bars

Cheese Ripple Bars

Cheese Batter:
Two 3-oz. pkgs. cream cheese, softened
2 eggs
1/4 cup sugar
2 tablespoons all-purpose flour
2 tablespoons (1/4 stick) butter, softened

Chocolate Batter:
1 cup all-purpose flour
1 cup sugar
3/4 teaspoon baking soda
3/4 teaspoon salt
1/2 cup milk
1 1/4 teaspoons vinegar
1/3 cup (5 1/3 tablespoons) butter, softened
3 envelopes (3 oz.) NESTLÉ® Choco Bake® Unsweetened Baking Chocolate Flavor
2 eggs
1 1/4 teaspoons vanilla extract

Cheese Batter: In small mixer bowl, beat cream cheese, eggs, sugar, flour and butter until creamy; set aside.

Chocolate Batter: Preheat oven to 350°F. Grease 13×9-inch baking pan. In large mixer bowl, combine flour, sugar, baking soda and salt. Beat in milk, vinegar, butter and Choco Bake®. Blend in eggs and vanilla extract until smooth. Pour into prepared pan. Spoon Cheese Batter over top. Swirl knife through batters to ripple slightly.

Bake 25 to 30 minutes. Cool completely in pan on wire rack; cut into 2×1-inch bars.
Makes about 4 dozen bars

Butterscotch Peanut Bars

1 (8 oz.) pkg. PHILADELPHIA BRAND® Cream Cheese, softened
1/2 cup packed brown sugar
1/2 cup granulated sugar
1/4 cup PARKAY® Margarine
1/2 cup milk
1 egg
2 teaspoons vanilla
2 1/4 cups flour
1 teaspoon CALUMET® Baking Powder
1/4 teaspoon salt
1 cup chopped salted peanuts
1 cup butterscotch chips
Butterscotch Frosting
1/2 cup chopped salted peanuts

• Preheat oven to 350°F.
• Beat cream cheese, sugars and 1/4 cup margarine in large mixing bowl at medium speed with electric mixer until well blended. Blend in 1/2 cup milk, egg and vanilla.
• Add combined dry ingredients; mix well. Stir in 1 cup peanuts and 1 cup butterscotch chips. Spread in greased 15×10×1-inch jelly roll pan.
• Bake 20 to 25 minutes or until wooden toothpick inserted in center comes out clean. Spread with Butterscotch Frosting. Sprinkle with 1/2 cup peanuts. Cut into bars.
Makes about 3 dozen bars

Butterscotch Frosting

1 cup butterscotch chips
1/2 cup creamy peanut butter
2 tablespoons PARKAY® Margarine
1 tablespoon milk

• Stir together all ingredients in small saucepan over low heat until smooth.

Prep time: 20 minutes
Cooking time: 25 minutes

"Cordially Yours" Chocolate Chip Bars

3/4 cup **BUTTER FLAVOR CRISCO®**
2 eggs
1/2 cup granulated sugar
1/4 cup firmly packed brown sugar
1 1/2 teaspoons vanilla
1 teaspoon almond extract
2 cups all-purpose flour
1 teaspoon baking soda
1/2 teaspoon cinnamon
1 can (21 ounces) cherry pie filling
1 1/2 cups milk chocolate big chips
Powdered sugar

1. Preheat oven to 350°F. Grease 15 1/2×10 1/2×1-inch pan with BUTTER FLAVOR CRISCO®.

2. Combine BUTTER FLAVOR CRISCO®, eggs, granulated sugar, brown sugar, vanilla and almond extract in large bowl. Beat at medium speed of electric mixer until well blended.

3. Combine flour, baking soda and cinnamon. Mix into creamed mixture at low speed until just blended. Stir in pie filling and chocolate chips. Spread in pan.

4. Bake 25 minutes or until lightly browned and top springs back when lightly pressed. Cool completely in pan on wire rack. Sprinkle with powdered sugar. Cut into 2 1/2×2-inch bars.

Makes 30 bars

Heath® Bars

1 cup butter, softened
1 cup brown sugar
1 egg yolk
1 teaspoon vanilla
2 cups flour
18 to 19 Original HEATH® Snack Size Bars, crushed, divided
1/2 cup finely chopped pecans

Preheat oven to 350°F. In large bowl, with electric mixer, cream butter well; blend in brown

Chocolate-Frosted Almond Shortbread

sugar, egg yolk and vanilla. By hand, mix in flour, 2/3 cup HEATH® Bars and nuts. Press into ungreased 15 1/2×10 1/2-inch jelly-roll pan.

Bake 18 to 20 minutes, or until lightly browned. Remove from oven and immediately sprinkle remaining HEATH® Bars over top. Cool slightly; cut into bars while warm.

Makes about 48 bars

Chocolate-Frosted Almond Shortbread

3/4 cup butter, softened
1/4 cup packed light brown sugar
1/4 cup powdered sugar
1 egg yolk
1 teaspoon almond extract
1 1/2 cups all-purpose flour
1/8 teaspoon baking soda
7 ounces (about 1 cup) almond paste
1/2 cup granulated sugar
1 egg
1/2 cup milk chocolate chips

Preheat oven to 350°F. Cover bottom of 9-inch pie pan with parchment or waxed paper.

Cream butter, brown sugar, powdered sugar, egg yolk and almond extract in large bowl. Blend in flour and baking soda until smooth. Press half of dough into prepared pie pan. Beat almond paste, granulated sugar and whole egg in small bowl until smooth. Spread over dough in pan. Roll out remaining half of dough on lightly floured surface into circle to fit on top of almond layer. Place over almond layer; press down to make smooth top.

Bake 30 to 40 minutes or until top appears very lightly browned and feels firm. Remove from oven; sprinkle chocolate chips over top. Let stand a few minutes until chips melt, then spread evenly over shortbread. Refrigerate until chocolate is set. Cut into slim wedges to serve.

Makes 16 to 20 cookies

Chocolate Macadamia Bars

- **12 squares (1 ounce each) bittersweet chocolate *or* 1 package (12 ounces) semisweet chocolate chips**
- **1 package (8 ounces) cream cheese, softened**
- **2/3 cup whipping cream or undiluted evaporated milk**
- **1 cup chopped macadamia nuts or almonds**
- **1 teaspoon vanilla, divided**
- **1 cup butter or margarine, softened**
- **1 1/2 cups sugar**
- **1 egg**
- **3 cups all-purpose flour**
- **1 teaspoon baking powder**
- **1/4 teaspoon salt**

Preheat oven to 375°F. Lightly grease 13×9-inch pan.

Combine chocolate, cream cheese and cream in large heavy saucepan. Stir over low heat until chocolate is melted and mixture is smooth. Remove from heat; stir in nuts and 1/2 teaspoon of the vanilla. Cream butter and sugar in large bowl. Beat in egg and remaining 1/2 teaspoon vanilla. Add flour, baking powder and salt, blending well. Press half of butter mixture in bottom of prepared pan. Spread chocolate mixture evenly over top. Sprinkle remaining butter mixture over chocolate.

Bake 35 to 40 minutes or until golden brown. Cool completely in pan on wire rack. Cut into 2×1 1/2-inch bars.

Makes about 3 dozen bars

Outlandish Oatmeal Bars

- **3/4 cup BUTTER FLAVOR CRISCO®**
- **3/4 cup firmly packed brown sugar**
- **1/2 cup granulated sugar**
- **1 egg**
- **1/4 cup apple butter**
- **2 tablespoons milk**
- **1 1/4 cups all-purpose flour**
- **1/2 teaspoon baking soda**
- **1/2 teaspoon salt**
- **2 1/2 cups quick oats (not instant or old fashioned), uncooked**
- **1 cup raspberry preserves, stirred**
- **3/4 cup white chocolate baking chips**

1. Preheat oven to 350°F. Grease 13×9×2-inch pan with BUTTER FLAVOR CRISCO®.

2. Combine BUTTER FLAVOR CRISCO®, brown sugar, granulated sugar, egg, apple butter and milk in large bowl. Beat at medium speed of electric mixer until well blended.

3. Combine flour, baking soda and salt. Mix into creamed mixture at low speed until just blended. Stir in oats, 1 cup at a time, with spoon until well blended.

4. Spread 1/2 of the dough in bottom of pan. Spread raspberry preserves over dough to 1/4 inch of sides. Mix white chocolate chips in remaining dough. Drop by spoonfuls over preserves. Spread evenly.

5. Bake 30 to 35 minutes or until golden brown. (Center will be soft.) Run spatula around edge of pan to loosen before cooling. Cool completely in pan on wire rack. Cut into 2×1 1/2-inch bars.

Makes 3 dozen bars

Awesome Apricot Oatmeal Bars

- **2/3 cup chopped dried apricots**
- **2/3 cup water**
- **1/2 cup apricot preserves**
- **1 tablespoon granulated sugar**
- **1/2 teaspoon almond extract**
- **1 cup BUTTER FLAVOR CRISCO®**
- **1 1/2 cups firmly packed brown sugar**
- **1 1/2 cups all-purpose flour**
- **1 1/2 cups quick oats (not instant or old fashioned), uncooked**
- **1 teaspoon baking powder**
- **1/2 teaspoon salt**

1. Combine apricots and water in small covered saucepan. Cook on medium heat about 10 minutes. Remove lid. Cook until apricots are tender and water has evaporated. Add preserves, granulated sugar and almond extract. Stir until preserves melt. Cool to room temperature.

2. Preheat oven to 350°F. Combine BUTTER FLAVOR CRISCO®, brown sugar, flour, oats, baking powder and salt in large bowl. Mix at low speed of electric mixer until well blended and crumbly.

3. Press 1/2 of the mixture in bottom of ungreased 13×9×2-inch pan. Spread filling evenly over crust. Sprinkle remaining crumb mixture over filling. Press down gently.

4. Bake 30 minutes or until crust is golden brown. Cool slightly. Run spatula around edge of pan to loosen. Cut into 2×1 1/2-inch bars. Cool completely in pan on wire rack.

Makes 3 dozen bars

Top to bottom: Awesome Apricot Oatmeal Bars, Outlandish Oatmeal Bars

Creative Pan Cookies

**2¼ cups all-purpose flour
1 teaspoon baking soda
½ teaspoon salt
1 cup (2 sticks) butter,
     softened
¾ cup granulated sugar
¾ cup firmly packed brown
     sugar
1 teaspoon vanilla extract
2 eggs
One 12-oz. pkg. (2 cups)
     NESTLÉ® Toll House®
     Semi-Sweet Chocolate
     Morsels
     Flavor Options, if desired
     (see below)**

Creative Pan Cookies

Preheat oven to 375°F. In small bowl, combine flour, baking soda and salt; set aside. In large mixer bowl, beat butter, granulated sugar, brown sugar and vanilla extract until creamy. Beat in eggs. Gradually beat in flour mixture. Stir in semi-sweet chocolate morsels and ingredients for 1 of the Flavor Options. Spread in ungreased 15½×10½×1-inch baking pan. Bake 18 to 20 minutes. Cool completely. Cut into 2-inch squares.

Makes about 35 squares

Flavor Options:
Granola-Nut: Stir in 2 cups granola cereal, 1 cup raisins and 1 cup chopped walnuts.

Apricot-Cashew: Stir in 2 cups granola cereal, 1 cup chopped dried apricots and 1 cup chopped dry-roasted cashews.

Apple-Oatmeal: Decrease all-purpose flour to 2 cups. Stir in 2¼ cups quick oats, uncooked, 1 cup diced peeled apples and ¾ teaspoon cinnamon.

Carrot-Pineapple: Increase all-purpose flour to 2¾ cups. Add ½ teaspoon cinnamon and ¼ teaspoon *each* allspice and nutmeg. Stir in 1 cup grated carrots, one 8-oz. can juice-packed crushed pineapple, *well drained,* and ¾ cup wheat germ.

Peanut Butter Bars

**½ cup BUTTER FLAVOR
     CRISCO®
1½ cups firmly packed brown
     sugar
⅔ cup JIF® Creamy or Extra
     Crunchy Peanut Butter
2 eggs
1 teaspoon vanilla
1½ cups all-purpose flour
½ teaspoon salt
¼ cup milk**

1. Preheat oven to 350°F. Grease 13×9×2-inch pan with BUTTER FLAVOR CRISCO®.
2. Combine BUTTER FLAVOR CRISCO®, brown sugar and JIF® Creamy Peanut Butter in large bowl. Beat at medium speed of electric mixer until well blended. Beat in eggs and vanilla.
3. Combine flour and salt. Add alternately with milk to creamed mixture at low speed. Beat until well blended. Spread in pan.
4. Bake for 28 to 32 minutes, or until golden brown and center is set. Cool in pan on wire rack. Top with frosting or glaze, if desired. Cut into 2¼×1½-inch bars.   *Makes 32 bars*

Frosting and Glaze Variations
"Peanut Butter Special"
Frosting: Combine 2 tablespoons BUTTER FLAVOR CRISCO® and ⅓ cup JIF® Creamy Peanut Butter in medium bowl. Stir

until smooth. Add 1¼ cups powdered sugar, 2 tablespoons milk and ½ teaspoon vanilla. Stir until well blended. Spread over top. Set aside until frosting is firm. Cut into bars.

Microwave Chocolate Chip Glaze: Combine 1 tablespoon BUTTER FLAVOR CRISCO®, ¼ cup semi-sweet chocolate chips and 3 tablespoons milk in medium microwave-safe bowl. Microwave at 50% (MEDIUM). Stir after 1 minute. Repeat until smooth (or melt on rangetop in small saucepan on very low heat). Add ½ cup powdered sugar and ¼ teaspoon vanilla. Stir until smooth. (Add small amount of hot milk if thinner consistency is desired.) Drizzle over top. Set aside until glaze is firm. Cut into bars.

Peanut Butter Glaze: Combine 1 tablespoon BUTTER FLAVOR CRISCO® and 1 tablespoon JIF® Creamy Peanut Butter in bowl. Stir until smooth. Add ¾ cup powdered sugar and 2 to 2½ tablespoons hot milk (use enough milk to obtain drizzling consistency). Stir until well blended. Drizzle over top. Sprinkle 2 tablespoons finely chopped peanuts over glaze. Set aside until glaze is firm. Cut into bars.

Orange Pumpkin Bars

Bars
1½ cups all-purpose flour
1 teaspoon baking powder
1 teaspoon pumpkin pie spice
½ teaspoon baking soda
½ teaspoon salt
1 cup solid packed canned pumpkin (not pumpkin pie filling)
¾ cup granulated sugar
⅔ cup CRISCO® Oil
2 eggs
¼ cup firmly packed light brown sugar
2 tablespoons orange juice
½ cup chopped nuts
½ cup raisins

Icing
1½ cups confectioners' sugar
2 tablespoons orange juice
2 tablespoons butter or margarine, softened
½ teaspoon grated orange peel

1. Preheat oven to 350°F. Grease and flour 12×8×2-inch baking dish.

2. For Bars, combine flour, baking powder, pumpkin pie spice, baking soda and salt in medium bowl. Set aside.

3. Combine pumpkin, granulated sugar, CRISCO® Oil, eggs, brown sugar and orange juice in large mixing bowl. Beat at low speed of electric mixer until blended, scraping bowl constantly. Add flour mixture. Beat at medium speed until smooth, scraping bowl frequently. Stir in nuts and raisins. Pour into prepared pan.

4. Bake 33 to 35 minutes, or until center springs back when touched lightly. Cool completely in pan on wire rack.

5. For Icing, combine the confectioners' sugar, orange juice, butter and orange peel. Beat at medium speed of electric mixer until smooth. Spread over top of cooled cake.

Makes about 24 bars

Magic Peanut Cookie Bars

½ cup margarine or butter
1½ cups graham cracker crumbs
1 (14-ounce) can EAGLE® Brand Sweetened Condensed Milk (NOT evaporated milk)
2 cups (about ¾ pound) chocolate-covered peanuts
1 (3½-ounce) can flaked coconut (1⅓ cups)

Preheat oven to 350°F (325°F for glass dish). In 13×9-inch baking pan, melt margarine in oven. Sprinkle crumbs over margarine; pour sweetened condensed milk evenly over crumbs. Top evenly with peanuts, then coconut; press down firmly. Bake 25 to 30 minutes or until lightly browned. Cool. Chill if desired. Cut into bars. Store loosely covered at room temperature.

Makes 24 to 36 bars

Pear Blondies

1 cup packed brown sugar
¼ cup butter or margarine, melted
1 egg
½ teaspoon vanilla
¾ cup all-purpose flour
½ teaspoon baking powder
½ teaspoon salt
1 cup chopped firm-ripe fresh U.S.A. Anjou, Bosc, Bartlett, Nelis or Seckel pears
⅓ cup semisweet chocolate chips

Preheat oven to 350°F. In medium bowl, mix brown sugar, butter, egg and vanilla; blend well. In small bowl, combine flour, baking powder and salt; stir into brown sugar mixture. Stir in pears and chips. Spread in greased 8-inch square pan. Bake 30 to 35 minutes or until golden brown. Cool completely in pan on wire rack. Cut into 2-inch squares.

Makes 16 bars

*Favorite recipe from **Oregon Washington California Pear Bureau***

Magic Peanut Cookie Bars

Top to bottom: Chocolate Almond Brownies (page 88), Chocolate Mint Cheesecake Bars, Streusel Caramel Bars

Streusel Caramel Bars

2 cups unsifted flour
³/₄ cup firmly packed light brown sugar
1 egg, beaten
³/₄ cup cold margarine or butter
³/₄ cup chopped nuts
24 EAGLE™ Brand Caramels, unwrapped
1 (14-ounce) can EAGLE® Brand Sweetened Condensed Milk (NOT evaporated milk)

Preheat oven to 350°F. In large bowl, combine flour, brown sugar and egg; cut in *1/2 cup* margarine until crumbly. Stir in nuts. Reserving 2 cups crumb mixture, press remainder firmly in bottom of greased 13×9-inch baking pan. Bake 15 minutes. Meanwhile, in heavy saucepan, over low heat, melt caramels with sweetened condensed milk and remaining *1/4 cup* margarine. Pour over prepared crust. Top with reserved crumb mixture. Bake 20 minutes or until bubbly. Cool. Cut into bars. Store loosely covered at room temperature.

Makes 24 to 36 bars

Chocolate Caramel Bars: Melt 2 (1-ounce) squares unsweetened chocolate with caramels, sweetened condensed milk and ¹/₄ cup margarine. Proceed as above.

Prep time: 30 minutes
Baking time: 35 minutes

Chocolate Mint Cheesecake Bars

1¼ cups unsifted flour
1 cup confectioners' sugar
½ cup unsweetened cocoa
¼ teaspoon baking soda
1 cup cold margarine or butter
1 (8-ounce) package cream cheese, softened
1 (14-ounce) can EAGLE® Brand Sweetened Condensed Milk (NOT evaporated milk)
2 eggs
1½ teaspoons peppermint extract
Green or red food coloring, optional
Easy Chocolate Glaze

Preheat oven to 350°F. In large bowl, combine the flour, confectioners' sugar, cocoa and baking soda; cut in margarine until crumbly (mixture will be dry). Press firmly on bottom of 13×9-inch baking pan. Bake 15 minutes.

Meanwhile, in large mixer bowl, beat cheese until fluffy. Gradually beat in sweetened condensed milk until smooth. Add eggs, extract and food coloring if desired; mix well. Pour over prepared crust.

Bake 20 minutes or until lightly browned around edges. Cool. Drizzle with Easy Chocolate Glaze. Chill. Cut into bars. Store covered in refrigerator.

Makes 24 to 36 bars

EASY CHOCOLATE GLAZE: In small saucepan, over low heat, melt 2 (1-ounce) squares semi-sweet chocolate with 2 tablespoons margarine or butter; stir until smooth. Remove from heat; stir in ½ teaspoon vanilla extract. Immediately drizzle over bars.

Makes about ¼ cup glaze

Prep time: 20 minutes
Baking time: 35 minutes

Chocolate Dream Bars

½ cup butter or margarine, softened
1½ cups packed light brown sugar, divided
1 egg yolk
1 cup plus 2 tablespoons all-purpose flour
2 eggs
1 cup (6 ounces) semisweet chocolate chips
½ cup chopped toasted walnuts

Preheat oven to 375°F. Grease 13×9-inch pan. Cream butter with ½ cup of the brown sugar and the egg yolk in large bowl until light and well blended. (There should be no sugar lumps.) Stir in the 1 cup flour until well blended. Press dough on bottom of prepared pan. Bake 12 to 15 minutes or until golden.

Meanwhile, beat remaining 1 cup brown sugar, the remaining 2 tablespoons flour and eggs in same bowl until light and frothy. Spread mixture over hot baked crust. Return to oven; bake about 15 minutes or until topping is set. Remove from oven; sprinkle chocolate chips over the top. Let stand a few minutes until chips melt, then spread evenly over bars. Sprinkle walnuts over chocolate. Cool in pan on wire rack. Cut into 2×1-inch bars.

Makes about 5 dozen bars

Toasted Pecan Toffee Bars

Toasted Pecan Toffee Bars

Bars
2 cups all-purpose flour
1 cup firmly packed brown sugar
1 cup LAND O LAKES® Butter, softened
½ teaspoon ground cinnamon
1 teaspoon vanilla
¾ cup chopped pecans, toasted
½ cup milk chocolate chips
Topping
½ cup milk chocolate chips
¼ cup chopped pecans, toasted

Preheat oven to 350°F. For Bars, in large mixer bowl, combine flour, brown sugar, butter, cinnamon and vanilla. Beat at low speed, scraping bowl often, until mixture is crumbly, 2 to 3 minutes. Stir in nuts and chocolate chips. Press in bottom of greased 13×9×2-inch baking pan. Bake for 25 to 30 minutes, or until edges are lightly browned.

For Topping, sprinkle chocolate chips over bars. Let stand 5 minutes to melt. Slightly swirl chips with tip of knife as they melt, leaving some whole for marbled effect. *Do not spread chips.* Sprinkle nuts over top. Cool completely in pan on wire rack. Cut into bars.

Makes about 3 dozen bars

Chocolate Streusel Bars

1³/₄ cups unsifted flour
1¹/₂ cups confectioners' sugar
¹/₂ cup unsweetened cocoa
1 cup cold margarine or
    butter
1 (8-ounce) package cream
    cheese, softened
1 (14-ounce) can EAGLE®
    Brand Sweetened
    Condensed Milk (NOT
    evaporated milk)
1 egg
2 teaspoons vanilla extract
¹/₂ cup chopped nuts

Preheat oven to 350°F. In large bowl, combine flour, sugar and cocoa. Cut in margarine until crumbly (mixture will be dry). Reserving 2 cups crumb mixture, press remainder firmly in bottom of 13×9-inch baking pan. Bake 15 minutes. In large mixer bowl, beat cheese until fluffy. Gradually beat in sweetened condensed milk until smooth. Add egg and vanilla; mix well. Pour over prepared crust. Combine nuts with reserved crumb mixture; sprinkle over cheese mixture. Bake 25 minutes or until bubbly. Cool. Chill. Cut into bars. Store covered in refrigerator.

Makes 24 to 36 bars

Chocolate Streusel Bars

Chocolate Raspberry Coconut Bars

Crust:
1¹/₂ cups all-purpose flour
    ¹/₄ cup firmly packed brown
        sugar
    ¹/₂ cup (1 stick) butter
Topping:
One 14-oz. can sweetened
        condensed milk
    ¹/₂ cup all-purpose flour
    ¹/₂ teaspoon baking powder
    ¹/₄ teaspoon salt
    2 eggs
One 6-oz. pkg. (1 cup) NESTLÉ®
        Toll House® Semi-Sweet
        Chocolate Morsels
One 3¹/₂-oz. can (1¹/₃ cups)
        flaked coconut, divided
    ¹/₂ cup pecans, chopped
    ¹/₂ cup raspberry preserves

Crust: Preheat oven to 350°F. Grease 13×9-inch baking pan. In small bowl, combine flour and brown sugar. With pastry blender or two knives, cut in butter until mixture resembles coarse crumbs. Press into bottom of the prepared pan. Bake 20 minutes.

Topping: In large mixer bowl, blend sweetened condensed milk, flour, baking powder, salt and eggs. Stir in semi-sweet chocolate morsels, 1 cup coconut and pecans. Pour over baked Crust.

Bake 25 minutes or until Topping is set. Remove from oven. Spread preserves over Topping. Sprinkle with remaining ¹/₃ cup coconut. Cool completely in pan on wire rack. Cut into 1¹/₂×1-inch bars.

Makes about 6 dozen bars

Apple Pie Bars

Crust
    Milk
    1 egg yolk, reserve egg
        white
2¹/₂ cups all-purpose flour
    1 teaspoon salt
    1 cup LAND O LAKES®
        Butter
Filling
    1 cup crushed corn flake
        cereal
    8 cups peeled, cored,
        ¹/₄-inch sliced, tart
        cooking apples (about
        8 to 10 medium)
    1 cup granulated sugar
1¹/₂ teaspoons ground
        cinnamon
    ¹/₂ teaspoon ground nutmeg
    1 reserved egg white
    2 tablespoons granulated
        sugar
    ¹/₂ teaspoon ground cinnamon
Glaze
    1 cup powdered sugar
    1 to 2 tablespoons milk
    ¹/₂ teaspoon vanilla

Preheat oven to 350°F. For Crust, add enough milk to egg yolk to measure ²/₃ cup; set aside. In medium bowl, combine flour and salt. Cut in butter until crumbly. With fork, stir in milk mixture until dough forms a ball; divide into halves. Roll out ¹/₂ of the dough, on lightly floured surface, into a 15×10-inch rectangle. Place on bottom of ungreased 15×10×1-inch jelly-roll pan.

For Filling, sprinkle cereal over top of crust; layer apples over cereal. In small bowl, combine 1 cup granulated sugar, 1¹/₂ teaspoons cinnamon and nutmeg. Sprinkle over apples. Roll remaining ¹/₂ of dough into a 15¹/₂×10¹/₂-inch rectangle; place over apples. In small bowl, with fork beat egg white until foamy; brush over top crust. In another small bowl, stir together

2 tablespoons granulated sugar and ½ teaspoon cinnamon; sprinkle over crust. Bake for 45 to 60 minutes, or until lightly browned.

For Glaze, in small bowl, stir together all glaze ingredients. Drizzle over warm bars. Cut into bars.

Makes about 3 dozen bars

Double Chocolate Pecan Pie Bars

Pastry for one 9-inch pie shell
2 eggs
¾ cup dark corn syrup
¾ cup sugar
2 tablespoons (¼ stick) butter, melted and cooled
1 teaspoon vanilla extract
⅛ teaspoon salt
One 6-oz. pkg. (1 cup) NESTLÉ® Toll House® Semi-Sweet Chocolate Morsels, divided
1 cup pecans, chopped
2 teaspoons vegetable shortening

Preheat oven to 425°F. On lightly floured board, roll pastry into 11-inch square; press into bottom and 1 inch up sides of 9-inch square baking pan. Bake 8 minutes. Remove from oven; set aside. *Turn oven control to 350°F.*

In large mixer bowl, beat eggs, corn syrup, sugar, butter, vanilla extract and salt until well blended. Stir in ¾ cup semi-sweet chocolate morsels and pecans. Pour into baked crust. Bake 45 to 50 minutes until set. Cool completely in pan on wire rack.

Melt remaining ¼ cup semi-sweet chocolate morsels and shortening, stirring until smooth. Drizzle over top. Refrigerate several hours. Cut into 2¼×1-inch bars.

Makes 32 bars

Apple Pie Bars

meal Apple
ares

1 cup BUTTER FLAVOR
    CRISCO®
1 cup firmly packed brown
    sugar
1 cup granulated sugar
2 eggs
⅓ cup apple juice
2 teaspoons vanilla
1½ cups all-purpose flour
2 teaspoons cinnamon
1 teaspoon baking powder
1 teaspoon baking soda
¼ teaspoon nutmeg
4 cups quick oats (not
    instant or old fashioned),
    uncooked
2 cups peeled, diced apples
½ cup raisins (optional)

1. Preheat oven to 350°F. Grease
15½×10½×1-inch pan with
BUTTER FLAVOR CRISCO®
2. Combine BUTTER FLAVOR
CRISCO®, brown sugar and
granulated sugar in large bowl.
Beat at medium speed of electric
mixer until well blended. Beat in
eggs, apple juice and vanilla.
3. Combine flour, cinnamon,
baking powder, baking soda
and nutmeg. Mix into creamed
mixture at low speed until
blended. Stir in oats, apples and
raisins with spoon. Spread in
prepared pan.
4. Bake 30 to 35 minutes, or
until browned and wooden
toothpick inserted in center
comes out clean. Cool completely
in pan on wire rack. Cut into
2½×1½-inch bars.

Makes 3½ dozen bars

*Chocolate Meringue Peanut
Squares*

Chocolate Meringue
Peanut Squares

Crust
1½ cups all-purpose flour
½ cup sugar
¾ cup LAND O LAKES®
    Butter, softened
2 egg yolks, reserve egg
    whites
2 teaspoons vanilla
Filling
2 reserved egg whites
⅓ cup sugar
1 cup chopped salted
    peanuts
½ cup milk chocolate chips

Preheat oven to 325°F. For
Crust, in large mixer bowl,
combine all crust ingredients.
Beat at low speed, scraping bowl
often, until mixture is crumbly, 1
to 2 minutes. Press onto bottom
of greased 13×9×2-inch baking
pan.
For Filling, in small bowl, beat
egg whites at high speed,
scraping bowl often, until soft
mounds form, 1 to 2 minutes.
Gradually add sugar; beat until
stiff peaks form, 1 to 2 minutes.
Fold in peanuts and chocolate
chips. Spread over crust. Bake
for 30 to 35 minutes, or until
lightly browned. Cool in pan on
wire rack. Cut into squares.

Makes about 3 dozen squares

Mocha Almond Bars

Bars
2¼ cups all-purpose flour
1 cup granulated sugar
1 cup LAND O LAKES®
    Butter, softened
1 egg
1 teaspoon instant coffee
    granules
1 cup sliced almonds
Glaze
¾ cup powdered sugar
1 to 2 tablespoons milk
¼ teaspoon almond extract

Preheat oven to 350°F. For Bars,
in small mixer bowl, combine
flour, granulated sugar, butter,
egg and instant coffee. Beat at
low speed, scraping bowl often,
until well mixed, 2 to 3 minutes.
Stir in nuts. Press in bottom of
greased 13×9×2-inch baking pan.
Bake for 25 to 30 minutes, or
until edges are lightly browned.
For Glaze, in small bowl, stir
together all glaze ingredients.
Drizzle glaze over warm bars.
Cool completely in pan on wire
rack. Cut into bars.

Makes about 3 dozen bars

Banana Date Bars

3 ripe, medium DOLE®
    Bananas, peeled
½ cup margarine, softened
1 cup brown sugar, packed
2 eggs
2 cups flour
1 teaspoon baking soda
1 teaspoon ground cinnamon
½ teaspoon baking powder
½ teaspoon ground nutmeg
¼ teaspoon salt
1 cup DOLE® Chopped Dates
1 cup chopped walnuts
    Powdered sugar

Preheat oven to 350°F. Grease
13×9-inch baking pan. In food
processor or blender, process 1
banana until pureed (½ cup).
Dice remaining two bananas.

In large bowl, cream margarine with brown sugar until light and fluffy. Beat in eggs, then pureed banana. Combine flour, baking soda, cinnamon, baking powder, nutmeg and salt; beat into creamed mixture until well blended. Fold in dates, nuts and diced bananas. Turn batter into prepared pan.

Bake for 25 minutes. Cool bars completely in pan on wire rack. Sprinkle with powdered sugar. Cut into bars.

Makes about 24 bars

Pineapple Walnut Bars

- 1 can (8¼ oz.) DOLE® Crushed Pineapple in Syrup*
- 2 cups flour
- 2 cups brown sugar, packed
- ½ cup margarine, softened
- 1 cup chopped walnuts
- 1 teaspoon ground cinnamon
- 1 teaspoon baking soda
- ¼ teaspoon salt
- 1 egg
- ¾ cup dairy sour cream
- 1 teaspoon vanilla extract
  Powdered sugar, optional

Preheat oven to 350°F. Drain pineapple well, pressing out excess syrup with back of spoon. Grease 13×9-inch baking pan.

In large bowl, combine flour, brown sugar and margarine; mix until fine crumbs form. Stir in walnuts. Press 2 cups mixture onto bottom of prepared baking pan. To remaining flour mixture, add cinnamon, baking soda and salt; blend well. Beat in egg, sour cream and vanilla until blended. Stir in pineapple. Spoon evenly over crust in pan.

Bake 40 minutes or until bars pull away from sides of pan and wooden toothpick inserted in center comes out clean. Cool completely in pan on wire rack. Dust with powdered sugar. Cut into bars.

Makes about 16 bars

*May use pineapple packed in juice if desired.

Frosted Honey Bars

Bars
- 1½ cups all-purpose flour
- 1 cup LAND O LAKES® Butter, melted
- 1 cup honey
- 3 eggs
- 1½ teaspoons baking soda
- 1 teaspoon ground cinnamon
- ¾ teaspoon salt
- 1½ cups shredded carrots (about 3 medium)
- ¾ cup chopped walnuts

Frosting
- 1 cup powdered sugar
- 1 package (8 ounces) cream cheese, softened
- 1 teaspoon milk
- 1 teaspoon vanilla

Preheat oven to 350°F. For Bars, in large mixer bowl, combine flour, butter, honey, eggs, baking soda, cinnamon and salt. Beat at low speed, scraping bowl often, until well mixed, 1 to 2 minutes. Stir in carrots and nuts. Pour into greased 15×10×1-inch jelly-roll pan. Bake for 20 to 25 minutes, or until top springs back when touched lightly in center. Cool completely in pan on wire rack.

For Frosting, in small mixer bowl, combine all frosting ingredients. Beat at medium speed, scraping bowl often, until smooth, 1 to 2 minutes. Spread with frosting. Cut into bars. Store, covered, in refrigerator.

Makes about 3 dozen bars

Frosted Honey Bars

Toffee Brownie Bars

Crust
- ¾ cup butter or margarine, softened
- ¾ cup firmly packed brown sugar
- 1 egg yolk
- ¾ teaspoon vanilla extract
- 1½ cups all-purpose flour

Filling
- 1 package DUNCAN HINES® Fudge Brownie Mix, Family Size
- 1 egg
- ⅓ cup water
- ⅓ cup CRISCO® Oil or PURITAN® Oil

Topping
- 1 package (12 ounces) milk chocolate chips, melted
- ¾ cup finely chopped pecans

1. Preheat oven to 350°F. Grease 15½×10½×1-inch pan.

2. For Crust, combine butter, brown sugar, egg yolk and vanilla extract in large bowl. Stir in flour. Spread in pan. Bake 15 minutes or until golden.

3. For Filling, prepare brownie mix following package directions. Spread over hot crust. Bake 15 minutes or until surface appears set. Cool 30 minutes.

4. For Topping, spread melted chocolate on top of brownie layer; garnish with pecans. Cool completely in pan on wire rack; cut into bars.

Makes about 48 brownies

Toffee Brownie Bars

Zesty Fresh Lemon Bars

Crust:
- ½ cup butter or margarine, softened
- ½ cup granulated sugar
  Grated peel of
  - ½ SUNKIST® Lemon
- 1¼ cups all-purpose flour

Filling:
- 1 cup packed brown sugar
- 1 cup chopped walnuts
- 2 eggs, slightly beaten
- ¼ cup all-purpose flour
  Grated peel of
  - ½ SUNKIST® Lemon
- ¼ teaspoon baking powder

Glaze:
- 1 cup powdered sugar
- 1 tablespoon butter or margarine, softened
- 2 tablespoons fresh-squeezed SUNKIST® Lemon Juice

To prepare Crust: Preheat oven to 350°F. In medium bowl, cream butter, granulated sugar and lemon peel. Gradually stir in flour to form soft dough. Press evenly in bottom of 13×9×2-inch pan. Bake 15 minutes.

To prepare Filling: In medium bowl, mix all filling ingredients. Spread over baked crust. Bake 20 minutes. Meanwhile, prepare Glaze.

To prepare Glaze: In small bowl, gradually blend small amount of powdered sugar into butter. Add lemon juice and remaining sugar; stir to blend well. Drizzle glaze over hot lemon bars. Cool completely in pan on wire rack; cut into bars.

Makes about 3 dozen bars

Walnut-Oat Topped Cookie Bars

2 cups unsifted flour
¾ cup sugar
½ cup margarine or butter, melted
2 eggs
1½ cups coarsely chopped walnuts
1 (14-ounce) can EAGLE® Brand Sweetened Condensed Milk (NOT evaporated milk)
1 cup quick-cooking oats, uncooked
1½ teaspoons vanilla extract
1 (6-ounce) package semi-sweet chocolate chips (1 cup)

Preheat oven to 350°F. In small mixer bowl, combine flour, sugar, margarine and eggs; beat until smooth. Spread into lightly greased 13×9-inch baking pan. In medium bowl, stir together *1 cup* walnuts, sweetened condensed milk, oats and vanilla. Spread evenly over cookie base. Top with chips and remaining *½ cup* walnuts; press down firmly. Bake 30 to 35 minutes or until golden brown. Cool. Chill. Cut into bars. Store loosely covered at room temperature.

Makes 24 to 36 bars

Chocolate Peanut Buddy Bars

1 cup peanut butter
6 tablespoons (¾ stick) butter or margarine, softened
1¼ cups sugar
3 eggs
1 teaspoon vanilla extract
1 cup all-purpose flour
¼ teaspoon salt
One 11½-oz. pkg. (2 cups) NESTLÉ® Toll House® Milk Chocolate Morsels, divided

Preheat oven to 350°F. In large mixer bowl, beat peanut butter and butter until smooth, about 1 minute. Add sugar, eggs and vanilla extract; beat until creamy. Gradually beat in flour and salt. Stir in 1 cup milk chocolate morsels. Spread in ungreased 13×9-inch baking pan. Bake 25 to 30 minutes until the edges begin to brown. Immediately sprinkle remaining 1 cup milk chocolate morsels over top. Let stand 5 minutes or until morsels become shiny and soft; spread evenly over top. When cool, refrigerate 5 to 10 minutes to set chocolate. Cut into 1½-inch squares.

Makes about 4 dozen bars

Mississippi Mud Bars

½ cup butter or margarine, softened
¾ cup packed brown sugar
1 teaspoon vanilla
1 egg
⅛ teaspoon baking soda
¼ teaspoon salt
1 cup plus 2 tablespoons all-purpose flour
1 cup (6 ounces) semisweet chocolate chips, divided
1 cup (6 ounces) white chocolate-flavored chips, divided
½ cup chopped walnuts or pecans

Preheat oven to 375°F. Line 9-inch square pan with foil; grease foil.

Cream butter and brown sugar in large bowl until blended and smooth. Beat in vanilla and egg until light. Blend in baking soda and salt. Add flour, mixing until well blended. Stir in ¾ cup *each* of the semisweet and white chocolate chips and the nuts. Spread dough in prepared pan. Bake 23 to 25 minutes or until center feels firm. Do not overbake. Remove from oven;

sprinkle rem
semisweet
chips over
minutes u
spread e
completel
until chocolate is
2×1-inch bars.

Makes about 3 dozen bars

Lemon Chocolate Bars

1⅓ cups plus 3 tablespoons unsifted flour
½ cup confectioners' sugar
2 tablespoons unsweetened cocoa
¾ cup cold margarine or butter
1½ cups granulated sugar
1 teaspoon baking powder
½ cup REALEMON® Lemon Juice from Concentrate
4 eggs, beaten
Quick Chocolate Drizzle

Preheat oven to 350°F. In large bowl, combine 1⅓ cups flour, confectioners' sugar and cocoa; cut in margarine until crumbly. Press in bottom of 13×9-inch baking pan; bake 20 minutes. Meanwhile, in medium bowl, combine granulated sugar, baking powder and remaining *3 tablespoons* flour. Add REALEMON® brand and eggs; mix well. Pour over baked crust; bake 20 minutes longer or until golden brown. Cool. Drizzle with Quick Chocolate Drizzle. Chill. Cut into bars. Store covered in refrigerator; serve at room temperature.

Makes 24 to 36 bars

QUICK CHOCOLATE DRIZZLE: In small saucepan, over low heat, melt 1 (1-ounce) square semi-sweet chocolate with 1 tablespoon margarine or butter. Immediately drizzle over bars.

Prep time: 15 minutes
Baking time: 40 minutes

CAKES & TORTES

Turn an ordinary day into a special occasion by baking a luscious cake. For a delightful ending to a simple supper, choose a moist carrot cake topped with a satiny smooth frosting or a buttery rich pound cake. Create a grand finale with an elegant multi-tiered torte, cream-filled cake roll or ever-popular chocolate layer cake. (For additional cake recipes, see the Jump-Start Baking, Especially for Kids and Festive Holiday Baking chapters.)

Bittersweet Chocolate Pound Cake

3 foil-wrapped bars (6 oz.) NESTLÉ® Unsweetened Chocolate Baking Bars
2 cups all-purpose flour
1 teaspoon baking soda
3/4 teaspoon baking powder
2 tablespoons NESCAFÉ® Classic Blend Instant Coffee
2 tablespoons hot water
Cold water
2 cups granulated sugar
1 cup (2 sticks) butter, softened
1 teaspoon vanilla extract
3 eggs
Viennese Glaze (recipe follows)
Confectioners' sugar, optional

Preheat oven to 325°F. Grease and flour 10-inch fluted tube or angel food cake pan. Melt unsweetened chocolate baking bars.

In small bowl, combine flour, baking soda and baking powder; set aside. In 2-cup measure, dissolve instant coffee in hot water; add cold water to measure 1½ cups.

In large mixer bowl, beat granulated sugar, butter and vanilla extract until creamy. Beat in eggs, 1 at a time. Stir in melted chocolate. Add flour mixture alternately with coffee mixture. Pour into prepared pan.

Bake 1 hour or until skewer inserted into center of cake comes out clean. Cool 30 minutes; remove from pan. Cool completely. Drizzle with Viennese Glaze; sprinkle with confectioners' sugar.
Makes 12 servings

Viennese Glaze

One 8-oz. pkg. (4 foil-wrapped bars) NESTLÉ® Semi-Sweet Chocolate Baking Bars
2/3 cup heavy or whipping cream
3 tablespoons confectioners' sugar
3/4 teaspoon vanilla extract

In medium saucepan over very low heat, melt semi-sweet chocolate baking bars with heavy cream and confectioners' sugar, stirring until smooth. Stir in vanilla extract; cool to room temperature.
Makes about 1²/₃ cups glaze

Bittersweet Chocolate Pound Cake

Almond Lemon Pound Cake

Almond Lemon Pound Cake

      2 cups cake flour
  1/2 teaspoon cream of tartar
  1/2 teaspoon salt
    **1 cup butter or margarine,
          softened**
    1 cup granulated sugar
    4 eggs
    5 tablespoons lemon juice
  **1 1/4 cups BLUE DIAMOND®
          Chopped Natural
          Almonds, toasted**
  1/2 cup powered sugar
  1/2 teaspoon vanilla

Preheat oven to 325°F. Grease
9×5×3-inch loaf pan.

In small bowl, combine flour,
cream of tartar and salt. In large
bowl, cream butter and
granulated sugar. Add eggs, 1 at
a time, beating well after each
addition. Beat in 2 tablespoons
of the lemon juice. Gradually add
flour mixture; mix thoroughly.
Fold in 1 cup of the almonds.
Pour batter into prepared pan.
Sprinkle top with remaining 1/4
cup almonds.

Bake 1 hour or until wooden
toothpick inserted into center
comes out clean. Meanwhile, in
small saucepan, combine
powdered sugar, remaining 3
tablespoons lemon juice and
vanilla. Stir over medium heat
until sugar is dissolved. Remove
cake from oven. Drizzle hot glaze
over top. Let cool in pan on wire
rack 15 minutes. Loosen edges;
remove from pan. Cool completely
on wire rack.   *Makes 1 loaf*

Kentucky Pound Cake

    3 cups all-purpose flour
    2 cups sugar
    1 cup sour cream
    **1 cup butter or margarine,
          softened**
    **1 tablespoon bourbon
          whiskey**
    1 teaspoon baking powder
  3/4 teaspoon salt
  1/2 teaspoon baking soda
    5 eggs
      **Bourbon Syrup (recipe
          follows)**

Preheat oven to 325°F. Grease
and lightly flour 12-cup Bundt®
or tube pan.

In large mixer bowl, combine all
ingredients *except* Bourbon
Syrup. Beat at low speed until
all ingredients are moistened.
Beat at high speed until smooth,
about 3 minutes. Pour batter
into prepared pan.

Bake 1 hour or until wooden toothpick inserted into center of cake comes out clean. Let cool in pan on wire rack 5 minutes. Meanwhile, prepare Bourbon Syrup.

Pierce cake deeply with fork in 6 evenly spaced places. Pour 3/4 cup hot Bourbon Syrup over cake. Let stand 5 minutes. Loosen edge; invert cake onto serving plate. Spoon or brush remaining syrup over cake. Cool completely.   *Makes 1 cake*

BOURBON SYRUP: In small saucepan, combine 3/4 cup sugar, 1/3 cup butter or margarine and 3 tablespoons water. Stir over low heat just until butter melts. Remove from heat; stir in 1 tablespoon bourbon whiskey.

Marble Pound Cake

    3¼ cups all-purpose flour
    1 tablespoon baking powder
    ½ teaspoon salt
    2 cups sugar
    1½ cups (3 sticks) butter, softened
    1½ teaspoons vanilla extract
    6 eggs
    1¼ cups milk
    4 envelopes (4 oz.) NESTLÉ®
       Choco Bake®
       Unsweetened Baking
       Chocolate Flavor
    Viennese Glaze (page 116)

Preheat oven to 325°F. Grease and flour 10-inch fluted tube pan. In small bowl, combine flour, baking powder and salt; set aside.

In large mixer bowl, beat sugar, butter and vanilla extract until creamy. Add eggs, 1 at a time, beating well after each addition. Gradually add flour mixture alternately with milk.

Divide batter in half (about 4 cups batter per half). Add Choco Bake® to one half; mix well.

Alternately spoon heaping tablespoonfuls of white and chocolate batters into prepared pan. Rotate pan clockwise then counterclockwise to level batter. Bake 1 hour and 15 minutes or until skewer inserted into center of cake comes out clean. Cool 15 minutes; remove from pan. Cool completely. Drizzle with Viennese Glaze.

Makes 12 to 16 servings

Sour Cream Pound Cake

    3 cups sifted all-purpose flour
    ¼ teaspoon ARM & HAMMER® Pure Baking Soda
    ¼ teaspoon salt
    3 cups granulated sugar
    1 cup (½ pound) butter or margarine, softened
    6 eggs
    1 cup sour cream
    1 teaspoon vanilla or lemon extract
    Confectioners' sugar

Preheat oven to 350°F. Grease and flour 10-inch tube pan. Sift together flour, baking soda and salt; set aside. Using an electric mixer, cream together granulated sugar and butter until light and fluffy in large bowl; add eggs, one at a time, beating well after each addition. Stir in sour cream and extract. Gradually mix dry ingredients into egg mixture until completely blended. Turn batter into prepared pan.

Bake 1 hour and 25 minutes or until wooden toothpick inserted in center comes out clean. Remove from pan; cool completely on wire rack. Before serving, sprinkle pound cake with confectioners' sugar.

Makes one 10-inch tube cake

Spicy Gingerbread

    1 cup MIRACLE WHIP® Salad Dressing
    1 cup sugar
    3 eggs
    3¾ cups flour
    2 teaspoons baking soda
    1 teaspoon ground ginger
    ½ teaspoon salt
    ½ teaspoon cinnamon
    ½ teaspoon ground cloves
    1 cup light molasses

• Preheat oven to 350°F.

• Beat salad dressing and sugar; blend in eggs.

• Gradually add combined sifted dry ingredients alternately with molasses, mixing well after each addition.

• Pour into greased and floured 13×9-inch baking pan.

• Bake 40 to 45 minutes or until wooden toothpick inserted in center comes out clean. Cool; cut into squares. Serve with ice cream, powdered sugar or whipped topping.

Makes about 12 servings

Spicy Gingerbread

Ginger Cake

1/2 **cup butter or margarine**
1/2 **cup light molasses**
1/2 **cup honey**
2 1/2 **cups sifted all-purpose
   flour**
1 **teaspoon baking powder**
1 **teaspoon baking soda**
2 **teaspoons ground ginger**
1/2 **teaspoon salt**
1/2 **teaspoon ground cinnamon**
1/4 **teaspoon ground cloves**
1/4 **teaspoon ground nutmeg**
1 **cup sugar**
1 **cup milk**
2 **eggs, slightly beaten
   Double Lemon Icing
   (recipe follows)**

Preheat oven to 350°F. Grease 8-inch square pan, line with waxed paper; grease again.

In small saucepan over low heat, melt butter. Remove from heat; stir in molasses and honey. In large bowl, combine flour, baking powder, baking soda, ginger, salt, cinnamon, cloves and nutmeg. Add sugar, milk and eggs; beat until blended. Add butter mixture; beat until well blended. Pour batter into prepared pan.

Bake 1 hour or until wooden toothpick inserted into center comes out clean. Let cool in pan on wire rack 15 minutes. Loosen edges; remove from pan. Peel off waxed paper. Cool completely on wire rack. Prepare Double Lemon Icing; spread evenly over cake.

Makes 6 to 8 servings

DOUBLE LEMON ICING: In a small bowl, combine 2 cups sifted confectioners' sugar, 2 tablespoons *each* softened butter or margarine and lemon juice, 1/2 teaspoon grated lemon peel and 1/4 teaspoon vanilla until smooth.

Sweetwater Ranch Spice Cake

2 1/2 **cups all-purpose flour**
1 **teaspoon baking powder**
1 **teaspoon ground cinnamon**
1/2 **teaspoon salt**
1/2 **teaspoon ground allspice**
1/2 **teaspoon ground ginger**
1/2 **teaspoon ground nutmeg**
1/2 **cup butter or margarine,
   softened**
1 1/2 **cups packed brown sugar**
2 **egg yolks**
1 **teaspoon baking soda**
1 1/4 **cups buttermilk**
1 **teaspoon vanilla extract
   Meringue Frosting (recipe
   follows)**
2/3 **cup coarsely chopped
   pecans**

Preheat oven to 350°F. Grease 13×9-inch baking pan; set aside.

Sift together flour, baking powder, cinnamon, salt, allspice, ginger and nutmeg. Beat butter in large bowl of electric mixer on medium speed until creamy. Add brown sugar; beat until fluffy. Beat in egg yolks. Dissolve baking soda in buttermilk. Add flour mixture to butter mixture alternately with buttermilk mixture, starting and ending with flour mixture. Stir in vanilla. Pour batter evenly into prepared pan. Prepare Meringue Frosting; spread over cake batter.

Bake 25 minutes; sprinkle with pecans. Continue baking 20 minutes or until wooden toothpick inserted in center comes out clean. Transfer to wire rack; let cool completely in pan.

Makes about 12 servings

Meringue Frosting

2 **egg whites**
1/2 **cup packed brown sugar**

Beat egg whites, using clean beaters and bowl, in medium bowl of electric mixer until stiff peaks form. Gradually add brown sugar, 2 tablespoons at a time, beating well after each addition. Beat until stiff peaks form.

Blueberry Upside-Down Cake

Topping:
2 **cups fresh or dry-pack
   frozen blueberries,
   rinsed and drained**
3/4 **cup granulated sugar**
2 **tablespoons flour**
2 **tablespoons lemon juice**
Batter:
1/2 **cup vegetable shortening**
1 **cup granulated sugar**
3 **eggs**
2 **cups all-purpose flour**
1 **tablespoon baking powder**
1 **teaspoon salt**
3/4 **cup milk**
1 1/2 **cups coarsely chopped
   nuts**
   **Grated rind of 1 orange
   Confectioners' sugar**

Preheat oven to 350°F. Grease 10×10×2-inch baking pan. For Topping, in medium bowl, combine blueberries, granulated sugar, flour and lemon juice. Spread mixture on bottom of prepared pan.

For Batter, in large bowl, cream shortening; gradually beat in granulated sugar. Add eggs one at a time, beating well after each addition. Sift flour, baking powder and salt together into small bowl. Alternately add dry ingredients and milk to creamed mixture, beginning and ending with dry ingredients. Fold in nuts and orange rind. Pour cake batter over blueberries.

Bake 45 minutes or until cake feels firm to the touch. Loosen edges and invert onto platter while still hot. Serve warm sprinkled with confectioners' sugar.

Makes one 10-inch square cake

Favorite recipe from **North American Blueberry Council**

Pineapple Upside Down Cake

Pineapple Upside Down Cake

Topping
- ½ cup butter or margarine
- 1 cup firmly packed brown sugar
- 1 can (20 ounces) pineapple slices, well drained
- Maraschino cherries, halved and drained
- Walnut halves

Cake
- 1 package DUNCAN HINES® Moist Deluxe Pineapple Supreme Cake Mix
- 1 package (4-serving size) vanilla instant pudding and pie filling mix
- 4 eggs
- 1 cup water
- ½ cup CRISCO® Oil or PURITAN® Oil

1. Preheat oven to 350°F.

2. For Topping, melt butter over low heat in 12-inch cast-iron skillet or skillet with oven-proof handle. Remove from heat. Stir in brown sugar; spread to cover bottom of skillet. Arrange pineapple slices, maraschino cherries and walnut halves in skillet. Set aside.

3. For Cake, combine cake mix, pudding mix, eggs, water and oil in large mixing bowl. Beat at medium speed with electric mixer for 2 minutes. Pour batter evenly over fruit in skillet. Bake 1 hour or until wooden toothpick inserted in center comes out clean. Invert onto serving plate.

Makes 16 to 20 servings

Tip: Cake can be made in a 13×9×2-inch pan. Bake at 350°F for 45 to 55 minutes or until wooden toothpick inserted in center comes out clean. Cake is also delicious using DUNCAN HINES® Moist Deluxe Yellow Cake Mix.

Pineapple Orange Chiffon Cake

Cake
- 3 eggs, separated
- 1½ cups sugar, divided
- 2 cups unsifted all-purpose flour
- 1 tablespoon baking powder
- 1 teaspoon salt
- 1 can (6 ounces) unsweetened pineapple juice
- ⅓ cup CRISCO® Oil
- ¼ cup milk
- 2 teaspoons grated orange peel

Filling
- ⅔ cup pineapple preserves
- ⅓ cup orange marmalade

Frosting
- 1 cup whipping cream
- ½ teaspoon grated orange peel
- ¼ cup confectioners' sugar

1. Preheat oven to 350°F. Grease and flour two 9-inch round cake pans.

2. For Cake, place egg whites in medium bowl. Beat at high speed of electric mixer until foamy. Add ½ cup sugar, 1 tablespoon at a time. Beat until stiff peaks form.

3. Combine remaining 1 cup sugar, flour, baking powder and salt in large bowl. Add pineapple juice, CRISCO® Oil, milk, orange peel and egg yolks. Beat at low speed of electric mixer until ingredients are moistened, scraping bowl constantly. Increase mixer speed to high; beat 2 minutes, scraping bowl occasionally. Fold in egg white mixture. Pour into prepared pans.

4. Bake 30 to 35 minutes, or until wooden toothpick inserted in center comes out clean. Cool 10 minutes. Turn out onto wire racks. Cool completely.

5. For Filling, combine pineapple preserves and orange marmalade in small bowl. Stir well. Spread half on top of one layer. Top with remaining layer. Spread top with remaining filling.

6. For Frosting, place whipping cream in chilled medium bowl. Beat at high speed of electric mixer until thickened. Add orange peel. Add confectioners' sugar gradually, beating at high speed until stiff peaks form. Spread on sides and top of cake. Serve immediately or refrigerate. Garnish with orange slices, if desired.

Makes 1 cake

Nectarine Almond Shortcake

Cake
- **½ cup slivered almonds, toasted (see Tip)**
- **1 package DUNCAN HINES® Moist Deluxe Lemon Supreme Cake Mix**

Almond Whipped Cream
- **1 cup whipping cream**
- **2 tablespoons confectioners sugar**
- **½ teaspoon almond extract**

Fruit
- **3 cups sliced fresh nectarines**
- **Additional nectarine slices, for garnish**
- **Additional whipped cream, for garnish**

1. Preheat oven to 350°F. Grease and flour one 9-inch round cake pan. Line another 9-inch round cake pan with aluminum foil. Spread almonds in foil-lined pan.

2. Prepare batter following package directions for original recipe. Pour into prepared pans. Bake and cool cake following package directions. Remove foil carefully from almond layer.

3. For almond whipped cream, in large bowl, beat whipping cream, confectioners sugar and almond extract until stiff.

4. To assemble cake, spread plain cake layer with whipped cream and sliced nectarines. Place almond cake layer on top. Refrigerate until ready to serve. Garnish with additional nectarine slices and whipped cream, if desired.

Makes about 12 servings

Tip: To toast slivered almonds, spread nuts in shallow baking pan. Bake at 350°F for about 5 minutes or until golden. (Watch closely as they burn quickly.) Stir occasionally for even browning.

Mile-High Buttermilk Cake

- **Lemon Filling (recipe follows)**
- **4 cups cake flour**
- **1 teaspoon baking soda**
- **½ teaspoon baking powder**
- **1 cup butter, softened**
- **3 cups sugar**
- **1 teaspoon lemon extract**
- **2 cups buttermilk**
- **6 egg whites**
- **Fluffy Frosting (recipe follows)**
- **Lemon slices and lemon leaves for garnish**

Preheat oven to 350°F. Grease three 9-inch round pans; line with waxed paper and grease again. Prepare Lemon Filling; set aside to cool.

In medium bowl, combine flour, baking soda and baking powder. In large bowl, cream butter. Add sugar; beat until fluffy. Beat in lemon extract. Add flour mixture alternately with buttermilk, beating well after each addition. Beat in egg whites. Divide batter evenly between prepared pans.

Bake 30 minutes or until wooden toothpick inserted into center comes out clean. Let cool in pans on wire racks 10 minutes. Loosen edges; remove from pans. Peel off waxed paper. Cool cakes completely on wire racks.

Prepare Fluffy Frosting. Reserve ¼ cup of the Lemon Filling. Place 1 cake layer on serving plate; spread with half the remaining filling. Top with second layer; spread with remaining filling. Top with third layer. Spread Fluffy Frosting over top and sides of cake; drizzle with reserved filling. If desired, garnish with lemon slices and lemon leaves.

Makes about 12 servings

Lemon Filling

- **1 cup sugar**
- **¼ cup cornstarch**
- **¼ teaspoon salt**
- **1 cup water**
- **3 egg yolks**
- **1 tablespoon butter**
- **4 teaspoons grated lemon peel**
- **½ cup fresh lemon juice**

In small saucepan, combine sugar, cornstarch and salt. Gradually stir in water. Cook, stirring constantly, over medium heat until thickened and bubbly. Cook and stir 2 minutes more. In small bowl, lightly beat egg yolks; gradually stir half the hot mixture into yolks. Gradually stir yolk mixture into remaining hot mixture in saucepan; cook and stir 2 minutes. Remove from heat; stir in butter and lemon peel until butter is melted. Blend in lemon juice. Cool slightly; cover with plastic wrap. Cool completely.

Fluffy Frosting

- **1 cup milk**
- **3 tablespoons all-purpose flour**
- **1 cup butter, softened**
- **1 cup sugar**

In small saucepan, combine milk and flour. Cook over medium heat, stirring constantly until thickened. Cook and stir 1 minute more. Cool slightly; cover with plastic wrap. Cool completely. In small bowl, cream butter. Add sugar; beat until fluffy. Beat in cooled milk mixture.

*Favorite recipe from **Wisconsin Milk Marketing Board** ©1991*

Nectarine Almond Shortcake

Easter Bonnet Cake

1 package (2-layer size)
yellow cake mix
2 packages (4-serving size
each) JELL-O® Instant
Pudding and Pie Filling,
Lemon Flavor
4 eggs
1 cup water
¼ cup vegetable oil
1½ cups cold milk
3½ cups (8 ounces) COOL
WHIP® Whipped Topping,
thawed
2⅔ cups (7 ounces) BAKER'S®
ANGEL FLAKE® Coconut
Cloth ribbon (optional)
Gumdrop Flowers*

Easter Bonnet Cake

Combine cake mix, 1 package of the pudding mix, eggs, water and oil in large bowl. Beat at low speed of electric mixer just to moisten, scraping sides of bowl often. Beat at medium speed 4 minutes. Measure 3¼ cups batter; pour into greased and floured 1½-quart metal or ovenproof glass bowl. Pour remaining batter into greased and floured 12-inch pizza pan. Bake at 350°F for 15 minutes for the pan and 50 minutes for the bowl or until cake tester inserted in centers comes out clean.

Cool cakes 10 minutes. Remove from pan and bowl; finish cooling on racks. If necessary, cut thin slice from flat end of bowl-shaped cake so that it will sit flat; split horizontally into 3 layers.

Pour milk into small bowl. Add remaining package of pudding mix. Beat with wire whisk until blended, 1 to 2 minutes.

Place 12-inch cake layer on large serving plate or tray. Spread layer with 1½ cups of the whipped topping. Center bottom layer of bowl-shaped cake on frosted layer; spread with ⅔ of the pudding. Add second layer; spread with remaining pudding. Add top layer, forming the crown.

Spread remaining whipped topping over crown. Sprinkle coconut over cake. Tie ribbon around cake crown to form hat band and bow and garnish with Gumdrop Flowers, if desired. Chill until ready to serve.

Makes about 16 servings

Prep time: 45 minutes
Baking time: 50 minutes

Gumdrop Flowers:

1. Flatten gumdrops with rolling pin on surface or sheet of waxed paper sprinkled with sugar. Roll until very thin (about ¹⁄₁₆ inch thick), turning frequently to coat with sugar.
2. Hold flattened gumdrop at center; overlap edges slightly to give petal effect, pressing piece together at base to resemble flower. For open blossom, bend gumdrop petals outward from center. Insert small piece of gumdrop in centers with wooden pick, if desired. Use wooden pick to attach flowers to cake if necessary.

Father's Day Tie

1 package DUNCAN HINES®
Moist Deluxe Cake Mix
(any flavor)
1 container (16 ounces)
DUNCAN HINES® Vanilla
Frosting
Food coloring
Colored sugar crystals

1. Preheat oven to 350°F. Grease and flour 13×9×2-inch pan.
2. Prepare, bake and cool cake following package directions. Invert cake onto large tray.
3. Frost sides and top of cake with vanilla frosting. Tint remaining frosting with food coloring. Outline shirt collar and tie on cake with colored frosting using decorator's tube (see Tip). Create your own design on tie with colored sugars and frosting. Personalize with frosting monogram or name, if desired.

Makes 12 to 16 servings

Tip: If decorator's tube is not available, place about ⅓ cup tinted frosting in small airtight plastic bag. Seal top and cut off a tiny bottom corner to use as tip. Refill as needed.

Orange Poppy Seed Cake

1 (8 oz.) container PHILADELPHIA BRAND® "Light" Pasteurized Process Cream Cheese Product
½ cup PARKAY® Margarine, softened
1 cup sugar
3 eggs, separated
2 cups flour
1 teaspoon CALUMET® Baking Powder
1 teaspoon baking soda
1 cup sour cream
2 tablespoons poppy seeds
1 tablespoon grated orange peel
½ cup sugar or 12 packets sugar substitute
⅓ cup orange-flavored liqueur
¼ cup orange juice
3 tablespoons powdered sugar

• Preheat oven to 350°F. Grease 10-inch fluted tube pan.

• Beat cream cheese product, margarine and 1 cup sugar in large mixing bowl at medium speed with electric mixer until well blended. Add egg yolks, one at a time, mixing well after each addition.

• Mix together flour, baking powder and soda; add to cream cheese mixture alternately with sour cream. Stir in poppy seeds and peel.

• Beat egg whites in small mixing bowl at high speed with electric mixer until stiff peaks form; fold into cream cheese mixture. Pour into prepared pan.

• Bake 50 minutes.

• Stir together ½ cup sugar, liqueur and orange juice in saucepan over low heat until sugar dissolves.

• Prick hot cake several times with fork. Pour syrup over cake; cool 10 minutes. Invert onto serving plate. Cool completely. Sprinkle with powdered sugar. Garnish with quartered orange slices, if desired.

Makes 12 to 16 servings

Prep time: 30 minutes
Cooking time: 50 minutes

Variation: Omit orange-flavored liqueur. Increase orange juice to ½ cup.

Lemon Loaf Cake

2 cups sifted cake flour
½ teaspoon ARM & HAMMER® Pure Baking Soda
¼ teaspoon salt
½ cup butter or margarine, softened
1 cup sugar
2 eggs
½ cup milk
4½ teaspoons lemon juice
1 teaspoon grated lemon peel

Preheat oven to 350°F. Grease and flour 8-inch square baking pan. In small bowl, sift together flour, baking soda and salt. Using an electric mixer, cream butter until light and fluffy in large bowl. Add sugar gradually, beating well after each addition. In separate bowl, beat eggs until thick and lemon-colored. Slowly beat eggs into butter mixture.

Combine milk and lemon juice. Alternately add dry ingredients and milk mixture to creamed mixture, beginning and ending with dry ingredients, and beating until smooth after each addition. Stir in lemon peel.

Turn into prepared pan. Bake 45 minutes or until wooden toothpick inserted in center comes out clean. Cool in pan 10 minutes. Remove from pan and cool on wire rack.

Makes one 8-inch square cake

Tony's Old-Fashioned Walnut Cake

1½ cups coarsely chopped SUN-MAID® Raisins
½ cup water
¼ cup bourbon
½ cup butter or margarine, softened
¾ cup sugar
1 egg
1½ cups all-purpose flour
1 teaspoon baking powder
1 teaspoon baking soda
¾ teaspoon salt
1 cup finely chopped DIAMOND® Walnuts

Preheat oven to 350°F. Grease 9-inch square pan; line bottom with waxed paper. In small saucepan, combine raisins, water and bourbon. Cover and bring to a boil over medium heat. Remove from heat and let stand, covered, 10 minutes.

In medium bowl, cream butter; gradually add sugar, continuing to beat until light and fluffy. Beat in egg. In small bowl, sift flour with baking powder, baking soda and salt. Add to creamed mixture alternately with raisin mixture. Stir in walnuts. Spoon into prepared pan.

Bake 30 minutes or until wooden toothpick inserted near center comes out clean. Cool in pan 10 minutes. Loosen edges; remove from pan. Cool completely on wire rack. Gently peel off paper. Serve plain or topped with your favorite icing.

Makes one 9-inch square cake

Harvest Raisin Apple Cakes

¼ **cup butter or margarine, softened**
¾ **cup granulated sugar**
1 **teaspoon ground cinnamon**
1 **teaspoon vanilla**
1 **cup all-purpose flour**
1 **teaspoon baking soda**
1½ **cups SUN-MAID® Raisins**
1½ **cups grated pared apples**
   Easy Lemon Icing (recipe follows)
   SUN-MAID® Raisins, for garnish
   Powdered sugar (optional)

Preheat oven to 350°F. Grease eight 6-ounce custard cups.

In large bowl, combine butter, granulated sugar, cinnamon and vanilla. Beat until thoroughly blended. In small bowl, combine flour and baking soda; stir half into butter mixture. Add raisins and apples, then remaining flour mixture. Blend thoroughly. Divide batter evenly between prepared custard cups. Place on baking sheet.

Bake about 30 minutes or until springy to the touch. Cool slightly. Loosen edges and invert onto wire racks to complete cooling. Ice with Easy Lemon Icing and garnish with additional raisins, or omit Easy Lemon Icing, if desired, and dust with powdered sugar.

Makes 8 small cakes

EASY LEMON ICING: In small bowl, combine 1¼ cups sifted powdered sugar with 1½ teaspoons lemon juice. Stir in enough water to make drizzling consistency. Stir in dash of ground cinnamon.

Note: Cakes may be baked in 12 greased 2¾-inch muffin cups. Bake in preheated 350°F oven about 20 minutes or until springy to the touch.

Fresh Apple Cake

Cake
1 **package DUNCAN HINES®
   Moist Deluxe Yellow
   Cake Mix**
3 **eggs**
1¼ **cups apple juice**
⅓ **cup CRISCO® Oil or
   PURITAN® Oil**
1 **teaspoon ground cinnamon**
2 **cups grated apples (about
   2 medium apples)**
½ **cup all-purpose flour**
1 **cup chopped pecans**
Frosting
3 **tablespoons butter or
   margarine**
3 **tablespoons brown sugar**
3 **tablespoons granulated
   sugar**
3 **tablespoons whipping
   cream**
½ **cup confectioners' sugar**
¼ **teaspoon vanilla extract**

1. Preheat oven to 350°F. Grease and flour 10-inch tube pan.

2. For cake, combine cake mix, eggs, apple juice, oil and cinnamon in large bowl. Beat at medium speed with electric mixer for 2 minutes. Toss apples with flour in medium bowl. Fold flour-coated apples and pecans into batter. Pour into prepared pan. Bake 45 minutes or until wooden toothpick inserted in center comes out clean. Cool in pan 25 minutes. Invert onto serving plate; cool completely.

3. For frosting, combine butter, brown sugar, granulated sugar and whipping cream in small heavy saucepan. Bring to a boil over medium heat; boil 1 minute. Remove from heat; cool for 20 minutes. Add confectioners' sugar and vanilla extract; blend with wooden spoon until smooth and thick. Spread frosting on cake. Garnish with pecans if desired.

Makes 12 to 16 servings

Tip: Apples may be grated in food processor fitted with shredding disc. If food processor is not available, use hand grater.

Fresh Apple Cake

Chocolate Applesauce Cake

**2½ cups all-purpose flour
⅓ cup unsweetened cocoa
2 teaspoons baking soda
¾ teaspoon salt
¾ cup shortening
1¾ cups sugar
2 eggs
1½ teaspoons vanilla
1½ cups applesauce
½ cup buttermilk**

Preheat oven to 350°F. Grease 13×9×2-inch baking pan.

In small bowl, combine flour, cocoa, baking soda and salt. In large bowl, cream shortening and sugar. Beat in eggs and vanilla. In small bowl, combine applesauce and buttermilk; mix well. Add dry ingredients to creamed mixture alternately with applesauce mixture; mix until well blended. Pour batter into prepared pan.

Bake 35 to 40 minutes or until wooden toothpick inserted in center comes out clean. Cool completely in pan on wire rack. Serve plain or top with your favorite frosting.

Makes about 12 servings

Favorite recipe from **Western New York Apple Growers Association, Inc.**

Chocolate Banana Cake

Preheat oven to 350°F. Grease and flour 13×9-inch baking pan.

In food processor or blender, process bananas until pureed (1½ cups). In large bowl, combine flour, granulated sugar, baking powder, baking soda and salt. Add pureed bananas, margarine and sour cream; beat 2 minutes. Add eggs; beat 2 minutes longer. Stir in dates and walnuts. Pour batter into prepared pan.

Bake 45 to 50 minutes or until wooden toothpick inserted in center comes out clean. Cool completely in pan on wire rack. Dust with powdered sugar.

Makes about 12 servings

Preheat oven to 350°F. Grease and flour two 9-inch round baking pans.

In food processor or blender, process bananas until pureed (1½ cups). In top of double boiler, over hot, not boiling, water, combine ½ cup pureed bananas, ⅓ cup sugar, 1 egg and chocolate. Heat, stirring constantly, until chocolate melts. Cool.

In large mixer bowl, beat remaining 1 cup sugar with shortening until light and fluffy. Add rum extract and remaining 2 eggs, 1 at a time, beating well after each addition. In small bowl, combine flour, baking soda and salt; beat into creamed mixture alternately with remaining bananas. Blend in chocolate mixture. Pour batter into prepared pans.

Bake 25 to 30 minutes, or until wooden toothpick inserted in center comes out clean. Cool 10 minutes in pans on wire racks. Remove from pans; cool completely on wire racks. Prepare Rum Fudge Frosting. Cut a paper-thin slice from top of each cake layer so frosting will soak into cake. Place one layer, cut-side up, on serving plate; spread with frosting. Top with remaining layer, cut-side up. Frost sides and top of cake. Garnish with additional banana slices, if desired.

Makes 8 to 10 servings

RUM FUDGE FROSTING: In top of double boiler, over hot, not boiling, water, melt 4 squares (1 oz. each) semi-sweet chocolate with 1 tablespoon butter. Stir in 3 tablespoons light corn syrup and 1 tablespoon rum. Cool to room temperature. Whisk in ½ cup whipping cream. Refrigerate until frosting is of spreading consistency.

Banana Date Nut Cake

**3 extra-ripe, medium DOLE®
    Bananas, peeled and cut
    into chunks
2½ cups flour
1 cup granulated sugar
1 teaspoon baking powder
1 teaspoon baking soda
½ teaspoon salt
¾ cup margarine, softened
½ cup dairy sour cream
3 eggs
1 cup DOLE® Chopped Dates
1 cup chopped walnuts
    Powdered sugar**

Chocolate Banana Cake

**3 extra-ripe, medium DOLE®
    Bananas, peeled and cut
    into chunks
1⅓ cups sugar
3 eggs
3 squares (1 oz. each)
    unsweetened chocolate
½ cup shortening
1 tablespoon rum extract
1¾ cups all-purpose flour
1 teaspoon baking soda
½ teaspoon salt
    Rum Fudge Frosting
    (recipe follows)**

Old-Fashioned Banana Cake

2¼ cups all-purpose flour
1⅔ cups sugar
1¼ teaspoons baking powder
1¼ teaspoons baking soda
1 teaspoon salt
1 can (5 fluid ounces) PET® Evaporated Milk
4 teaspoons vinegar
⅔ cup shortening
1¼ cups mashed ripe bananas (about 4)
3 eggs
Butter Cream Frosting (recipe follows)

Preheat oven to 350°F. Grease and flour two 9-inch round cake pans.

In large mixer bowl, combine flour, sugar, baking powder, baking soda and salt. Mix evaporated milk with vinegar; add to dry ingredients alternately with shortening and bananas. Beat 2 minutes at medium speed. Add eggs; beat 2 minutes. Pour batter into prepared pans.

Bake 30 to 35 minutes or until wooden toothpick inserted in center comes out clean. Cool in pans on wire racks 10 minutes; remove from pans. Cool completely on wire racks. Frost with Butter Cream Frosting.

Makes about 12 servings

Butter Cream Frosting

½ cup butter or margarine, softened
¼ cup PET® Evaporated Milk
2 teaspoons vanilla
4½ cups (1 pound) powdered sugar, sifted

In small bowl, beat butter, evaporated milk and vanilla. Gradually beat in powdered sugar; continue beating until frosting is smooth and of spreading consistency.

Carrot-Coconut Cake

Blueberry Carrot Cake

1 cup vegetable oil
1 cup firmly packed brown sugar
1 teaspoon vanilla
1 cup MOTT'S® Chunky Apple Sauce
2 eggs
2½ cups all-purpose flour
2 teaspoons baking soda
2 teaspoons cinnamon
½ teaspoon salt
2 cups shredded carrots
½ cup chopped walnuts
1 cup fresh blueberries

Preheat oven to 350°F. Grease 12-cup fluted tube pan. In large bowl, combine oil, brown sugar, vanilla, apple sauce and eggs; mix well. Stir in flour, baking soda, cinnamon and salt; mix well. Stir in carrots and walnuts. Gently stir in blueberries. Pour into prepared pan.

Bake 50 to 60 minutes or until wooden toothpick inserted in center comes out clean. Cool 15 minutes; invert onto serving plate. Cool completely. If desired, serve with whipped cream and fresh blueberries.

Makes about 16 servings

Carrot-Coconut Cake

2 cups all-purpose flour
2½ teaspoons baking powder
2 teaspoons ground cinnamon
¾ cup BLUE BONNET® Margarine, softened
1½ cups sugar
3 eggs
½ cup milk
2 cups grated carrots
1⅓ cups flaked coconut
½ cup chopped walnuts
1 (8-ounce) can crushed pineapple in its own juice, undrained
Coconut Cream Cheese Frosting (recipe follows)
Toasted flaked coconut and carrot flowers, for garnish

Preheat oven to 350°F. Grease two 9-inch round cake pans.

In small bowl, combine flour, baking powder and cinnamon; set aside.

In medium bowl, with electric mixer at medium speed, beat margarine, sugar and eggs until creamy. Alternately stir in milk and flour mixture until blended. Mix in carrots, coconut, walnuts and pineapple with juice until blended. Spread batter into prepared pans.

Bake 40 minutes or until wooden toothpick inserted in center comes out clean. Cool in pans on wire racks 10 minutes. Remove from pans; cool completely on wire racks. Frost cake with Coconut Cream Cheese Frosting. Garnish with coconut and carrot flowers.

Makes about 12 servings

COCONUT CREAM CHEESE FROSTING: In medium bowl, with electric mixer at medium speed, beat 1 (3-ounce) package softened cream cheese and ¼ cup softened BLUE BONNET® Margarine until smooth. Add 1 (16-ounce) package confectioners' sugar alternately with 2 tablespoons milk and ½ teaspoon vanilla extract, beating until smooth. Stir in ½ cup toasted flaked coconut.

Fabulous Carrot Cake

1 can (20 oz.) DOLE®
   Crushed Pineapple
1 cup margarine, softened
1 cup brown sugar, packed
1 cup granulated sugar
4 eggs
1 pound carrots, shredded
   (4 cups)
1 cup DOLE® Raisins
2 teaspoons vanilla extract
3 cups all-purpose flour
2 teaspoons baking soda
1 teaspoon ground cinnamon
1 teaspoon ground ginger
½ teaspoon salt

Preheat oven to 350°F. Grease and flour 13×9-inch baking pan. Drain pineapple well. In large bowl, cream margarine and sugars until light and fluffy. Beat in eggs. Beat in pineapple, carrots, raisins and vanilla. In small bowl, combine flour, baking soda, cinnamon, ginger and salt. Gradually beat into pineapple mixture until well blended. Pour into prepared pan. Bake 50 to 60 minutes or until wooden toothpick inserted in center comes out clean. Cool completely in pan on wire rack. Spread cake with favorite cream cheese frosting or dust with powdered sugar.

Makes about 20 servings

Lemon Angel Roll

Lemon Angel Roll

1 (14½- or 16-ounce)
   package angel food cake
   mix, plus ingredients to
   prepare mix
   Confectioners' sugar
1 (14-ounce) can EAGLE®
   Brand Sweetened
   Condensed Milk (NOT
   evaporated milk)
⅓ cup REALEMON® Lemon
   Juice from Concentrate
2 teaspoons grated lemon
   rind
   Yellow food coloring,
   optional
1 (4-ounce) container frozen
   non-dairy whipped
   topping, thawed
½ cup flaked coconut, tinted
   yellow* if desired

Preheat oven to 350°F. Line 15×10-inch jellyroll pan with aluminum foil, extending foil 1 inch over ends of pan.

Prepare cake mix as package directs. Spread batter evenly into prepared pan. Bake 30 minutes or until top springs back when lightly touched. *Immediately* turn onto towel sprinkled with confectioners' sugar. Peel off foil; beginning at narrow end, roll up cake with towel, jellyroll-fashion. Cool thoroughly.

Meanwhile, in medium bowl, combine sweetened condensed milk, REALEMON® brand, rind and food coloring if desired; mix well. Fold in whipped topping. Unroll cake; trim edges. Spread with half the lemon filling; reroll. Place on serving plate, seam-side down; spread remaining filling over roll. Garnish with coconut. Chill. Store in refrigerator.

Makes 8 to 10 servings

***To tint coconut:** Combine coconut, ½ teaspoon water and 2 drops yellow food coloring in small plastic bag or bowl; shake or mix well.

Southern Jam Cake

1 cup margarine or butter,
   softened
1 cup sugar
5 eggs
1 (16-ounce) jar BAMA®
   Blackberry Jam or
   Preserves
1 cup BAMA® Strawberry
   Preserves
3 cups unsifted flour
1 tablespoon baking soda
2 teaspoons ground allspice
2 teaspoons ground
   cinnamon
½ teaspoon ground cloves
1 cup BORDEN® or MEADOW
   GOLD® Buttermilk
   Maple Frosting
   Chopped nuts, optional

Preheat oven to 350°F. Grease three 9-inch round layer cake pans; line with waxed paper.

In large mixer bowl, beat margarine and sugar until fluffy. Add eggs, 1 at a time, beating well after each addition. Stir in jam and preserves. Stir together dry ingredients; add alternately with buttermilk to jam mixture. Pour batter into prepared pans. Bake 40 minutes or until wooden toothpick inserted near center comes out clean. Cool 5 minutes; remove from pans. Cool completely. Frost with Maple Frosting; garnish with nuts if desired.

Makes one 9-inch cake

MAPLE FROSTING: In mixer bowl, beat 1 (8-ounce) package cream cheese until fluffy. Add 1½ pounds sifted confectioners' sugar (about 6 cups), 2 teaspoons maple flavoring and 1 tablespoon milk; mix well. Add additional milk, 1 teaspoon at a time, for desired consistency.

Rainbow Cupcakes

Cake
  **1 package DUNCAN HINES®
    Moist Deluxe Fudge
    Marble Cake Mix
  Red and green food
    coloring**
Frosting
  **1 pound confectioners sugar
    (3½ to 4 cups)
  ½ cup BUTTER FLAVOR
    CRISCO®
  ⅓ cup milk
  1 teaspoon vanilla extract
  Red and green food
    coloring
  2 tablespoons cocoa
  Assorted colored decors**

1. Preheat oven to 350°F. Place 2½-inch paper liners in 24 muffin cups.

2. For Cake, set aside cocoa packet. Prepare cake mix following package directions. Divide batter into thirds and place in 3 different bowls. Stir cocoa packet into one. Add 5 drops red food coloring to another. Add 5 drops green food coloring to the third. Stir each just until blended.

3. Layer 1 tablespoon of each color batter into each muffin cup. Bake 20 to 25 minutes. Cool completely.

4. For Frosting, combine sugar, BUTTER FLAVOR CRISCO®, milk and vanilla extract in medium bowl. Beat at low speed with electric mixer until blended. Scrape bowl. Beat at high speed for 2 minutes.

5. Divide frosting into thirds and place in 3 different bowls. Add cocoa to one. Add a few drops red food coloring to another. Add a few drops green food coloring to the third. Stir each until well blended. Frost cupcakes with a small amount of each color frosting. Sprinkle with colored decors.   *Makes 24 cupcakes*

Rainbow Cupcakes

Birthday Cakelets

  **2 packages DUNCAN HINES®
    Moist Deluxe Devil's
    Food Cake Mix
  6 large eggs
  1 cup CRISCO® Oil or
    PURITAN® Oil
  2⅔ cups water
  2 cups light corn syrup
  4 large egg whites
  ⅛ teaspoon salt
  Red food coloring
  ½ teaspoon peppermint
    extract**

1. Preheat oven to 350°F. Grease and flour two 13×9×2-inch pans.

2. Combine dry cake mix, whole eggs, oil and water in large mixer bowl. Mix, bake and cool cakes as directed on package. Freeze cooled cakes at least 2 hours.

3. For frosting, heat syrup to boiling. Beat egg whites in large mixer bowl at medium speed until frothy. Add salt and continue beating until soft peaks form. Turn mixer to high speed and gradually add hot corn syrup, beating until soft peaks form. Fold in food coloring to tint delicate pink. Fold in peppermint extract.

4. Draw heart on 3-inch square of cardboard; cut out. Set heart pattern on lower left corner of one cake. Cut around pattern through cake. Cut out 11 more hearts before removing cake pieces. Repeat with remaining cake.

5. Frost sides and tops of each cake heart. Insert pink birthday candle in center of each heart.
     Makes about 24 servings

Tip: Before frosting cakes, brush off any loose crumbs, which will mix in with the frosting. If necessary, apply a thin coating of frosting first to seal in any remaining crumbs.

Chocolate Peanut Butter Cupcakes

**1 package DUNCAN HINES®
Moist Deluxe Cake Mix,
any chocolate flavor
1½ cups JIF® Peanut Butter
¾ cup chopped peanuts**

1. Preheat oven to 350°F. Place 2½-inch paper liners in 24 muffin cups. Prepare, bake and cool cupcakes following package directions.
2. Stir peanut butter to soften. Spread 1 tablespoon on top of each cupcake. Dip in chopped peanuts. *Makes 24 cupcakes*

Tip: To make Snowball Cupcakes, frost with DUNCAN HINES® Vanilla Frosting. Sprinkle with flaked coconut.

Raisin Fudge Cups

**Crust:
2 cups chocolate sandwich
cookie crumbs
¼ cup butter or margarine,
melted
Filling:
1 package (6 ounces) real
semisweet chocolate
pieces
¼ cup butter or margarine
1 egg, beaten
½ teaspoon vanilla
⅔ cup all-purpose flour
⅓ cup packed brown sugar
1 teaspoon baking powder
¼ teaspoon salt
1 cup miniature
marshmallows
1 cup SUN-MAID® Raisins**

To prepare Crust: In medium bowl, combine cookie crumbs and the ¼ cup melted butter; mix well. Evenly divide and press mixture onto bottoms and sides of twelve 2½-inch muffin cups; set aside.

To prepare Filling: Preheat oven to 350°F. In medium saucepan, melt chocolate and butter over low heat. Remove from heat and stir in egg, vanilla, flour, brown sugar, baking powder and salt; blend well. Stir in marshmallows and raisins. Evenly divide mixture into crumb-lined cups. Bake 15 to 20 minutes (centers should still be soft). Cool in pan on wire rack 10 minutes. Loosen edges and remove from muffin cups while still warm. Cool completely on wire rack.
Makes 1 dozen cupcakes

Lemon Peach Kalach

**1 can (16 oz.) California cling
peach slices in juice or
extra light syrup
½ cup butter, softened
¾ cup sugar, divided
4 eggs
1 cup flour
½ teaspoon baking powder
½ teaspoon salt
½ teaspoon grated lemon
peel
¼ teaspoon nutmeg
1 cup low-fat ricotta cheese
1 teaspoon vanilla**

Preheat oven to 350°F. Grease and flour 8½-inch springform pan. Drain peaches reserving 3 tablespoons liquid; save remainder of liquid for other uses.

In large bowl, cream butter with ½ cup sugar. Add 3 eggs, 1 at a time, beating well after each addition. Stir in reserved 3 tablespoons peach liquid. In small bowl, combine flour, baking powder, salt, lemon peel and nutmeg. Add dry ingredients to creamed mixture; mix until smooth. Spoon batter into prepared pan.

Bake 25 minutes. In small bowl, combine remaining egg, ¼ cup sugar, ricotta cheese and vanilla; mix well. Remove pan from oven. Spoon ricotta mixture over cake; top with peach slices. Return to

oven; bake 10 minutes longer or until top is set. Cool slightly. Loosen edge of cake from pan; cool completely in pan. Serve immediately or refrigerate until ready to serve.
Makes about 8 servings

Favorite recipe from **California Cling Peach Advisory Board**

Pumpkin-Bran Cake

**2 cups NABISCO® 100% Bran
½ cup milk
3 eggs
1 can (16 ounces) solid pack
pumpkin
¾ cup BLUE BONNET®
Margarine, melted
2½ cups all-purpose flour
2 cups granulated sugar
1½ teaspoons pumpkin pie
spice
1 teaspoon baking soda
½ teaspoon DAVIS® Baking
Powder
1¼ cups PLANTERS® Walnuts,
chopped
2 teaspoons grated orange
peel
½ cup powdered sugar
1 to 1½ teaspoons milk**

Preheat oven to 325°F. Grease 13×9×2-inch pan.

In large bowl, combine bran, ½ cup milk and eggs; let stand 5 minutes. Blend in pumpkin and margarine. Stir in flour, granulated sugar, spice, baking soda, baking powder, ¾ cup of the walnuts and the orange peel. Pour batter into prepared pan; sprinkle with remaining ½ cup walnuts.

Bake 1 hour or until wooden toothpick inserted into center comes out clean. Let cool in pan on wire rack 10 minutes. Loosen edges; remove from pan. Invert cake again so nut side is up. Cool completely on wire rack. In small bowl, mix powdered sugar and 1 teaspoon milk. Add additional milk, if necessary, to make glaze of desired consistency. Drizzle glaze over cake.
Makes about 12 servings

Triple Chocolate Pear Cake

**2 cups grated fresh
    California Bartlett pears
2 squares (1 ounce each)
    unsweetened chocolate
3 cups flour
1 tablespoon unsweetened
    cocoa
1½ teaspoons baking powder
1½ teaspoons cinnamon
1 teaspoon baking soda
1 teaspoon salt
1½ cups vegetable oil
2 cups sugar
4 large eggs
1 teaspoon vanilla extract
1 cup semisweet chocolate
    chips
1 cup whipping cream,
    whipped
    Pear slices for garnish**

Preheat oven to 350°F. Butter and flour 10-inch Bundt® pan. Place pears in sieve over bowl; squeeze out excess liquid. Chop unsweetened chocolate; place in bowl over hot water to melt.

In small bowl, combine flour, cocoa, baking powder, cinnamon, baking soda and salt. In large mixer bowl, beat oil and sugar at medium speed until well combined. Add eggs, 1 at a time, beating well after each addition. Beat in vanilla extract and melted chocolate. Add dry ingredients, mixing just until blended. Stir in pears and chocolate chips. Pour batter into prepared pan.

Bake 1 hour and 40 minutes or until wooden toothpick inserted into center of cake comes out clean. Let cool in pan on wire rack 15 minutes. Remove from pan; cool completely on wire rack.

To assemble, slice cake horizontally into 3 layers. Place bottom layer on serving plate; spread with ⅓ of the whipped cream. Add center layer; spread with ⅓ whipped cream. Place final layer on top; pipe remaining whipped cream decoratively over cake. Garnish with pear slices. Serve cake immediately.

Makes about 8 servings

Favorite recipe from **California Tree Fruit Agreement**

Premier White Layer Cake with Raspberry Filling

**Cake:
Two 6-oz. pkgs. (6 foil-wrapped
    bars) NESTLÉ® Premier
    White Baking Bars,
    broken up
¼ cup milk
2 cups all-purpose flour
¾ teaspoon baking soda
½ teaspoon salt
¼ teaspoon baking powder
¾ cup sugar
½ cup (1 stick) butter,
    softened
1 teaspoon vanilla extract
4 eggs
¾ cup sour cream
Raspberry Filling:
1½ cups heavy or whipping
    cream
¾ cup fresh or thawed frozen
    raspberries
3 tablespoons sugar
    White Buttercream (recipe
    follows)
    Raspberries and mint
    sprigs, for garnish**

Cake: Preheat oven to 350°F. Grease two 9-inch round baking pans; line bottoms with waxed paper. Melt over hot (not boiling) water, Premier White baking bars with milk, stirring until smooth.

In small bowl, combine flour, baking soda, salt and baking powder; set aside. In large mixer bowl, beat sugar and butter until light and fluffy. Gradually blend in melted baking bar mixture and vanilla extract. Add eggs, 1 at a time, beating well after each addition. Add flour mixture alternately with sour cream. Pour into prepared pans.

Bake 35 minutes or until wooden toothpick inserted into center comes out clean. Cool 15 minutes; remove from pans. Cool completely.

Raspberry Filling: In small mixer bowl, combine heavy cream, raspberries and sugar; beat until stiff peaks form. Refrigerate until ready to use.

Prepare White Buttercream. Split cake layers horizontally in half. Place 1 layer on cake plate; spread with ⅓ of Raspberry Filling. Repeat with remaining layers and Filling. Frost cake with White Buttercream. Garnish with raspberries and mint. Store in refrigerator.

Makes 10 to 12 servings

White Buttercream

**One 6-oz. pkg. (3 foil-wrapped
    bars) NESTLÉ® Premier
    White Baking Bars,
    broken up
¼ cup heavy or whipping
    cream
1 cup (2 sticks) cold butter,
    cut into pieces
1 cup confectioners' sugar**

Melt over hot (not boiling) water, Premier White baking bars with heavy cream, stirring until smooth. Transfer to large mixer bowl; cool to room temperature.

Gradually beat in cold butter and confectioners' sugar; continue beating until light and fluffy. Buttercream may be made 1 to 2 days ahead of time and refrigerated; beat until light and fluffy before using.

Makes about 3 cups frosting

Premier White Layer Cake with Raspberry Filling

Almond Sherry Cake

Filling
  1/3 **cup firmly packed brown sugar**
  1/4 **cup flour**
  3 **tablespoons firm butter**
  1/2 **teaspoon cinnamon**
  3/4 **cup BLUE DIAMOND®
     Sliced Natural Almonds,
     toasted**

Cake
  1 **package (18 1/2 ounces)
     yellow cake mix (*NOT*
     pudding type)**
  4 **large eggs**
  3/4 **cup cream sherry**
  3/4 **cup vegetable oil**
  1 **package (3 3/4 ounces)
     instant vanilla
     pudding mix**
  1/2 **teaspoon nutmeg**

Glaze
  2 **cups sifted powdered
     sugar**
  1/3 **cup melted butter**
  1 **tablespoon cream sherry**
  1 **to 2 teaspoons hot water**
  1/4 **cup BLUE DIAMOND®
     Sliced Natural Almonds,
     toasted, for garnish**

To prepare Filling, in large bowl, combine brown sugar, flour, butter and cinnamon until crumbly. Stir in almonds; reserve.

To prepare Cake, preheat oven to 350°F. Grease and flour 10-inch Bundt® pan. In large mixer bowl, combine all Cake ingredients. Mix at low speed 1 minute, scraping bowl constantly. Mix at medium speed 3 minutes, scraping bowl occasionally (or beat by hand 5 minutes). Pour half of batter into prepared pan; sprinkle evenly with Filling. Pour in remaining cake batter.

Bake 45 to 50 minutes or until cake springs back when touched lightly in center. Cool on wire rack 15 minutes. Remove from pan; cool completely on rack. Meanwhile, prepare Glaze. Combine powdered sugar, melted butter, and sherry. Stir in enough water to make glaze of desired consistency. Glaze top of cake and garnish with almonds.

Makes one 10-inch cake

Almond Sherry Cake

Heart and Kisses Cake

  1 **package DUNCAN HINES®
     Moist Deluxe Cake Mix
     (any flavor)**
  5 **cups confectioners sugar**
  3/4 **cup CRISCO® Shortening**
  1/2 **cup water**
  1/3 **cup non-dairy creamer**
  2 **teaspoons vanilla extract**
  1/2 **teaspoon salt
     Red food coloring
     Chocolate kiss candies**

1. Preheat oven to 350°F. Grease and flour one 8-inch round and one 8-inch square pan.

2. Prepare cake as directed on package. Pour 2 cups batter into round pan and 3 cups batter into square pan. Bake and cool cake following package directions.

3. For frosting, combine confectioners sugar, shortening, water, non-dairy creamer, vanilla extract and salt in large bowl. Beat at medium speed with electric mixer for 3 minutes. Beat at high speed for 5 minutes. Add more confectioners sugar to thicken or more water to thin as needed. Reserve 1 1/2 cups frosting for decorating, if desired. Tint remaining frosting pink with red food coloring.

4. Place square cake on serving platter bottom side up. Cut round cake in half. Place each half top side up next to square as shown in diagram. Spread pink frosting on cake. Use reserved frosting for writing Valentine greeting and decorating edges. Garnish with chocolate kiss candies.

Makes 16 to 20 servings

Tip: For a lovely presentation, assemble cake on large cookie sheet or serving platter covered with lace doilies.

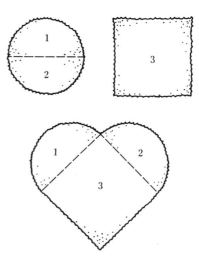

One-Step Chocolate Cake Roll

**1 (14-ounce) can EAGLE®
  Brand Sweetened
  Condensed Milk (NOT
  evaporated milk)
2 egg yolks plus 3 eggs
½ cup flaked coconut
½ cup chopped nuts
¼ cup margarine or butter,
  melted
2 teaspoons vanilla extract
1 cup granulated sugar
⅔ cup unsifted flour
⅓ cup unsweetened cocoa
⅓ cup water
  Confectioners' sugar
  Easy Chocolate Glaze
  (page 109)**

Preheat oven to 350°F. Line 15×10-inch jellyroll pan with aluminum foil, extending foil 1 inch over ends of pan. Grease aluminum foil.

In medium bowl, combine sweetened condensed milk, *2 egg yolks*, coconut, nuts, margarine and *1 teaspoon* vanilla; mix well. Spread evenly into prepared pan. In large mixer bowl, beat *3 eggs* at high speed until fluffy. Gradually beat in granulated sugar then beat 2 minutes. Add remaining ingredients except confectioners' sugar and Easy Chocolate Glaze; beat 1 minute. Pour evenly over coconut mixture.

Bake 20 to 25 minutes or until cake springs back when lightly touched. Sprinkle generously with confectioners' sugar. *Immediately* turn onto towel. Peel off foil; beginning at narrow end, roll up cake, jellyroll-fashion. *Do not roll up towel with cake.* Place on serving plate, seam-side down. Cool. Sprinkle with additional confectioners' sugar and drizzle with Easy Chocolate Glaze if desired.
Makes 8 to 10 servings

Prep time: 30 minutes
Baking time: 25 minutes

Droste® Chocolate Cream Roll

**6 eggs, separated
1¼ cups granulated sugar,
  divided
½ teaspoon vanilla
¾ cup cake flour
½ teaspoon baking powder
  Powdered sugar
2 cups whipping cream
⅓ cup DROSTE® Cocoa
2 tablespoons brandy
  DROSTE® Tulips for
  garnish**

Preheat oven to 350°F. Grease 15½×10½×1-inch jelly-roll pan and line with waxed paper.

In large bowl, beat egg yolks, ¾ cup of the granulated sugar and the vanilla until thick and lemon colored. In small bowl, combine flour and baking powder; beat into yolk mixture. In large mixer bowl, beat egg whites at high speed until stiff but not dry peaks form. Fold egg whites into yolk mixture. Spread batter in prepared pan.

Bake 15 to 20 minutes or until wooden toothpick inserted into center comes out clean. Immediately invert cake onto towel sprinkled with powdered sugar; remove waxed paper. While still warm, roll up cake and towel beginning at short end; cool completely.

In large bowl, beat whipping cream, remaining ½ cup granulated sugar, DROSTE® Cocoa and brandy until stiff peaks form. Unroll cake. Reserve ½ cup cocoa mixture for garnish; spread remaining cocoa mixture over cake. Reroll cake; sprinkle with powdered sugar. Garnish cake with reserved cocoa mixture and DROSTE® Tulips.
Refrigerate until serving time.
Makes 8 to 10 servings

Rich Double Chocolate Cream Torte

**Brownie
1 package DUNCAN HINES®
  Brownies Plus Milk
  Chocolate Chunks Mix
3 eggs
⅓ cup water
⅓ cup CRISCO® Oil or
  PURITAN® Oil
½ cup finely chopped nuts
Chocolate Butter Cream
1 package (6 ounces) semi-
  sweet chocolate chips,
  melted
½ cup butter or margarine,
  softened
1 cup whipping cream,
  chilled and divided
Whipped Cream
2 tablespoons sugar
1 tablespoon chocolate
  jimmies**

1. Preheat oven to 350°F. Grease and flour 9-inch round pan.

2. For Brownie, combine brownie mix, eggs, water, oil and nuts. Stir with spoon until well blended, about 50 strokes. Pour into pan. Bake 35 to 40 minutes. Cool 30 minutes. Run knife around edge of pan. Invert onto serving platter.

3. For Chocolate Butter Cream, stir together melted chocolate, butter and 2 tablespoons whipping cream. Spread over top of brownie.

4. For Whipped Cream, beat remaining whipping cream and sugar with electric mixer on high speed for 1 to 3 minutes or until thick. Spread over chocolate butter cream. Sprinkle with chocolate jimmies.
Refrigerate until ready to serve.
Makes 8 to 12 servings

Orange Coconut Fudge Cake

1 can (6 ounces) CITRUS HILL® Orange Juice Concentrate, thawed

Cake
1 package DUNCAN HINES® Butter Recipe Fudge Cake Mix
³/₄ cup CITRUS HILL® Orange Juice (see step #2 below)
3 eggs
¹/₂ cup butter or margarine, softened
2 tablespoons orange liqueur, optional

Frosting
1 cup evaporated milk
³/₄ cup sugar
3 egg yolks
¹/₄ cup butter or margarine
2 tablespoons CITRUS HILL® Frozen Orange Juice concentrate, thawed (see step #2 below)
1 teaspoon vanilla extract
2 cups chopped pecans
1 cup flaked coconut

1. Preheat oven to 375°F. Grease and flour two 9-inch round cake pans.

2. Measure 2 tablespoons orange juice concentrate. Set aside for frosting. Reconstitute remaining concentrate using ¹/₃ cup less water than package directions.

Orange Coconut Fudge Cake

3. For Cake, combine cake mix, orange juice, eggs, butter and liqueur in large bowl. Mix, bake and cool cake following package directions.

4. For Frosting, combine evaporated milk, sugar, egg yolks and butter in medium saucepan. Cook on medium heat, stirring constantly, until mixture comes to boil and thickens. Remove from heat. Add reserved orange juice concentrate and vanilla extract; stir well. Add pecans and coconut. Cool. Place one cake layer on serving plate. Spread with thin layer of frosting. Top with second cake layer. Frost top and sides with remaining frosting. Refrigerate until ready to serve.

Makes 12 to 16 servings

Tip: Garnish cake with orange slices or twists.

Black Forest Torte

2 cups sugar
1³/₄ cups all-purpose flour
³/₄ cup HERSHEY'S® Cocoa
1¹/₂ teaspoons baking powder
1¹/₂ teaspoons baking soda
1 teaspoon salt
2 eggs
1 cup milk
¹/₂ cup vegetable oil
2 teaspoons vanilla extract
1 cup boiling water
1 can (21 ounces) cherry pie filling, chilled
1 container (4 ounces) frozen whipped topping, thawed
Sliced almonds (optional)

Preheat oven to 350°F. Grease and flour two 9-inch round baking pans.

In large mixer bowl, blend sugar, flour, cocoa, baking powder, baking soda and salt. Add eggs, milk, oil and vanilla; beat on medium speed 2 minutes. Remove from mixer; stir in boiling water (batter will be thin). Pour batter into prepared pans.

Bake 30 to 35 minutes or until wooden toothpick inserted in center comes out clean. Cool 10 minutes; remove from pans. Cool completely on wire rack.

Place one layer on serving plate. Spread half of pie filling over layer to within ¹/₂ inch of edge. Spoon or pipe border of whipped topping around edge. Top with second cake layer. Spread remaining pie filling to within ¹/₂ inch of edge. Make border around top edge with remaining topping. Garnish with sliced almonds, if desired. Refrigerate until just before serving.

Makes 10 to 12 servings

Chocolate Chips Pecan Torte

1 cup butter or margarine, melted
1¹/₂ cups sugar
1¹/₂ teaspoons vanilla extract
3 eggs, separated
²/₃ cup HERSHEY'S® Cocoa
¹/₂ cup all-purpose flour
3 tablespoons water
³/₄ cup finely chopped pecans
¹/₈ teaspoon cream of tartar
¹/₈ teaspoon salt
2 cups (12-ounce package) HERSHEY'S® Semi-Sweet Chocolate Chips, divided
Royal Chip Glaze (recipe follows)
Sweetened whipped cream or pecan halves (optional)

Preheat oven to 350°F. Line bottom of 9-inch springform pan with foil; grease foil and side of pan with butter.

In large mixer bowl, combine melted butter, sugar and vanilla; beat well. Add egg yolks, one at a time, beating after each addition. Blend in cocoa, flour and water; beat well. Stir in chopped pecans.

In small mixer bowl, with clean set of beaters, beat egg whites, cream of tartar and salt until stiff peaks form; carefully fold into chocolate mixture with 1 cup chocolate chips, reserving remaining chips for glaze. Pour mixture into prepared pan.

Bake 45 minutes or until top begins to crack slightly. (Cake will not test done in center.) Cool in pan on wire rack 1 hour. Cover; refrigerate until firm. Loosen cake from rim of pan; remove rim.

Prepare Royal Chip Glaze; pour over cake, allowing glaze to run down sides. With spatula, spread glaze evenly on top and sides of cake. Garnish with sweetened whipped cream or pecan halves, if desired. Cover; refrigerate leftovers.

Makes 10 to 12 servings

ROYAL CHIP GLAZE: In small saucepan, melt remaining 1 cup chocolate chips with ¼ cup milk over very low heat, stirring constantly, until mixture is smooth; do not boil. Remove from heat; cool, stirring occasionally, until mixture thickens, 10 to 15 minutes.

Variation: One 10-ounce package HERSHEY'S® Premium Semi Sweet Chocolate Chunks may be substituted for chocolate chips.

Top to bottom: Black Forest Torte, Triple Layer Chocolate Mousse Cake

Triple Layer Chocolate Mousse Cake

2 cups sugar
1¾ cups all-purpose flour
¾ cup HERSHEY'S® Cocoa or HERSHEY'S® Premium European Style Cocoa
1½ teaspoons baking powder
1½ teaspoons baking soda
1 teaspoon salt
2 eggs
1 cup milk
½ cup vegetable oil
2 teaspoons vanilla extract
1 cup boiling water
Chocolate Mousse (recipe follows)
Sliced almonds (optional)
Chocolate curls (optional)

Preheat oven to 350°F. Grease and flour three 8-inch round baking pans.

In large mixer bowl, mix together sugar, flour, cocoa, baking powder, baking soda and salt. Add eggs, milk, oil and vanilla; beat on medium speed 2 minutes. Remove from mixer; stir in boiling water (batter will be thin). Pour batter into prepared pans.

Bake 30 to 35 minutes or until wooden toothpick inserted in center comes out clean. Cool 10 minutes; remove from pans. Cool completely on wire racks. Prepare Chocolate Mousse. Fill and frost layers with Mousse. Garnish with almonds and chocolate curls, if desired. Refrigerate at least 1 hour. Cover; refrigerate leftovers.

Makes 10 to 12 servings

Chocolate Mousse

1 teaspoon unflavored gelatin
2 tablespoons cold water
¼ cup boiling water
1 cup sugar
½ cup HERSHEY'S® Cocoa
2 cups chilled whipping cream
2 teaspoons vanilla extract

In small bowl, sprinkle gelatin over cold water; let stand 1 minute to soften. Add boiling water; stir until gelatin is completely dissolved and mixture is clear. Cool slightly. In large cold mixer bowl, stir together sugar and cocoa; add whipping cream and vanilla. Beat at medium speed, scraping bottom of bowl occasionally, until stiff peaks form; pour in gelatin mixture and beat until well blended. Refrigerate about 30 minutes.

Makes about 2 cups mousse

Chocolate Dream Torte

Chocolate Dream Torte

**1 package DUNCAN HINES®
Moist Deluxe Dark Dutch
Fudge Cake Mix**
**1 package (6 ounces) semi-
sweet chocolate chips,
melted, for garnish**
**1 container (8 ounces) frozen
whipped topping, thawed
and divided**
**1 container (16 ounces)
DUNCAN HINES® Milk
Chocolate Frosting**
**3 tablespoons finely
chopped dry roasted
pistachios**

1. Preheat oven to 350°F. Grease
and flour two 9-inch round cake
pans. Prepare, bake and cool
cake following package
directions.
2. For chocolate hearts garnish,
spread melted chocolate to ⅛-
inch thickness on waxed-paper-
lined cookie sheet. Cut shapes
with heart cookie cutter when
chocolate begins to set.
Refrigerate until firm. Push out
heart shapes. Set aside.
3. Split each cake layer in half
horizontally. Spread one-third
whipped topping on one cake
layer. Place second layer on top
of filling. Repeat with remaining
layers and whipped topping.
Frost sides and top with milk
chocolate frosting. Sprinkle
pistachios on top. Position
chocolate hearts by pushing
points down into cake.
Refrigerate until ready to serve.
Makes about 12 servings

Cocoa Chiffon Cake

2 cups sugar, divided
1½ cups cake flour
⅔ cup HERSHEY'S® Cocoa
2 teaspoons baking powder
1 teaspoon salt
½ teaspoon baking soda
½ cup vegetable oil
**7 eggs, separated, at room
temperature**
¾ cup cold water
2 teaspoons vanilla extract
**½ teaspoon cream of tartar
Vanilla Icing (recipe
follows)**

Preheat oven to 325°F. In large
bowl, stir together 1¾ cups
sugar, cake flour, cocoa, baking
powder, salt and baking soda.
Add oil, egg yolks, water and
vanilla; beat until smooth. In
large mixer bowl, beat egg
whites and cream of tartar until
soft peaks form. Gradually add
remaining ¼ cup sugar, beating
until stiff peaks form. Gradually
pour chocolate batter over beaten
egg whites, folding with rubber
spatula just until blended. Pour
into ungreased 10-inch tube pan.
Bake 1 hour and 20 minutes or
until top springs back when
touched lightly. Invert pan on
heat-proof funnel until
completely cool. Remove cake
from pan; invert onto serving
plate. Spread top of cake with
Vanilla Icing, allowing some to
drizzle down sides.
Makes 12 to 16 servings

Vanilla Icing

⅓ cup butter or margarine
2 cups powdered sugar
1½ teaspoons vanilla extract
2 to 4 tablespoons hot water

In medium saucepan, melt
butter over low heat. Remove
from heat. Stir in powdered
sugar and vanilla. Stir in water,
1 tablespoon at a time, until
icing is smooth and of desired
consistency.
Makes about 1¼ cups icing

Choco-Lemon Delight

**1 package DUNCAN HINES®
Moist Deluxe Devil's
Food Cake Mix**
Filling
1 cup granulated sugar
3 tablespoons cornstarch
⅛ teaspoon salt
1 cup water
2 egg yolks, slightly beaten
**1 teaspoon grated lemon
peel**
**2 tablespoons butter or
margarine**
**2 tablespoons lemon juice
Confectioners sugar
Frozen non-dairy whipped
topping, thawed, for
garnish**

1. Preheat oven to 350°F. Grease
and flour two 9-inch round cake
pans.
2. Prepare, bake and cool cake
following package directions for
original recipe.
3. To make Filling, combine
granulated sugar, cornstarch and
salt in saucepan. Stir in water.
Cook on medium heat, stirring
constantly, until mixture comes
to a full boil. Boil and stir 1
minute. Remove from heat.
Gradually stir in egg yolks and
lemon peel. Cook on medium
heat until filling comes to a boil.
Reduce heat to low; cook 1
minute. Remove from heat. Add
butter; stir until melted. Stir in
lemon juice. Refrigerate 1 hour.
4. Place one cake layer on
serving plate. Spread with lemon
filling. Place second layer on top.
Sift confectioners sugar over
cake. Garnish with dollops of
whipped topping around edge, if
desired.
Makes 12 to 16 servings
Tip: You can get about 1
teaspoon grated peel and 2
tablespoons juice from 1 small
lemon.

Toll House® Cake

Toll House® Cake

Cake:
>1 cup (2 sticks) butter, softened
>1 cup firmly packed brown sugar
>²/₃ cup granulated sugar
>½ teaspoon salt
>4 eggs
>2 teaspoons vanilla extract
>2 cups all-purpose flour
>One 12-oz. pkg. (2 cups) NESTLÉ® Toll House® Semi-Sweet Chocolate Mini Morsels, divided

Frosting:
>1 cup NESTLÉ® Toll House® Semi-Sweet Chocolate Mini Morsels, reserved from 12-oz. pkg.
>1½ cups sifted confectioners' sugar
>¾ cup (1½ sticks) butter, softened
>2 teaspoons vanilla extract

Cake: Preheat oven to 350°F. Grease bottom of 15½×10½×1-inch baking pan and line with waxed paper; set aside.

In large mixer bowl, beat butter, brown sugar, granulated sugar and salt until creamy. Add eggs, 1 at a time, beating well after each addition. Beat in vanilla extract. Gradually beat in flour.

Stir in 1 cup mini morsels. Spread in prepared pan. Bake 20 to 25 minutes until top springs back when lightly pressed. Cool completely.

Frosting: Melt remaining 1 cup mini morsels; set aside. In small mixer bowl, beat confectioners' sugar and butter until creamy. Add melted chocolate and vanilla extract; blend until smooth.

Loosen cake from sides of pan. Invert onto lightly floured cloth towel. Peel off waxed paper. Trim edges of cake. Cut cake crosswise into four 3¾×10½-inch sections. Spread about ¼ cup frosting on 1 cake layer. Top with second cake layer. Repeat layers of frosting and cake. Frost entire cake with remaining frosting.

Makes about 10 servings

Old-Fashioned Chocolate Cake

>1½ cups sugar
>¾ cup (1½ sticks) butter, softened
>2 eggs
>1 teaspoon vanilla extract
>2 cups all-purpose flour
>1 cup water
>²/₃ cup NESTLÉ® Cocoa
>1½ teaspoons baking soda
>½ teaspoon salt

Preheat oven to 350°F. Grease and flour two 9-inch round baking pans.

In large mixer bowl, beat sugar, butter, eggs and vanilla extract until light and fluffy, about 5 minutes. Add flour, water, cocoa, baking soda and salt. Beat until blended and smooth. Pour into prepared pans.

Bake 28 to 33 minutes until wooden toothpick inserted into center comes out clean. Cool 5 minutes; remove from pans. Cool completely. Fill and frost with favorite frosting.

Makes 10 to 12 servings

Cocoa-Cola Cake

>2 cups sugar
>2 cups all-purpose flour
>½ cup vegetable oil
>½ cup butter or margarine
>⅓ cup HERSHEY'S® Cocoa
>⅓ cup regular cola (not diet)
>1½ cups miniature marshmallows
>½ cup buttermilk or sour milk*
>1 teaspoon baking soda
>2 eggs, slightly beaten
>1 teaspoon vanilla extract
>Chocolate Nut Frosting (recipe follows)

Preheat oven to 350°F. Grease 13×9×2-inch baking pan.

In large mixer bowl, combine sugar and flour; set aside. In saucepan, over medium heat, combine oil, butter, cocoa and cola; heat to boiling, stirring constantly. Add chocolate mixture to sugar mixture; beat until smooth. Stir in marshmallows. Add buttermilk, baking soda, eggs and vanilla; blend well. Pour batter into prepared pan.

Bake 40 to 45 minutes or until wooden toothpick inserted in center comes out clean. Meanwhile, prepare Chocolate Nut Frosting; spread over warm cake. Cool completely in pan on wire rack.

Makes 12 to 15 servings

***To sour milk:** Combine 1½ teaspoons white vinegar plus milk to equal ½ cup.

Chocolate Nut Frosting

>3²/₃ cups (1 pound) powdered sugar
>½ cup butter or margarine
>6 tablespoons regular cola (not diet)
>3 tablespoons HERSHEY'S® Cocoa
>½ to 1 cup coarsely chopped pecans
>1 teaspoon vanilla extract

In small mixer bowl, place powdered sugar; set aside. In small saucepan over medium heat, combine butter, cola and cocoa; cook, stirring constantly, until mixture boils. Pour hot mixture over powdered sugar; beat until smooth and slightly thickened. Stir in pecans and vanilla.

Makes about 2½ cups frosting

Black Magic Cake

2 cups sugar
1¾ cups all-purpose flour
¾ cup HERSHEY'S® Cocoa
2 teaspoons baking soda
1 teaspoon baking powder
1 teaspoon salt
2 eggs
1 cup strong black coffee *or* 2 teaspoons powdered instant coffee plus 1 cup boiling water
1 cup buttermilk or sour milk*
½ cup vegetable oil
1 teaspoon vanilla extract

Preheat oven to 350°F. Grease and flour two 9-inch round baking pans or one 13×9×2-inch baking pan.

In large mixer bowl, blend sugar, flour, cocoa, baking soda, baking powder and salt. Add eggs, coffee, buttermilk, oil and vanilla; beat 2 minutes on medium speed (batter will be thin). Pour batter into prepared pans.

Bake 30 to 35 minutes for round pans, 35 to 40 minutes for rectangular pan or until wooden toothpick inserted in center comes out clean. Cool 10 minutes; remove from pans. Cool completely on wire rack. Frost as desired.

Makes 10 to 12 servings

To sour milk: Combine 1 tablespoon white vinegar plus milk to equal 1 cup.

Midnight Torte

Midnight Torte

Cake:
One 6-oz. pkg. (1 cup) NESTLÉ® Toll House® Semi-Sweet Chocolate Morsels
1¼ cups water, divided
2¼ cups all-purpose flour
1 teaspoon baking soda
¾ teaspoon salt
1½ cups sugar
¾ cup (1½ sticks) butter, softened
1 teaspoon vanilla extract
3 eggs

Filling:
¼ cup NESTLÉ® Cocoa
¼ cup sugar
2 cups heavy or whipping cream

Glaze:
6 tablespoons (¾ stick) butter
⅓ cup corn syrup
2 tablespoons water
One 12-oz. pkg. (2 cups) NESTLÉ® Toll House® Semi-Sweet Chocolate Morsels

Cake: Preheat oven to 375°F. Grease and flour two 9×1½-inch round baking pans. Melt semi-sweet chocolate morsels with ¼ cup water, stirring until smooth; set aside.

In small bowl, combine flour, baking soda and salt; set aside. In large mixer bowl, beat sugar, butter and vanilla extract until creamy. Add eggs, 1 at a time, beating well after each addition. Blend in chocolate mixture. Gradually blend in flour mixture alternately with remaining 1 cup water. Pour into prepared pans. Bake 30 to 35 minutes until wooden toothpick inserted into center comes out clean. Cool 10 minutes; remove from pans and cool completely. Split layers in half horizontally.

Filling: In small mixer bowl, stir cocoa and sugar until smooth. Add heavy cream. Beat at medium speed until soft peaks form. Place 1 split cake layer on serving plate; spread with ⅓ of Filling. Repeat with remaining layers and Filling.

Glaze: In 2-quart saucepan, combine butter, corn syrup and water. *Heat to boiling* over low heat, stirring constantly; remove from heat. Stir in semi-sweet chocolate morsels until smooth. Cool to room temperature. Spread over top and side of cake. Refrigerate cake a few minutes to set glaze. Store in refrigerator.

Makes 10 to 12 servings

Hot Fudge Pudding Cake

1¼ cups granulated sugar, divided
1 cup all-purpose flour
7 tablespoons HERSHEY'S® Cocoa, divided
2 teaspoons baking powder
¼ teaspoon salt
½ cup milk
⅓ cup butter or margarine, melted
1½ teaspoons vanilla extract
½ cup packed light brown sugar
1¼ cups hot water
Whipped topping

Preheat oven to 350°F. In large bowl, combine ¾ cup granulated sugar, flour, 3 tablespoons cocoa, baking powder and salt. Blend in milk, butter and vanilla; beat until smooth. Pour batter into ungreased 8- or 9-inch square baking pan. Stir together remaining ½ cup granulated sugar, brown sugar and remaining 4 tablespoons cocoa; sprinkle mixture evenly over batter. Pour hot water over top; do not stir.

Bake 35 to 40 minutes or until center is almost set. Let stand 15 minutes; spoon into dessert dishes, spooning sauce from bottom of pan over top. Garnish with whipped topping.

Makes 8 to 10 servings

Hot Fudge Pudding Cake

Chocolate-Filled Boston Cream Pie

2 cups all-purpose flour
1½ cups sugar
3½ teaspoons baking powder
1 teaspoon salt
¼ cup butter or margarine, softened
¼ cup shortening
1 cup milk
3 eggs
1 teaspoon vanilla extract
Chocolate Cream Filling (recipe follows)
Quick Chocolate Glaze (recipe follows)

Preheat oven to 350°F. Grease and flour two 9-inch round baking pans.

In large mixer bowl, combine all ingredients except Chocolate Cream Filling and Quick Chocolate Glaze; mix on low speed 30 seconds. Increase speed to high; beat 3 minutes. Pour batter into prepared pans.

Bake 30 to 35 minutes or until wooden toothpick inserted in center comes out clean. Cool 10 minutes; remove from pans. Cool completely on wire racks.

Meanwhile, prepare Chocolate Cream Filling. Place one cake layer on serving plate; spread with filling. Top with second cake layer; refrigerate. Prepare Quick Chocolate Glaze. Spoon hot glaze on top of cake, allowing glaze to drizzle down sides. Refrigerate before serving. Refrigerate leftovers.

Makes 10 to 12 servings

Chocolate Cream Filling

⅔ cup sugar
2 tablespoons cornstarch
⅛ teaspoon salt
1½ cups milk
2 egg yolks, slightly beaten
1 square (1 ounce) HERSHEY'S® Premium Unsweetened Baking Chocolate, broken up
2 teaspoons vanilla extract

In medium saucepan, stir together sugar, cornstarch and salt; gradually stir in milk and egg yolks. Add chocolate. Cook, over medium heat, stirring constantly, until mixture boils; boil, stirring constantly, 1 minute or until chocolate flecks disappear. Remove from heat; stir in vanilla. Pour into bowl; press plastic wrap directly onto surface. Cool slightly; refrigerate.

Quick Chocolate Glaze

1 square (1 ounce) HERSHEY'S® Premium Unsweetened Baking Chocolate
1 tablespoon butter or margarine
¼ cup sugar
1 tablespoon cornstarch Dash salt
⅓ cup water
½ teaspoon vanilla extract

In saucepan, over low heat, melt chocolate with butter; stir in sugar, cornstarch and salt until smooth. Gradually stir in water. Increase heat to medium; heat to boiling, stirring constantly. Remove from heat; stir in vanilla.

Chocolate Sheet Cake

1¼ cups margarine or butter
½ cup unsweetened cocoa
2 tablespoons instant coffee
1 cup water
2 cups unsifted flour
1½ cups firmly packed light brown sugar
1 teaspoon baking soda
1 teaspoon ground cinnamon
½ teaspoon salt
1 (14-ounce) can EAGLE® Brand Sweetened Condensed Milk (NOT evaporated milk)
2 eggs
1 teaspoon vanilla extract
1 cup confectioners' sugar
1 cup toasted slivered almonds or pecans

Preheat oven to 350°F. Grease 15×10-inch jellyroll pan.

In small saucepan, melt *1 cup* margarine; stir in *¼ cup* cocoa and *1 tablespoon* coffee, then water. Bring to a boil; remove from heat. In large mixer bowl, combine flour, brown sugar, baking soda, cinnamon and salt. Add cocoa mixture; mix well. Stir in *⅓ cup* sweetened condensed milk, eggs and vanilla. Pour into prepared pan.

Bake 15 minutes or until cake springs back when lightly touched. In small saucepan, melt remaining *¼ cup* margarine; stir in remaining *¼ cup* cocoa and *1 tablespoon* coffee. Add remaining sweetened condensed milk; stir in confectioners' sugar and nuts. Spread on warm cake.

Makes one 15×10-inch cake

Chocolate Berry Torte

Double Chocolate Snack Cake

1²/₃ **cups all-purpose flour**
1 **cup packed light brown sugar**
¼ **cup HERSHEY'S® Cocoa**
1 **teaspoon baking soda**
¼ **teaspoon salt**
1 **cup water**
⅓ **cup vegetable oil**
1 **teaspoon white vinegar**
¾ **teaspoon vanilla extract**
½ **cup HERSHEY'S® Semi-Sweet Chocolate Chips**

Preheat oven to 350°F. Grease and flour an 8-inch square baking pan.

In large bowl, stir together flour, brown sugar, cocoa, baking soda and salt. Add water, vegetable oil, vinegar and vanilla; beat with spoon or wire whisk until smooth. Pour batter into prepared pan. Sprinkle chocolate chips over top.

Bake 35 to 40 minutes or until wooden toothpick inserted in center comes out clean. Cool in pan on wire rack.

Makes 6 to 8 servings

Chocolate Berry Torte

1 **package (2-layer size) chocolate cake mix**
1 **package (4-serving size) JELL-O® Instant Pudding and Pie Filling, Chocolate or Chocolate Fudge Flavor**
4 **eggs**
1 **cup water**
¼ **cup vegetable oil**
3 **cups cold milk**
2 **tablespoons chocolate or coffee liqueur (optional)**
2 **packages (4-serving size each) JELL-O® Instant Pudding and Pie Filling, French Vanilla or Vanilla Flavor**
1³/₄ **cups (4 ounces) COOL WHIP® Whipped Topping, thawed**
2 **pints strawberries**

Combine cake mix, chocolate pudding mix, eggs, water and oil in large bowl. Blend at low speed of electric mixer just to moisten, scraping sides of bowl often. Beat at medium speed 4 minutes.

Pour into 2 greased and floured 9-inch round cake pans. Bake at 350°F for 35 to 40 minutes or until cake tester inserted in centers comes out clean. Cool in pans 15 minutes. Remove from pans; finish cooling on racks.

Pour milk and liqueur into large bowl. Add vanilla pudding mix. Beat with wire whisk until well blended, 1 to 2 minutes. Let stand 5 minutes. Fold in whipped topping. Chill 15 minutes.

Cut each cake layer in half horizontally. Reserve a few strawberries for garnish; slice remaining strawberries. Place 1 cake layer on serving plate; top with ¼ of the pudding mixture and ⅓ of the sliced strawberries. Repeat layers, using remaining cake, pudding mixture and sliced strawberries, ending with pudding mixture. Chill at least 1 hour. Garnish with reserved strawberries.

Makes about 12 servings

Prep time: 30 minutes
Baking time: 35 minutes

Cocoa Oatmeal Cake

1¹/₃ cups boiling water
1 cup quick-cooking rolled oats, uncooked
¹/₂ cup butter or margarine, softened
1 cup granulated sugar
1 cup packed light brown sugar
2 eggs
1¹/₂ cups all-purpose flour
¹/₂ cup HERSHEY'S® Cocoa
1 teaspoon baking powder
1 teaspoon baking soda
¹/₄ teaspoon ground cinnamon
1 cup finely chopped, peeled apple
1 cup chopped nuts
Vanilla Glaze (recipe follows)

In small bowl, pour boiling water over rolled oats; let stand 15 minutes. Preheat oven to 350°F. Grease and flour 13×9×2-inch baking pan.

In large mixer bowl, beat butter, granulated sugar, brown sugar and eggs until light and fluffy; blend in oat mixture. Stir together flour, cocoa, baking powder, baking soda and cinnamon; add to butter mixture, mixing well. Stir in apple and chopped nuts. Pour batter into prepared pan.

Bake 30 to 35 minutes or until wooden toothpick inserted in center comes out clean. Cool in pan on wire rack. Drizzle Vanilla Glaze over top in decorative design.
Makes 12 to 15 servings

Vanilla Glaze

1 cup powdered sugar
1 tablespoon butter or margarine, softened
1 to 2 tablespoons hot water
¹/₂ teaspoon vanilla extract

In bowl, beat all ingredients with spoon or wire whisk until smooth.

Mississippi Mud Cake

¹/₂ cup butter or margarine, softened
1 cup sugar
1 teaspoon vanilla extract
3 eggs
³/₄ cup all-purpose flour
¹/₃ cup HERSHEY'S® Cocoa
¹/₂ teaspoon baking powder
Dash salt
1 cup chopped pecans
One-Bowl Buttercream Frosting (recipe follows)
1 package (10¹/₂ ounces) miniature marshmallows

Preheat oven to 350°F. Grease 13×9×2-inch baking pan.

In large mixer bowl, beat butter, sugar and vanilla until creamy. Add eggs, one at a time, beating well after each addition. Stir together flour, cocoa, baking powder and salt; blend into butter mixture. Stir in pecans. Spoon batter into prepared pan.

Bake 15 to 18 minutes or until top is barely soft to the touch. Meanwhile, prepare One-Bowl Buttercream Frosting. Remove cake from oven; immediately place marshmallows over top. Return cake to oven 2 to 3 minutes or until marshmallows become soft. Gently spread marshmallows over cake; immediately spread frosting over marshmallow layer. Cool thoroughly before cutting cake into squares.
Makes 12 to 15 servings

One-Bowl Buttercream Frosting

6 tablespoons butter or margarine, softened
2²/₃ cups powdered sugar
¹/₂ cup HERSHEY'S® Cocoa
¹/₃ cup milk
1 teaspoon vanilla extract

In small mixer bowl, beat butter. Blend in powdered sugar and cocoa alternately with milk; beat to desired spreading consistency (additional milk may be needed). Blend in vanilla.
Makes about 2 cups frosting

Chocolate Cherry Upside-Down Cake

1 tablespoon cold water
1 tablespoon cornstarch
¹/₄ to ¹/₂ teaspoon almond extract (optional)
1 can (21 ounces) cherry pie filling
1²/₃ cups all-purpose flour
1 cup sugar
¹/₄ cup HERSHEY'S® Cocoa
1 teaspoon baking soda
¹/₂ teaspoon salt
1 cup water
¹/₃ cup vegetable oil
1 teaspoon white vinegar
¹/₂ teaspoon vanilla extract
Sweetened whipped cream

Preheat oven to 350°F. In medium bowl, stir together 1 tablespoon water, cornstarch and almond extract, if desired, until cornstarch is dissolved. Stir in pie filling; blend well. Spread mixture evenly on bottom of ungreased 9-inch square baking pan; set aside. In large bowl, stir together flour, sugar, cocoa, baking soda and salt. Add 1 cup water, oil, vinegar and vanilla; beat with spoon or wire whisk until batter is smooth and well blended. Pour batter evenly over cherries.

Bake 40 to 45 minutes or until wooden pick inserted in center comes out clean. Cool 10 minutes; invert onto serving plate. Serve warm with whipped cream.
Makes about 8 servings

Chocolate Cherry Upside-Down Cake

Sour Cream Brownie Cake

- **1 cup BORDEN® or MEADOW GOLD® Butter**
- **2 (1-ounce) squares unsweetened chocolate**
- **1 cup water**
- **2 cups firmly packed brown sugar**
- **2 cups unsifted flour**
- **1 teaspoon baking soda**
- **½ teaspoon salt**
- **1 (8-ounce) container BORDEN® or MEADOW GOLD® Sour Cream**
- **2 eggs**
- **1 tablespoon vanilla extract**
- **1 cup chopped nuts, optional**
- **Fudgy Frosting**

Preheat oven to 350°F. Grease and flour 15×10×1-inch jellyroll pan.

In saucepan, melt butter and chocolate with water. Combine dry ingredients. In mixer bowl, beat sour cream, eggs, vanilla and chocolate mixture until well combined. Add flour mixture; beat until smooth. Stir in nuts. Pour into prepared pan.

Bake 25 minutes or until wooden toothpick inserted in center of cake comes out clean. Cool. Frost with Fudgy Frosting.

Makes one 15×10-inch cake

FUDGY FROSTING: In mixer bowl, beat 2 cups confectioners' sugar, ½ cup BORDEN® or MEADOW GOLD® Sour Cream, 1 tablespoon butter, softened, 2 (1-ounce) squares unsweetened chocolate, melted, and 1 teaspoon vanilla until smooth.

Prep time: 20 minutes
Baking time: 25 minutes

Toll House® Crumbcake

Toll House® Crumbcake

Topping:
- **½ cup firmly packed brown sugar**
- **2 tablespoons (¼ stick) butter, softened**
- **1 tablespoon all-purpose flour**
- **½ cup nuts, chopped**
- **One 12-oz. pkg. (2 cups) NESTLÉ® Toll House® Semi-Sweet Chocolate Mini Morsels, divided**

Cake:
- **2 cups all-purpose flour**
- **1 teaspoon baking powder**
- **1 teaspoon baking soda**
- **¼ teaspoon salt**
- **1 cup granulated sugar**
- **½ cup (1 stick) butter, softened**
- **1 teaspoon vanilla extract**
- **3 eggs**
- **1 cup sour cream**
- **1½ cups NESTLÉ® Toll House® Semi-Sweet Chocolate Mini Morsels, reserved from 12-oz. pkg.**

Topping: In small bowl, mix brown sugar, butter and flour. Stir in nuts and ½ cup mini morsels; set aside.

Cake: Preheat oven to 350°F. Grease 13×9-inch baking pan. In small bowl, combine flour, baking powder, baking soda and salt; set aside. In large mixer bowl, beat granulated sugar, butter and vanilla extract until creamy. Add eggs, 1 at a time, beating well after each addition. Gradually beat in flour mixture alternately with sour cream. Fold in remaining 1½ cups mini morsels. Spread in pan. Sprinkle Topping evenly over batter. Bake 45 to 50 minutes until wooden toothpick inserted into center comes out clean. Cool; cut into 2-inch squares.

Makes about 24 squares

CHEESECAKES

Cheesecake has earned the status of dessert classic, and rightly so. No other dessert is quite as extravagant as an incredibly smooth and creamy cheesecake. The sumptuous selection offered here is impressive and includes strawberry, lemon, mocha, chocolate, praline and piña colada—plus an assortment of cheesecake bars and mini cheesecakes. (For additional cheesecake recipes, see the Jump-Start Baking and Festive Holiday Baking chapters.)

Autumn Cheesecake

1 cup graham cracker crumbs
½ cup finely chopped pecans
3 tablespoons sugar
½ teaspoon cinnamon
¼ cup PARKAY® Margarine, melted
2 (8 oz.) pkgs. PHILADELPHIA BRAND® Cream Cheese, softened
½ cup sugar
2 eggs
½ teaspoon vanilla
4 cups thin peeled apple slices
⅓ cup sugar
½ teaspoon cinnamon
¼ cup chopped pecans

• Preheat oven to 350°F.
• Stir together crumbs, finely chopped pecans, 3 tablespoons sugar, ½ teaspoon cinnamon and margarine; press onto bottom of 9-inch springform pan. Bake 10 minutes.
• Beat cream cheese and ½ cup sugar in large mixing bowl at medium speed with electric mixer until well blended. Add eggs, one at a time, mixing well after each addition. Blend in vanilla; pour over crust.
• Toss apples with combined ⅓ cup sugar and ½ teaspoon cinnamon. Spoon apple mixture over cream cheese layer; sprinkle with chopped pecans.
• Bake 1 hour and 10 minutes. Loosen cake from rim of pan; cool before removing rim of pan. Chill.   *Makes 10 to 12 servings*

Prep time: 25 minutes plus chilling
Cooking time: 1 hour 10 minutes

Variation: Omit pecans in crust.

Chocolate and Orange Cheesecake

1 cup vanilla wafer crumbs
¼ cup (½ stick) butter, melted
1¾ cups sugar, divided
2 foil-wrapped bars (4 oz.) NESTLÉ® Semi-Sweet Chocolate Baking Bars
3 (8-oz.) pkgs. cream cheese, softened
4 eggs
1½ cups sour cream
2 teaspoons vanilla extract
2 teaspoons grated orange rind
Whipped cream and orange rind, for garnish

In small bowl, combine vanilla wafer crumbs, butter and ¼ cup sugar; pat firmly into bottom of greased 9-inch springform pan. Melt semi-sweet chocolate baking bars; set aside. In large mixer bowl, beat cream cheese and remaining 1½ cups sugar until creamy. Add eggs, 1 at a time, beating well after each addition. Stir in sour cream and vanilla extract. Combine 3 cups cream cheese mixture with melted chocolate. Pour into crust. Freeze 30 to 45 minutes until batter sets.

Preheat oven to 325°F. Stir grated orange rind into remaining cream cheese mixture. Gently spoon orange mixture over chocolate layer. Bake 1½ hours or until cheesecake is set. Turn off oven. Let stand in oven with door ajar about 1 hour. Cool in pan on wire rack. Remove side of pan; refrigerate until serving time. Garnish with whipped cream and orange rind.
Makes 12 to 16 servings

Autumn Cheesecake

Premier White Cheesecake

Premier White Cheesecake

**1¼ cups chocolate wafer
    crumbs
⅓ cup (5⅓ tablespoons)
    butter, melted
½ cup sugar, divided
One 6-oz. pkg. (3 foil-wrapped
    bars) NESTLÉ® Premier
    White Baking Bars
Two 8-oz. pkgs. cream cheese,
    softened
2 eggs
1 teaspoon vanilla extract
Premier White Wedges, for
    garnish (recipe follows)
Raspberries, for garnish**

Preheat oven to 375°F. In small
bowl, combine chocolate wafer
crumbs, butter and ¼ cup sugar;
press evenly into 9-inch pie
plate; refrigerate.

Melt over hot (not boiling) water,
Premier White baking bars. In
large mixer bowl, beat cream
cheese and remaining ¼ cup
sugar until smooth. Add eggs, 1
at a time, beating well after each
addition. Blend in melted baking
bars and vanilla extract. Pour
into prepared crust.

Bake 30 minutes or until edges
are very lightly browned. Cool
completely. Store in refrigerator.
Garnish with Premier White
Wedges and raspberries.

Makes 8 to 10 servings

PREMIER WHITE WEDGES:
Melt over hot (not boiling) water,
2 foil-wrapped bars (4 oz.)
NESTLÉ® Premier White
Baking Bars with 2 tablespoons
vegetable shortening, stirring
until smooth. Spread in waxed
paper or foil-lined 8-inch round
pan. Refrigerate until softly set,
but not hard. With tip of knife,
score circle into 8 to 10 wedges;
loosen circle from edge of pan.
Refrigerate until firm, about 20
minutes. Remove wedges from
pan; use as garnish.

Cocoa-Nut Meringue Cheesecake

**1 (7 oz.) pkg. BAKER'S®
    ANGEL FLAKE® Coconut,
    toasted
¼ cup chopped pecans
3 tablespoons PARKAY®
    Margarine, melted
2 (8 oz.) pkgs.
    PHILADELPHIA BRAND®
    Cream Cheese, softened
⅓ cup sugar
3 tablespoons unsweetened
    cocoa
2 tablespoons cold water
1 teaspoon vanilla
3 eggs, separated
    Dash of salt
1 (7 oz.) jar KRAFT®
    Marshmallow Creme
½ cup chopped pecans**

• Preheat oven to 350°F.

• Stir together coconut, ¼ cup
pecans and margarine in small
bowl. Press onto bottom of 9-inch
springform pan.

• Beat cream cheese, sugar,
cocoa, water and vanilla in large
mixing bowl at medium speed
with electric mixer until well
blended. Blend in egg yolks;
pour over crust.

• Bake 30 minutes. Loosen cake
from rim of pan; cool before
removing rim of pan.

• Beat egg whites and salt until
foamy; gradually add
marshmallow creme, beating
until stiff peaks form.

• Sprinkle ½ cup pecans on
cheesecake to within ½ inch of
edge. Carefully spread
marshmallow creme mixture
over top of cheesecake to seal.

• Bake 15 minutes. Cool.
Makes 10 to 12 servings

Prep time: 25 minutes plus
chilling
Baking time: 45 minutes

Chocolate Caramel Pecan Cheesecake

2 cups vanilla wafer crumbs
6 tablespoons PARKAY®
    Margarine, melted
1 (14 oz.) bag KRAFT®
    Caramels
1 (5 oz.) can evaporated milk
1 cup chopped pecans
2 (8 oz.) pkgs.
    PHILADELPHIA BRAND®
    Cream Cheese, softened
½ cup sugar
2 eggs
1 cup BAKER'S® Real Semi-
    Sweet Chocolate Chips,
    melted
1 teaspoon vanilla

• Preheat oven to 350°F.

• Mix together crumbs and margarine; press onto bottom and sides of 9-inch springform pan. Bake 10 minutes.

• Microwave caramels with milk in small microwave-safe bowl on HIGH 4 to 5 minutes or until melted, stirring every minute. Pour over crust; top with pecans.

• Beat cream cheese and sugar in large mixing bowl at medium speed with electric mixer until well blended.

• Add eggs, one at a time, mixing well after each addition. Blend in chocolate and vanilla; pour over pecans.

• Place pan on cookie sheet. Bake 45 minutes. Loosen cake from rim of pan; cool before removing rim of pan. Chill several hours or overnight.

Makes 10 to 12 servings

Prep time: 35 minutes plus chilling
Baking time: 45 minutes

Classic Cheesecake

⅓ cup PARKAY® Margarine,
    softened
⅓ cup sugar
1 egg
1¼ cups flour
2 (8 oz.) pkgs.
    PHILADELPHIA BRAND®
    Cream Cheese, softened
½ cup sugar
1 tablespoon lemon juice
1 teaspoon grated lemon
    peel
½ teaspoon vanilla
3 eggs
1 cup sour cream
1 tablespoon sugar
1 teaspoon vanilla

• Preheat oven to 450°F.

• Beat margarine and ⅓ cup sugar until light and fluffy; blend in one egg. Add flour; mix well. Spread dough onto bottom and 1½ inches up sides of 9-inch springform pan. Bake 5 minutes.

• Beat cream cheese, ½ cup sugar, juice, peel and ½ teaspoon vanilla in large mixing bowl at medium speed with electric mixer until well blended.

• Add three eggs, one at a time, mixing well after each addition. Pour into crust.

• Reduce oven temperature to 325°F. Continue baking 50 minutes.

• Stir together sour cream, 1 tablespoon sugar and 1 teaspoon vanilla in small bowl. Spread evenly over cake; continue baking 10 minutes. Loosen cake from rim of pan; cool before removing rim of pan. Chill.

• Serve with BIRDS EYE® Frozen Quick Thaw Strawberries in Syrup, thawed, if desired.

Makes 10 to 12 servings

Prep time: 30 minutes plus chilling
Cooking time: 1 hour 5 minutes

Chocolate Caramel Pecan Cheesecake

Marble Cheesecake

Cocoa Crumb Crust (recipe follows)
3 packages (8 ounces each) cream cheese, softened
1 cup sugar, divided
1/2 cup dairy sour cream
2 1/2 teaspoons vanilla extract, divided
3 tablespoons all-purpose flour
3 eggs
1/4 cup HERSHEY'S® Cocoa
1 tablespoon vegetable oil

Prepare Cocoa Crumb Crust; set aside. Heat oven to 450°F.

In large mixer bowl, on medium speed, beat cream cheese, 3/4 cup sugar, sour cream and 2 teaspoons vanilla until smooth. Gradually add flour, blending well. Add eggs, 1 at a time, beating well after each addition; set aside. In medium bowl, stir together cocoa and remaining 1/4 cup sugar. Add oil, remaining 1/2 teaspoon vanilla and 1 1/2 cups of cream cheese mixture; blend well. Spoon plain and chocolate batters alternately over crust, ending with dollops of chocolate on top; gently swirl with spatula or knife for marbled effect.

Bake 10 minutes. Without opening oven door, *reduce oven temperature to 250°F;* continue baking 30 minutes. Turn off oven; leave cheesecake in oven 30 minutes without opening door. Remove from oven. Loosen cheesecake from rim of pan; cool to room temperature. Refrigerate several hours or overnight; remove rim of pan. Cover; refrigerate leftovers.

Makes 10 to 12 servings

COCOA CRUMB CRUST: Preheat oven to 350°F. In medium bowl, stir together 1 1/4 cups vanilla wafer crumbs, 1/3 cup powdered sugar and 1/3 cup HERSHEY'S® Cocoa; blend in 1/4 cup melted butter or margarine. Press mixture onto bottom and 1/2 inch up side of 9-inch springform pan. Bake 8 to 10 minutes. Cool.

Creamy Baked Cheesecake

1 1/4 cups graham cracker crumbs
1/4 cup sugar
1/3 cup margarine or butter, melted
2 (8-ounce) packages cream cheese, softened
1 (14-ounce) can EAGLE® Brand Sweetened Condensed Milk (NOT evaporated milk)
3 eggs
1/4 cup REALEMON® Lemon Juice from Concentrate
1 (8-ounce) container BORDEN® or MEADOW GOLD® Sour Cream, at room temperature
Raspberry Topping, optional

Preheat oven to 300°F. Combine crumbs, sugar and margarine; press firmly on bottom of 9-inch springform pan. In large mixer

Marble Cheesecake

bowl, beat cheese until fluffy. Gradually beat in sweetened condensed milk until smooth. Add eggs and REALEMON® brand; mix well. Pour into prepared pan.

Bake 50 to 55 minutes or until center is set; top with sour cream. Bake 5 minutes longer. Cool. Chill. Serve with Raspberry Topping if desired. Refrigerate leftovers.

Makes one 9-inch cheesecake

RASPBERRY TOPPING: Thaw 1 (10-ounce) package frozen red raspberries; reserve syrup. In small saucepan, combine 2/3 cup reserved syrup, 1/4 cup red currant jelly *or* red raspberry jam and 1 tablespoon cornstarch. Cook and stir until slightly thickened and clear. Cool. Stir in raspberries.

Makes about 1 1/3 cups topping

Prep time: 30 minutes
Baking time: 55 minutes

Chocolate Truffle Cheesecake

Chocolate Truffle Cheesecake

- **1 cup chocolate wafer crumbs**
- **3 tablespoons PARKAY® Margarine, melted**
- **2 (8 oz.) pkgs. PHILADELPHIA BRAND® Cream Cheese, softened**
- **2/3 cup sugar**
- **2 eggs**
- **1 cup BAKER'S® Real Semi-Sweet Chocolate Chips, melted**
- **1/2 teaspoon vanilla**
  Creamy Raspberry Sauce

- Preheat oven to 350°F.
- Stir together crumbs and margarine in small bowl. Press onto bottom of 9-inch springform pan. Bake 10 minutes.
- Beat cream cheese and sugar in large mixing bowl at medium speed with electric mixer until well blended.

- Add eggs, one at a time, mixing well after each addition.
- Blend in chocolate chips and vanilla; pour over crust.
- Bake 45 minutes. Loosen cake from rim of pan; cool before removing rim of pan. Chill.
- Spoon Creamy Raspberry Sauce onto each serving plate. Place slice of cheesecake over sauce. Garnish as desired.

Makes 10 to 12 servings

Creamy Raspberry Sauce

- **1 (10 oz.) pkg. BIRDS EYE® Quick Thaw Red Raspberries in a Lite Syrup, thawed**
- **3 tablespoons whipping cream**

- Place raspberries in food processor or blender container; process until smooth. Strain. Stir in cream.

Prep time: 30 minutes plus chilling
Cooking time: 45 minutes

Apple Sauce Cheesecake

Apple Sauce Cheesecake

12 oz. cream cheese, softened
1/2 cup sugar
2 eggs
1 1/2 cups MOTT'S® Regular Apple Sauce, divided
1 teaspoon vanilla
1 (9-inch) graham cracker crust*
1/4 cup graham cracker crumbs *or* chopped nuts (optional)
Raspberry Peach Topping (recipe follows)

Preheat oven to 350°F. In medium bowl, beat cream cheese, sugar and eggs until smooth. Stir in 1 cup apple sauce and vanilla. Pour into graham cracker crust. Bake 40 to 45 minutes or until center is just set. Gently spread remaining 1/2 cup apple sauce over cheesecake. Cool; refrigerate several hours. Just before serving, sprinkle with graham cracker crumbs. Serve with Raspberry Peach Topping.   *Makes 8 servings*

*Tip: To prepare in 9-inch springform pan, make filling 1 1/2 times the recipe. Bake at 350°F for 60 to 65 minutes.

Raspberry Peach Topping

1 (10-oz.) pkg. frozen raspberries in syrup, thawed
1/3 cup red currant jelly
1 tablespoon cornstarch
1 (16-oz.) can peach slices, drained *or* 1 1/2 cups fresh peach slices

Drain raspberries; reserve syrup. Set raspberries aside. Add enough water to syrup to equal 3/4 cup. In small saucepan, combine syrup, jelly and cornstarch; stir to dissolve cornstarch. Cook and stir over medium heat until clear, thickened and jelly is melted. Stir in raspberries. Chill. Arrange peach slices on cheesecake; drizzle with some raspberry sauce. Serve with additional sauce.

Piña Colada Cheesecake

1 (3 1/2-ounce) can flaked coconut, toasted (1 1/3 cups)
1 cup vanilla wafer crumbs (about 26 wafers)
1/4 cup margarine or butter, melted
3 (8-ounce) packages cream cheese, softened
3 eggs
2 tablespoons flour
1 (15-ounce) can COCO LOPEZ® Cream of Coconut
1/4 cup light rum
1 (8-ounce) can juice-pack crushed pineapple, drained, reserving juice
1 teaspoon cornstarch

Preheat oven to 300°F. In small bowl, combine coconut, crumbs and margarine; press firmly on bottom of 9-inch springform pan.

In large mixer bowl, beat cheese until fluffy. Add eggs and flour; beat until smooth. Gradually beat in cream of coconut and then rum. Pour mixture into prepared pan.

Bake 1 hour and 5 to 10 minutes or until cake springs back when lightly touched or until set. Carefully loosen top of cheesecake from edge of pan with knife tip. Cool to room temperature.

In small pan, combine reserved pineapple juice and cornstarch; cook and stir until slightly thickened. Remove from heat; stir in pineapple. Spoon onto top of cooled cheesecake. Chill. Refrigerate leftovers.

Makes one 9-inch cheesecake

Prep time: 20 minutes
Baking time: 70 minutes

Kahlúa® Fantasy Chocolate Cheesecake

Chocolate Crumb Crust (recipe follows)
1 1/2 cups semi-sweet chocolate pieces
1/4 cup KAHLÚA®
2 tablespoons butter
2 large eggs, beaten
1/3 cup sugar
1/4 teaspoon salt
1 cup sour cream
2 packages (8 ounces each) cream cheese, softened
Whipped cream (optional)
Chocolate leaves (optional)

Prepare Chocolate Crumb Crust. Preheat oven to 350°F. In small saucepan, over medium heat, melt chocolate with KAHLÚA® and butter; stir until smooth. Set aside.

In large bowl, combine eggs, sugar and salt. Add sour cream; blend well. Add cream cheese to egg mixture; beat until smooth. Gradually blend in chocolate mixture. Turn into prepared crust.

Bake 40 minutes or until filling is barely set in center. Remove from oven; let stand at room temperature 1 hour. Refrigerate several hours or overnight. Garnish, if desired, with whipped cream and chocolate leaves.

Makes 12 to 14 servings

Chocolate Crumb Crust

1 1/3 cups chocolate wafer crumbs
1/4 cup butter, softened
1 tablespoon sugar

In small bowl, combine chocolate wafer crumbs, butter and sugar. Press firmly in bottom of 9-inch springform pan.

New York Style Cheesecake

New York Style Cheesecake

1¼ cups graham cracker crumbs
¼ cup sugar
⅓ cup margarine or butter, melted
4 (8-ounce) packages cream cheese, softened
1 (14-ounce) can EAGLE® Brand Sweetened Condensed Milk (NOT evaporated milk)
4 eggs
⅓ cup unsifted flour
1 tablespoon vanilla extract
½ teaspoon grated lemon rind

Preheat oven to 300°F. Combine crumbs, sugar and margarine; press firmly on bottom of 9-inch springform pan. In large mixer bowl, beat cheese until fluffy. Gradually beat in sweetened condensed milk until smooth. Add eggs, flour, vanilla and rind; mix well. Pour mixture into prepared pan.

Bake 1 hour or until lightly browned. Cool. Chill. Garnish as desired. Refrigerate leftovers.

Makes one 9-inch cheesecake

Black Forest Cheesecake Delight

1 cup chocolate wafer crumbs
3 tablespoons PARKAY® Margarine, melted
2 (8 oz.) pkgs. PHILADELPHIA BRAND® Cream Cheese, softened
⅔ cup sugar
2 eggs
1 cup BAKER'S® Semi-Sweet Chocolate Chips, melted
¼ teaspoon almond extract
1 (21 oz.) can cherry pie filling
COOL WHIP® Whipped Topping, thawed

• Preheat oven to 350°F.
• Mix together crumbs and margarine in small bowl; press onto bottom of 9-inch springform pan. Bake 10 minutes.
• Beat cream cheese and sugar in large mixing bowl at medium speed with electric mixer until well blended.
• Add eggs, one at a time, mixing well after each addition. Blend in chocolate and extract; pour over crust.

• Bake 45 minutes. Loosen cake from rim of pan; cool before removing rim of pan. Chill. Top cheesecake with pie filling and whipped topping.

Makes 10 to 12 servings

Prep time: 20 minutes plus chilling
Baking time: 45 minutes

Orange Cheesecake

1½ cups vanilla wafer crumbs (about 36 wafers)
¼ cup margarine or butter, melted
3 (8-ounce) packages cream cheese, softened
1 (14-ounce) can EAGLE® Brand Sweetened Condensed Milk (NOT evaporated milk)
¼ cup frozen orange juice concentrate, thawed
3 eggs
1 teaspoon grated orange rind
Fresh orange sections
Orange Glaze

Preheat oven to 300°F. Combine crumbs and margarine; press firmly on bottom of 9-inch springform pan *or* 13×9-inch baking pan.

In large mixer bowl, beat cheese until fluffy. Gradually beat in sweetened condensed milk until smooth. Add juice concentrate, eggs and rind; mix well. Pour into prepared pan.

Bake 55 to 60 minutes or until set. Cool. Top with orange sections then Orange Glaze. Chill. Refrigerate leftovers.

Makes one 9-inch cheesecake

ORANGE GLAZE: In small saucepan, combine ¼ cup sugar and 2 teaspoons cornstarch. Add ½ cup orange juice and ¼ teaspoon grated orange rind; mix well. Over medium heat, cook and stir until thickened. Remove from heat; cool slightly. (For 13×9-inch pan, double all glaze ingredients.)

Heavenly Dessert Cheesecake

1 tablespoon graham cracker crumbs
1 cup low fat (1% to 2%) cottage cheese
2 (8 oz.) pkgs. PHILADELPHIA BRAND® "Light" Neufchatel Cheese, softened
²/₃ cup sugar
2 tablespoons flour
3 eggs
2 tablespoons skim milk
¼ teaspoon almond extract or vanilla

• Preheat oven to 325°F.
• Lightly grease bottom of 9-inch springform pan. Sprinkle with crumbs. Dust bottom; remove excess crumbs.
• Place cottage cheese in food processor or blender container. Cover; process until smooth.
• Beat cottage cheese, neufchatel cheese, sugar and flour in large mixing bowl at medium speed with electric mixer until well blended.
• Add eggs, one at a time, mixing well after each addition. Blend in milk and extract; pour into pan.
• Bake 45 to 50 minutes or until center is almost set. (Center of cheesecake appears soft but firms upon cooling.) Loosen cake from rim of pan; cool before removing rim of pan. Chill.
• Top with fresh strawberry slices or blueberries, if desired.
Makes 10 to 12 servings

Prep time: 15 minutes plus chilling
Baking time: 50 minutes

Variation: Prepare pan as directed; omit blender method. Place cottage cheese in large bowl of electric mixer; beat at high speed until smooth. Add neufchatel cheese, sugar and flour, mixing at medium speed until well blended. Continue as directed.

Almond Cheesecake

Almond Cheesecake

¾ cup graham cracker crumbs
½ cup slivered almonds, toasted and finely chopped
¼ cup sugar
¼ cup margarine or butter, melted
3 (8-ounce) packages cream cheese, softened
1 (14-ounce) can EAGLE® Brand Sweetened Condensed Milk (NOT evaporated milk)
3 eggs
1 teaspoon almond extract
Almond Praline Topping

Preheat oven to 300°F. Combine crumbs, almonds, sugar and margarine; press firmly on bottom of 9-inch springform pan *or* 13×9-inch baking pan.

In large mixer bowl, beat cheese until fluffy. Gradually beat in sweetened condensed milk until smooth. Add eggs and extract; mix well. Pour mixture into prepared pan.

Bake 55 to 60 minutes or until set. Cool. Top cheesecake with Almond Praline Topping. Chill. Refrigerate leftovers.
Makes one 9-inch cheesecake

ALMOND PRALINE TOPPING: In small saucepan, combine ⅓ cup firmly packed dark brown sugar and ⅓ cup BORDEN® or MEADOW GOLD® Whipping Cream. Cook and stir until sugar dissolves. Simmer 5 minutes. Remove from heat; stir in ½ cup chopped toasted slivered almonds. Spoon evenly over cake. (For 13×9-inch pan, double all topping ingredients; simmer 10 to 12 minutes.)

Heath® Bar Cheesecake

Crust:
1¾ cups vanilla wafer crumbs
⅓ cup butter or margarine, melted
2 tablespoons sugar
Filling:
3 packages (8 ounces each) cream cheese, softened
1 cup sugar
3 eggs
1 cup sour cream
½ teaspoon vanilla
1 package (9 ounces) HEATH® English Toffee Snack Size Bars, chilled

Preheat oven to 350°F. For Crust, combine crumbs, butter and sugar; press mixture on bottom and 1 inch up side of 9-inch springform pan. Refrigerate.

For Filling, in large mixer bowl, beat cream cheese and sugar until fluffy. Add eggs, 1 at a time, beating well after each addition. Blend in sour cream and vanilla until smooth. Pour cheese mixture into crust.

Bake 1 hour or until filling is just firm when pan is tapped. Remove from oven; let cool 10 to 15 minutes.

While cake is cooling, unwrap 18 to 19 HEATH® English Toffee Snack Size Bars. Place chilled bars in freezer bag; crush with mallet until bars are desired size. Sprinkle crushed toffee bars over top of warm cake. Cool completely on wire rack. Refrigerate until ready to serve.
Makes about 12 servings

Amaretto Cheesecake

**3/4 cup graham cracker
crumbs**
**1/2 cup slivered almonds,
toasted and finely
chopped**
1/4 cup sugar
**1/4 cup margarine or butter,
melted**
**3 (8-ounce) packages cream
cheese, softened**
**1 (14-ounce) can EAGLE®
Brand Sweetened
Condensed Milk (NOT
evaporated milk)**
2 eggs
**1/4 cup amaretto liqueur
Chocolate Amaretto Glaze**

Preheat oven to 300°F. Combine
crumbs, almonds, sugar and
margarine; press firmly on
bottom of 9-inch springform pan.

In large mixer bowl, beat cheese
until fluffy. Gradually beat in
sweetened condensed milk until
smooth. Add eggs and amaretto;
mix well. Pour mixture into
prepared pan.

Bake 55 to 60 minutes or until
center is set. Cool. Drizzle with
Chocolate Amaretto Glaze. Chill.
Refrigerate leftovers.
Makes one 9-inch cheesecake

Prep time: 30 minutes
Baking time: 1 hour

**CHOCOLATE AMARETTO
GLAZE:** In small saucepan, over
low heat, melt 1 (1-ounce) square
unsweetened chocolate with 1
tablespoon margarine or butter
and dash salt, stirring
constantly until smooth. Remove
from heat. Stir in 3/4 cup
confectioners' sugar, 3 to 4
teaspoons boiling water and 1 1/2
teaspoons amaretto. Stir until
smooth and well blended.
Immediately drizzle or spread
over cheesecake.
Makes about 1/3 cup glaze

Chocolate Chip Cheesecake Supreme

Chocolate Chip Cheesecake Supreme

**1 cup chocolate wafer
crumbs**
**3 tablespoons PARKAY®
Margarine, melted**
**3 (8 oz.) pkgs.
PHILADELPHIA BRAND®
Cream Cheese, softened**
3/4 cup sugar
1/4 cup flour
3 eggs
1/2 cup sour cream
1 teaspoon vanilla
**1 cup mini semi-sweet
chocolate pieces**

• Preheat oven to 350°F.

• Stir together crumbs and
margarine in small bowl. Press
onto bottom of 9-inch springform
pan. Bake 10 minutes.

• Reduce oven temperature to
325°F.

• Beat cream cheese, sugar and
flour in large mixing bowl at
medium speed with electric
mixer until well blended.

• Add eggs, one at a time,
mixing well after each addition.
Blend in sour cream and vanilla.
Stir in chocolate pieces. Pour
over crust.

• Bake 55 minutes.

• Loosen cake from rim of pan;
cool before removing rim of pan.
Chill. Garnish with whipped
cream and fresh mint, if desired.
Makes 10 to 12 servings

Prep time: 20 minutes plus
chilling
Baking time: 55 minutes

Mocha Cheesecake

> **Chocolate Cookie Crust
> (recipe follows)**
> **4 packages (3 ounces each)
> cream cheese, softened**
> **2½ tablespoons butter or
> margarine, softened**
> **1 cup sugar**
> **2 eggs**
> **5 tablespoons HERSHEY'S®
> Cocoa**
> **¾ teaspoon vanilla extract**
> **1 tablespoon powdered
> instant coffee**
> **1 teaspoon boiling water**
> **1 cup dairy sour cream**

Prepare Chocolate Cookie Crust;
set aside. Preheat oven to 325°F.
In large mixer bowl, beat
together cream cheese and
butter; gradually beat in sugar.
Add eggs, one at a time, beating
well after each addition. Beat in
cocoa and vanilla. Dissolve
instant coffee in water; stir into
cheese mixture. Add sour cream;
blend well. Pour into prepared
crust.

Bake 30 minutes. Turn off oven;
without opening door leave
cheesecake in oven 15 minutes.
Loosen cheesecake from rim of
pan; cool to room temperature.
Refrigerate several hours or
overnight. Remove rim of pan.
Refrigerate leftovers.

Makes 10 to 12 servings

Chocolate Cookie Crust

> **22 chocolate wafers (½ of
> 8½-ounce package)**
> **¼ cup cold butter or
> margarine, cut into
> ½-inch pieces**
> **⅛ teaspoon ground cinnamon**

Crush wafers in food processor or
blender to form fine crumbs. In
small bowl, mix crumbs, butter
and cinnamon until evenly
blended. Press mixture evenly on
bottom of 9-inch springform pan.

Easy Chocolate Cheesecake

> **2 packages (4 oz. each)
> BAKER'S® GERMAN'S®
> Sweet Chocolate**
> **⅓ cup heavy cream**
> **2 eggs**
> **⅔ cup corn syrup**
> **1½ teaspoons vanilla**
> **2 packages (8 oz. each)
> cream cheese, cut into
> cubes**
> **Crumb Crust (recipe
> follows)**

Microwave* 1½ packages (6 oz.)
of the chocolate and the cream in
microwavable bowl at HIGH 2
minutes. *Stir until chocolate is
completely melted.*

Blend eggs, corn syrup and
vanilla in blender until smooth.
With blender running, gradually
add cream cheese; blend until
smooth. Add chocolate; blend.

Pour into crust. Bake at 325°F
for 45 minutes or until set. Cool
on rack. Cover; chill. Melt
remaining 2 ounces chocolate,
drizzle over top.

Makes about 8 servings

*Range Top: Heat chocolate and
cream in saucepan over very low
heat, stirring until chocolate is
melted. Remove from heat;
continue as above.

Easy Chocolate Cheesecake

CRUMB CRUST: In 9-inch pie
plate or 9×3-inch springform
pan, combine 1¾ cups chocolate
cookie or graham cracker
crumbs, 2 tablespoons sugar and
⅓ cup butter or margarine,
melted, until well mixed. Press
evenly in pie plate or on bottom
and 1¼ inches up side of pan.

Praline Cheesecake

> **1 cup graham cracker
> crumbs**
> **3 tablespoons granulated
> sugar**
> **3 tablespoons PARKAY®
> Margarine, melted**
> **3 (8 oz.) pkgs.
> PHILADELPHIA BRAND®
> Cream Cheese, softened**
> **¾ cup packed dark brown
> sugar**
> **2 tablespoons flour**
> **3 eggs**
> **2 teaspoons vanilla**
> **½ cup finely chopped pecans
> LOG CABIN® Syrup
> Pecan halves**

• Preheat oven to 350°F.

• Stir together crumbs,
granulated sugar and margarine
in small bowl. Press onto bottom
of 9-inch springform pan. Bake
10 minutes.

• Increase oven temperature to
450°F.

• Beat cream cheese, brown
sugar and flour in large mixing
bowl at medium speed with
electric mixer until well blended.

• Add eggs, 1 at a time, mixing
well after each addition. Blend
in vanilla; stir in chopped
pecans. Pour over crust. Bake 10
minutes.

• Reduce oven temperature to
250°F; continue baking 30
minutes. Loosen cake from rim
of pan; cool before removing rim.
Chill. Brush with syrup and top
with pecan halves.

Makes 10 to 12 servings

Prep time: 25 minutes plus
chilling
Cooking time: 40 minutes

Strawberry Chocolate Chip Cheesecake

Pastry Crust (recipe follows)
3 packages (8 ounces each) cream cheese, softened
3/4 cup sugar
1 package (10 ounces) frozen sliced strawberries with syrup, thawed
2/3 cup all-purpose flour
3 eggs
1 teaspoon strawberry extract
4 or 5 drops red food color (optional)
1 cup HERSHEY'S® MINI CHIPS® Semi-Sweet Chocolate
Sweetened whipped cream (optional)
Fresh strawberries (optional)

Prepare Pastry Crust; set aside. *Decrease oven temperature to 350°F.*

In large mixer bowl, beat cream cheese and sugar until smooth. Puree strawberries with syrup in food processor or blender; add to cream cheese mixture. Blend in flour, eggs, strawberry extract and food color. Stir in MINI CHIPS® chocolate. Pour into prepared crust.

Bake 10 minutes; without opening oven door, *decrease oven temperature to 250°F;* continue baking 50 to 60 minutes or until set. Loosen cheesecake from rim of pan; cool to room temperature. Refrigerate several hours or overnight; remove rim of pan. Serve topped with sweetened whipped cream and strawberries.

Makes 10 to 12 servings

Pastry Crust

1/3 cup butter or margarine, softened
1/3 cup sugar
1 egg
1 1/4 cups all-purpose flour

Preheat oven to 450°F. In small mixer bowl, beat butter and sugar until creamy; blend in egg. Add flour; mix well. Spread dough on bottom and 1 1/2 inches up side of 9-inch springform pan. Bake 5 minutes; cool.

Double Lemon Cheesecake

1 1/4 cups graham cracker crumbs
1/4 cup sugar
1/3 cup margarine or butter, melted
4 (8-ounce) packages cream cheese, softened
1 (14-ounce) can EAGLE® Brand Sweetened Condensed Milk (NOT evaporated milk)
4 eggs
2 tablespoons flour
1/4 cup REALEMON® Lemon Juice from Concentrate
Lemon Glaze

Preheat oven to 350°F. Combine crumbs, sugar and margarine; press firmly on bottom of 9-inch springform pan.

In large mixer bowl, beat cheese until fluffy. Gradually beat in sweetened condensed milk until smooth. Add eggs and flour; mix well. Stir in REALEMON® brand. Pour into prepared pan.

Bake 1 hour or until lightly browned. Cool. Top with Lemon Glaze. Chill. Serve cheesecake with fresh strawberries if desired. Refrigerate leftovers.

Makes one 9-inch cheesecake

LEMON GLAZE: In small saucepan, combine 1/3 cup sugar, 1 tablespoon cornstarch and dash salt. Add 1/3 cup water, 1/4 cup REALEMON® brand and 1 egg yolk; mix well. Over medium heat, cook and stir until thickened and bubbly. Remove from heat; add 1 tablespoon margarine or butter. Stir until well blended. Cool slightly.

Makes about 3/4 cup glaze

Chocolate Festival Cheesecake

Cocoa Crumb Crust (page 150)
3 packages (8 ounces each) cream cheese, softened
1 1/4 cups sugar
1/4 cup HERSHEY'S® Cocoa
1/2 cup dairy sour cream
2 teaspoons vanilla extract
2 tablespoons all-purpose flour
3 eggs
Assorted fresh fruit, sliced (optional)
Sweetened whipped cream or whipped topping (optional)

Prepare Cocoa Crumb Crust; set aside. *Increase oven temperature to 450°F.*

In large mixer bowl, combine cream cheese, sugar, cocoa, sour cream and vanilla; beat on medium speed until smooth. Add flour and eggs; beat well. Pour into prepared crust.

Bake 10 minutes. Without opening oven, *decrease oven temperature to 250°F;* continue baking 30 minutes. (Cheesecake may not appear set in middle.) Turn off oven; leave cheesecake in oven 30 minutes without opening door. Remove from oven. Loosen cheesecake from rim of pan; cool to room temperature. Refrigerate several hours or overnight; remove rim of pan. Garnish with sliced fruit and whipped cream, if desired. Cover; refrigerate leftovers.

Makes 10 to 12 servings

Chocolate Festival Cheesecake

Fruit Melange Cheesecake

Graham Cracker Crumb Crust (recipe follows)
2½ **pounds cream cheese, softened**
¾ **cup whipping cream**
⅓ **cup fresh lemon juice**
1 **tablespoon vanilla**
1¾ **cups sugar**
8 **large eggs, slightly beaten**
1 **kiwi**
½ **small pineapple**
10 to 12 **strawberries**
6 **seeded black grapes or blackberries**
½ **cup red currant jelly**
1 **teaspoon water**

Prepare Graham Cracker Crumb Crust. Beat cream cheese in large bowl at medium speed until smooth. Gradually beat in cream, juice and vanilla; beat until smooth. Gradually beat in sugar. Add ¼ cup of eggs at a time, beating well after each addition.

Pour batter into prepared crust; smooth top. Bake in 350°F oven 70 minutes or until cake is set 3 inches in from edge and center is puddinglike. (For firmer cheesecake, bake 10 minutes longer or until center is just set.) Cool completely on wire rack, away from drafts. Remove sides of pan. Refrigerate, uncovered, at least 8 hours.

Top cheesecake with fruit 1 to 3 hours before serving. Cut kiwi and pineapple into small wedges or slices. Cut strawberries lengthwise in half. Arrange all fruit on cheesecake.

Melt jelly and water in small saucepan over low heat, stirring constantly. Brush evenly over fruit. Refrigerate, uncovered, at least 1 hour to set glaze. Serve cold.   *Makes 10 to 12 servings*

Graham Cracker Crumb Crust

1 to 2 **tablespoons butter, softened**
2 **cups graham cracker crumbs**
6 **tablespoons butter, melted**

Preheat oven to 350°F. Coat bottom and sides of 10-inch springform pan with softened butter. Thoroughly combine crumbs and melted butter. Press mixture on bottom and side of pan; refrigerate 5 minutes. Bake 5 minutes. Cool on wire rack 30 minutes before filling.

Rum Raisin Cheesecake

1 **cup old fashioned or quick oats, uncooked**
¼ **cup chopped nuts**
3 **tablespoons PARKAY® Margarine, melted**
3 **tablespoons packed brown sugar**
2 (8 oz.) **pkgs. PHILADELPHIA BRAND® Cream Cheese, softened**
⅓ **cup granulated sugar**
¼ **cup flour**
2 **eggs**
½ **cup sour cream**
3 **tablespoons rum**
2 **tablespoons PARKAY® Margarine**
⅓ **cup packed brown sugar**
⅓ **cup raisins**
¼ **cup chopped nuts**
2 **tablespoons old fashioned or quick oats, uncooked**

Fruit Melange Cheesecake

- Preheat oven to 350°F.
- Stir together 1 cup oats, ¼ cup nuts, 3 tablespoons margarine and 3 tablespoons brown sugar in small bowl. Press onto bottom of 9-inch springform pan. Bake 15 minutes.
- Beat cream cheese, granulated sugar and 2 tablespoons flour in large mixing bowl at medium speed with electric mixer until well blended.
- Add eggs, one at a time, mixing well after each addition. Blend in sour cream and rum; mix well. Pour over crust.
- Cut 2 tablespoons margarine into combined remaining 2 tablespoons flour and ⅓ cup brown sugar until mixture resembles coarse crumbs. Stir in raisins, ¼ cup nuts and 2 tablespoons oats. Sprinkle over cream cheese mixture.
- Bake 50 minutes. Loosen cake from rim of pan; cool before removing rim of pan. Chill.

Makes 10 to 12 servings

Prep time: 25 minutes plus chilling
Cooking time: 50 minutes

Citrus Fruit Cheesecake

    1 cup graham cracker
        crumbs
    ⅓ cup packed brown sugar
    ¼ cup PARKAY® Margarine,
        melted
    4 (8 oz.) pkgs.
        PHILADELPHIA BRAND®
        Cream Cheese, softened
    1 cup granulated sugar
    4 eggs
    2 tablespoons shredded
        orange peel
        Assorted sliced fresh fruit

- Preheat oven to 325°F.
- Stir crumbs, brown sugar and margarine in small bowl. Press onto bottom of 9-inch springform pan. Bake 10 minutes.
- Beat cream cheese and granulated sugar in large mixing bowl at medium speed

with electric mixer until well blended.
- Add eggs, one at a time, mixing well after each addition. Blend in peel; pour over crust.
- Bake 50 minutes.
- Loosen cake from rim of pan; cool before removing rim of pan. Chill.
- Top with fruit. Garnish with lime peel, if desired.

Makes 10 to 12 servings

Prep time: 20 minutes plus chilling
Cooking time: 50 minutes

Black-Eyed Susan Cheesecakes

    24 vanilla wafer cookies
    2 packages (8 ounces each)
        cream cheese, softened
    ½ cup sugar
    2 eggs
    ½ teaspoon vanilla extract
    1 cup REESE'S® Peanut
        Butter Chips
    ½ cup HERSHEY'S® Semi-
        Sweet Chocolate Chips
    3 tablespoons butter

Preheat oven to 350°F. Line muffin pans with foil-laminated paper bake cups (2 inches in diameter); place one vanilla wafer in bottom of each cup.

In large mixer bowl, beat together cream cheese and sugar. Add eggs and vanilla; beat well. Stir in peanut butter chips. Spoon 1 heaping tablespoon cream cheese mixture into each muffin cup.

Bake 15 minutes or just until set, but not browned. Cool.

In small microwave-safe bowl, place chocolate chips and butter. Microwave at HIGH (100%) 30 seconds to 1 minute or until chips are melted and mixture is smooth when stirred. Drop teaspoonfuls of chocolate mixture onto center of each cheesecake, letting white show around edge. Refrigerate; cover when chocolate is set.

Makes about 2 dozen cheesecakes

Party Chocolate Cheesecake Cups

    **Graham Shells (recipe
        follows)
    2 packages (8 ounces each)
        cream cheese, softened
    1 cup dairy sour cream
    1¼ cups sugar
    ⅓ cup HERSHEY'S® Cocoa
    2 tablespoons flour
    3 eggs
    1 teaspoon vanilla extract
    Sour Cream Topping
        (recipe follows)
    Cherry pie filling**

Prepare Graham Shells; set aside. Preheat oven to 350°F.

In large mixer bowl, beat cream cheese and sour cream. Stir together sugar, cocoa and flour; add to cream cheese mixture, blending well. Add eggs, 1 at a time, beating well after each addition. Blend in vanilla. Fill each prepared Graham Shell almost full with cheese mixture (mixture rises only slightly during baking.)

Bake 15 to 20 minutes or just until set. Turn off oven; let cheese cups remain in oven 45 minutes without opening door.

Prepare Sour Cream Topping; spread heaping teaspoonful on each cup. Cool completely; refrigerate. Garnish with dollop of cherry pie filling just before serving.

Makes 2 dozen cheesecakes

GRAHAM SHELLS: Line 24 muffin cups (2½ inches in diameter) with paper baking cups. In bowl, stir together 1½ cups graham cracker crumbs, ⅓ cup sugar and ¼ cup melted butter or margarine. Press about 1 tablespoon mixture onto bottom of each cup.

SOUR CREAM TOPPING: In bowl, stir together 1 cup dairy sour cream, 2 tablespoons sugar and 1 teaspoon vanilla extract; stir until sugar dissolves.

Mini Cheesecakes

1½ cups graham cracker or chocolate wafer crumbs
¼ cup sugar
¼ cup margarine or butter, melted
3 (8-ounce) packages cream cheese, softened
1 (14-ounce) can EAGLE® Brand Sweetened Condensed Milk (NOT evaporated milk)
3 eggs
2 teaspoons vanilla extract
Fruit preserves or fresh fruit, optional

Preheat oven to 300°F. Grease* or paper-line 24 (2½-inch) muffin cups. Combine crumbs, sugar and margarine; press equal portions onto bottoms of prepared muffin cups. In large mixer bowl, beat cheese until fluffy. Gradually beat in sweetened condensed milk until smooth. Add eggs and vanilla; mix well. Spoon equal amounts of mixture (about 3 tablespoons) into prepared cups.

Bake 20 minutes or until cakes spring back when lightly touched or until set. Cool. Chill. Garnish with fruit preserves or fresh fruit if desired. Refrigerate leftovers.

Makes about 2 dozen cheesecakes

*If greased muffin cups are used, cool baked cheesecakes. Freeze 15 minutes; remove from pans. Proceed as above.

Chocolate: Add 1 (6-ounce) package semi-sweet chocolate chips (1 cup), melted, to batter; mix well. Proceed as above. Bake 20 to 25 minutes.

Prep time: 35 minutes
Baking time: 20 minutes

Mini Cheesecakes

Cheesecake Macaroon Bars

1 cup flour
1 cup ground almonds
½ cup PARKAY® Margarine, softened
⅓ cup packed brown sugar
¼ teaspoon salt
¼ teaspoon almond extract
2 (8 oz.) pkgs. PHILADELPHIA BRAND® Cream Cheese, softened
¾ cup granulated sugar
1 tablespoon lemon juice
3 eggs
1½ cups BAKER'S® ANGEL FLAKE® Coconut, toasted
1½ cups sour cream
3 tablespoons granulated sugar
2 teaspoons vanilla

• Preheat oven to 350°F.
• Beat flour, almonds, margarine, brown sugar, salt and extract in small mixing bowl at medium speed with electric mixer until blended. Press onto bottom of 13×9-inch baking pan.
• Bake 8 to 10 minutes or until lightly browned.
• Beat cream cheese, ¾ cup granulated sugar and lemon juice in large mixing bowl at medium speed with electric mixer until well blended.
• Add eggs, one at a time, mixing well after each addition. Stir in 1 cup coconut; pour over crust.
• Bake 25 minutes. Cool 5 minutes.
• Stir together sour cream, 3 tablespoons granulated sugar and vanilla in small bowl until smooth; carefully spread over coconut mixture.
• Bake 5 to 7 minutes or until set. Sprinkle with remaining ½ cup coconut; cool. Cut into bars.
Makes about 3 dozen bars

Prep time: 30 minutes plus cooling
Cooking time: 32 minutes

German Chocolate Cheesecake Squares

1½ cups graham cracker crumbs
½ cup sugar
½ cup margarine or butter, melted
3 (8-ounce) packages cream cheese, softened
1 (14-ounce) can EAGLE® Brand Sweetened Condensed Milk (NOT evaporated milk)
2 (4-ounce) packages sweet cooking chocolate, melted
3 eggs
1 tablespoon vanilla extract
Coconut Pecan Topping

German Chocolate Cheesecake Squares

Preheat oven to 350°F. Combine crumbs, sugar and margarine; press in bottom of 15×10-inch jellyroll pan. In large mixer bowl, beat cheese until fluffy. Gradually beat in sweetened condensed milk until smooth. Add remaining ingredients except Coconut Pecan Topping; mix well. Pour mixture into prepared pan.

Bake 20 minutes or until center is set. Cool. Top with Coconut Pecan Topping. Chill. Cut into squares. Garnish as desired. Refrigerate leftovers.

Makes one 12 to 15 servings

COCONUT PECAN TOPPING: In heavy saucepan, combine 1 (14-ounce) can EAGLE® Brand Sweetened Condensed Milk (NOT evaporated milk) and 3 egg yolks; mix well. Add ½ cup margarine or butter. Over medium-low heat, cook and stir until thickened and bubbly, 8 to 10 minutes. Remove from heat; stir in 1 (3½-ounce) can flaked coconut (1⅓ cups), 1 cup chopped pecans and 1 teaspoon vanilla. Cool 10 minutes.

Makes about 2¾ cups topping

Prep time: 30 minutes
Baking time: 20 minutes

Peanut Butter Cheesecake Squares

Base
1½ cups graham cracker crumbs
3 tablespoons sugar
¼ cup BUTTER FLAVOR CRISCO®, melted
1 tablespoon milk
Filling
1 package (3 ounces) cream cheese, softened
¼ cup JIF® Creamy Peanut Butter
¼ cup sugar
¼ cup milk
1 egg
½ cup chopped peanuts
Drizzle
¼ cup semi-sweet chocolate chips
1 teaspoon BUTTER FLAVOR CRISCO®

1. Preheat oven to 350°F. For Base, combine crumbs and sugar in small bowl. Combine melted BUTTER FLAVOR CRISCO® and milk; stir in crumbs. Press lightly into 8×8×2-inch pan. Bake 20 to 22 minutes.
2. For Filling, beat cream cheese and peanut butter in small bowl at medium speed of electric mixer until well blended. Add sugar, milk and egg; beat well. Stir in chopped nuts. Spread over baked crust; return to oven. Bake 20 to 22 minutes, or until cheesecake is set.
3. For Drizzle, melt chocolate chips and BUTTER FLAVOR CRISCO® on very low heat or at 50% power in microwave. Stir to combine. Drizzle from end of spoon back and forth over top of cheesecake. Chill. Cut into 2×2-inch squares. Cover; store in refrigerator.

Makes 16 squares

Hint: Graham cracker crumbs can be made using a food processor or rolling pin. Store extra crumbs in tightly covered container.

Preparation time: 20 minutes
Bake time: 20 to 22 minutes

Two-Tone Cheesecake Bars

2 cups finely crushed creme-filled chocolate sandwich cookies (about 24 cookies)
3 tablespoons margarine or butter, melted
3 (8-ounce) packages cream cheese, softened
1 (14-ounce) can EAGLE® Brand Sweetened Condensed Milk (NOT evaporated milk)
3 eggs
2 teaspoons vanilla extract
2 (1-ounce) squares unsweetened chocolate, melted
Easy Chocolate Icing

Preheat oven to 300°F. Combine crumbs and margarine; press firmly in bottom of 13×9-inch baking pan. In large mixer bowl, beat cheese until fluffy. Gradually beat in sweetened condensed milk until smooth. Add eggs and vanilla; mix well. Pour half the batter evenly over prepared crust. Stir melted chocolate into remaining batter; pour evenly over yellow batter.

Bake 55 to 60 minutes or until set. Cool. Top with Easy Chocolate Icing. Chill. Cut into bars. Refrigerate leftovers.

Makes 24 to 36 bars

EASY CHOCOLATE ICING: In small saucepan, over low heat, melt 2 (1-ounce) squares unsweetened chocolate with 2 tablespoons margarine or butter and a dash salt. Remove from heat; add 1¾ cups confectioners' sugar and 3 tablespoons hot water; mix well. *Immediately* spread over bars.

Makes about 1 cup icing

PIES & TARTS

What better way to show off your baking skills than with a glorious pie or tart bursting with seasonal fruit. Tart crisp apples, sweet red cherries, and juicy ripe peaches are just a few of the fruits enveloped in tender, flaky pie crusts. Airy meringue, crunchy nut and decadent chocolate pies will add variety to your repertoire. (For additional pie recipes, see the Jump-Start Baking and Festive Holiday Baking chapters.)

Toll House® Pie

2 eggs
½ cup all-purpose flour
½ cup granulated sugar
½ cup firmly packed light brown sugar
¾ cup (1½ sticks) butter, softened
One 6-oz. pkg. (1 cup) NESTLÉ® Toll House® Semi-Sweet Chocolate Morsels
1 cup walnuts, chopped
One 9-inch unbaked pie shell* Whipped cream or ice cream, optional

Preheat oven to 325°F. In large mixer bowl, beat eggs at high speed until foamy, about 3 minutes. Beat in flour, granulated sugar and brown sugar until well blended. Beat in butter. Stir in semi-sweet chocolate morsels and walnuts. Pour into pie shell.

Bake 55 to 60 minutes until knife inserted halfway between edge and center comes out clean and top is golden brown. Cool completely. Serve with whipped cream or ice cream.

Makes 6 to 8 servings

*If using frozen pie shell, use deep-dish style; thaw completely. Place on cookie sheet; increase baking time by 10 minutes.

Chocolate Hazelnut Tart

Crust:
1 cup all-purpose flour
¼ cup sugar
3 tablespoons NESTLÉ® Cocoa
¼ teaspoon baking soda
⅛ teaspoon salt
¼ cup (½ stick) butter
1 egg
Filling:
3 foil-wrapped bars (6 oz.) NESTLÉ® Semi-Sweet Chocolate Baking Bars
2 eggs
2 egg yolks
½ cup sugar
½ cup light corn syrup
2 tablespoons butter, softened
2 cups finely chopped hazelnuts, toasted

Crust: Preheat oven to 325°F. In small mixer bowl, mix flour, sugar, cocoa, baking soda and salt. With pastry blender or 2 knives, cut in butter until mixture is crumbly. Stir in egg. Press dough onto bottom and up sides of 9-inch tart pan with removable bottom. Bake 20 minutes.

Filling: Melt semi-sweet chocolate baking bars; set aside. In small mixer bowl, beat eggs, egg yolks, sugar and corn syrup until blended. Beat in butter and melted chocolate. Stir in hazelnuts. Pour into Crust. Bake 30 minutes or until Filling is set. Cool completely. Remove tart from pan.

Makes 6 to 8 servings

Toll House® Pie

CLASSIC CRISCO® CRUST

8, 9 or 10-Inch Single Crust
1⅓ cups all-purpose flour
½ teaspoon salt
½ cup CRISCO® Shortening
3 tablespoons cold water

8 or 9-Inch Double Crust
2 cups all-purpose flour
1 teaspoon salt
¾ cup CRISCO® Shortening
5 tablespoons cold water

10-Inch Double Crust
2⅔ cups all-purpose flour
1 teaspoon salt
1 cup CRISCO® Shortening
7 to 8 tablespoons cold water

1. Spoon flour into measuring cup and level. Combine flour and salt in medium bowl.

2. Cut in CRISCO® using pastry blender (or 2 knives) until flour is blended to form pea-size chunks.

3. Sprinkle with water, 1 tablespoon at a time. Toss lightly with fork until dough will form a ball.

For Single Crust Pies

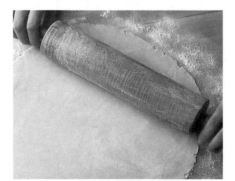

4. Press dough between hands to form 5- to 6-inch "pancake." Flour rolling surface and rolling pin lightly. Roll dough into circle. (Or, flour "pancake" lightly on both sides. Roll between sheets of waxed paper or plastic wrap on dampened countertop.)

5. Trim 1 inch larger than upside-down pie plate. Loosen dough carefully.

6. Fold dough into quarters. Unfold and press into pie plate. Fold edge under and flute.

7. For recipes using a **baked** pie crust, heat oven to 425°F. Prick bottom and sides thoroughly with fork (50 times) to prevent shrinkage. Bake 10 to 15 minutes or until lightly browned.

For recipes using an **unbaked** pie crust, follow baking directions given in that recipe.

For Double Crust Pies

1. Divide dough in half. Roll each half separately. Transfer bottom crust to pie plate. Trim edge evenly with pie plate. Moisten pastry edge with water.

2. Add desired filling to unbaked pie crust. Lift top crust onto filled pie. Trim ½ inch beyond edge of pie plate. Fold top edge under bottom crust. Flute. Cut slits in top crust to allow steam to escape.

3. Bake according to specific recipe directions.

Decorative Tips
Fork Edge

Press pastry to rim of pie plate using 4-tined fork. Leave about 1¼ inches between marks. Go around crust edge again, filling in spaces with fork held at an angle.

Woven Lattice Top

1. Leave overhang on bottom crust. Cut top crust into ten ½-inch strips. Place 5 strips evenly across filling. Fold every other strip back. Lay first strip across in opposite direction.

2. Continue in this pattern, folding back every other strip each time you add a cross strip.

3. Trim ends of lattice strips even with crust overhang. Press together, fold edge under and flute.

Rope Edge

Fold overhang under and make stand-up edge. Press thumb into pastry at an angle. Pinch pastry between thumb and knuckle of index finger, rolling knuckle towards thumb. Place thumb in groove left by finger and continue around edge.

Cutouts

Trim edge even with pie plate. Cut desired shapes (about ¾ inch in size) from remaining pastry using small cookie cutter, thimble or bottle cap. Moisten pastry edge. Place cutouts on pastry edge, slightly overlapping. Press into place.

Lemon Pastry

1 cup unsifted flour
½ teaspoon salt
⅓ cup shortening
1 egg
1 tablespoon REALEMON®
Lemon Juice from
Concentrate

Preheat oven to 400°F. In medium bowl, combine flour and salt; cut in shortening until crumbly. In small bowl, beat egg and REALEMON® brand; sprinkle over flour mixture. Stir until dough forms a ball. On floured surface, roll out to about ⅛-inch thickness. Line 9-inch pie plate; flute edges. Prick with fork. Bake 12 to 15 minutes or until golden.

Makes one 9-inch pastry shell

Prep time: 5 minutes
Baking time: 15 minutes

Brownie Fudge Pie

1 can (14 ounces) sweetened
condensed milk
½ cup DROSTE® Cocoa
¼ cup butter or margarine
3 eggs, beaten
3 tablespoons all-purpose
flour
1 teaspoon vanilla
1 cup pecans, chopped
1 cup flaked coconut
1 (9-inch) unbaked pie shell
Whipped cream

Preheat oven to 350°F. In medium saucepan, combine sweetened condensed milk, DROSTE® Cocoa and butter. Stir over low heat until butter is melted and mixture is well blended. Remove from heat; cool slightly. Stir in eggs, flour, vanilla, pecans and coconut; mix well. Pour into unbaked pie shell.

Bake 50 minutes or until center is firm. Cool on wire rack. Serve warm with whipped cream.

Makes about 10 servings

Chocolate Mousse Filled Tartlets

Chocolate Custard Pie

1 (9-inch) unbaked pastry
shell
2 (1-ounce) squares semi-
sweet chocolate
1 (14-ounce) can EAGLE®
Brand Sweetened
Condensed Milk (NOT
evaporated milk)
3 eggs, well beaten
1½ cups water
2 teaspoons vanilla extract
1 (4-ounce) container frozen
non-dairy whipped
topping, thawed

Preheat oven to 425°F. In heavy saucepan, over low heat, melt chocolate with sweetened condensed milk. Remove from heat. Stir in eggs; mix well. Add water and vanilla; mix well. Pour into pastry shell.

Bake 10 minutes. *Reduce oven temperature to 300°F;* continue baking 25 to 30 minutes or until knife inserted near center comes out clean. Cool. Chill. Spread whipped topping over pie. Refrigerate leftovers.

Makes one 9-inch pie

Chocolate Mousse Filled Tartlets

½ cup butter or margarine,
softened
1 package (3 ounces) cream
cheese, softened
¼ cup confectioners' sugar
1 cup all-purpose flour
Chocolate Mousse Filling
(recipe follows)
Whipped cream, fresh
strawberries, chopped
nuts or chocolate curls

In small mixer bowl, cream butter and cream cheese. Add confectioners' sugar; beat until smooth and fluffy. Add flour; blend thoroughly. Cover; chill about 1 hour.

Preheat oven to 350°F. Shape chilled mixture into 2 dozen 1-inch balls; place each ball into ungreased 1¾-inch muffin cup. Press dough onto bottoms and sides of cups.

Bake 15 minutes or until edges are brown. Cool on wire rack; remove from pans. Prepare Chocolate Mousse Filling. With star tip in pastry bag, pipe mousse into tart shells. (Or, spoon mousse into shells, if desired.) Garnish with whipped cream, strawberries, chopped nuts or chocolate curls. Chill about 1 hour.

Makes 24 tartlets

Chocolate Mousse Filling

1 teaspoon unflavored
gelatin
1 tablespoon cold water
2 tablespoons boiling water
½ cup sugar
¼ cup HERSHEY'S® Cocoa
1 cup chilled whipping cream
1 teaspoon vanilla extract

In custard cup, sprinkle gelatin over cold water; let stand 1 minute to soften. Add boiling water; stir until gelatin is completely dissolved and mixture is clear. Cool slightly.

In small cold mixer bowl, stir together sugar and cocoa. Add whipping cream and vanilla;

whipping cream and vanilla; beat on medium speed, scraping bottom of bowl occasionally, until stiff peaks form. Pour in gelatin mixture; beat until well blended.
Makes about 2 cups filling

Chocolate Amaretto Pie

1 (9-inch) unbaked pastry shell
1 (3-ounce) package cream cheese, softened
2 (1-ounce) squares unsweetened chocolate, melted
1/8 teaspoon salt
1 (14-ounce) can EAGLE® Brand Sweetened Condensed Milk (NOT evaporated milk)
2 eggs
1/4 to 1/3 cup amaretto liqueur
1 cup sliced or chopped almonds, toasted if desired

Preheat oven to 350°F. In large mixer bowl, beat cheese, chocolate and salt until well blended. Gradually beat in sweetened condensed milk until smooth. Add eggs; mix well. Stir in liqueur and almonds. Pour into pastry shell.

Bake 30 to 35 minutes or until center is set. Cool. Serve warm or chilled. Garnish as desired. Refrigerate leftovers.
Makes one 9-inch pie

Prep time: 15 minutes
Baking time: 35 minutes

Chocolate Amaretto Pie

Caramel Apple Pie

2 1/2 cups thinly sliced Jonathan apples
1/2 cup sugar
1/4 cup flour
25 caramels, unwrapped
3 tablespoons milk
1 PET-RITZ® Regular Pie Crust Shell
1/2 cup chopped pecans LA CREME® Whipped Topping, thawed

Preheat oven and baking sheet to 400°F. In medium bowl, combine apples, sugar and flour; set aside. In top of double boiler over hot (not boiling) water, melt caramels with milk, stirring frequently. Stir in apple mixture. Spoon mixture into pie shell; top with nuts.

Place pie in oven on baking sheet. Bake 25 minutes. Cool at least 1 hour. Serve warm or cold; top with whipped topping.
Makes about 6 servings

Daisy Apple Pie

Crust
Unbaked 9-inch Classic CRISCO® *Double* Crust prepared with BUTTER FLAVOR CRISCO® (page 166)
Filling
5 or 6 large Rambo or Granny Smith apples, peeled and sliced
1/2 to 1 cup firmly packed brown sugar
2 tablespoons quick cooking tapioca
1/4 teaspoon cinnamon
1/8 teaspoon nutmeg
2 tablespoons butter or margarine, melted
1 tablespoon lemon juice
1 teaspoon vanilla
Glaze
1 egg
3 or 4 tablespoons milk
1 teaspoon granulated sugar

1. Preheat oven to 400°F. For Filling, combine apples, brown sugar, tapioca, spices, butter, juice and vanilla. Spoon into unbaked pie shell. Moisten pastry edge with water.

2. Cover with top crust. Fold top edge under bottom crust; flute with fingers or fork. Cut slits or design in top crust or prick with fork for escape of steam.

3. For Glaze, combine egg and milk in small bowl. Brush on top crust; sprinkle with sugar.

4. Bake 10 minutes. *Reduce oven temperature to 350°F.* Bake for 40 minutes. Cool until barely warm or to room temperature.
Makes one 9-inch pie

Deep Dish Apple-Cot Pie

Pastry for 1-crust pie
3 pounds all-purpose apples, cored, pared and sliced (about 8 cups)
1 tablespoon REALEMON® Lemon Juice from Concentrate
1/2 cup unsifted flour
1/2 to 3/4 cup sugar
1 1/2 teaspoons ground cinnamon
1 teaspoon ground nutmeg
1 (16-ounce) jar BAMA® Apricot or Peach Preserves
1 egg yolk plus 2 tablespoons water, optional

Preheat oven to 375°F. In large bowl, sprinkle apples with REALEMON® brand. Combine flour, sugar and spices; toss with apples. Add preserves; mix well. Turn into well-buttered 12×7-inch baking dish.

Roll pastry 1 1/2 inches larger than baking dish; cut slits near center. Place pastry over apples; turn under edges, seal and flute. For a more golden crust, mix egg yolk and water; brush over pie. Bake 40 to 45 minutes or until golden brown. Serve warm.
Makes 8 to 10 servings

Maple Apple Pie

Crust
> Unbaked 9-inch Classic
> **CRISCO®** *Double* Crust
> (page 166)

Filling
> **7 cups peeled, sliced baking**
>   **apples (about**
>   **2½ pounds)**
> **¾ cup pure maple syrup***
> **2 tablespoons cornstarch**

Nut Layer
> **½ cup chopped pecans**
> **2 tablespoons pure maple**
>   **syrup***
> **1 teaspoon butter or**
>   **margarine**

Glaze
> **1 tablespoon pure maple**
>   **syrup***

1. Preheat oven to 375°F.

2. For Filling, place apple slices in large microwave-safe bowl; cover with waxed paper. Microwave at 100% (HIGH) 2 minutes; stir. Repeat 2 times or until apples start to soften.

3. Combine syrup and cornstarch in microwave-safe measuring cup; stir. Microwave at 100% (HIGH) 2 minutes; stir. Repeat until mixture starts to thicken. Pour over cooked apples. Cool.

4. For Nut Layer, combine pecans, syrup and butter in small microwave-safe bowl. Microwave at 100% (HIGH) 1 minute; stir. Microwave at 50% (MEDIUM) 1 minute; stir to break up. Cool.

5. Spoon filling into unbaked pie shell. Top with nut mixture. Moisten pastry edge with water.

6. Roll top crust same as bottom. Cut into ten ½-inch strips. Make lattice top over filling. Trim ends of strips even with crust overhang; press together. Fold edge under; flute with fingers or fork.

7. Bake 1 hour or until apples start to bubble. Remove from oven.

8. For Glaze, brush syrup on top crust. Return to oven for 5 minutes. Cool until barely warm or to room temperature before serving.

Makes one 9-inch pie

*Substitute maple flavor pancake and waffle syrup, if desired.

Apple Walnut Upside-Down Pie

> **Pastry for 2-crust pie**
> **¼ cup firmly packed light**
>   **brown sugar**
> **2 tablespoons margarine or**
>   **butter, melted**
> **½ cup chopped walnuts**
> **2 pounds all-purpose apples,**
>   **cored, pared and sliced**
>   **(about 5 cups)**
> **⅔ to 1 cup granulated sugar**
> **2 to 3 tablespoons flour**
> **2 tablespoons REALEMON®**
>   **Lemon Juice from**
>   **Concentrate**
> **1 teaspoon ground cinnamon**

Preheat oven to 400°F. In 9-inch pie plate, combine brown sugar and margarine; spread over bottom. Sprinkle nuts evenly over sugar mixture.

Apple Walnut Upside-Down Pie

Divide pastry in half; roll each into 12-inch circle. Carefully line prepared pie plate with 1 pastry circle; *do not press* into nut mixture. Trim even with edge of plate.

Combine remaining ingredients; turn into prepared pie plate. Cover with remaining pastry circle; prick with fork. Trim top crust even with edge of plate; seal crust edges with water. Roll edges *toward center* of pie (crust edge should *not* touch rim of plate). Place aluminum-foil-lined baking sheet on bottom oven rack to catch drippings.

Bake 40 to 45 minutes or until golden brown. Let stand 2 minutes; carefully run knife tip around edge of pie plate to loosen pie. Invert onto serving plate. Serve warm with ice cream if desired.

Makes one 9-inch pie

Apple Pie with Cheddar Pastry

Crust:
> **1⅔ cups sifted all-purpose**
>   **flour**
> **¼ teaspoon salt**
> **1 cup (4 oz.) finely shredded**
>   **sharp Wisconsin**
>   **Cheddar cheese**
> **½ cup (1 stick) butter, chilled,**
>   **cut into ½-inch pieces**
> **¼ cup ice water**

Filling:
> **5 to 6 cups baking apples,**
>   **pared, cored and thinly**
>   **sliced**
> **½ to ⅔ cup granulated or**
>   **brown sugar**
> **1 tablespoon cornstarch**
> **¼ teaspoon cinnamon**
> **⅛ teaspoon nutmeg**
> **⅛ teaspoon salt**
> **2 tablespoons butter**

For crust: Preheat oven to 450°F. In large bowl, sift together flour and salt. Stir in cheese; mix well. Cut in butter, using pastry blender or two knives, until mixture resembles coarse crumbs. Sprinkle with water, 1 tablespoon at a time, until flour is moistened and dough almost cleans side of bowl. Divide dough in half; shape each half into flattened round. Roll out each half separately on lightly floured surface into 11-inch circle. Carefully fit one crust into 9-inch pie plate.

For filling: Place apples in large bowl. Combine sugar, cornstarch, spices and salt in small bowl; sprinkle over apples. Stir gently until well coated.

Spoon filling into pie shell; dot with butter. Cover with top crust; cut slits in center to allow steam to escape. Fold edge of top crust under edge of bottom crust; flute edge.

Bake 10 minutes. *Reduce oven temperature to 350°F;* continue baking an additional 35 to 40 minutes. Cool on wire rack.

Makes 6 to 8 servings

Favorite recipe from **Wisconsin Milk Marketing Board** ©*1991*

Streusel-Topped Apple Custard Pie

Applesauce Spice Pie

- 1 (9-inch) unbaked pastry shell
- 1 (16-ounce) jar applesauce
- ³/₄ cup firmly packed light brown sugar
- 4 eggs
- ¹/₄ cup REALEMON® Lemon Juice from Concentrate
- 2 tablespoons margarine or butter, melted
- 1 tablespoon flour
- ³/₄ teaspoon salt
- ¹/₂ teaspoon ground cinnamon
- ¹/₄ teaspoon ground nutmeg

Preheat oven to 425°F. In large mixer bowl, combine all ingredients except pastry shell; mix well. Pour into pastry shell. Bake 15 minutes. *Reduce oven temperature to 325°F;* bake 30 minutes longer or until wooden toothpick inserted near edge comes out clean. Cool. Serve warm with ice cream or whipped cream if desired. Refrigerate leftovers.

Makes one 9-inch pie

Streusel-Topped Apple Custard Pie

- 1 (9-inch) unbaked pastry shell
- 4 medium all-purpose apples, pared and sliced (about 4 cups)
- 2 eggs
- 1 (14-ounce) can EAGLE® Brand Sweetened Condensed Milk (NOT evaporated milk)
- ¹/₄ cup margarine or butter, melted
- ¹/₂ teaspoon ground cinnamon Dash ground nutmeg
- ¹/₂ cup firmly packed light brown sugar
- ¹/₂ cup unsifted flour
- ¹/₄ cup cold margarine or butter
- ¹/₄ cup chopped nuts

Place rack in lower third of oven; preheat oven to 425°F. Arrange apples in pastry shell. In medium bowl, beat eggs. Add sweetened condensed milk, melted margarine, cinnamon and nutmeg; mix well. Pour over apples. In medium bowl, combine brown sugar and flour; cut in cold margarine until crumbly. Stir in nuts; sprinkle over pie.

Bake 10 minutes. *Reduce oven temperature to 375°F;* continue baking 35 to 40 minutes or until golden brown. Cool. Refrigerate leftovers.

Makes one 9-inch pie

Harvest Fruit Custard Tart

1 (9- or 10-inch) unbaked
    pastry shell
1½ cups BORDEN® or
    MEADOW GOLD® Sour
    Cream
1 (14-ounce) can EAGLE®
    Brand Sweetened
    Condensed Milk (NOT
    evaporated milk)
¼ cup frozen apple juice
    concentrate, thawed
1 egg
1½ teaspoons vanilla extract
¼ teaspoon ground cinnamon
¾ pound all-purpose apples
    or pears, cored, pared
    and thinly sliced (about
    2 cups)
1 tablespoon margarine or
    butter
    Cinnamon Glaze

Preheat oven to 375°F. Bake
pastry shell 15 minutes.
Meanwhile, in large mixer bowl,
beat sour cream, sweetened
condensed milk, juice
concentrate, egg, vanilla and
cinnamon; pour into prepared
pastry shell.

Bake 30 minutes or until set.
Cool. In skillet, cook apples in
margarine until tender-crisp.
Arrange on pie; drizzle with
Cinnamon Glaze. Refrigerate
leftovers.

Makes one 9- or 10-inch pie

CINNAMON GLAZE: In small
saucepan, mix ¼ cup thawed
frozen apple juice concentrate,
1 teaspoon cornstarch and ¼
teaspoon ground cinnamon; cook
and stir until thickened.

Makes about ¼ cup glaze

Harvest Fruit Custard Tart

Orange Blossom Pie

**1 (14-ounce) can EAGLE®
   Brand Sweetened
   Condensed Milk (NOT
   evaporated milk)
4 egg yolks
1/2 cup orange juice
1 tablespoon grated orange
   rind
1 (6-ounce) packaged
   graham cracker crumb
   pie crust
1 (3-ounce) package cream
   cheese, softened
1/3 cup confectioners' sugar
1/4 cup BORDEN® or MEADOW
   GOLD® Sour Cream
1/4 teaspoon vanilla extract**

Preheat oven to 325°F. In large bowl, combine sweetened condensed milk, egg yolks, orange juice and rind; mix well. Pour into crust (mixture will be thin).

Bake 35 minutes or until knife inserted near center comes out clean.

Meanwhile, in small mixer bowl, combine remaining ingredients; beat until smooth. Spread evenly over pie. Bake 10 minutes longer. Cool. Chill. Garnish as desired. Refrigerate leftovers.
Makes 6 to 8 servings

California Plum Flan

**1 pie crust stick
   (5½ ounces), plus
   ingredients to prepare
   pie crust
Yogurt Custard (recipe
   follows)
2 cups fresh California
   plums, sliced
3 tablespoons apricot
   preserves, sieved**

Preheat oven to 400°F. Prepare pie crust according to package directions. Roll out pie crust; line bottom and side of 9-inch flan pan. Turn edge under and flute. Prick bottom and sides with fork. Bake 15 minutes or until golden. Cool.

Pour Yogurt Custard into cooled shell; return to oven 8 to 10 minutes or until barely set. Chill. Arrange plums decoratively over flan. Brush with apricot preserves.
Makes about 6 servings

YOGURT CUSTARD: Combine 1 cup plain low-fat yogurt, 2 egg yolks, 1/4 cup sugar, 2 tablespoons flour and 1/4 teaspoon orange zest.

*Favorite recipe from **California Tree Fruit Agreement***

Whole Wheat Pear Pie

**Whole Wheat Pie Shell
   (recipe follows)
4 to 5 Western winter pears
2/3 cup whole wheat flour
1/2 cup granulated sugar
1 teaspoon ground cinnamon
2 tablespoons lemon juice
1/4 cup packed brown sugar
1/4 cup butter or margarine,
   softened
Additional pear slices
   (optional)**

Preheat oven to 350°F. Prepare Whole Wheat Pie Shell. Core and slice unpeeled pears.

In large bowl, toss pear slices with 2 tablespoons of the flour, the granulated sugar, 3/4 teaspoon of the cinnamon and the lemon juice. Spoon into unbaked pie shell. In small bowl, combine brown sugar, butter, remaining flour and remaining 1/4 teaspoon cinnamon; sprinkle over top of pie.

Bake 50 minutes. If desired, garnish with additional pear slices. *Makes one 9-inch pie*

WHOLE WHEAT PIE SHELL: In medium bowl, combine 1¼ cups whole wheat flour, 2 tablespoons granulated sugar, 1/3 cup vegetable oil and 3 tablespoons milk; mix well. (Mixture will be crumbly.) Press onto bottom and side of 9-inch pie plate.

*Favorite recipe from **Oregon Washington California Pear Bureau***

California Plum Flan

Peach Pie

Crust
Unbaked 10-inch Classic
CRISCO® *Double* Crust
prepared with ½ cup
CRISCO® and ½ cup
BUTTER FLAVOR
CRISCO® (page 166)

Filling
1 can (1 pound 13 ounces)
yellow cling peaches in
heavy syrup
3 tablespoons cornstarch
1 cup sugar, divided
3 tablespoons reserved
peach syrup
3 eggs
⅓ cup buttermilk
½ cup butter or margarine,
melted
1 teaspoon vanilla

Glaze
2 tablespoons butter or
margarine, melted
2 tablespoons sugar

1. Preheat oven to 400°F.

2. For Filling, drain peaches, reserving 3 tablespoons syrup. Cut peaches into small pieces; place in large bowl.

3. Combine cornstarch and 2 to 3 tablespoons sugar in medium bowl. Stir in reserved peach syrup. Add remaining sugar, eggs and buttermilk; mix well. Stir in melted butter and vanilla; pour over peaches. Stir until peaches are coated.

4. Pour filling into unbaked pie shell. Moisten pastry edge with water; cover with top crust. Fold top edge under bottom crust; flute with fingers or fork. Cut slits or design in top crust or prick with fork for escape of steam.

5. For Glaze, brush top crust with melted butter; sprinkle with sugar.

6. Bake 45 minutes. Cool to room temperature before serving.

Makes one 10-inch pie

Peach Tart

Crust
1 cup all-purpose flour,
divided
½ teaspoon salt
¼ cup CRISCO® Oil
2 tablespoons plus
1½ teaspoons cold water

Filling
5 tablespoons peach
preserves, divided
¼ cup flour
6 fresh peaches, peeled and
sliced, *or* 2 cans
(16 ounces each) peach
slices, drained
1 teaspoon hot water

Glaze
3 tablespoons peach
preserves

1. Preheat oven to 375°F.

2. For Crust, combine flour and salt in small bowl; set aside.

3. Beat CRISCO® Oil and cold water in small bowl until thickened and creamy; add immediately to flour mixture. Stir with fork until ingredients are moistened. (If dough seems dry, add 1 to 2 tablespoons CRISCO® Oil.)

4. Shape pastry into ball; flatten slightly. Place pastry between sheets of waxed paper. Roll into circle at least 2 inches larger than inverted 9-inch pie plate or quiche dish. Remove waxed paper; fit dough into pie plate. Trim and flute edges.

5. For Filling, combine 3 tablespoons peach preserves and flour in small bowl; stir well. Spread in bottom of pastry shell. Arrange peach slices, overlapping slightly, in pastry shell. Mix remaining 2 tablespoons peach preserves and hot water in small bowl; brush on peaches.

6. Bake 40 to 45 minutes, or until peaches are tender and pastry is light brown.

7. For Glaze, heat 3 tablespoons peach preserves in small saucepan on moderate heat; brush over peaches. Cool completely.

Makes one 9-inch tart

Peach Amaretto Cheese Pie

1 (9-inch) unbaked pastry
shell
1 (8-ounce) package cream
cheese, softened
1 (14-ounce) can EAGLE®
Brand Sweetened
Condensed Milk (NOT
evaporated milk)
2 eggs
3 tablespoons amaretto
liqueur
1½ teaspoons almond extract
3 medium peaches, peeled,
seeded and sliced *or*
1 (16-ounce) package
frozen peach slices,
thawed and well drained
2 tablespoons BAMA® Peach
Preserves

Preheat oven to 375°F. Bake pastry shell 15 minutes. Meanwhile, in large mixer bowl, beat cheese until fluffy. Gradually beat in sweetened condensed milk until smooth. Add eggs, *2 tablespoons* amaretto and *1 teaspoon* extract; mix well. Pour into prepared pastry shell. Bake 25 minutes or until set. Cool. Arrange peach slices on top of pie. In small saucepan, combine preserves, remaining *1 tablespoon* amaretto and remaining *½ teaspoon* extract; over low heat, cook and stir until hot. Spoon over top of pie. Chill. Refrigerate leftovers.

Makes one 9-inch pie

Prep time: 20 minutes
Baking time: 40 minutes

Peach Pie

Deep-Dish Peach Pie

Pastry for 1-crust pie
1 cup plus 1 tablespoon sugar
2 tablespoons cornstarch
3 pounds peaches, seeded, pared and sliced (about 6 cups)
2 tablespoons REALEMON® Lemon Juice from Concentrate
2 tablespoons margarine or butter, melted
¼ teaspoon almond extract
1 egg yolk plus 2 tablespoons water
2 tablespoons sliced almonds

Preheat oven to 375°F. In small bowl, combine *1 cup* sugar and cornstarch.

In large bowl, toss peaches with REALEMON® brand; add sugar mixture, margarine and extract. Turn into 8-inch square baking dish. Roll pastry to 9-inch square; cut slits near center. Place pastry over filling; turn under edges, seal and flute. Mix egg yolk and water; brush over entire surface of pie. Sprinkle with remaining *1 tablespoon* sugar and almonds.

Bake 45 to 50 minutes or until golden brown.

Makes 6 to 8 servings

Deep-Dish Peach Pie

Canned Peach Pie: Omit fresh peaches. Reserving ½ cup syrup, drain 2 (29-ounce) cans peach slices. Combine sugar and cornstarch as above. Toss peaches with REALEMON® brand and reserved syrup; stir in sugar mixture, margarine and extract. Proceed as above.

Utah's Best Cherry Pie

Crust
Unbaked 9-inch Classic CRISCO *Double* Crust (page 166)
Filling
1 cup sugar
2 tablespoons plus 1½ teaspoons cornstarch
⅛ teaspoon cinnamon
⅛ teaspoon salt
½ cup peach or apricot nectar
⅓ cup Chambord liqueur (optional)
2 tablespoons butter or margarine
3½ cups frozen unsweetened pitted red tart cherries, thawed and well drained

1. Preheat oven to 425°F.
2. For Filling, combine sugar, cornstarch, cinnamon and salt in medium saucepan. Stir in peach nectar and Chambord (if used). Cook and stir until thick and clear. Add butter; stir until melted. Cool.
3. Add cherries; stir until blended. Pour into unbaked pie shell. Moisten edge with water.
4. Roll top crust same as bottom; cut into strips. Weave lattice top over filling. Trim ends of lattice strips even with crust overhang; press together. Fold edge under; flute edge high. Cover edge of pie with foil to prevent overbrowning.
5. Bake 30 minutes. Remove foil; continue baking 10 minutes. Cool until barely warm or to room temperature before serving.   *Makes one 9-inch pie*

Cherry-Berry Delight Pie

Crust
Unbaked 9-Inch Classic CRISCO *Double* Crust prepared with ¼ cup plus 2 tablespoons each CRISCO® and BUTTER FLAVOR CRISCO® (page 166)
Cherry Layer
About 5 cups frozen unsweetened pitted red tart cherries*
⅓ cup plus 1 tablespoon granulated sugar, divided
1 tablespoon plus 1½ teaspoons quick cooking tapioca, divided
3 teaspoons cornstarch, divided
½ teaspoon almond extract
½ teaspoon vanilla
Cream Cheese Layer
1 package (8 ounces) cream cheese, softened
½ cup confectioners sugar
⅓ cup chopped almonds
½ teaspoon almond extract
½ teaspoon vanilla
Raspberry Layer
1 cup fresh raspberries, drained
2 tablespoons granulated sugar
1 tablespoon cornstarch
Topping
1 egg white, lightly beaten
Granulated sugar
Chopped almonds and flake coconut (optional)

1. For Cherry Layer thaw and drain enough cherries to yield 3 to 4 cups fruit and ½ cup juice. Combine cherries, ⅓ cup granulated sugar, 1 tablespoon tapioca, 1½ teaspoons cornstarch, almond extract and vanilla in large bowl.

*If using fresh cherries, use 3 to 4 cups in pie. Mash and press additional cherries through sieve or colander to obtain ½ cup juice.

Cherry-Berry Delight Pie

2. Combine ½ cup reserved cherry juice, remaining 1 tablespoon granulated sugar, 1½ teaspoons tapioca and 1½ teaspoons cornstarch in small saucepan. Place on medium heat; cook, stirring constantly, 3 to 4 minutes. Cool slightly. Pour over cherries; mix gently until coated. Set aside.

3. For Cream Cheese Layer, combine cream cheese and confectioners sugar in small bowl; beat at medium speed of electric mixer until well blended. Add almonds, almond extract and vanilla; beat until well blended. Spread on bottom of unbaked pie shell.

4. For Raspberry Layer, combine raspberries, granulated sugar and cornstarch; mix carefully. Spoon over cream cheese layer.

5. Preheat oven to 400°F. Spoon cherry mixture over raspberries. Moisten pastry edge with water.

6. Cover with top crust. Fold top edge under bottom crust; flute with fingers or fork. Cut slits or design in top crust or prick with fork for escape of steam.

7. For Topping, brush pastry with egg white. Sprinkle lightly with granulated sugar.

8. Bake 15 minutes. *Reduce oven temperature to 350°F.* Bake 40 minutes. Sprinkle with chopped almonds and coconut 5 minutes before end of baking time, if desired. Cool until barely warm or to room temperature before serving. *Makes one 9-inch pie*

Sour Cherry Pie

Crust

Unbaked 9-inch Classic CRISCO® *Double* Crust prepared with BUTTER FLAVOR CRISCO® (page 166)

Filling

3 pounds pitted red tart cherries frozen with sugar, thawed*

1/3 cup firmly packed brown sugar

1/3 cup granulated sugar

1/4 cup cornstarch

1/2 teaspoon cinnamon

1 1/2 tablespoons BUTTER FLAVOR CRISCO®

1 tablespoon vanilla

1 teaspoon almond extract

Glaze

Milk

Granulated sugar

1. Preheat oven to 425°F.

2. For Filling, drain cherries, reserving 1½ cups juice. Combine brown sugar, granulated sugar, cornstarch and cinnamon in saucepan; stir in reserved cherry juice. Cook and stir until mixture is thick and bubbly. Boil and stir 1 minute. Add cherries; cook 1 minute or until mixture comes to a boil. Remove from heat. Add shortening, vanilla and almond extract; mix well. Spoon filling into unbaked pie shell.

3. Cover with top crust. Fold top edge under bottom crust; flute with fingers or fork. Cut slits or design in top crust or prick with fork for escape of steam.

4. For Glaze, brush crust with milk; sprinkle with granulated sugar.

5. Bake 15 minutes. *Reduce oven temperature to 350°F.* Bake 25 minutes or until crust is golden brown. Cool until barely warm or to room temperature before serving.   *Makes one 9-inch pie*

***Substitution:** 2 cans (1 pound each) red tart cherries packed in water; reserve only 1 cup of the liquid.

Sour Cherry Pie

Strawberry Tart Glace

1/2 (15 oz.) pkg. refrigerated pie crust (1 crust)

2 (8 oz.) pkgs. PHILADELPHIA BRAND® Cream Cheese, softened

1/2 cup sugar

1 tablespoon milk

1/4 teaspoon vanilla

1 qt. strawberries

1 tablespoon cornstarch

1/4 cup cold water

Few drops red food coloring (optional)

• Preheat oven to 450°F.

• On lightly floured surface, roll pastry to 12-inch circle. Place in 10-inch quiche dish. Trim edges; prick bottom and sides of pastry with fork. Bake 9 to 11 minutes or until golden brown.

• Beat cream cheese, 1/4 cup sugar, milk and vanilla in large mixing bowl at medium speed with electric mixer until well blended. Spread onto bottom of crust.

• Puree 1 cup strawberries. Top cream cheese mixture with remaining strawberries.

• Stir together remaining 1/4 cup sugar and cornstarch in saucepan; gradually add pureed strawberries and water. Cook, stirring constantly, over medium heat until mixture is clear and thickened. Stir in food coloring. Pour over strawberries; chill.

Makes 8 servings

Prep time: 40 minutes plus chilling

Cooking time: 11 minutes

Variations:

• Substitute 9-inch pie plate for 10-inch quiche dish.

• Substitute almond extract for vanilla.

• Substitute PHILADELPHIA BRAND® "Light" Neufchatel Cheese for Cream Cheese.

Apple Raspberry Tart

Pastry
 1 cup all-purpose flour
 ½ teaspoon salt
 ⅓ cup shortening
 2 to 3 tablespoons cold
   water

Filling
 1 egg, separated
 1 (23-oz.) jar MOTT'S®
   Chunky Apple Sauce
 1 cup fresh raspberries *or*
   1 (10-oz.) pkg. frozen
   raspberries, thawed and
   drained
 2 tablespoons granulated
   sugar
 ½ teaspoon cinnamon

Topping
 ¾ cup all-purpose flour
 ½ cup firmly packed brown
   sugar
 ½ teaspoon cinnamon
 ⅓ cup margarine or butter,
   softened

Preheat oven to 400°F. For
Pastry, in medium bowl, combine
flour and salt. Using pastry
blender or 2 knives, cut
shortening into flour mixture
until particles are size of small
peas. Gradually add water,
tossing with fork until
moistened. Gather pastry into
ball; flatten. Roll out on lightly
floured surface into circle 1½
inches larger than inverted 9-
inch tart pan with removable
bottom. Fold dough in half; place
in pan. Unfold; press in bottom
and up sides of pan. Trim edges
if necessary. Bake 5 minutes.
Remove from oven; *reduce oven
temperature to 375°F.* In small
bowl, beat egg white. Brush over
entire surface of partially baked
crust. Reserve yolk for filling.

For Filling, in medium bowl,
combine apple sauce, raspberries,
granulated sugar, cinnamon and
egg yolk. Pour into pan.

For Topping, in medium bowl,
combine all topping ingredients;
sprinkle over fruit. Bake 40 to
50 minutes until topping is
golden brown. Cool; remove sides
of pan. Serve with whipped cream.
Makes about 8 servings

Blueberry Pie

Crust
   Unbaked 8-inch Classic
   CRISCO® *Double* Crust
   (page 166)

Filling
 3 cups fresh blueberries
 ⅔ to 1 cup sugar
 ¼ cup all-purpose flour
 ½ teaspoon cinnamon
 1 to 2 tablespoons butter or
   margarine

Topping
   Sugar

1. Preheat oven to 375°F.
2. For Filling, place blueberries
in large bowl. Combine sugar,
flour and cinnamon; sprinkle
over blueberries, tossing lightly
to coat. Spoon into unbaked pie
shell; dot with butter. Moisten
pastry edge with water.
3. Cover with top crust. Fold top
edge under bottom crust; flute
with fingers or fork. Cut slits or
design in top crust or prick with
fork for escape of steam.
4. For Topping, sprinkle top crust
lightly with sugar.
5. Bake 45 to 60 minutes or
until golden brown and filling
bubbles. Cool until barely warm
or to room temperature before
serving.   *Makes one 8-inch pie*

Rhubarb Pie

Crust
   Unbaked 9-inch Classic
   CRISCO® *Double* Crust
   (page 166)

Filling
 ¾ cup sugar
 3 tablespoons all-purpose
   flour
 1 egg, beaten
 2 cups chopped red rhubarb
 ½ cup frozen raspberries
 ½ cup cran/raspberry sauce

1. Preheat oven to 425°F.
2. For Filling, sift sugar and
flour into large bowl. Add egg;
beat thoroughly. Stir in rhubarb,
raspberries and sauce. Spoon
filling into unbaked pie shell.
Moisten pastry edge with water.
3. Cover with top crust. Fold top
edge under bottom crust; flute
with fingers or fork. Cut slits or
design in top crust or prick with
fork for escape of steam. Cover
edge of pastry with foil to
prevent overbrowning, if
necessary.
4. Bake 10 minutes. *Reduce oven
temperature to 350°F.* Bake 45
minutes or until golden brown.
Cool until barely warm or to
room temperature before
serving.   *Makes one 9-inch pie*

Apple Raspberry Tart

Celia's Flat Fruit Pie

Celia's Flat Fruit Pie

- **2 packages (8 ounces each) mixed dried fruit (pitted prunes, pears, apples, apricots and peaches)**
- **3 cups water**
- **½ cup sugar**
- **½ teaspoon ground cinnamon**
- **¼ teaspoon ground cloves**
- **1 teaspoon lemon juice Flaky Pastry (recipe follows)**

Combine fruit, water, sugar, cinnamon and cloves in 3-quart pan. Cook, stirring occasionally, over medium heat until sugar is dissolved. Cover; reduce heat and simmer 45 minutes or until fruit is tender.

Pour cooked fruit and liquid into blender or food processor fitted with metal blade; process to make coarse puree. (Puree should measure 3 cups. If puree measures more, return to pan and cook, stirring frequently, to reduce to 3 cups.) Stir in lemon juice. Let cool. While fruit is cooling, prepare Flaky Pastry.

Preheat oven to 400°F. Roll one pastry ball on lightly floured board to 13-inch circle about ⅛ inch thick. Fold pastry into quarters. Place in 12-inch pizza pan; unfold. Trim edge of pastry to leave ½-inch overhang.

Spread fruit puree in even layer over pastry. Roll out second ball to 13-inch circle; place over filling. Cut slits or design in center. Fold edge of top crust under edge of bottom crust; flute edge.

Bake 35 to 40 minutes or until pastry is golden brown. Place pie on wire rack. Let cool 1 hour before cutting into thin wedges.

Makes about 12 servings

Flaky Pastry

- **3⅓ cups all-purpose flour**
- **¾ teaspoon salt**
- **1 cup shortening or lard**
- **6 to 8 tablespoons cold water**

Combine flour and salt in medium bowl. With fingers, pastry blender or 2 knives, rub or cut shortening into flour mixture until it resembles fine crumbs. Gradually add water; stir with fork until mixture forms dough. Shape into 2 balls. Wrap in plastic wrap; refrigerate 30 minutes.

Choco-Cherry Macaroon Pie

- **1 (9-inch) unbaked pastry shell**
- **2 (1-ounce) squares unsweetened chocolate**
- **¼ cup margarine or butter**
- **1 (14-ounce) can EAGLE® Brand Sweetened Condensed Milk (NOT evaporated milk)**
- **¾ cup water**
- **2 eggs, well beaten**
- **1 teaspoon vanilla extract**
- **⅛ teaspoon salt**
- **1 (3½-ounce) can flaked coconut (1⅓ cups)**
- **½ cup red candied cherries, chopped**

Preheat oven to 350°F. In large heavy saucepan, over low heat, melt chocolate with margarine. Stir in sweetened condensed milk, water and eggs; *mix well.* Remove from heat; stir in remaining ingredients except pastry shell. Pour into pastry shell.

Bake 35 to 40 minutes or until center is set. Cool. Serve warm or chilled. Garnish as desired. Refrigerate leftovers.

Makes one 9-inch pie

Old-Fashioned Buttermilk Pie

- **1 (9-inch) unbaked pastry shell**
- **3 eggs**
- **1¼ cups sugar**
- **3 tablespoons flour**
- **¼ teaspoon ground nutmeg**
- **1 cup BORDEN® or MEADOW GOLD® Buttermilk**
- **⅓ cup BORDEN® or MEADOW GOLD® Butter, melted**
- **1 teaspoon vanilla extract**

Preheat oven to 400°F. In large mixer bowl, beat eggs. Add sugar, flour and nutmeg; mix well. Beat in remaining ingredients except pastry shell. Pour into pastry shell.

Bake 10 minutes. *Reduce oven temperature to 325°F;* continue baking 35 to 40 minutes or until knife inserted 1 inch from edge comes out clean. Cool. Serve with fresh fruit if desired. Refrigerate leftovers.

Makes one 9-inch pie

Raisin Sour Cream Pie

- **1 cup sour cream**
- **1 cup sugar**
- **1 cup raisins**
- **2 eggs, slightly beaten**
- **2 teaspoons vinegar**
- **½ teaspoon salt**
- **¼ teaspoon cinnamon**
- **⅛ teaspoon ground cloves**
- **1 KEEBLER® Ready-Crust® Graham Cracker Pie Crust**

Preheat oven to 350°F. In large bowl, mix sour cream, sugar, raisins, eggs, vinegar, salt, cinnamon and cloves. Pour mixture into pie crust.

Bake 40 minutes or until knife inserted in center of pie comes out clean. Cool slightly. Serve with whipped topping, if desired.

Makes 6 to 8 servings

Classic Raisin Pie

2 cups SUN-MAID® Raisins
1 cup *each* orange juice and
water
½ cup sugar
2 tablespoons cornstarch
1 teaspoon ground allspice
½ cup chopped DIAMOND®
Walnuts
1 tablespoon lemon juice
Pastry for double-crust
9-inch pie
1 egg, beaten, for glaze
Sugar, for glaze

Preheat oven to 425°F. In medium saucepan, combine raisins, orange juice and water; bring to boil over high heat. Reduce heat to low; simmer 5 minutes.

In small bowl, combine sugar, cornstarch and allspice; mix well. Stir into raisin mixture. Cook and stir over medium heat until thickened, about 1 minute. Remove from heat; stir in walnuts and lemon juice. Cool 10 minutes; pour into pastry-lined 9-inch pie plate. Cover with top crust; seal and flute edges. Cut leaves from leftover pastry to decorate top of pie, if desired. Cut slits for steam to escape. Brush with beaten egg; sprinkle generously with sugar.

Bake 10 minutes; *reduce heat to 375°F* and bake 25 to 30 minutes longer or until filling is bubbly and crust is golden. Cover with foil, if needed, to prevent overbrowning. Cool on wire rack about ½ hour before cutting. Serve warm or at room temperature with ice cream or whipped cream, if desired.

Makes one 9-inch pie

Lemon Sponge Pie

1 (9-inch) unbaked pastry
shell
3 eggs, separated
1 (14-ounce) can EAGLE®
Brand Sweetened
Condensed Milk (NOT
evaporated milk)
⅓ cup REALEMON® Lemon
Juice from Concentrate
2 tablespoons flour
2 teaspoons grated lemon
rind
Yellow food coloring,
optional

Preheat oven to 375°F. Bake pastry shell 10 minutes; remove from oven. *Reduce oven temperature to 350°F.*

In large mixer bowl, combine remaining ingredients except egg whites; mix well. In small mixer bowl, beat egg whites until stiff but not dry; fold into lemon mixture. Pour into prepared pastry shell.

Bake 25 minutes or until set. Cool. Serve warm or chilled. Garnish as desired. Refrigerate leftovers.   *Makes one 9-inch pie*

Lemon Sponge Pie

Lemon Tartlets

Cream Cheese Tartlet
Shells (recipe follows)
1¼ cups sugar
¾ cup unsalted butter
¾ cup fresh lemon juice
7 eggs
1 teaspoon grated lemon
peel

Prepare Cream Cheese Tartlet Shells.

Preheat oven to 350°F. In large nonaluminum saucepan, combine sugar, butter and lemon juice. Cook over medium heat, stirring constantly, until sugar is dissolved. Remove from heat.

In large mixer bowl, beat eggs lightly. Continue beating at low speed, slowly adding half the hot lemon mixture. Mix just until thoroughly combined. Gradually stir egg mixture into remaining lemon mixture in saucepan. Cook over low heat, stirring constantly, until mixture thickens to consistency of light pudding, about 3 minutes. Remove from heat; stir in lemon peel. Immediately pour lemon filling into shallow heatproof dish; cool completely. Spoon about 2 teaspoons cooled lemon filling into each unbaked tartlet shell, filling about two-thirds full.

Bake 20 to 25 minutes or until bottoms of pastries are crisp and light brown. Let cool 10 minutes in pans on wire racks. Remove tartlets from pans to wire racks to cool completely. (It may be necessary to tap pans against counter to loosen tartlets.)

Makes about 4 dozen tartlets

Raspberry-Topped Lemon Pie

CREAM CHEESE TARTLET SHELLS: In large bowl, beat 1 cup softened butter and 2 packages (3 ounces each) softened cream cheese until light and fluffy. Stir in 2 cups all-purpose flour with spoon just until mixture forms a ball. Divide dough into thirds. Wrap each portion; refrigerate 1 hour. Roll out dough, one third at a time, ⅛ inch thick on lightly floured surface. Cut out with 2¼-inch round cutter. Gently press dough rounds into ungreased fluted 2-inch tartlet pan cups or 1¾-inch muffin pan cups. Refrigerate tartlet shells until ready to fill and bake.

Raspberry-Topped Lemon Pie

- 1 (10-ounce) package frozen red raspberries in syrup, thawed
- 1 tablespoon cornstarch
- 3 egg yolks*
- 1 (14-ounce) can EAGLE® Brand Sweetened Condensed Milk (NOT evaporated milk)
- ½ cup REALEMON® Lemon Juice from Concentrate
- Yellow food coloring, optional
- 1 (6-ounce) packaged graham cracker crumb pie crust
- Whipped topping

Preheat oven to 350°F. In small saucepan, combine raspberries and cornstarch; cook and stir until mixture thickens and is clear. In medium bowl, beat egg yolks; stir in sweetened condensed milk, REALEMON® brand and food coloring if desired. Pour into crust.

Bake 8 minutes. Spoon raspberry mixture evenly over top. Chill 4 hours or until set. Top with whipped topping. Garnish as desired. Refrigerate leftovers.

Makes 6 to 8 servings

*Use only Grade A clean, uncracked eggs.

Creamy Mock Cheese Pie

- 1 (9-inch) graham cracker crumb crust
- 1 (16-ounce) container BORDEN® or MEADOW GOLD® Sour Cream
- 1 (14-ounce) can EAGLE® Brand Sweetened Condensed Milk (NOT evaporated milk)
- 3 tablespoons presweetened lemonade flavor drink mix
- BAMA® Peach Preserves, optional

Preheat oven to 350°F. In medium bowl, combine sour cream, sweetened condensed milk and drink mix; mix well. Pour into prepared crust.

Bake 25 to 30 minutes. Cool. Chill at least 2 hours. Garnish with preserves if desired. Refrigerate leftovers.

Makes one 9-inch pie

Tip: Other fruit preserves can be substituted for peach preserves.

ReaLemon® Meringue Pie

Lemon Meringue Pie

Crust
Baked 9-inch Classic
CRISCO® *Single* Crust
(page 166)

Filling
1½ cups sugar
¼ cup cornstarch
3 tablespoons all-purpose
flour
¼ teaspoon salt
1½ cups hot water
3 egg yolks, beaten
2 tablespoons butter or
margarine
1½ teaspoons grated lemon
peel
⅓ cup plus 1 tablespoon
fresh lemon juice

Meringue
½ cup sugar, divided
1 tablespoon cornstarch
½ cup cold water
4 egg whites
¾ teaspoon vanilla

1. Preheat oven to 350°F.
2. For Filling, combine sugar, cornstarch, flour and salt in medium saucepan. Add water gradually, stirring constantly. Cook and stir on medium heat until mixture boils and thickens. Reduce temperature to low; stir constantly for 8 minutes. Remove from heat. Gradually stir about one-third of hot mixture into egg yolks; mix well. Return mixture to saucepan. Bring to second boil on medium-high heat. Reduce heat to low; cook and stir for 4 minutes. Remove from heat; stir in butter and lemon peel. Add lemon juice slowly; mix well. Spoon into baked pie shell.
3. For Meringue, combine 2 tablespoons sugar, cornstarch and water in small saucepan; stir until cornstarch dissolves. Cook and stir on medium heat until mixture is clear. Cool.
4. Combine egg whites and vanilla in large bowl. Beat at high speed of electric mixer until soft peaks form. Gradually add remaining 6 tablespoons sugar, 1 tablespoon at a time, beating well after each addition. Add cornstarch mixture to meringue and continue beating until stiff peaks form. Spread over filling, covering completely and sealing to edge of pie shell.
5. Bake 12 to 15 minutes or until meringue is lightly browned. Cool to room temperature before serving.
Makes one 9-inch pie

ReaLemon® Meringue Pie

1 (9-inch) baked pastry shell
1⅔ cups sugar
6 tablespoons cornstarch
½ cup REALEMON® Lemon
Juice from Concentrate
4 eggs, separated*
1½ cups boiling water
2 tablespoons margarine or
butter
¼ teaspoon cream of tartar
Mint leaves, optional

Preheat oven to 350°F. In heavy saucepan, combine 1⅓ cups sugar and cornstarch; add REALEMON® brand. In small bowl, beat egg yolks; add to REALEMON® brand mixture. Gradually add water, stirring constantly. Over medium heat, cook and stir until mixture boils and thickens, about 8 to 10 minutes. Remove from heat. Add margarine; stir until melted. Pour into prepared pastry shell.
In small mixer bowl, beat egg whites with cream of tartar until soft peaks form; gradually add remaining ⅓ cup sugar, beating until stiff but not dry. Spread on top of pie, sealing carefully to edge of shell.
Bake 12 to 15 minutes or until golden brown. Cool. Chill before serving. Garnish with mint if desired. Refrigerate leftovers.
Makes one 9-inch pie
*Use only Grade A clean, uncracked eggs.

Key Lime Pie

1 (9- or 10-inch) baked pastry
shell or graham cracker
crumb crust*
6 egg yolks**
2 (14-ounce) cans EAGLE®
Brand Sweetened
Condensed Milk (NOT
evaporated milk)
1 (8-ounce) bottle REALIME®
Lime Juice from
Concentrate
Yellow or green food
coloring, optional
Whipped cream or whipped
topping

Preheat oven to 350°F. In large mixer bowl, beat egg yolks with sweetened condensed milk. Stir in REALIME® brand and food coloring if desired. Pour into prepared pastry shell; bake 12 minutes. Cool. Chill. Top with whipped cream. Garnish as desired. Refrigerate leftovers.
Makes one 9- or 10-inch pie
Key Lime Meringue Pie: Omit whipped cream. Prepare filling as above, reserving 4 egg whites; do not bake. In small mixer bowl, beat egg whites with ¼ teaspoon cream of tartar to soft peaks; gradually add ½ cup sugar, beating until stiff but not dry. Spread on top of pie, sealing carefully to edge of pastry shell. Bake in preheated 350°F oven 15 minutes or until lightly browned. Cool. Chill.
*If using frozen packaged pie shell or 6-ounce packaged graham cracker crumb pie crust, use 1 can EAGLE® Brand Sweetened Condensed Milk, 3 egg yolks and ½ cup REALIME® brand. Bake 8 minutes. Proceed as above.
**Use only Grade A clean, uncracked eggs.

Butterscotch Caramel Pear Tart

Butterscotch Caramel Pear Tart

> **Pastry for one 9-inch pie shell**
> **One 16-oz. can pear halves**
> **³/₄ cup sugar, divided**
> **2 tablespoons cornstarch**
> **2 cups heavy or whipping cream**
> **1 teaspoon grated fresh ginger, optional**
> **1 cup (half of 12-oz. pkg.) NESTLÉ® Butterscotch Flavored Morsels**
> **Additional whipped cream, optional**

Preheat oven to 425°F. On lightly floured board, roll pastry into 11-inch circle. Fit into 9- to 10-inch tart pan with removable bottom. Trim overhang to ¹/₂ inch. Fold overhang into pan; press firmly against side. Prick pastry to prevent puffing. Bake 10 to 14 minutes until lightly browned. Cool completely.

Drain pears, reserving 1 cup liquid; set aside. In 2-quart saucepan, combine ¹/₂ cup sugar and cornstarch; gradually stir in heavy cream, reserved pear liquid and ginger. Cook over medium heat, stirring constantly, until mixture *boils*.

Boil 1 minute, stirring constantly. Stir in butterscotch morsels until smooth. Pour into prepared crust.

Thinly slice pears lengthwise. Arrange pear slices in slightly overlapping circle around edge of tart. Arrange a few slices in center of tart.

In small saucepan, heat remaining ¹/₄ cup sugar over medium heat, stirring frequently, until melted and golden brown; drizzle over pear slices. Refrigerate until filling is cool and set, about 2 hours. To serve, remove tart from pan; slide onto serving plate. Cut into wedges. Garnish with whipped cream.

Makes 8 to 10 servings

Raspberry Crumb Pie

> **Pastry for 8-inch single crust pie**
> **¹/₂ to ³/₄ cup DOMINO® Granulated Sugar**
> **3 tablespoons cornstarch**
> **4¹/₂ cups fresh raspberries***
> **1 tablespoon lemon juice**
> **1 tablespoon butter, cut into bits**
> **Crumb Topping (recipe follows)**

Preheat oven to 400°F. In large bowl, combine sugar and cornstarch. Gently fold in raspberries and lemon juice. Turn into pastry-lined pie plate. Dot with butter and top with Crumb Topping. Bake 1 hour or until juices near center are bubbly. Check crust halfway through baking time; cover crust with foil if necessary to prevent overbrowning.

Makes one 8-inch pie

*Or use individually quick-frozen raspberries (no sugar or syrup added). Increase cornstarch to 3¹/₂ tablespoons and baking time to 1 hour and 10 minutes.

CRUMB TOPPING: In small bowl, combine ¹/₂ cup all-purpose flour, ¹/₃ cup DOMINO® Light Brown Sugar, dash of cinnamon and 3 tablespoons softened butter or margarine until mixture is crumbly, pressing together slightly with fingers if necessary to form larger crumbs.

Apple, Blackberry, Cranberry Pie

> **1 KEEBLER® Ready-Crust® Butter-Flavored Pie Crust**
> **1 egg yolk, slightly beaten**
> **2¹/₂ cups sliced and peeled apples**
> **¹/₂ cup frozen blackberries, drained and thawed**
> **¹/₂ cup fresh or frozen cranberries, thawed**
> **³/₄ cup sugar**
> **2 tablespoons cornstarch**
> **1 tablespoon flour**

Preheat oven to 375°F. Brush pie crust with egg yolk; bake 5 minutes.

In large bowl, combine apples, blackberries, cranberries, sugar and cornstarch. Sprinkle flour in bottom of pie crust. Spoon fruit mixture into crust. Bake 45 minutes.

Makes 6 to 8 servings

Hint: To keep cranberries for year-round use, simply freeze an entire bag of cranberries purchased from the grocery store. They keep up to one year.

Deep-Dish Pumpkin Pie

1³/₄ cups unsifted flour
  ¹/₃ cup firmly packed brown
    sugar
  ¹/₃ cup granulated sugar
  1 cup cold margarine or
    butter, cut into small
    pieces
  1 cup chopped nuts
  1 (16-ounce) can pumpkin
    (about 2 cups)
  1 (14-ounce) can EAGLE®
    Brand Sweetened
    Condensed Milk (NOT
    evaporated milk)
  2 eggs
  1 teaspoon ground cinnamon
  ¹/₂ teaspoon ground allspice
  ¹/₂ teaspoon salt

Preheat oven to 350°F. In medium bowl, combine flour and sugars; cut in margarine until crumbly. Stir in nuts. Reserving 1 cup crumb mixture, press remainder firmly on bottom and halfway up side of 12×7-inch baking dish.

In large mixer bowl, combine remaining ingredients except reserved crumb mixture; mix well. Pour into prepared dish. Top with reserved crumb mixture.

Bake 55 minutes or until golden. Cool. Serve with ice cream if desired. Refrigerate leftovers.

Makes 8 to 10 servings

Deep-Dish Pumpkin Pie

Sweet Potato Meringue Pie

Nut Layer
  ²/₃ cup chopped pecans
  ²/₃ cup firmly packed brown
    sugar
  3 tablespoons butter or
    margarine
Crust
  Unbaked 9-inch Classic
  CRISCO® Single Crust
  (page 166)
Filling
  1¹/₄ cups mashed cooked or
    canned sweet potatoes
  ²/₃ cup granulated sugar
  3 egg yolks
  ¹/₂ cup evaporated milk
  ¹/₂ cup flake coconut, toasted
    and crumbled
  6 tablespoons butter or
    margarine, melted
  ¹/₂ teaspoon vanilla
Meringue
  3 egg whites
  ¹/₈ teaspoon salt
  1 jar (7 ounces) marshmallow
    creme
  Toasted flake coconut
    (optional)

1. For Nut Layer, place pecans, brown sugar and butter in baking pan. Broil until butter melts and pecans are toasted. Stir to coat pecans. Cool.

2. Preheat oven to 350°F.

3. Sprinkle sugared pecans in bottom of unbaked pie shell.

4. For Filling, combine potatoes, granulated sugar, egg yolks, evaporated milk, coconut, butter and vanilla; mix until well blended. Pour over nuts in pie shell.

5. Bake 45 minutes. Remove from oven.

6. For Meringue, *increase oven temperature to 375°F.*

7. Beat egg whites and salt until soft peaks form. Gradually add marshmallow creme; beat until stiff peaks form. Spread over filling, covering completely and sealing to edge of pie. Sprinkle with coconut, if desired.

8. Bake 8 to 10 minutes or until lightly browned. Cool to room temperature before serving.

Makes one 9-inch pie

Luscious Sweet Potato Pie

  1 (9-inch) unbaked pastry
    shell
  1 pound (2 medium) sweet
    potatoes or yams,
    cooked and peeled
  ¹/₂ cup margarine or butter,
    softened
  1 (14-ounce) can EAGLE®
    Brand Sweetened
    Condensed Milk (NOT
    evaporated milk)
  ¹/₄ cup orange-flavored
    liqueur or 2 teaspoons
    grated orange rind
  1 teaspoon ground cinnamon
  ¹/₂ teaspoon ground nutmeg
  ¹/₄ teaspoon salt
  2 eggs, beaten

Preheat oven to 350°F. In large mixer bowl, mash sweet potatoes with margarine; add remaining ingredients except pastry shell and eggs. Beat until smooth and well blended. Stir in eggs. Pour into pastry shell.

Bake 50 to 55 minutes or until knife inserted near center comes out clean. Cool. Refrigerate leftovers.

Makes one 9-inch pie

Tip: 1 (16- or 17-ounce) can sweet potatoes or yams, drained, can be substituted for fresh. Melt margarine. Proceed as above.

Apple Butter Yam Pie

Apple Butter Yam Pie

1 (9-inch) unbaked pastry
    shell
1 cup hot mashed yams or
    sweet potatoes (about
    ³/₄ pound raw)
½ cup margarine or butter,
    softened
½ cup firmly packed light
    brown sugar
2 tablespoons flour
1 (15-ounce) jar BAMA®
    Apple Butter
½ cup BORDEN® or MEADOW
    GOLD® Milk
1½ teaspoons grated orange
    rind
¼ teaspoon salt
3 eggs
    Whipped cream and nuts,
    optional

Preheat oven to 400°F. In large
mixer bowl, beat yams,
margarine, brown sugar and
flour until well blended. Add
apple butter, milk, rind, salt and
eggs; beat well. Turn into pastry
shell.

Bake 10 minutes. *Reduce oven
temperature to 350°F;* bake 50
minutes longer or until knife
inserted near edge comes out
clean. Cool. Serve warm or
chilled. Garnish with whipped
cream and nuts if desired.
Refrigerate leftovers.

    Makes one 9-inch pie

Tip: Canned yams can be
substituted for fresh yams; melt
margarine. Proceed as above.

Banana Split Dessert Pizza

1 (14-ounce) can EAGLE®
    Brand Sweetened
    Condensed Milk (NOT
    evaporated milk)
½ cup BORDEN® or MEADOW
    GOLD® Sour Cream
6 tablespoons REALEMON®
    Lemon Juice from
    Concentrate
1 teaspoon vanilla extract
½ cup plus 1 tablespoon
    margarine or butter,
    softened
¼ cup firmly packed brown
    sugar
1 cup unsifted flour
¼ cup quick-cooking oats
¼ cup finely chopped nuts
3 medium bananas, sliced
1 (8-ounce) can sliced
    pineapple, drained and
    cut in half
    Maraschino cherries and
    nuts
1 (1-ounce) square semi-
    sweet chocolate

Preheat oven to 375°F. Lightly
grease pizza pan or baking sheet.
In medium bowl, combine
sweetened condensed milk, sour
cream, *¼ cup* REALEMON®
brand and vanilla; mix well.
Chill.

In large mixer bowl, beat *½ cup*
margarine and brown sugar
until fluffy; add flour, oats and
nuts. Mix well. On prepared pan,
press dough into 12-inch circle,
forming rim around edge. Prick
with fork.

Bake 10 to 12 minutes or until
golden brown. Cool. Arrange 2
bananas on cooled crust. Spoon
chilled filling evenly over
bananas. Dip remaining banana
slices in remaining *2 tablespoons*
REALEMON® brand; arrange on
top along with pineapple,
cherries and additional nuts.

In small saucepan, over low
heat, melt chocolate with
remaining *1 tablespoon*
margarine; drizzle over pizza.
Chill. Refrigerate leftovers.

    Makes one 12-inch pizza

Tip: Crust and filling can be
made in advance and held until
ready to assemble. Cover crust
and store at room temperature;
store filling in refrigerator.

Banana Berry Brownie Pizza

⅓ cup cold water
1 (15 oz.) pkg. brownie mix
¼ cup oil
1 egg
1 (8 oz.) pkg. PHILADELPHIA
    BRAND® Cream Cheese,
    softened
¼ cup sugar
1 egg
1 teaspoon vanilla
    Strawberry slices
    Banana slices
2 (1 oz.) squares BAKER'S®
    Semi-Sweet Chocolate,
    melted

- Preheat oven to 350°F.
- Bring water to boil.
- Mix together brownie mix,
water, oil and egg in large bowl
until well blended. Pour into
greased and floured 12-inch
pizza pan.
- Bake 25 minutes.
- Beat cream cheese, sugar, egg
and vanilla in small mixing bowl
at medium speed with electric
mixer until well blended. Pour
over crust.
- Bake 15 minutes. Cool. Top
with fruit; drizzle with chocolate.
Garnish with mint leaves, if
desired.

    Makes 10 to 12 servings

Prep time: 35 minutes
Cooking time: 40 minutes

Microwave Tip: To melt
chocolate, place unwrapped
chocolate squares in small bowl.
Microwave on HIGH 1 to 2
minutes or until almost melted.
Stir until smooth.

Banana Berry Brownie Pizza

Mocha Walnut Tart

1 (9-inch) unbaked pastry
   shell
2 (1-ounce) squares
   unsweetened chocolate
1/4 cup margarine or butter
1 (14-ounce) can EAGLE®
   Brand Sweetened
   Condensed Milk (NOT
   evaporated milk)
1/4 cup water
2 eggs, well beaten
1/4 cup coffee-flavored liqueur
1 teaspoon vanilla extract
1/8 teaspoon salt
1 cup walnuts, toasted and
   chopped

Preheat oven to 350°F. In
medium saucepan, over low heat,
melt chocolate and margarine.
Stir in sweetened condensed
milk, water and eggs; *mix well.*
Remove from heat; stir in
remaining ingredients except
walnuts and pastry shell. Pour
into shell; top with walnuts.
Bake 40 to 45 minutes or until
center is set. Cool. Serve warm
or chilled. Garnish as desired.
Refrigerate leftovers.

Makes one 9-inch tart

Peanut Pie

Crust
   **Baked 9-inch Classic
   CRISCO® *Single* Crust
   prepared with BUTTER
   FLAVOR CRISCO®
   (page 166)**
Filling
   1/2 cup granulated sugar
   1/4 cup firmly packed brown
      sugar
   1/4 cup all-purpose flour
   2 tablespoons cornstarch
   1/4 teaspoon salt
   3 cups milk
   1/2 cup peanut butter chips
   4 egg yolks
   3 tablespoons butter or
      margarine
   1 1/2 teaspoons vanilla
   1 bag (7 ounces) chocolate
      covered peanuts,
      chopped

1. Preheat oven to 350°F.
2. For Filling, combine
granulated sugar, brown sugar,
flour, cornstarch and salt in
large saucepan. Gradually add
milk and peanut butter chips.
Cook and stir on medium heat
until thick and bubbly. Reduce
heat; cook and stir 2 minutes.
3. Beat egg yolks lightly in small
bowl. Gradually stir 1 cup hot
milk mixture into yolks. Return
egg mixture to saucepan; bring
to gentle boil. Cook and stir on
low heat 2 minutes. Remove from
heat. Stir in butter and vanilla.
Pour mixture into prebaked and
cooled pie shell. Sprinkle with
peanuts.
Bake at 350°F for 12 minutes.
Cool to room temperature before
serving.

Makes one 9-inch pie

Peanut Pie

Best-Ever Walnut Pie

1 1/2 cups dark corn syrup
   4 eggs, lightly beaten
   1/2 teaspoon salt
1 1/2 cups packed brown sugar
   2 teaspoons vanilla
   2 cups DIAMOND® Walnuts
   1 (9-inch) unbaked pie shell
      Whipped cream, for
      garnish

Preheat oven to 400°F. In large
bowl, combine syrup, eggs, salt,
brown sugar and vanilla. Stir
briskly until well blended; do not
beat because mixture should not
become foamy. Stir in walnuts.
Pour mixture into unbaked pie
shell.

Bake 10 minutes. *Reduce oven
temperature to 350°F;* bake 40 to
50 minutes longer or just until
center trembles slightly when
pie is gently shaken. Cool on
wire rack. Garnish with whipped
cream, if desired.

Makes 8 to 10 servings

Golden Ambrosia Pecan Pie

Crust

Unbaked 9-inch Classic CRISCO® *Single* Crust prepared with BUTTER FLAVOR CRISCO® (page 166)

Filling

3 eggs, beaten
³/₄ cup light corn syrup
¹/₂ cup granulated sugar
3 tablespoons firmly packed brown sugar
2 tablespoons butter or margarine, melted
3 tablespoons thawed orange juice concentrate
2 tablespoons cornstarch
1 teaspoon grated orange peel
1 teaspoon vanilla
¹/₂ teaspoon coconut flavor or extract
1¹/₂ cups chopped pecans
²/₃ cup flake coconut

1. Preheat oven to 350°F.

2. For Filling, combine eggs, corn syrup, granulated sugar, brown sugar and melted butter in large bowl. Stir well.

3. Combine orange juice concentrate, cornstarch, orange peel, vanilla and coconut flavor. Add to egg mixture; stir well. Stir in pecans and coconut; pour into unbaked pastry shell. Cover edge with foil to prevent overbrowning.

4. Bake at 350°F for 35 minutes. Remove foil; return to oven for 15 to 20 minutes or until set. Cool to room temperature before serving.

Makes one 9-inch pie

Golden Ambrosia Pecan Pie

Maple Pecan Pie

Bake 45 minutes or until top is firm and just begins to crack. Cool at least 3 hours before cutting to serve. Garnish with whipped topping and additional pecans, if desired.

Makes 8 servings

Prep time: 15 minutes
Baking time: 45 minutes

Honey Crunch Pecan Pie

Crust
   Unbaked 9-inch Classic CRISCO® *Single* Crust prepared with BUTTER FLAVOR CRISCO® (page 166)

Filling
   4 eggs, lightly beaten
   ¼ cup firmly packed brown sugar
   ¼ cup granulated sugar
   ½ teaspoon salt
   1 cup light corn syrup
   2 tablespoons butter or margarine, melted
   1 tablespoon bourbon
   1 teaspoon vanilla
   1 cup chopped pecans

Topping
   ⅓ cup firmly packed brown sugar
   3 tablespoons butter or margarine
   3 tablespoons honey
   1½ cups pecan halves

1. Preheat oven to 350°F.

2. For Filling, combine eggs, brown sugar, granulated sugar, salt, corn syrup, butter, bourbon, vanilla and chopped pecans; mix well. Spoon into unbaked pie shell.

3. Bake 15 minutes. Cover edge of pastry with foil; bake 20 minutes. Remove from oven.

Maple Pecan Pie

   1 (9-inch) unbaked pastry shell
   3 eggs, beaten
   1 cup CARY'S®, VERMONT MAPLE ORCHARDS or MACDONALD'S Pure Maple Syrup
   ½ cup firmly packed light brown sugar
   2 tablespoons butter or margarine, melted
   1 teaspoon vanilla extract
   1¼ cups pecan halves or pieces

Place rack in lowest position in oven; preheat oven to 350°F. In medium bowl, combine all ingredients except pastry shell. Pour into pastry shell.

Bake 35 to 40 minutes or until golden. Cool. Chill if desired. Refrigerate leftovers.

Makes one 9-inch pie

Pudding Pecan Pie

   1 cup light or dark corn syrup
   1 package (4-serving size) JELL-O® Instant Pudding and Pie Filling, Butterscotch, French Vanilla or Vanilla Flavor
   ¾ cup evaporated milk
   1 egg, slightly beaten
   1 cup chopped pecans
   1 unbaked 8-inch pie shell
   COOL WHIP® Whipped Topping, thawed (optional)

Preheat oven to 375°F. Pour corn syrup into medium bowl. Blend in pie filling mix. Gradually add evaporated milk and egg, stirring until well blended. Add pecans. Pour into pie shell.

4. For Topping, combine brown sugar, butter and honey in medium saucepan. Cook about 2 minutes or until sugar dissolves. Add pecan halves; stir until coated. Spoon evenly over pie. Keep edge of pastry covered with foil. Bake 10 to 20 minutes or until topping is bubbly and golden brown. Cool to room temperature before serving.

Makes one 9-inch pie

Fudgy Pecan Pie

1 (9-inch) unbaked pastry shell
1 (4-ounce) package sweet cooking chocolate *or* 2 (1-ounce) squares unsweetened chocolate
¼ cup margarine or butter
1 (14-ounce) can EAGLE® Brand Sweetened Condensed Milk (NOT evaporated milk)
½ cup water
2 eggs, well beaten
1 teaspoon vanilla extract
⅛ teaspoon salt
1¼ cups pecan halves or pieces

Preheat oven to 350°F. In medium saucepan, over low heat, melt chocolate with margarine. Stir in sweetened condensed milk, water and eggs; *mix well.* Remove from heat; stir in remaining ingredients except pastry shell. Pour into pastry shell.

Bake 40 to 45 minutes or until center is set. Cool slightly. Serve warm or chilled. Garnish as desired. Refrigerate leftovers.

Makes one 9-inch pie

Simply Superb Pecan Pie

3 eggs, beaten
1 cup sugar
½ cup dark corn syrup
1 teaspoon vanilla
6 tablespoons butter or margarine, melted, cooled
1 cup pecan pieces or halves
1 (9-inch) unbaked pie shell

Preheat oven to 350°F. In large bowl, beat eggs, sugar, corn syrup, vanilla and butter. Stir in pecans. Pour into unbaked pie shell.

Bake 45 to 60 minutes or until knife inserted halfway between edge and center comes out clean. Cool on wire rack.

Makes one 9-inch pie

Favorite recipe from **National Pecan Marketing Council, Inc.**

Pecan Tartlets

Cream Cheese Tartlet Shells (page 183)
2 eggs
1½ cups packed dark brown sugar
2 teaspoons butter or margarine, melted
2 teaspoons vanilla
2 cups finely chopped pecans

Prepare Cream Cheese Tartlet Shells.

Preheat oven to 350°F. In medium bowl using wire whisk, lightly beat eggs. Whisk in brown sugar, butter and vanilla until thoroughly blended. Stir in pecans. Spoon about 1 teaspoon filling into each unbaked tartlet shell, filling about half full.

Bake 20 to 25 minutes or until bottoms of pastries are crisp and light brown. Let cool 10 minutes in pans on wire racks. Remove tartlets from pans to wire racks to cool completely. (It may be necessary to tap pans against counter to loosen tartlets.)

Makes about 4 dozen tartlets

Fudgy Pecan Pie

DESSERTS

If you miss the old-fashioned goodness of desserts like Mom used to make, you'll love this collection of tempting recipes. Prepare one of the comforting crisps and cobblers teeming with fruit or a warm and inviting bread pudding delicately scented with cinnamon. From creamy baked custards to flaky filled pastries, these classics will rekindle fond dessert memories and create new ones. (For additional dessert recipes, see the Jump-Start Baking and Festive Holiday Baking chapters.)

Baked Almond Pudding

¼ cup firmly packed brown sugar
¾ cup slivered almonds, toasted
1 (14-ounce) can EAGLE® Brand Sweetened Condensed Milk (NOT evaporated milk)
5 eggs
1 cup (½ pint) BORDEN® or MEADOW GOLD® Whipping Cream
¼ cup water
½ teaspoon almond extract
Additional toasted almonds, optional

Preheat oven to 325°F. In 8-inch round layer cake pan, sprinkle brown sugar; set aside.

In blender or food processor container, grind nuts; add sweetened condensed milk, eggs, *½ cup* cream, water and extract. Blend thoroughly. Pour into prepared pan; set in larger pan. Fill larger pan with 1 inch hot water.

Bake 40 to 45 minutes or until knife inserted near center comes out clean. Cool. Chill; invert onto serving plate. Beat remaining *½ cup* cream for garnish; top with additional almonds if desired. Refrigerate leftovers.

Makes 8 to 10 servings

Fruit Glazed Baked Custards

3 eggs
1 (14-ounce) can EAGLE® Brand Sweetened Condensed Milk (NOT evaporated milk)
1 cup water
1 teaspoon vanilla extract
½ cup red currant jelly
2 tablespoons orange-flavored liqueur *or* orange juice
1 tablespoon cornstarch
Few drops red food coloring, optional
Fresh strawberries or other fruit

Preheat oven to 350°F. In medium mixing bowl, beat eggs; stir in sweetened condensed milk, water and vanilla. Pour equal portions of mixture into six 6-ounce custard cups. Set cups in shallow pan; fill pan with 1 inch hot water.

Bake 45 to 50 minutes or until knife inserted in center comes out clean. Cool.

In small saucepan, combine jelly, liqueur and cornstarch. Cook and stir until jelly melts and mixture comes to a boil. Stir in food coloring if desired. Cool to room temperature.

Invert custards onto serving plates. Top with sauce and strawberries. Refrigerate leftovers.

Makes 6 servings

Clockwise from top: Baked Almond Pudding, Fruit Glazed Baked Custards, Caramel Flan (page 196)

Caramel Flan

³/₄ cup sugar
4 eggs
1³/₄ cups water
1 (14-ounce) can EAGLE®
Brand Sweetened
Condensed Milk (NOT
evaporated milk)
½ teaspoon vanilla extract
⅛ teaspoon salt

Preheat oven to 350°F. In heavy skillet, over medium heat, cook sugar, stirring constantly until melted and caramel-colored. Pour into ungreased 9-inch round layer cake pan, tilting to coat bottom completely. In medium bowl, beat eggs; stir in water, sweetened condensed milk, vanilla and salt. Pour over caramelized sugar; set cake pan in larger pan. Fill larger pan with 1 inch hot water.

Bake 55 to 60 minutes or until knife inserted near center comes out clean. Cool. Chill thoroughly. Loosen side of flan with knife; invert onto serving plate with rim. Garnish as desired. Refrigerate leftovers.

Makes 10 to 12 servings

Caramel Pumpkin Flan

³/₄ cup sugar, divided
4 eggs
1 cup canned pumpkin
1 teaspoon ground cinnamon
¼ teaspoon salt
¼ teaspoon ground ginger
¼ teaspoon ground allspice
¼ teaspoon ground nutmeg
1 cup half-and-half
½ teaspoon vanilla extract
Boiling water

Preheat oven to 350°F. Melt ½ cup sugar in 8-inch skillet over medium heat, stirring constantly, until sugar is caramelized. Immediately pour

caramel syrup into 1-quart soufflé dish or other baking dish 7 to 8 inches in diameter. Tilt dish so syrup flows over bottom and slightly up side. Let cool 10 minutes.

Beat eggs slightly on medium speed in large bowl of electric mixer. Add remaining ¼ cup sugar, pumpkin, cinnamon, salt, ginger, allspice and nutmeg. Beat to blend thoroughly. Add half-and-half and vanilla; beat until smooth. Pour into caramel-lined dish. Set dish in larger pan. Pour boiling water into larger pan to depth of 1½ inches. Bake 45 to 50 minutes or until knife inserted in center comes out clean. Remove from water bath; place on wire rack to cool. Refrigerate, loosely covered, 6 hours or until next day.

To unmold, run knife around edge of dish; cover with rimmed serving plate. Holding plate in place, invert dish. Flan and caramel will slide onto plate. Cut into wedges to serve; spoon caramel over top.

Makes about 6 servings

Raisin Rice Pudding Soufflé

Granulated sugar
1³/₄ cups cooked rice
2 cups half-and-half
5 eggs, separated
½ cup granulated sugar
2 tablespoons all-purpose
flour
1 teaspoon ground nutmeg
1 can (8 ounces) crushed
unsweetened pineapple,
drained
1 cup SUN-MAID® Raisins
½ teaspoon salt
Powdered sugar, for
garnish

Preheat oven to 400°F. Butter 3-quart soufflé dish. Dust with granulated sugar; set aside.

In medium saucepan, combine rice and half-and-half; bring to boil over medium-high heat. In large bowl, beat egg yolks, ¼ cup of the granulated sugar, the flour and nutmeg. Gradually stir in rice mixture, then add pineapple and raisins; set aside to cool.

In another large bowl, beat egg whites and salt until soft peaks form; gradually beat in remaining ¼ cup granulated sugar. Gently fold whites into cooled raisin-rice mixture. Pour into prepared dish. Place in shallow pan partly filled with hot water.

Bake 35 to 40 minutes or until puffy and golden brown. Serve at once, dusted with powdered sugar. *Makes 6 to 8 servings*

Old-Fashioned Rice Custard

1½ cups milk
3 eggs, beaten
½ cup sugar
½ teaspoon vanilla extract
¼ teaspoon salt
³/₄ cup cooked rice
½ cup seedless golden
raisins

Preheat oven to 350°F. Grease 1-quart baking dish. Combine milk, eggs, sugar, vanilla and salt in large bowl. Stir in rice and raisins. Pour into prepared dish. Place dish in larger pan filled with about 1 inch hot water.

Bake, uncovered, 1 hour and 15 minutes or until light golden brown, stirring once after 30 minutes.

Makes about 4 servings

Favorite recipe from **USA Rice Council**

Peachy Rice Dessert

- **1 can (16 ounces) sliced peaches in juice or syrup**
- **3 cups cooked rice**
- **1/2 cup jam, jelly or preserves (any flavor)**
- **1 tablespoon lemon juice**
- **Ground cinnamon (optional)**
- **Whipped cream (optional)**

Preheat oven to 375°F. Grease six 1-cup baking dishes. Drain peaches; reserve 6 tablespoons juice. Combine reserved juice, rice, jam and lemon juice in large bowl. Spoon into prepared baking dishes; top with peach slices. Sprinkle with cinnamon, if desired. Cover.

Bake 20 minutes. Serve warm with whipped cream, if desired.

Makes 6 servings

Favorite recipe from **USA Rice Council**

Chocolate Cinnamon Bread Pudding

- **4 cups soft white bread cubes (5 slices bread)**
- **1/2 cup chopped nuts**
- **3 eggs**
- **1/4 cup unsweetened cocoa**
- **2 teaspoons vanilla extract**
- **1 teaspoon ground cinnamon**
- **1/2 teaspoon salt**
- **1 (14-ounce) can EAGLE® Brand Sweetened Condensed Milk (NOT evaporated milk)**
- **2 3/4 cups water**
- **2 tablespoons margarine or butter, melted**
- **Cinnamon Cream Sauce**

Preheat oven to 350°F. Butter 9-inch square baking pan. Place bread cubes and nuts in prepared pan.

In large bowl, beat eggs, cocoa, vanilla, cinnamon and salt; add sweetened condensed milk, water and margarine. Pour evenly over bread, moistening completely.

Bake 40 to 45 minutes or until knife inserted in center comes out clean. Cool slightly. Serve warm with Cinnamon Cream Sauce. Refrigerate leftovers.

Makes 6 to 8 servings

CINNAMON CREAM SAUCE: In medium saucepan, combine 1 cup (1/2 pint) BORDEN® or MEADOW GOLD® Whipping Cream, 2/3 cup firmly packed brown sugar, 1 teaspoon vanilla extract and 1/2 teaspoon ground cinnamon. Bring to a boil; reduce heat and boil rapidly 6 to 8 minutes or until thickened, stirring occasionally. Cool slightly. Serve warm.

Makes about 1 cup sauce

Prep time: 30 minutes
Baking time: 45 minutes

Banana Bread Pudding

- **2 extra-ripe, medium DOLE® Bananas, peeled and cut into chunks**
- **4 slices bread, cubed**
- **1/4 cup DOLE® Raisins**
- **1 1/4 cups milk**
- **2 firm, medium DOLE® Bananas**
- **2 eggs, lightly beaten**
- **1/2 cup sugar**
- **1 tablespoon margarine, softened**
- **1 teaspoon vanilla extract**
- **1/2 teaspoon ground nutmeg**
- **1/4 teaspoon salt**

Preheat oven to 350°F. Grease 1 1/2-quart casserole dish. Puree extra-ripe bananas in blender or food processor (1 cup).

In large bowl, combine bread cubes and raisins. Stir in pureed bananas and milk. Let stand 5 minutes. Slice firm bananas; stir into bread mixture. Stir in eggs, sugar, margarine, vanilla, 1/4 teaspoon nutmeg and salt. Pour into prepared dish. Sprinkle with remaining 1/4 teaspoon nutmeg.

Place casserole in large pan. Pour boiling water into pan to come 2 inches up sides of dish. Bake 1 hour. Serve warm.

Makes about 8 servings

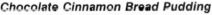

Chocolate Cinnamon Bread Pudding

Bread Pudding

**4 cups soft white bread
    cubes (5 slices)
3 eggs
1 teaspoon ground cinnamon
3 cups water
1 (14-ounce) can EAGLE®
    Brand Sweetened
    Condensed Milk (NOT
    evaporated milk)
2 tablespoons margarine or
    butter, melted
2 teaspoons vanilla extract
½ teaspoon salt**

Preheat oven to 350°F. Place
bread cubes in buttered 9-inch
square baking pan. In large
bowl, beat eggs and cinnamon;
stir in remaining ingredients.
Pour evenly over bread,
moistening completely.

Bake 45 to 50 minutes or until
knife inserted in center comes
out clean. Cool. Serve warm or
chilled. Refrigerate leftovers.

Makes 6 to 8 servings

Tip: For a softer, more custard-
like bread pudding, decrease
bread cubes to 3 cups (4 slices).

Apple Bread Pudding: Arrange
2 cups pared, chopped all-
purpose apples (3 medium) and
½ cup raisins, then bread in
baking pan. Increase margarine
to ¼ cup. Reduce water to 1¾
cups. Proceed as above.

Pineapple Bread Pudding: Add
1 (8- or 8¼-ounce) can crushed
pineapple, undrained, to bread
cubes. Reduce water to 2¾ cups.
Proceed as above.

**Blueberry 'n' Spice Bread
Pudding:** Add 2 cups fresh *or*
thawed dry-pack frozen
blueberries to bread cubes.
Increase margarine to ¼ cup.
Reduce cinnamon to ½ teaspoon
and add ½ teaspoon ground
nutmeg. Reduce water to 1½
cups. Proceed as above.

Baked Lemon Sponge Pudding

**2 eggs, separated
1 cup *undiluted*
    CARNATION® Evaporated
    Milk
⅓ cup sugar
⅓ cup all-purpose flour
3 tablespoons lemon juice
2 tablespoons butter or
    margarine, melted
2 teaspoons lemon zest,
    grated
¼ cup sugar
    Lemon zest
    Raspberry Sauce (recipe
    follows)**

Preheat oven to 350°F. In
medium bowl, beat egg yolks
with wire whisk. Blend in
evaporated milk, *⅓ cup* sugar,
flour, lemon juice, butter, and *2
teaspoons* lemon zest. In small
mixer bowl, beat egg whites just
until soft peaks form. Gradually
add *¼ cup* sugar, beating just
until stiff peaks form and sugar
is dissolved. Do not overbeat.
Carefully fold beaten egg whites
into lemon mixture. Spoon into
six 6-ounce ungreased baking
dishes. Place dishes in 13×9×2-
inch baking pan. Fill outer pan
with hot water to 1-inch depth.
Bake 35 to 45 minutes or until
light golden brown. Carefully
remove puddings from hot water
bath. Sprinkle with lemon zest.
Serve immediately with
Raspberry Sauce.

Makes 6 servings

RASPBERRY SAUCE: In small
saucepan, combine 1½ cups
(12-ounce package) whole,
unsweetened frozen raspberries
and ¼ cup sugar. Cook and stir
until sugar is dissolved. Puree in
blender or food processor. Strain
mixture through sieve into bowl
to remove seeds. Serve warm.

Baked Lemon Sponge Pudding

Orange Bread Pudding

Orange Rum Sauce (recipe
follows)
3 tablespoons butter
1/2 loaf (1 pound) day-old
French bread
5 eggs
1 egg white
2/3 cup granulated sugar
1/3 cup packed brown sugar
1/4 teaspoon ground cinnamon
2 cups milk
1 cup orange juice
1 tablespoon vanilla extract
1/2 cup raisins
1/4 cup pine nuts
Boiling water

Prepare Orange Rum Sauce;
refrigerate until ready to use.
Preheat oven to 350°F. Butter 3-
quart baking dish or casserole
dish with 1 tablespoon butter.
Cut bread into 1-inch slices; cut
each slice, with crust, into 1-inch
cubes to make 8 cups. Beat eggs
and egg white in large bowl of
electric mixer on medium speed
until foamy. Gradually beat in
granulated sugar, brown sugar
and cinnamon. Stir in milk,
orange juice, vanilla, raisins and
pine nuts. Add bread cubes; mix
well, pushing bread into liquid
so each piece is moistened. Pour
bread mixture into prepared
dish. Dot top with remaining 2
tablespoons butter. Set dish in
larger pan. Pour boiling water
into larger pan to depth of 1½
inches.
Bake, uncovered, 45 minutes or
until top of pudding is golden
brown and knife inserted in
center comes out clean. Remove
pudding from water bath and
place on wire rack to cool 30
minutes. Serve warm with
Orange Rum Sauce. To reheat
pudding, bake, covered, in 350°F
oven 15 minutes or until
warmed.
Makes about 8 servings

Orange Rum Sauce

1/4 cup butter or margarine,
softened
1 egg yolk*
1½ cups powdered sugar
2 tablespoons rum
1 teaspoon grated orange
peel

Beat butter in small bowl of
electric mixer on medium speed
until creamy. Beat in egg yolk.
Add powdered sugar; beat until
light and fluffy. Add rum; beat
until well blended. Stir in peel.
Cover and refrigerate up to 2
days. Serve chilled sauce over
warm pudding.
Makes about 1 cup sauce
*Use clean, uncracked egg.

Blueberry Clafouti

1/2 cup butter, softened
2/3 cup sugar
4 eggs
1 cup all-purpose flour
1 tablespoon lemon juice
1 teaspoon vanilla
1/4 teaspoon ground nutmeg
1/8 teaspoon salt
1 pint blueberries
Whipped cream, optional

Preheat oven to 375°F. Grease
9-inch quiche dish or cake pan.
In large mixing bowl, beat
together butter and sugar until
light and fluffy. Beat in eggs
until thoroughly blended. Add
remaining ingredients except
blueberries and whipped cream;
beat until smooth. Reserve 8
blueberries for garnish, if
desired. Fold remaining
blueberries into batter. Pour into
prepared pan.
Bake 40 to 50 minutes or until
lightly browned and knife
inserted in center comes out
clean. Cool on wire rack. Cut
into wedges and serve warm or
cool garnished with whipped
cream and reserved blueberries,
if desired. *Makes 8 servings*

*Favorite recipe from **American Egg
Board***

Blueberry Clafouti

Blueberry Crumble

1 teaspoon lemon juice
4 cups fresh or dry-pack
frozen blueberries,
rinsed and drained
1/2 cup granulated sugar
2 tablespoons all-purpose
flour
1¼ cups rolled oats, uncooked
1/2 cup firmly packed brown
sugar
1/2 teaspoon cinnamon
1/4 cup butter or margarine

Preheat oven to 375°F. Sprinkle
lemon juice over blueberries in
large bowl. Combine granulated
sugar and flour; add to
blueberries, tossing with fork to
coat. Place in 8-inch square
baking dish. Combine remaining
ingredients in small bowl,
mixing until crumbly. Sprinkle
over blueberries. Bake 25 to 30
minutes. Serve warm with ice
cream.
Makes about 6 servings

*Favorite recipe from **North American
Blueberry Council***

Old-Fashioned Apple Crisp

½ to ¾ cup granulated sugar
1 tablespoon cornstarch
¾ teaspoon ground cinnamon
¼ cup REALEMON® Lemon Juice from Concentrate
6 cups pared and sliced all-purpose apples (about 2½ pounds)
⅓ cup raisins
1 cup quick-cooking oats, uncooked
½ cup unsifted flour
⅓ cup firmly packed light brown sugar
¼ teaspoon ground nutmeg
⅓ cup margarine or butter, melted
Cream or ice cream, optional

Preheat oven to 350°F. In large bowl, combine granulated sugar, cornstarch, cinnamon and REALEMON® brand; mix well. Add apples and raisins; mix well. Turn into 8-inch square baking dish. In small bowl, combine remaining ingredients except cream; sprinkle evenly over apples.
Bake 30 to 40 minutes or until apples are tender. Serve warm with cream or ice cream if desired.

Makes 4 to 6 servings

Old-Fashioned Apple Crisp

Butterscotch Apple Pecan Cobbler

Filling:
One 12-oz. pkg. (2 cups) NESTLÉ® Toll House® Butterscotch Flavored Morsels
¼ cup firmly packed brown sugar
¼ cup all-purpose flour
½ teaspoon cinnamon
2½ lbs. tart apples, peeled and diced

Topping:
½ cup all-purpose flour
¼ cup firmly packed brown sugar
¼ cup (½ stick) butter
1 cup chopped pecans
¾ cup quick or old-fashioned oats, uncooked
Whipped cream or ice cream, optional

Filling: Preheat oven to 375°F. In small bowl, combine butterscotch morsels, brown sugar, flour and cinnamon; set aside. Place apples in ungreased 13×9-inch baking pan; sprinkle morsel mixture over apples. Bake 20 minutes.

Topping: In small bowl, combine flour and brown sugar. With pastry blender or 2 knives, cut in butter until crumbly. Stir in pecans and oats. Sprinkle over hot apple mixture. Bake 30 to 40 minutes longer until apples are tender. Cool slightly. Serve warm with whipped cream or ice cream.

Makes 10 to 12 servings

Butterscotch Apple Pecan Cobbler

Cheese Apple Crisp

4 cups peeled, sliced apples
¼ cup cold water
1 cup firmly packed brown sugar
⅔ cup quick-cooking rolled oats, uncooked
⅓ cup flour
½ teaspoon cinnamon
⅛ teaspoon salt
⅓ cup butter
¾ cup shredded Wisconsin Cheddar cheese (Aged or Medium)

Preheat oven to 350°F. Arrange apple slices in bottom of greased 8-inch baking dish; sprinkle with water. In large bowl, combine brown sugar, oats, flour, cinnamon and salt. Cut in butter until mixture resembles coarse crumbs. Reserve ¼ cup of mixture for topping. Stir cheese into remainder and spread over apples; sprinkle with reserved topping. Bake 25 to 30 minutes or until apples are tender.

Makes about 6 servings

Favorite recipe from **Wisconsin Milk Marketing Board** ©*1991*

Blueberry Pear Cream Cheese Crisp

2 cups old fashioned or quick oats, uncooked
1 cup flour
1/3 cup granulated sugar
1/3 cup packed brown sugar
1/2 cup PARKAY® Margarine, melted
2 (8 oz.) containers PHILADELPHIA BRAND® "Light" Pasteurized Process Cream Cheese Product
1/2 cup granulated sugar
2 eggs
2 tablespoons lemon juice
1 tablespoon grated lemon peel
2 pears, peeled, cored, sliced, cut in half crosswise
1 pt. blueberries

• Preheat oven to 325°F.
• Mix together oats, flour, 1/3 cup granulated sugar and brown sugar in medium bowl until well blended. Stir in margarine.
• Reserve 1 cup oat mixture for topping. Press remaining oat mixture onto bottom of 13×9-inch baking pan. Bake 10 minutes.
• Beat cream cheese product and 1/2 cup granulated sugar in large mixing bowl at medium speed with electric mixer until well blended. Add eggs, one at a time, mixing well after each addition. Stir in lemon juice and peel, pour over crust.
• Layer pears evenly over cream cheese mixture; top with blueberries. Sprinkle reserved oat mixture over fruit.
• Bake 45 minutes. Serve warm with vanilla ice cream, if desired.

Makes about 16 servings

Prep time: 20 minutes
Cooking time: 45 minutes

Peach Cobbler

Maple Pear Crisp

6 cups cored, pared and sliced pears (about 2 1/2 pounds)
1/2 cup CARY'S®, VERMONT MAPLE ORCHARDS or MACDONALD'S Pure Maple Syrup
1/4 cup margarine or butter, melted
1 cup quick-cooking oats, uncooked
1/2 cup unsifted flour
1/4 cup firmly packed light brown sugar
1/2 teaspoon ground cinnamon
6 tablespoons cold margarine or butter

Preheat oven to 375°F. In medium bowl, combine pears, pure maple syrup and 1/4 cup melted margarine. Turn into 8- or 9-inch square baking pan. In medium bowl, combine oats, flour, brown sugar and cinnamon; cut in *6 tablespoons* cold margarine until crumbly. Sprinkle evenly over pear mixture.
Bake 35 to 40 minutes or until bubbly. Serve warm with ice cream and pure maple syrup if desired. *Makes 6 to 8 servings*

Prep time: 20 minutes
Baking time: 35 minutes

Peach Cobbler

1/2 cup sugar
1 tablespoon cornstarch
1/4 teaspoon cinnamon
Dash of nutmeg
1/3 cup water
4 cups sliced peaches *or* 1 bag (20 ounces) individual quick frozen peach slices

Biscuit Topping:
1 cup all-purpose flour
2 tablespoons sugar
1 1/2 teaspoons baking powder
1/4 teaspoon salt
1/4 cup BUTTER FLAVOR CRISCO®
1 egg, slightly beaten
1/4 cup milk

1. Preheat oven to 400°F. Combine sugar, cornstarch, cinnamon and nutmeg in medium saucepan. Add water; stir to mix. Add peach slices. Cook on medium-high heat until mixture comes to boil. Simmer 1 minute, stirring constantly. Pour into 8×8×2-inch glass baking dish or 2-quart baking dish. Place in oven.

2. For biscuit topping, combine flour, sugar, baking powder and salt. Cut in BUTTER FLAVOR CRISCO® until coarse crumbs form.

3. Combine egg and milk. Add all at once to flour mixture; stir just until moistened. Remove baking dish from oven; drop biscuit mixture in 8 mounds on top of hot fruit. Bake 20 minutes or until golden brown. Serve warm with ice cream or cream.

Makes about 8 servings

Deep Dish Peach Cobbler

Deep Dish Peach Cobbler

**1 package DUNCAN HINES®
    Moist Deluxe Spice
    Cake Mix
1 cup quick-cooking oats
    (not instant or old-
    fashioned), uncooked
1 cup chopped walnuts
³/₄ cup butter or margarine,
    melted
6 cups peeled and sliced
    peaches (about 6 large)
¹/₂ cup water
3 tablespoons brown sugar
2 tablespoons cornstarch
1 tablespoon plus
    1 teaspoon lemon juice
Whipped topping, for
    garnish
Ice cream (optional)
Nutmeg, for garnish**

1. Preheat oven to 350°F. Grease and flour 13×9×2-inch pan.
2. Combine cake mix, oats, nuts and butter in large bowl; stir until well blended. Press 2¹/₂ cups mixture in bottom of pan. Set aside remaining mixture.
3. Combine peaches, water and brown sugar in large saucepan. Simmer on low heat 5 minutes, stirring occasionally. Combine cornstarch and lemon juice in cup. Gradually add to peaches; stir until thickened. Pour over crust. Sprinkle reserved crumbs evenly over peaches. Bake 25 to 30 minutes or until topping is lightly browned. Serve with whipped topping or ice cream sprinkled with nutmeg, if desired.

Makes 10 to 12 servings

Fruited Shortcakes

**1¹/₃ cups SPOON SIZE®
    Shredded Wheat*, finely
    rolled (about 1 cup
    crumbs)
²/₃ cup all-purpose flour
1 teaspoon baking powder
¹/₂ teaspoon ground cinnamon
2 eggs
³/₄ cup milk
¹/₄ cup honey
2 tablespoons BLUE
    BONNET® Margarine,
    melted
1 teaspoon grated lemon
    peel
3 cups cut-up mixed fresh or
    drained canned fruit
1 tablespoon lemon juice
Lowfat vanilla yogurt**

Preheat oven to 375°F. Grease 8×8×2-inch baking pan. In medium bowl, combine cereal, flour, baking powder and cinnamon; set aside.

In small bowl, beat together eggs, milk, 2 tablespoons honey, margarine and lemon peel; blend into cereal mixture. Pour into prepared pan.

Bake 20 to 25 minutes or until toothpick inserted in center comes out clean. Cool slightly in pan on wire rack.

Meanwhile, in medium bowl, toss fruit with lemon juice and remaining 2 tablespoons honey. Cut warm cake into 9 squares. Serve immediately topped with fruit mixture and a dollop of yogurt.   *Makes 9 servings*

*Three NABISCO® Shredded Wheat Biscuits may be substituted.

Strawberry-Banana Shortcake

**1 cup skim milk
4 egg whites
6 tablespoons BLUE
    BONNET® Margarine,
    melted
3 medium, ripe bananas
1³/₄ cups all-purpose flour
1 cup NABISCO® 100% Bran
¹/₂ cup firmly packed light
    brown sugar
2¹/₂ teaspoons baking powder
1 teaspoon ground cinnamon
1 pint strawberries, sliced
3 tablespoons orange juice
Mint sprigs, for garnish**

Preheat oven to 350°F. Grease two 8-inch round baking pans. In large bowl, with electric mixer at low speed, blend milk, egg whites, margarine and 1 mashed banana. Add flour, bran, brown sugar, baking powder and cinnamon; beat at medium speed for 30 seconds. Spread in prepared pans.

Bake 30 minutes or until knife inserted in center comes out clean. Remove from pans; cool on wire racks.

Mash or puree ³/₄ cup strawberry slices with 2 tablespoons orange juice. Slice remaining 2 bananas; toss with remaining strawberries and 1 tablespoon orange juice. Place one cake layer on serving plate. Top with half the puree and half the fruit mixture; repeat layers. Garnish with mint if desired.

Makes about 10 servings

Chocolate Soufflé for Two

Almond Custard Sauce (recipe follows)
3 tablespoons HERSHEY'S® Cocoa
2 tablespoons all-purpose flour
2 tablespoons butter or margarine, softened
⅓ cup milk
½ teaspoon vanilla extract
⅓ cup sugar, divided
2 eggs, separated

Prepare Almond Custard Sauce at least 1 hour before serving. Lightly butter 3-cup soufflé dish; dust with sugar.

In small bowl, stir together cocoa and flour. Add butter, blending well; set aside. In medium saucepan, over low heat, heat milk until very hot; do not boil. Add cocoa mixture; cook over low heat, stirring constantly, until thickened. Remove from heat; stir in vanilla and all but 1 tablespoon sugar. Cool slightly. Add egg yolks, one at a time, beating with wooden spoon after each addition; cool to room temperature.

Preheat oven to 350°F. In large mixer bowl, beat egg whites until soft peaks form; gradually add reserved 1 tablespoon sugar and beat until stiff peaks form. Fold one-fourth of beaten whites into chocolate mixture; carefully fold chocolate mixture into remaining whites. Pour into prepared dish.

Bake 25 minutes. Serve soufflé immediately with refrigerated sauce.   *Makes 2 servings*

Almond Custard Sauce

1 cup milk
2 egg yolks*
2 tablespoons sugar
¼ teaspoon vanilla extract
1 teaspoon almond-flavored liqueur or ¼ teaspoon almond extract

In small saucepan, over low heat, heat milk until very hot; do not boil. Meanwhile, in small bowl, beat together egg yolks and sugar. Slowly pour in hot milk, stirring constantly, until blended. Return mixture to saucepan; cook over medium-low heat, stirring constantly, until mixture is slightly thickened and coats a metal spoon. Do not boil. Remove from heat; pour into bowl. (If custard should start to curdle, beat vigorously with rotary beater until smooth.) Cool quickly by placing in refrigerator for 5 minutes; stir in vanilla and liqueur. Cover; refrigerate until just before serving.

Makes about 1 cup sauce
*Use clean, uncracked eggs.

Luscious Cream Puffs

Cream Puffs:
1 cup water
½ cup BUTTER FLAVOR CRISCO®
½ teaspoon salt
1 cup all-purpose flour
4 eggs
Filling:
¾ cup granulated sugar
5 tablespoons cornstarch
Dash of salt
3¼ cups milk (or use part half-and-half)
3 egg yolks, slightly beaten*
2 tablespoons BUTTER FLAVOR CRISCO®
1 teaspoon vanilla
Confectioners sugar

1. Preheat oven to 400°F. Grease 2 baking sheets. For Cream Puffs, combine water, BUTTER FLAVOR CRISCO® and salt in medium saucepan; bring to boil. Stir in flour all at once. Cook and stir until mixture forms a ball. Remove from heat. Add eggs, one at a time, beating well after each addition.

*Use clean, uncracked eggs.

2. Drop dough by rounded tablespoonfuls onto prepared baking sheets (6 per sheet). Bake at least 30 minutes or until golden brown and dry. Cool away from drafts.

3. For Filling, combine granulated sugar, cornstarch and salt in large saucepan; stir in milk. Cook on medium heat, stirring constantly, until smooth and thickened. Gradually stir a little hot mixture into egg yolks. Stir egg mixture back into remaining hot mixture. Cook 2 or 3 minutes longer. Stir in BUTTER FLAVOR CRISCO® and vanilla. Cool.

4. Cut off tops of cream puffs; pull out any soft dough. Spoon filling into cream puffs; replace tops. Sprinkle with confectioners sugar. Serve immediately or refrigerate.

Makes 10 to 12 servings

Banana-Pineapple Cream Puffs

Cream Puff Pastry
1 cup water
⅓ cup butter, cut into pieces
1 tablespoon sugar
¼ teaspoon salt
1 cup all-purpose flour
4 eggs
Filling
¼ cup granulated sugar
3 tablespoons butter
¼ cup *plus* 1½ teaspoons cold water
½ teaspoon lemon juice
1 tablespoon rum
1 can (8 ounces) pineapple chunks in natural juice, drained and halved
1 envelope KNOX® Unflavored Gelatine
2 cups (1 pint) whipping or heavy cream
¼ cup confectioners sugar
½ cup sliced banana (about ½ medium)

Cream Puff Pastry: Preheat oven to 400°F. Grease baking sheets; set aside. In medium saucepan, combine water, butter, sugar and salt. Bring to a boil, then remove from heat. All at once, with wooden spoon, vigorously stir in flour until mixture comes away from sides of saucepan and forms a ball. Let stand 5 minutes to cool slightly. Add eggs, 1 at a time, beating well after each addition until dough is smooth. On greased baking sheets, using about ¼ cup for each, drop mixture in mounds, about 2 inches apart; swirl top of each mound. Immediately bake 30 minutes. With tip of sharp knife, quickly cut a slit into side of each puff. Bake an additional 10 minutes or until golden brown. Turn off oven and open door slightly; let cream puffs stand in oven 1 hour. Cool completely on wire rack.

Filling: In medium saucepan, combine granulated sugar, butter, 1½ teaspoons cold water and lemon juice. Cook over medium heat, stirring constantly, until sugar is completely dissolved and mixture turns tan. Remove from heat. Slowly stir in rum, then pineapple; set aside to cool.

In small saucepan, sprinkle unflavored gelatine over remaining ¼ cup cold water; let stand 1 minute. Stir over low heat until gelatine is completely dissolved, about 3 minutes.

In large, chilled bowl, while beating cream on low speed, gradually add gelatine mixture, then beat on medium speed until mixture thickens, about 5 minutes. Gradually add confectioners sugar and continue beating on medium speed until stiff peaks form, about 2 minutes. Gently fold in pineapple mixture and chill at least 1 hour. One hour before serving, slice cream puffs in half horizontally; remove doughy inside. Generously fill each with cream mixture, then top with banana slices. Replace top, then sprinkle, if desired, with additional confectioners sugar. *Makes 12 cream puffs*

Cheese Strudel with Fresh Fruit

Cheese Strudel with Fresh Fruit

12 phyllo strudel sheets
½ cup butter, melted
1 envelope KNOX® Unflavored Gelatine
¼ cup cold water
1 container (15 ounces) ricotta cheese
½ cup milk
½ cup sugar
1 egg
⅛ teaspoon ground nutmeg
½ cup currants or raisins (optional)
⅓ cup slivered blanched almonds, toasted
Suggested Fruit*

Preheat oven to 350°F. Unfold phyllo strudel sheets; cover with waxed paper, then damp cloth. Brush 1 sheet at a time with melted butter. Place 6 buttered sheets across 9-inch pie plate, extending sheets over sides; press gently into pie plate (see illustration). Place remaining 6 buttered sheets in opposite direction across pie plate, extending sheets over sides, to form cross; press gently into pie plate. Fold over extended sheets to form decorative border on rim of pie plate. Pierce center and sides with fork. Bake 15 minutes or until golden; cool on wire rack.

Meanwhile, in small saucepan, sprinkle unflavored gelatine over cold water; let stand 1 minute. Stir over low heat until gelatine is completely dissolved, about 3 minutes.

In blender or food processor, process ricotta, milk, sugar, egg and nutmeg until smooth. While processing, through feed cap, gradually add gelatine mixture and process until blended; gently stir in currants and almonds. Pour into prepared pie plate. Chill until thickened, about 15 minutes. Top with Suggested Fruit, then brush, if desired, with apple or apricot jam, melted; chill until firm, about 3 hours.

Makes about 8 servings

*Suggested Fruit: Use any one of the following—fresh or canned sliced peaches or apricots; fresh sliced nectarines or plums, or pitted cherries.

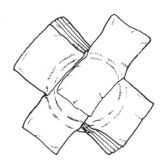

Napoleon Tarts

through stripes in an up and down motion to feather lines. Chill until ready to serve. Serve with remaining sauce.

Makes 8 servings

Prep time: 20 minutes
Baking time: 12 minutes

Quick Chocolate Sauce

   ³/₄ **cup light corn syrup**
   1 package (4-serving size)
      JELL-O® Instant Pudding
      and Pie Filling,
      Chocolate or Chocolate
      Fudge Flavor
   ³/₄ **cup evaporated milk or half**
      and half

Pour corn syrup into small bowl. Blend in pudding mix. Gradually add evaporated milk, stirring constantly. Let stand 10 minutes or until slightly thickened.

Makes about 2 cups sauce

Prep time: 20 minutes

Note: Store leftover sauce in covered container in refrigerator.

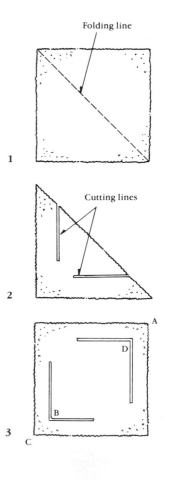

Napoleon Tarts

   1 package (17¼ ounces)
      frozen puff pastry sheets
   1 cup cold milk
   1 cup (½ pint) sour cream
   1 package (4-serving size)
      JELL-O® Instant Pudding
      and Pie Filling, any flavor
   Quick Chocolate Sauce
      (recipe follows)

Thaw pastry as directed on package. Preheat oven to 375°F. Unfold pastry. Cut each sheet into 4 squares. Fold each square in half diagonally. (See Diagram 1.) Cut along 2 unfolded edges, leaving ½-inch rim all around (do not cut completely through to center). (See Diagram 2.) Unfold pastry. Fold outer top righthand corner (A) over to inner bottom lefthand corner (B); fold outer bottom lefthand corner (C) over to inner top righthand corner (D). (See Diagram 3.) Repeat with remaining squares.

Place pastries on baking sheets. Pierce bottom of each pastry in several places with fork. Bake for 12 to 15 minutes or until golden. If pastry rises in center, gently press down with fork. Cool on wire rack.

Mix milk and sour cream in small bowl until smooth. Add pudding mix. Beat with wire whisk until well blended, 1 to 2 minutes. Let stand 5 minutes or until slightly thickened.

Spoon 1 tablespoon Quick Chocolate Sauce onto bottom of each tart shell. Spoon pudding mixture into shells.

Drizzle each tart with 1 teaspoon Quick Chocolate Sauce in stripes. Pull wooden toothpick

Crispy Apple Turnovers

Filling:
 1³/₄ cups pared, chopped tart
      cooking apples (about
      2 medium)
 ¹/₃ cup water
 ¹/₃ cup firmly packed brown
      sugar
 ¹/₄ teaspoon cinnamon
 ¹/₈ teaspoon nutmeg
 1 tablespoon all-purpose
   flour
 1 teaspoon granulated sugar
 1 tablespoon butter or
   margarine
Pastry:
 2 cups all-purpose flour
 2 tablespoons granulated
   sugar
 1 teaspoon salt
 ³/₄ cup CRISCO® Shortening
 5 tablespoons cold water
Glaze:
 ¹/₂ cup confectioners sugar
 1 tablespoon milk
 ¹/₄ teaspoon vanilla

1. Preheat oven to 425°F. For
Filling, combine apples and
water in small saucepan. Cook
on high heat until mixture
comes to boil, stirring frequently.
Reduce heat to low; simmer 5
minutes. Stir in brown sugar,
cinnamon and nutmeg; simmer 5
minutes, stirring frequently.

2. Combine flour and granulated
sugar. Stir into apple mixture;
bring to boil. Boil 1 minute; stir
in butter.

3. For Pastry, combine flour,
granulated sugar and salt in
medium bowl. Cut in CRISCO®
using pastry blender (or 2
knives) until mixture resembles
coarse crumbs. Sprinkle with
water, 1 tablespoon at a time.
Toss lightly with fork until
dough forms ball.

4. Flour rolling surface and
rolling pin lightly. Divide dough
in half. Roll each half to ¹/₁₆-inch
thickness. Use lid from 3 pound
CRISCO® can as pattern to cut 6
(5¹/₄-inch) circles from each half.
Reroll dough as necessary.

5. Place about 1 tablespoon of
apple filling on each dough
circle. Moisten edges with water;
fold in half over filling. Press
with fork to seal.

6. Place on ungreased baking
sheet; prick tops with fork. Bake
20 minutes or until golden
brown. Cool 10 minutes on wire
rack.

7. For Glaze, combine
confectioners sugar, milk and
vanilla in small bowl; stir well.
Drizzle over turnovers. Serve
warm or cool.

Makes 12 turnovers

Apples in Cheddar Pastry

 2 cups all-purpose flour
 ¹/₄ teaspoon salt
 ¹/₂ cup (1 stick) butter, cut
   into pieces
 1 cup (4 ounces) finely
   shredded Wisconsin
   Medium Cheddar cheese
 6 tablespoons cold water
 6 small Golden Delicious
   apples, peeled and cored
 4 tablespoons granulated
   sugar
 2 tablespoons brown sugar
 ¹/₃ cup chopped pecans
   Milk
   Lemon Nutmeg Sauce
   (recipe follows)

Preheat oven to 400°F. Blend
flour and salt in medium bowl.
Using pastry blender or 2
knives, cut in butter until coarse
crumbs form. Stir in cheese. Add
water gradually, tossing gently
until moisture is absorbed.
Shape into ball.

On lightly floured surface, roll
dough to 19×12-inch rectangle.
Cut off 1-inch strip to make an
18×12-inch rectangle; reserve
strip. Cut remaining dough into
six 6-inch squares. Place 1 apple
(upside down) in center of each
square.

In small bowl, combine sugars
and nuts. Stuff center of each
apple with sugar mixture. Fold
dough up tightly around each
apple, sealing seams well. Place
on ungreased cookie sheet, seam-
side down. Brush dough with
milk and prick with fork. Cut
leaf design out of reserved
dough; brush with milk and
place on top of apples.

Bake 30 minutes or until apples
are fork tender. If pastry browns
too quickly, cover with foil. While
apples are baking, prepare
Lemon Nutmeg Sauce. To serve,
place dumplings on individual
dessert dishes and spoon warm
sauce over each. Serve
immediately.

Makes 6 servings

Lemon Nutmeg Sauce

 1 tablespoon cornstarch
 ¹/₂ cup granulated sugar
 1 cup water
 2 tablespoons fresh lemon
   juice
 2 tablespoons butter
 1 teaspoon finely grated
   lemon peel
 ¹/₈ teaspoon nutmeg
   Pinch of salt

Combine cornstarch and
granulated sugar in medium
saucepan. Gradually stir in
water. Cook and stir over
medium heat until thickened.
Remove from heat; add lemon
juice, butter, lemon peel, nutmeg
and salt, stirring until butter
melts.

*Favorite recipe from **Wisconsin Milk
Marketing Board** ©1991*

Pear Dumplings

2½ cups water
½ cup plus 2 tablespoons sugar
2 tablespoons cinnamon imperials candies
½ teaspoon nutmeg
1 teaspoon cinnamon
1½ cups all-purpose flour
2 teaspoons baking powder
½ teaspoon salt
½ cup margarine, softened
1 cup KELLOGG'S® ALL-BRAN® Cereal
¾ cup skim milk
3 large pears, cored, peeled and cut in half crosswise

1. Preheat oven to 375°F. In 2-quart saucepan, combine water, the ½ cup sugar, cinnamon candies and ¼ teaspoon of the nutmeg. Cook over medium heat, stirring occasionally, until mixture starts to boil; remove from heat.

2. Combine remaining 2 tablespoons sugar, ¼ teaspoon nutmeg and cinnamon in small bowl. Set aside. In medium-size mixing bowl, mix together flour, baking powder and salt. With pastry blender or 2 knives, cut in margarine until mixture resembles coarse crumbs. Combine KELLOGG'S® ALL-BRAN® Cereal and milk. Let stand 2 to 3 minutes or until milk is absorbed. Add cereal mixture to flour mixture, stirring with fork until dough forms a ball. Divide dough evenly into 6 pieces.

3. On lightly floured surface, roll each dough piece into 7-inch round; place 1 pear half on each. Sprinkle ⅙ of the sugar-cinnamon mixture over each pear half. Gently pull dough up and around pear, molding dough around pear and sealing completely. Place in 13×9×2-inch baking pan. Pour hot cinnamon syrup over dumplings.

Pear Dumplings

4. Bake 35 minutes or until pears are tender. Baste twice during baking with syrup around dumplings. Serve warm or cold.   *Makes 6 servings*

Nectarine Dumplings: Substitute 6 medium-size nectarines, peeled and pitted, for pears.

Apple Dumplings: Substitute 6 small cooking apples, peeled and cored, for pears.

Creamy Dutch Apple Dessert

¼ cup margarine or butter
1½ cups graham cracker crumbs
1 (14-ounce) can EAGLE® Brand Sweetened Condensed Milk (NOT evaporated milk)
1 (8-ounce) container BORDEN® or MEADOW GOLD® Sour Cream
¼ cup REALEMON® Lemon Juice from Concentrate
1 (21-ounce) can apple pie filling
¼ cup chopped walnuts
¼ teaspoon ground cinnamon

Preheat oven to 350°F. In 10×6-inch baking dish, melt margarine in oven. Sprinkle crumbs over margarine; mix well. Press firmly on bottom of dish.

In medium bowl, combine sweetened condensed milk, sour cream and REALEMON® brand; spread evenly over crumbs. Spoon pie filling evenly over creamy layer.

Bake 25 to 30 minutes or until set. Cool slightly. Before serving, combine nuts and cinnamon; sprinkle over apple layer. Serve warm or chilled. Refrigerate leftovers.

Makes 10 to 12 servings

Brownie Fudge Dessert

½ cup HERSHEY'S® Cocoa
1 cup butter or margarine
3 tablespoons vegetable oil
1 cup sugar
4 eggs, slightly beaten
2 teaspoons vanilla extract
½ cup all-purpose flour
30 pecan halves
Ice cream or sweetened whipped cream

Preheat oven to 350°F. In top of double boiler over hot, not boiling, water, combine cocoa, butter and oil; stir until butter is melted. Remove from heat; stir in sugar. Stir in eggs and vanilla just until blended; stir in flour. Pour batter into ungreased 9-inch square baking pan; arrange pecan halves evenly on top. Place 9-inch pan in 13×9-inch baking pan; place both in oven. Pour hot water to depth of 1 inch into larger pan.

Bake 40 to 45 minutes or until knife inserted ½ inch from edge comes out clean and brownie-like crust has formed; do not overbake. Remove from water bath; let cool on wire rack until warm. Scoop onto serving plates and top with ice cream. May also be served cold, cut into squares; serve with sweetened whipped cream.

Makes about 8 servings

Kahlúa® Chocolate Nut Squares

1¼ cups sifted all-purpose
   flour
¾ teaspoon baking powder
½ teaspoon salt
½ cup butter, softened
¾ cup brown sugar, packed
1 large egg
¼ cup plus 1 tablespoon
   KAHLÚA®
1 cup (6 ounces) semisweet
   chocolate pieces
⅓ cup chopped walnuts or
   pecans
   Brown Butter Icing (recipe
   follows)
   Nut halves (optional)

Preheat oven to 350°F. Grease 11×7-inch baking pan. In small bowl, resift flour with baking powder and salt; set aside. In large mixing bowl, cream butter and brown sugar; beat in egg. Stir in ¼ cup KAHLÚA®, then flour mixture; blend well. Fold in chocolate pieces and nuts. Spread evenly in prepared pan. Bake 30 minutes or until top springs back when touched lightly in center. Do not overbake.

Remove from oven; cool in pan 15 minutes. Brush top with remaining 1 tablespoon KAHLÚA®. Cool completely. Spread with Brown Butter Icing. When icing is set, cut into 2×1½-inch bars. Garnish with nut halves, if desired.
Makes about 2 dozen bars

Brown Butter Icing

2 tablespoons butter
1 tablespoon KAHLÚA®
2 teaspoons milk or cream
1⅓ cups powdered sugar,
   sifted

In saucepan, heat butter until lightly browned. Remove from heat. Add KAHLÚA®, milk and sifted powdered sugar; beat until smooth.

Kiwifruit Squares

1¼ cups flour
⅓ cup powdered sugar,
   divided
½ cup butter or margarine
1 cup granulated sugar
2 California kiwifruit, pared
   and pureed (about
   ⅓ cup)
2 eggs, beaten
½ teaspoon baking powder
½ teaspoon grated lime peel
1 teaspoon lime juice

Preheat oven to 350°F. In small bowl, combine flour and ¼ cup powdered sugar; cut in butter until mixture resembles coarse crumbs. Pat on bottom of 9-inch square pan. Bake 15 minutes. Combine granulated sugar, kiwifruit, eggs, baking powder, lime peel and lime juice; pour over baked crust. Return to oven; bake 25 minutes. Cool. Sprinkle with remaining powdered sugar. Cut into 16 squares.
Makes 16 squares

*Favorite recipe from **California Kiwifruit Commission***

Creamy Cherry n' Oat Squares

1¼ cups old fashioned or
   quick oats, uncooked
⅓ cup PARKAY® Margarine,
   melted
¼ cup sugar
1 (8 oz.) pkg. PHILADELPHIA
   BRAND® Cream Cheese,
   softened
¼ cup sugar
1 egg
1 (21 oz.) can cherry pie
   filling

• Preheat oven to 400°F.

• Stir together oats, margarine and ¼ cup sugar in small bowl; press onto bottom of greased 8-inch square pan. Bake 15 minutes.

• Reduce oven temperature to 350°F.

• Beat cream cheese and ¼ cup sugar in small mixing bowl at medium speed with electric mixer until well blended. Blend in egg.

• Pour over crust. Bake 10 to 15 minutes or until set. Spread pie filling over cream cheese mixture; continue baking 15 minutes. Chill.
Makes 8 servings

Prep time: 25 minutes
Cooking time: 15 minutes

Kiwifruit Squares

Cashew Peanut Butter Bars

1 cup unsifted flour
¼ cup firmly packed brown sugar
½ teaspoon baking powder
¼ teaspoon baking soda
½ cup cold margarine or butter
1 tablespoon vanilla extract
3 cups CAMPFIRE® Miniature Marshmallows
1 (14-ounce) can EAGLE® Brand Sweetened Condensed Milk (NOT evaporated milk)
1 cup peanut butter flavored chips *or* ½ cup creamy peanut butter
1 (3-ounce) can chow mein noodles
1 cup coarsely chopped cashews *or* peanuts

Preheat oven to 350°F. In medium bowl, combine flour, brown sugar, baking powder and baking soda; cut in margarine and *1 teaspoon* vanilla until crumbly. Press mixture firmly on bottom of ungreased 13×9-inch baking pan.

Bake 15 minutes or until lightly browned. Top evenly with marshmallows; bake 2 minutes longer or until marshmallows begin to puff. Remove from oven; cool.

Meanwhile, in heavy saucepan, over medium heat, combine sweetened condensed milk and peanut butter chips; cook and stir until slightly thickened, 6 to 8 minutes. Remove from heat; stir in noodles, nuts and remaining *2 teaspoons* vanilla. Spread evenly over marshmallows. Cool. Chill. Cut into bars. Store loosely covered at room temperature.
Makes 24 to 36 bars

Cashew Peanut Butter Bars

Chocolate-Cherry Squares

1 cup all-purpose flour
⅓ cup butter or margarine
½ cup packed light brown sugar
½ cup chopped nuts
Cream Cheese Filling (recipe follows)
Red candied cherries, halved

Preheat oven to 350°F. In large mixer bowl, combine flour, butter and brown sugar; blend on low speed 2 to 3 minutes to form fine crumbs. Stir in nuts. Reserve ¾ cup crumb mixture for topping; press remaining crumbs onto bottom of ungreased 9-inch square baking pan. Bake 10 minutes or until lightly browned.

Meanwhile, prepare Cream Cheese Filling; spread over warm crust. Sprinkle reserved crumb mixture over top; garnish with cherry halves. Return to oven. Bake 25 minutes or until lightly browned. Cool in pan on wire rack. Cut into squares. Store, covered, in refrigerator.

Makes about 3 dozen squares

Cream Cheese Filling

1 package (8 ounces) cream cheese, softened
½ cup sugar
⅓ cup HERSHEY'S® Cocoa
¼ cup milk
1 egg
½ teaspoon vanilla extract
½ cup chopped red candied cherries

In small mixer bowl, beat cream cheese and sugar until fluffy. Add cocoa, milk, egg and vanilla; beat until smooth. Fold in cherries.

Caramel Apple Oat Squares

1¾ cups unsifted flour
1 cup quick-cooking oats, uncooked
½ cup firmly packed brown sugar
½ teaspoon baking soda
½ teaspoon salt
1 cup cold margarine or butter
1 cup chopped walnuts
20 EAGLE® Brand Caramels, unwrapped
1 (14-ounce) can EAGLE® Brand Sweetened Condensed Milk (NOT evaporated milk)
1 (21-ounce) can apple pie filling

Preheat oven to 375°F. In large bowl, combine flour, oats, brown sugar, baking soda and salt; cut in margarine until crumbly. Reserving 1½ cups crumb mixture, press remainder on bottom of 13×9-inch baking pan. Bake 15 minutes. Add nuts to reserved crumb mixture.

In heavy saucepan, over low heat, melt caramels with

Caramel Apple Oat Squares

sweetened con[...] stirring until [...] apple pie fill[...] crust; top wi[...] then reserve[...] Bake 20 minutes or [...] Cool. Serve warm with ice cream.

Makes 10 to 12 servings

Prep time: 30 minutes
Baking time: 35 minutes

Cherry Pineapple Trifle

1 package DUNCAN HINES® Moist Deluxe Yellow Cake Mix
1 package (4-serving size) vanilla instant pudding and pie filling mix
1 can (15¼ ounces) crushed pineapple, drained
1 can (21 ounces) cherry pie filling
1 package (12 ounces) flaked coconut (3½ cups)
2 cups chopped pecans
2 containers (8 ounces each) frozen whipped topping, thawed

1. Preheat oven to 350°F. Grease and flour two 9-inch round cake pans. Prepare, bake and cool cake following package directions.

2. Prepare instant pudding following directions. Refrigerate until ready to use.

3. Crumble one cake layer in 6-quart trifle dish. Layer half each of pudding, pineapple, cherry pie filling, coconut, pecans and whipped topping. Repeat layers, beginning with crumbling second cake layer and ending with remaining pecans. Refrigerate until ready to serve.

Makes 24 to 32 servings

Tip: If a trifle dish is not available, use a 6-quart clear glass bowl with straight sides.

Pear Dessert Squares

Filling:
- 3 or 4 fresh California Bartlett pears
- 4 tablespoons cornstarch
- 1/3 cup sugar
- 1/2 teaspoon cinnamon
- 1/4 teaspoon salt
- 3/4 cup water
- 2 1/2 tablespoons lemon juice
- 2 tablespoons butter
- 1 teaspoon vanilla extract
- 2 tablespoons currants or raisins

Pastry Shell:
- 2 cups flour
- 1/2 teaspoon salt
- 3 tablespoons sugar
- 3/4 cup butter
- 3 egg yolks
- 1 1/2 tablespoons lemon juice

Topping:
- 2 tablespoons sugar
- 1/4 cup ground walnuts
- 1 cup reserved pastry dough

For Filling, pare, halve, core and slice enough pears to measure 4 cups. In large bowl, toss pears with 2 tablespoons cornstarch; set aside. In small saucepan, combine sugar, remaining 2 tablespoons cornstarch, cinnamon and salt. Stir in water and juice. Cook over medium heat, stirring constantly, until thickened. Add butter and vanilla extract. Stir in currants; set aside.

For Pastry Shell, preheat oven to 375°F. Mix flour, salt and sugar in mixing bowl; cut in butter with pastry blender or beat with mixer until well combined. Mixture will be moist and crumbly. Mix in yolks and juice. Reserve 1 cup dough for topping; press remainder into bottom and 1 1/4 inches up sides of 8-inch square baking pan. Bake 10 minutes. Spoon into shell.

For Topping, combine sugar and nuts. Stir into reserved pastry dough; crumble over filling. Bake an additional 35 to 40 minutes. Serve warm or chilled.

Makes 8 servings

Favorite recipe from **California Tree Fruit Agreement**

Chocolate Mint Dessert

- 1 cup all-purpose flour
- 1 cup sugar
- 1/2 cup butter or margarine, softened
- 4 eggs
- 1 1/2 cups (16-ounce can) HERSHEY'S® Syrup
- Mint Cream Center (recipe follows)
- Chocolate Chip Glaze (recipe follows)

Preheat oven to 350°F. Grease 13×9×2-inch baking pan. In large mixer bowl, combine flour, sugar, butter, eggs and syrup; beat until smooth. Pour batter into prepared pan. Bake 25 to 30 minutes or until top springs back when touched lightly. Cool completely in pan on wire rack. Spread Mint Cream Center on cake. Cover; refrigerate. Pour Chocolate Chip Glaze over chilled dessert. Cover; refrigerate at least 1 hour before serving.

Makes about 12 servings

MINT CREAM CENTER: In small mixer bowl, combine 2 cups powdered sugar, 1/2 cup softened butter or margarine and 2 tablespoons green creme de menthe; beat until smooth.

(One tablespoon water, 1/2 to 3/4 teaspoon mint extract and 3 drops green food color may be substituted for creme de menthe.)

CHOCOLATE CHIP GLAZE: In small saucepan, over very low heat, melt 6 tablespoons butter or margarine and 1 cup HERSHEY'S® Semi-Sweet Chocolate Chips. Remove from heat; stir until smooth. Cool slightly.

Southern Yam Dessert Squares

- 2 cups quick-cooking oats, uncooked
- 1 1/2 cups unsifted flour
- 1/2 teaspoon baking soda
- 1/2 teaspoon salt
- 1 cup margarine or butter, softened
- 1 cup firmly packed light brown sugar
- 1 teaspoon vanilla extract
- 1/2 cup chopped nuts
- 1 pound yams or sweet potatoes, cooked, peeled and mashed (about 2 cups)
- 1 (14-ounce) can EAGLE® Brand Sweetened Condensed Milk (NOT evaporated milk)
- 2 eggs, beaten
- 1 1/2 teaspoons ground allspice *or* pumpkin pie spice
- 1 teaspoon grated orange rind

Preheat oven to 350°F. Combine oats, flour, baking soda and salt; set aside.

In large mixer bowl, beat margarine, brown sugar and vanilla until fluffy. Add dry ingredients; mix until crumbly. Reserving 1 cup crumb mixture, press remainder firmly on bottom of 13×9-inch baking dish. Bake 10 minutes.

Southern Yam Dessert Squares

Meanwhile, stir nuts into reserved crumb mixture. In large mixer bowl, beat remaining ingredients until well blended. Pour over prepared crust. Top with reserved crumb mixture. Bake 25 to 30 minutes or until golden brown. Cool. Serve warm or chilled. Garnish as desired. Refrigerate leftovers.

Makes 8 to 10 servings

Tip: 1 (16- or 17-ounce) can sweet potatoes, drained and mashed, *or* 1 (16-ounce) can pumpkin can be substituted for yams.

Apple Pumpkin Desserts

- 1 (21-ounce) can apple pie filling
- 1 (16-ounce) can pumpkin (about 2 cups)
- 1 (14-ounce) can EAGLE® Brand Sweetened Condensed Milk (NOT evaporated milk)
- 2 eggs
- 1 teaspoon ground cinnamon
- 1/2 teaspoon ground nutmeg
- 1/2 teaspoon salt
- 1 cup gingersnap cookie crumbs (about 18 cookies)
- 2 tablespoons margarine or butter, melted

Preheat oven to 400°F. Lightly grease 8 to 10 custard cups. Spoon equal portions of apple pie filling into prepared cups. In large mixer bowl, combine pumpkin, sweetened condensed milk, eggs, cinnamon, nutmeg and salt; mix well. Spoon equal portions over apple filling. Combine crumbs and margarine. Sprinkle over pumpkin filling. Place cups on 15×10-inch jellyroll pan. Bake 10 minutes. *Reduce oven temperature to 350°F;* bake 15 minutes longer or until set. Cool. Serve warm. Refrigerate leftovers.

Makes 8 to 10 servings

Prep time: 20 minutes
Baking time: 25 minutes

Apple Pumpkin Desserts

German Apple Torte

- 1/3 cup PARKAY® Margarine, softened
- 1/3 cup sugar
- 1 egg
- 1 1/4 cups flour
- 2 (8 oz.) pkgs. PHILADELPHIA BRAND® "Light" Neufchatel Cheese, softened
- 1/3 cup sugar
- 2 tablespoons flour
- 1/2 teaspoon vanilla
- 2 eggs
- 1 1/4 cups peeled chopped apple
- 1/4 cup sliced almonds
- 1/3 cup KRAFT® Grape or Red Currant Jelly, heated

• Preheat oven to 425°F.

• Beat margarine and sugar in small mixing bowl until light and fluffy. Blend in egg. Add flour; mix well.

• Spread dough onto bottom and 1 1/4 inches up side of 9-inch springform pan.

• Bake 5 to 7 minutes or until crust is lightly browned.

• Beat neufchatel cheese, sugar, flour and vanilla in large mixing bowl at medium speed with electric mixer until well blended.

• Add eggs, one at a time, mixing well after each addition. Pour into crust. Top with apples and almonds. Bake 10 minutes.

• Reduce oven temperature to 350°F; continue baking 30 minutes. Drizzle with jelly. Loosen cake from rim of pan; cool before removing rim of pan. Chill several hours or overnight.

Makes 10 to 12 servings

Prep time: 25 minutes plus chilling
Cooking time: 40 minutes

P-START BAKING

There's always time to bake when you turn to this chapter of fuss-free recipes. Convenience foods, such as cake mixes, biscuit mixes and frozen puff pastry, get these delicious baked goods off to a quick start. Prepare freshly baked breads and muffins, elegant cakes and cheesecakes, foolproof pies and desserts, and delightful cookies and brownies—all in less time and with less effort. They're perfect to serve at impromptu gatherings or as everyday family treats.

Cream Cheese and Pecan Danish

1 sheet frozen puff pastry, thawed
2 (3 oz.) pkgs. PHILADELPHIA BRAND® Cream Cheese, softened
¼ cup powdered sugar
1 egg
1 teaspoon vanilla
¾ cup chopped pecans
Creamy Glaze

• Preheat oven to 375°F.
• Unfold pastry; roll to 15×10-inch rectangle. Place in 15×10×1-inch jelly roll pan.
• Beat 6 ounces cream cheese, ¼ cup sugar, egg and vanilla in small mixing bowl at medium speed with electric mixer until well blended. Stir in ½ cup pecans.
• Spread cream cheese mixture over pastry to within 3 inches from each side.
• Make 2-inch cuts at 1-inch intervals on long sides of rectangle. Crisscross strips over filling.
• Bake 25 to 30 minutes or until golden brown. Cool.
• Drizzle with Creamy Glaze. Sprinkle with remaining ¼ cup pecans.

Makes 10 to 12 servings

Creamy Glaze

1 (3 oz.) pkg. PHILADELPHIA BRAND® Cream Cheese, softened
¾ cup powdered sugar
1 tablespoon milk

• Beat ingredients until smooth.

Prep time: 20 minutes
Cooking time: 30 minutes

Orange Spice Muffins

⅓ cup firmly packed brown sugar
¼ cup margarine or butter, softened
1 egg, beaten
¾ cup BORDEN® or MEADOW GOLD® Milk
½ cup orange juice
1 tablespoon grated orange peel
3 cups biscuit baking mix
1 (9-ounce) package NONE SUCH® Condensed Mincemeat, crumbled
2 tablespoons granulated sugar
2 teaspoons ground cinnamon

Preheat oven to 375°F. In large bowl, beat brown sugar and margarine until fluffy. Add egg, milk, orange juice and peel; mix well. Stir in biscuit mix and mincemeat only until moistened (do not overmix). Fill greased or paper-lined 2½-inch muffin cups ¾ full. In small bowl, combine granulated sugar and ground cinnamon; sprinkle evenly over muffins. Bake 18 to 22 minutes or until golden brown. Remove from pan; serve warm.

Makes about 18 muffins

Cream Cheese and Pecan Danish

Fruit Blossom Muffins

²/₃ cup **BAMA®** Blackberry
    Jam or Orange
    Marmalade
½ cup orange juice
 1 egg, slightly beaten
 2 cups biscuit baking mix
²/₃ cup chopped pecans
¼ cup sugar
 1 tablespoon flour
½ teaspoon ground cinnamon
¼ teaspoon ground nutmeg
 2 to 3 teaspoons cold
    margarine or butter

Preheat oven to 400°F. In
medium bowl, combine jam,
orange juice and egg. Add biscuit
mix; stir only until moistened
(batter will be slightly lumpy).
Stir in nuts. Fill greased or
paper-lined 2½-inch muffin cups
²/₃ full. In small bowl, combine
sugar, flour and spices; cut in
margarine until crumbly.
Sprinkle over batter. Bake 15 to
20 minutes or until golden
brown. Remove from pans; serve
warm.

Makes about 12 muffins

Fruit Diamonds

Fruit Diamonds

 1 (8-ounce) package
    refrigerated crescent
    rolls
¾ cup of your favorite
    conserve
    Granulated sugar

Preheat oven to 350°F. Unroll
dough and place on waxed paper.
Pinch all seams together. Cover
with another piece of waxed
paper. Roll into 16×12-inch
rectangle; cut into twelve 4×4-
inch squares. Place 1 tablespoon
of your favorite conserve in
center of each square. Fold
opposite corners towards center
and pinch together. Sprinkle
with granulated sugar; place on
ungreased baking sheet. Bake 8
to 10 minutes.

Makes 12 fruit diamonds

Favorite recipe from **Kerr Corporation**

Garlic Monkey Bread

 2 packages (10 ounces each)
    refrigerated buttermilk
    biscuit dough
 6 tablespoons unsalted
    IMPERIAL® Margarine,
    melted
1½ tablespoons chopped
    parsley
 1 tablespoon finely chopped
    onion
¾ teaspoon **LAWRY'S®** Garlic
    Powder with Parsley
½ teaspoon **LAWRY'S®**
    Seasoned Salt

Preheat oven to 375°F. Separate
biscuit dough. In small bowl,
combine remaining ingredients.
Dip each biscuit into margarine
mixture to coat. In Bundt® pan
or 1½-quart casserole, place 1
layer of dipped biscuits in
bottom, slightly overlapping to
fit. Arrange remaining biscuits
in a zig-zag fashion, placing
some towards the center and
some towards the outside edge.
Pour any remaining margarine
mixture over biscuits. Bake 15 to
20 minutes or until golden
brown. Invert onto serving plate;
serve warm.

Makes 10 servings

Presentation: A perfect last-
minute bread idea to serve with
homemade soup or salad.

Hint: If top biscuits brown too
quickly, cover with foil and
continue baking.

Bacon Brunch Buns

Bacon Brunch Buns

1 loaf (1 pound) frozen bread
    dough
2 tablespoons (½ package)
    **HIDDEN VALLEY
    RANCH®** Original Ranch®
    with Bacon Salad
    Dressing Mix
¼ cup unsalted butter or
    margarine, melted
1 cup (4 ounces) shredded
    Cheddar cheese
2 egg yolks
1½ tablespoons cold water
3 tablespoons sesame seeds

Thaw bread dough following
package directions. On floured
board, roll dough into rectangle
about 18×7 inches. In small
bowl, whisk together salad
dressing mix and butter. Spread
mixture on dough; sprinkle with
cheese. Starting at 18-inch side,
roll up tightly, jelly-roll style,
pinching seam to seal. Cut into
16 slices. Place slices cut-side
down on greased jelly-roll pan.
Cover with plastic wrap; let rise
in warm place (80° to 85°F)
until doubled in bulk, about
1 hour.

Preheat oven to 375°F. In small
bowl, beat egg yolks and water;
brush mixture over buns.
Sprinkle with sesame seeds.
Bake until golden brown, 25 to
30 minutes. Serve warm.

Makes 16 buns

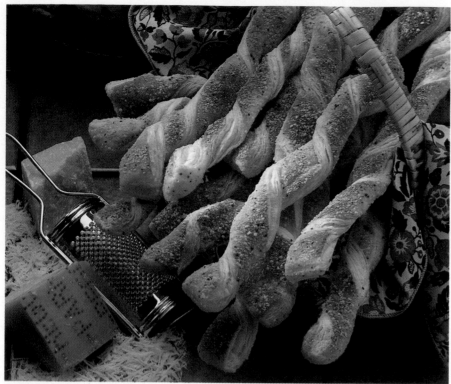

Crispie Cheese Twists

Crispie Cheese Twists

1/2 cup grated Parmesan
     cheese
3/4 teaspoon LAWRY'S®
     Seasoned Pepper
1/2 teaspoon LAWRY'S® Garlic
     Powder with Parsley
1 package (17³/4 ounces)
     frozen puff pastry,
     thawed
1 egg white, lightly beaten

Preheat oven to 350°F. In small
bowl, combine Parmesan cheese,
Seasoned Pepper and Garlic
Powder with Parsley. Unfold
pastry sheets onto cutting board.
Brush pastry lightly with egg
white; sprinkle each sheet with
1/4 of the cheese mixture. Lightly
press into pastry; turn over and
repeat. Cut each sheet into 12
(1-inch-wide) strips; twist. Place
on greased cookie sheet. Bake 15
minutes or until golden brown.
Makes 2 dozen twists
Presentation: Serve in a napkin-
lined basket. Place layer of
plastic wrap over napkin to
protect it.

Tabasco® Onion Bread

2 tablespoons instant
     minced onion
1/3 cup water
1½ cups biscuit baking mix
1 egg, slightly beaten
1/2 cup milk
1/2 teaspoon TABASCO®
     Pepper Sauce
1/2 teaspoon caraway seeds,
     optional
2 tablespoons butter, melted

Preheat oven to 400°F. Soak
instant minced onion in water 5
minutes. Combine biscuit mix,
egg, milk and TABASCO®
Pepper Sauce; stir until blended.
Stir in onion. Turn into greased
8-inch pie plate; sprinkle with
caraway seeds. Brush melted
butter over top. Bake 20 to 25
minutes or until bread is golden
brown.   *Makes 1 loaf*

Peachy Cinnamon Coffeecake

1 package DUNCAN HINES®
     Bakery Style Cinnamon
     Swirl with Crumb
     Topping Muffin Mix
1 can (8¹/4 ounces) juice
     pack sliced yellow cling
     peaches
1 egg

1. Preheat oven to 400°F. Grease
8-inch square or 9-inch round
baking pan.
2. Drain peaches, reserving juice.
Add water to reserved juice to
equal ³/4 cup liquid. Chop
peaches.
3. Combine muffin mix, egg and
³/4 cup peach liquid in medium
bowl; fold in peaches. Pour batter
into pan. Knead swirl packet 10
seconds before opening. Squeeze
contents on top of batter and
swirl with knife. Sprinkle
topping over batter. Bake 28 to
33 minutes for 8-inch pan (or 20
to 25 minutes for 9-inch pan) or
until golden. Serve warm.
Makes 9 servings

Savory Corn Muffins

1 egg, beaten
³/4 cup MIRACLE WHIP® Salad
     Dressing
1 (4-oz.) can chopped green
     chilies, drained
1 (8¹/2-oz.) pkg. corn
     muffin mix

Preheat oven to 400°F. Combine
egg, salad dressing and chilies,
mixing until well blended. Add
muffin mix, mixing just until
moistened. Spoon into greased
medium-size muffin pan, filling
each cup ²/3 full. Bake 15
minutes. Loosen edge of muffins;
remove from pan. Cool on wire
rack.   *Makes about 12 muffins*

Preparation time: 10 minutes
Baking time: 15 minutes

Peachy Cinnamon Coffeecake

Blueberry Orange Loaf

Blueberry Orange Loaf

**1 package DUNCAN HINES®
    Bakery Style Blueberry
    with Crumb Topping
    Muffin Mix
¹/₂ teaspoon baking powder
2 egg whites
²/₃ cup CITRUS HILL® Orange
    Juice
1 teaspoon grated orange
    peel**

1. Preheat oven to 350°F. Grease 8×4-inch or 9×5-inch loaf pan.
2. Rinse blueberries with cold water and drain.
3. Empty muffin mix into bowl. Add baking powder; stir to combine and break up any lumps. Add egg whites and orange juice; stir until moistened, about 50 strokes. Fold in blueberries and orange peel. Pour into pan; sprinkle topping from packet over batter. Bake 45 to 55 minutes or until wooden toothpick inserted in center comes out clean. Cool in pan 10 minutes. Loosen loaf from pan; invert onto cooling rack. Turn right side up; cool competely.

Makes 1 loaf

Walnut Coffee Strip

**2¹/₂ cups buttermilk baking mix
¹/₂ cup milk
1 egg, beaten
3 tablespoons butter or
    margarine, softened
¹/₄ cup granulated sugar
¹/₂ teaspoon ground cinnamon
³/₄ cup diced mixed candied
    fruits
¹/₂ cup chopped DIAMOND®
    Walnuts
    Powdered Sugar Frosting
    (recipe follows)**

Preheat oven to 400°F. In medium bowl, combine baking mix, milk and egg; stir until soft dough is formed. Turn dough out onto floured board; knead lightly. Roll out into 12×9-inch rectangle. In small bowl, mix butter, sugar and cinnamon; spread over dough. Sprinkle with candied fruits and walnuts. Roll up, jelly-roll fashion, starting from 12-inch side. Cut roll into 8 slices and overlap on greased baking sheet.

Bake 20 to 25 minutes or until lightly browned. Drizzle with Powdered Sugar Frosting while warm; serve immediately.

Makes 8 servings

POWDERED SUGAR FROSTING: In small bowl, mix ³/₄ cup sifted powdered sugar with 2 teaspoons hot water and ¹/₄ teaspoon vanilla.

Spicy Oatmeal Raisin Cookies

**1 package DUNCAN HINES®
    Moist Deluxe Spice
    Cake Mix
4 egg whites
1 cup quick-cooking oats
    (not instant or old-
    fashioned), uncooked
¹/₂ cup CRISCO® Oil or
    PURITAN® Oil
¹/₂ cup raisins**

1. Preheat oven to 350°F. Grease cookie sheets.
2. Combine cake mix, egg whites, oats and oil in large bowl. Beat on low speed with electric mixer until blended. Stir in raisins. Drop by rounded teaspoons onto cookie sheets. Bake 7 to 9 minutes or until lightly browned. Cool 1 minute on cookie sheets. Remove to cooling rack.

Makes about 4 dozen cookies

Spiced Chip Cookies

**1 package (18.25 or
    18.5 ounces) spice
    cake mix
1 cup quick-cooking rolled
    oats, uncooked
³/₄ cup butter or margarine,
    softened
2 eggs
2 cups HERSHEY'S® Milk
    Chocolate Chips
¹/₂ cup coarsely chopped nuts**

Preheat oven to 350°F. In large mixer bowl, combine cake mix, oats, butter and eggs; mix well. Stir in milk chocolate chips and nuts. Drop by rounded teaspoonfuls onto ungreased cookie sheet.

Bake 10 to 12 minutes or until very lightly browned. Cool slightly; remove from cookie sheet. Cool completely on wire rack.

Makes about 4 dozen cookies

Peanut Butter Glazed Chocolate Cookies

**1 package (15 ounces)
  golden sugar cookie mix
1/2 cup HERSHEY'S® Cocoa
1 egg
2 tablespoons water
  About 2 cups pecan halves
  Peanut Butter Chip Glaze
  (recipe follows)**

Preheat oven to 350°F. In large bowl, combine cookie mix and enclosed flavor packet, cocoa, egg and water; mix with spoon or fork until thoroughly blended. To form base for cookies, on cookie sheet arrange 3 pecan halves with tips touching in center; repeat for each cookie. Shape dough into 1-inch balls; gently press 1 ball onto each pecan cluster until pecans adhere.

Bake 8 to 10 minutes or until almost set; do not overbake. Cool slightly; remove from cookie sheet to wire rack. Cool completely. Place waxed paper or foil under rack of cookies. Gently spoon or drizzle thin coating of Peanut Butter Chip Glaze onto each cookie. Allow glaze to set.

Makes about 3 1/2 dozen cookies

PEANUT BUTTER CHIP GLAZE: In top of double boiler over hot, not boiling, water, melt 1 cup REESE'S® Peanut Butter Chips and 2 tablespoons shortening (not butter, margarine or oil), stirring constantly to blend; remove from heat and use immediately. *Or,* in small microwave-safe bowl, place peanut butter chips and shortening. Microwave at HIGH (100%) 45 seconds; stir. If necessary, microwave at HIGH additional 15 seconds or until melted and smooth when stirred. Use immediately.

Chocolate Peanut Butter Chip Cookies

Chocolate Peanut Butter Chip Cookies

**8 (1-ounce) squares semi-
  sweet chocolate
3 tablespoons margarine or
  butter
1 (14-ounce) can EAGLE®
  Brand Sweetened
  Condensed Milk (NOT
  evaporated milk)
2 cups biscuit baking mix
1 egg
1 teaspoon vanilla extract
1 cup peanut butter flavored
  chips**

Preheat oven to 350°F. In large saucepan, over low heat, melt chocolate and margarine with sweetened condensed milk; remove from heat. Add biscuit mix, egg and vanilla; with mixer, beat until smooth. Cool to room temperature. Stir in chips. Shape into 1 1/4-inch balls. Place 2 inches apart on ungreased cookie sheets.

Bake 6 to 8 minutes or until tops are slightly crusted (*do not overbake*). Cool. Store tightly covered at room temperature.

Makes about 4 dozen cookies

Triple Chocolate Cookies

**1 package DUNCAN HINES®
  Moist Deluxe Swiss
  Chocolate Cake Mix
1/2 cup butter or margarine,
  melted
1 egg
1/2 cup semi-sweet chocolate
  chips
1/2 cup milk chocolate chips
1/2 cup coarsely chopped
  white chocolate
1/2 cup chopped pecans**

1. Preheat oven to 375°F.
2. Combine cake mix, melted butter and egg in large bowl. Stir in all 3 chocolates and pecans.
3. Drop dough by rounded tablespoonfuls onto ungreased cookie sheets. Bake 9 to 11 minutes. Cool 1 minute on cookie sheet. Remove to cooling rack.

Makes 3 1/2 to 4 dozen cookies

Lemon Cookies

Lemon Cookies

**1 package DUNCAN HINES®
Moist Deluxe Lemon
Supreme Cake Mix
2 eggs
1/3 cup CRISCO® Oil or
PURITAN® Oil
1 tablespoon lemon juice
3/4 cup chopped nuts or flaked
coconut
Confectioners sugar**

1. Preheat oven to 375°F. Grease cookie sheets.
2. Combine cake mix, eggs, oil and lemon juice in large bowl. Beat at low speed with electric mixer until well blended. Add nuts. Shape into 1-inch balls. Place on cookie sheets, 1 inch apart. Bake 6 to 7 minutes or until lightly browned. Cool 1 minute on cookie sheets. Remove to cooling rack. Dust with confectioners sugar.

Makes about 3 dozen cookies

Chocolate Candy Cookies

**2/3 cup MIRACLE WHIP® Salad
Dressing
1 two-layer devil's food
cake mix
2 eggs
1 (8 oz.) pkg. multicolored
milk chocolate candies**

• Preheat oven to 375°F.
• Blend salad dressing, cake mix and eggs at low speed with electric mixer until moistened. Beat on medium speed 2 minutes. Stir in candies.
• Drop rounded teaspoonfuls of dough, 2 inches apart, onto greased cookie sheet.
• Bake 9 to 11 minutes or until almost set. (Cookies will still appear soft.) Cool 1 minute; remove from cookie sheet.

Makes about 4 1/2 dozen cookies

Prep time: 10 minutes
Cooking time: 11 minutes per batch

Swiss Chocolate Crispies

**1 package DUNCAN HINES®
Moist Deluxe Swiss
Chocolate Cake Mix
1/2 cup BUTTER FLAVOR
CRISCO®
1/2 cup butter or margarine,
softened
2 eggs
2 tablespoons water
3 cups crisp rice cereal,
divided**

1. Combine cake mix, BUTTER FLAVOR CRISCO®, butter, eggs and water in large bowl. Beat at low speed with electric mixer for 2 minutes. Fold in 1 cup cereal. Refrigerate 1 hour.
2. Crush remaining 2 cups cereal into coarse crumbs.
3. Preheat oven to 350°F. Grease cookie sheets. Shape dough into 1-inch balls. Roll in crushed cereal. Place on cookie sheets about 1 inch apart.
4. Bake 11 to 13 minutes. Cool 1 minute on cookie sheets. Remove to cooling rack.

Makes about 4 dozen cookies

Double Nut Chocolate Chip Cookies

**1 package DUNCAN HINES®
Moist Deluxe Yellow
Cake Mix
1/2 cup butter or margarine,
melted
1 egg
1 cup semi-sweet chocolate
chips
1/2 cup finely chopped pecans
1 cup sliced almonds,
divided**

1. Preheat oven to 375°F. Grease cookie sheet.
2. Combine cake mix, butter and egg in large bowl. Mix at low speed with electric mixer until just blended. Stir in chocolate chips, pecans and 1/4 cup almonds. Shape rounded

tablespoonfuls dough into balls. Place remaining 3/4 cup almonds in shallow bowl. Press tops of cookies in almonds. Place on cookie sheet, 1 inch apart.
3. Bake 9 to 11 minutes or until lightly browned. Cool 2 minutes on cookie sheet. Remove to cooling rack.

Makes 3 to 3 1/2 dozen cookies

Cherry Chocolate Chip Cookies

**1 package DUNCAN HINES®
Moist Deluxe Yellow
Cake Mix
1/2 cup butter or margarine,
melted
1 egg
1 package (6 ounces) semi-
sweet chocolate chips
1/2 cup chopped pecans
1/4 cup chopped maraschino
cherries, drained**

1. Preheat oven to 375°F.
2. Combine cake mix, butter and egg in large bowl. Stir in chocolate chips, pecans and maraschino cherries.
3. Drop by slightly rounded teaspoonfuls onto ungreased cookie sheets. Bake 10 to 12 minutes or until lightly browned. Cool 1 minute on cookie sheet. Remove to cooling rack.

Makes 3 1/2 to 4 dozen cookies

Chocolate Oat Chewies

Chocolate Oat Chewies

**1 package DUNCAN HINES®
    Moist Deluxe Devil's
    Food Cake Mix
1⅓ cups old-fashioned oats,
    uncooked
1 cup flaked coconut,
    toasted and divided
¾ cup butter or margarine,
    melted
2 eggs, beaten
1 teaspoon vanilla extract
5 bars (1.55 ounces each)
    milk chocolate, cut into
    rectangles**

1. Preheat oven to 350°F.
2. Combine cake mix, oats, ½ cup coconut, melted butter, eggs and vanilla extract in large bowl. Cover and chill 15 minutes.
3. Shape dough into 1-inch balls. Place balls 2 inches apart on ungreased cookie sheet. Bake 12 minutes or until tops are slightly cracked. Remove from oven. Press one milk chocolate rectangle into center of each cookie. Sprinkle with remaining ½ cup coconut. Remove to cooling rack.

Makes about 4½ dozen cookies

Chewy Double Chocolate Brownies

**2 eggs, beaten
½ cup MIRACLE WHIP® Salad
    Dressing
¼ cup cold water
1 (21.5-oz.) pkg. fudge
    brownie mix
1 (6-oz.) pkg. semi-sweet
    chocolate pieces**

Preheat oven to 350°F. Combine eggs, salad dressing and water; mix well. Stir in brownie mix, mixing just until moistened. Add chocolate pieces; mix lightly. Pour into greased 13×9-inch baking pan.
Bake 30 minutes or until edges begin to pull away from sides of pan. Cool completely on wire rack. Cut into squares.
Makes about 2 dozen brownies

Preparation time: 5 minutes
Baking time: 30 minutes plus cooling

Berry Bars

**1 package DUNCAN HINES®
    Blueberry Muffin Mix
1 cup old-fashioned oats,
    uncooked
¼ cup firmly packed brown
    sugar
¼ cup plus 2 tablespoons
    butter or margarine
½ cup raspberry preserves**

1. Preheat oven to 375°F. Grease 8-inch square pan. Rinse blueberries with cold water and drain.
2. Combine dry muffin mix, oats and brown sugar in large bowl. Cut in butter using pastry blender or 2 knives; reserve 1½ cups. Press remaining crumb mixture in pan.
3. Fold blueberries into preserves. Spread on top of crumb mixture. Sprinkle with 1½ cups reserved crumbs. Pat evenly on berry mixture. Bake 20 to 25 minutes or until golden. Cool completely. Cut into bars.
Makes about 1½ dozen bars

Chocolate Chip Raspberry Jumbles

**1 package DUNCAN HINES®
    Chocolate Chip
    Cookie Mix
½ cup seedless red raspberry
    preserves**

1. Preheat oven to 350°F. Prepare chocolate chip cookie mix following package directions. Reserve ½ cup dough.
2. Spread remaining dough into ungreased 9-inch square pan. Spread preserves over base. Drop teaspoonfuls of reserved dough randomly over top. Bake 20 to 25 minutes or until golden brown.
Makes about 16 bars

Tip: For delicious flavor variations, try strawberry or blackberry preserves.

Chocolate Chip Raspberry Jumbles

Cappucino Bon Bons

1 package DUNCAN HINES®
Fudge Brownie Mix,
Family Size
2 eggs
⅓ cup water
⅓ cup CRISCO® Oil or
PURITAN® Oil
1½ tablespoons FOLGERS®
Instant Coffee
1 teaspoon ground cinnamon
Whipped topping
Cinnamon

1. Preheat oven to 350°F. Place 2-inch foil cupcake liners on cookie sheet.
2. Combine brownie mix, eggs, water, oil, instant coffee and cinnamon. Stir with spoon until well blended, about 50 strokes. Fill each cupcake liner with 1 measuring tablespoon batter.
3. Bake 12 to 15 minutes or until wooden toothpick inserted in center comes out clean. Cool completely. Garnish with whipped topping and a dash of cinnamon. Refrigerate until ready to serve.

Makes about 40 bon bons

Tip: To make larger bon bons, use twelve 2½-inch foil cupcake liners and fill with ¼ cup batter. Bake for 28 to 30 minutes.

Quick Rocky Road Brownies

1 (20 to 23 oz.) pkg.
brownie mix
2 cups KRAFT® Miniature
Marshmallows
1 cup BAKER'S® Real Semi-
Sweet Chocolate Chips,
melted
¼ cup milk
½ cup coarsely chopped nuts

• Prepare brownie mix and bake as directed on package for cake-type brownies.
• Immediately sprinkle marshmallows over brownies; continue baking until marshmallows begin to melt.

• Melt chips with milk over low heat, stirring until smooth. Drizzle over marshmallows; sprinkle with nuts.
• Cool; cut into bars.

Makes about 2 dozen brownies

Prep time: 5 minutes
Cooking time: 30 minutes

Buckeye Cookie Bars

1 (18¼- or 18½-ounce)
package chocolate
cake mix
¼ cup vegetable oil
1 egg
1 cup chopped peanuts
1 (14-ounce) can EAGLE®
Brand Sweetened
Condensed Milk (NOT
evaporated milk)
½ cup peanut butter

Preheat oven to 350°F (325°F for glass dish). In large mixer bowl, combine cake mix, oil and egg; beat on medium speed until crumbly. Stir in peanuts. Reserving 1½ cups crumb mixture, press remainder firmly on bottom of greased 13×9-inch baking pan.

In medium bowl, beat sweetened condensed milk with peanut butter until smooth; spread over prepared crust. Sprinkle with reserved crumb mixture.

Bake 25 to 30 minutes or until set. Cool. Cut into bars. Store loosely covered at room temperature.

Makes 24 to 36 bars

Cappucino Bon Bons

Cheesecake Topped Brownies

Cheesecake Topped Brownies

1 (21.5- or 23.6-ounce) package fudge brownie mix
1 (8-ounce) package cream cheese, softened
2 tablespoons margarine or butter, softened
1 tablespoon cornstarch
1 (14-ounce) can EAGLE® Brand Sweetened Condensed Milk (NOT evaporated milk)
1 egg
1 teaspoon vanilla extract
Ready-to-spread chocolate frosting, optional

Preheat oven to 350°F. Prepare brownie mix as package directs. Spread into well-greased 13×9-inch baking pan. In small mixer bowl, beat cheese, margarine and cornstarch until fluffy. Gradually beat in sweetened condensed milk, then egg and vanilla until smooth. Pour evenly over brownie batter.

Bake 45 minutes or until top is lightly browned. Cool. Spread with frosting if desired. Cut into bars. Store covered in refrigerator.

Makes 36 to 40 brownies

Raspberry-Glazed Brownies

1 package DUNCAN HINES® Brownies Plus Milk Chocolate Chunks Mix
1 square (1 ounce) unsweetened chocolate, melted
2 tablespoons butter or margarine, softened
2 tablespoons light corn syrup
1 cup confectioners sugar
1 tablespoon milk
1 teaspoon vanilla extract
2 tablespoons seedless red raspberry jam

1. Preheat oven to 350°F. Grease and flour 13×9×2-inch pan. Prepare, bake and cool brownies following package directions.
2. Combine melted chocolate, butter and corn syrup in medium bowl. Stir in confectioners sugar, milk and vanilla extract. Add raspberry jam; mix well. Spread on top of cooled brownies.

Makes about 24 brownies

Tip: For delicious flavor variations, use your favorite jam or preserves, such as orange marmalade, apricot or strawberry preserves.

Decadent Brownies

1 (20 to 23 oz.) pkg. brownie mix
1 (14 oz.) bag KRAFT® Caramels
2 tablespoons milk
1 (6 oz.) pkg. BAKER'S® Real Semi-Sweet Chocolate Chips
1 cup chopped nuts

• Prepare and bake brownies according to package directions.
• While brownies are baking, melt caramels with milk over low heat, stirring frequently.
• Top hot brownies with caramel mixture; sprinkle with chocolate chips and nuts.
• Cool slightly; chill. Cut into bars.

Makes about 2½ dozen brownies

Prep time: 15 minutes
Cooking time: 35 minutes

Microwave Tip: To microwave caramels, combine caramels and milk in microwave-safe 1½-quart bowl; microwave on HIGH 2½ to 3½ minutes or until smooth when stirred, stirring after each minute.

Fudgy Cookie Wedges

1 (20-ounce) package
   refrigerated cookie
   dough, any flavor
1 (12-ounce) package semi-
   sweet chocolate chips
2 tablespoons margarine or
   butter
1 (14-ounce) can EAGLE®
   Brand Sweetened
   Condensed Milk (NOT
   evaporated milk)
1 teaspoon vanilla extract
   Chopped nuts

Preheat oven to 350°F. Divide
cookie dough into thirds. With
floured hands, press on bottom of
three aluminum foil-lined 9-inch
round cake pans *or* press into
9-inch circles on ungreased
baking sheets. Bake 10 to 12
minutes or until golden. Cool.

In heavy saucepan, over medium
heat, melt chips and margarine
with sweetened condensed milk
and vanilla. Cook and stir until
thickened, about 5 minutes.
Spread over cookie circles; top
with nuts. Chill. Cut into
wedges. Store loosely covered at
room temperature.

Makes 36 wedges

Microwave: Bake cookie dough
as above. In 1-quart glass
measure, combine remaining
ingredients except nuts. Cook on
100% power (high) 4 minutes,
stirring after each minute.
Proceed as above.

Apple Nut Bars

3 cups finely chopped
   all-purpose apples
   (4 medium)
1 (16.1-ounce) package nut
   bread mix
1 (14-ounce) can EAGLE®
   Brand Sweetened
   Condensed Milk (NOT
   evaporated milk)
1 cup chopped nuts
3 eggs
2 teaspoons vanilla extract
1½ teaspoons ground
   cinnamon
½ teaspoon ground nutmeg
   Cream Cheese Frosting

Preheat oven to 350°F. I
bowl, combine all ingredie
except frosting; mix well. Po
into greased and floured 15×1
inch jellyroll pan. Bake 30
minutes or until golden. Cool.
Spread with frosting. Cut into
bars. Garnish as desired. Store
covered at room temperature.

Makes 36 to 48 bars

CREAM CHEESE FROSTING:
In small mixer bowl, beat
2 (3-ounce) packages cream
cheese, softened, ½ cup
margarine or butter, softened,
and 1 teaspoon vanilla until
fluffy. Add 4 cups sifted
confectioners' sugar; mix
well. *Makes 2½ cups frosting*

German Chocolate Snackin' Bars

1 (4-ounce) package sweet
   cooking chocolate
¼ cup margarine or butter
1 (14-ounce) can EAGLE®
   Brand Sweetened
   Condensed Milk (NOT
   evaporated milk)
2 eggs
½ cup biscuit baking mix
1 teaspoon vanilla extract
1 (7-ounce) package flaked
   coconut (2⅔ cups)
1 cup chopped pecans

Preheat oven to 350°F (325°F
for glass dish). In medium
saucepan, over low heat, melt
chocolate with margarine.
Remove from heat; stir in ½ *cup*
sweetened condensed milk, eggs,
biscuit mix and vanilla. Spread
evenly into greased 13×9-inch
baking pan.

In medium bowl, combine
remaining sweetened condensed
milk and coconut. Spoon in
small amounts evenly over
chocolate mixture. Sprinkle with
nuts; press down firmly.

Bake 25 minutes or until wooden
toothpick inserted near center
comes out clean. Cool. Cut into
bars. Store loosely covered at
room temperature.

Makes 24 to 36 bars

Fudgy Cookie Wedges

...HINES®
...ow

... grated fresh carrots
1 can (8 ounces) crushed
    pineapple, undrained
½ cup water
3 eggs
½ cup CRISCO® Oil or
    PURITAN® Oil
½ cup finely chopped pecans
2 teaspoons cinnamon

Frosting
2 packages (3 ounces each)
    cream cheese, softened
⅓ cup butter or margarine,
    softened
1½ teaspoons vanilla extract
3½ cups confectioners sugar
1 teaspoon milk

1. Preheat oven to 350°F. Grease
and flour 13×9×2-inch pan.

2. For Cake, combine cake mix,
carrots, pineapple, water, eggs,
oil, pecans and cinnamon in
large bowl. Beat at low speed
with electric mixer until
moistened. Beat at medium
speed for 2 minutes. Pour batter
into pan. Bake 35 to 40 minutes
or until wooden toothpick
inserted in center comes out
clean. Cool in pan.

3. For Frosting, combine cream
cheese, butter and vanilla
extract in large bowl; beat at
medium speed with electric
mixer until smooth. Gradually
add confectioners sugar and
milk, mixing well. Spread on
cooled cake. Refrigerate until
ready to serve.

Makes 16 servings

Carrot Cake

Easy Choco-Applesauce Cake

1 (15-ounce) jar applesauce
1 (14-ounce) can EAGLE®
    Brand Sweetened
    Condensed Milk (NOT
    evaporated milk)
½ cup margarine or butter,
    melted
3 eggs
1 (1-ounce) square
    unsweetened chocolate,
    melted
2 teaspoons vanilla extract
2½ cups biscuit baking mix
½ teaspoon ground cinnamon
¾ cup chopped nuts
1 (16-ounce) can ready-to-
    spread chocolate
    frosting

Preheat oven to 325°F. Lightly
grease 15×10-inch jellyroll pan.

In large mixer bowl, beat
applesauce, sweetened condensed
milk, margarine, eggs, chocolate
and vanilla. Add biscuit mix and
cinnamon; mix well. Stir in nuts.
Turn into prepared pan.

Bake 25 to 30 minutes or until
wooden toothpick inserted near
center comes out clean. Cool.
Frost with chocolate frosting.

Makes one 15×10-inch cake

Peanut Butter Pudding Cake

1 package (13.5 ounces)
    applesauce raisin snack
    cake mix
2¼ cups water, divided
2 cups REESE'S® Peanut
    Butter Chips, divided
1⅓ cups packed light brown
    sugar
1 tablespoon butter or
    margarine
1 tablespoon lemon juice
    Whipped topping

Preheat oven to 350°F. In 9-inch
square baking pan, combine cake
mix and 1 cup water; mix with
fork until smooth. Stir in 1 cup
peanut butter chips. Sprinkle
remaining 1 cup chips over
batter.

In saucepan over medium heat,
combine brown sugar, remaining
1¼ cups water, butter and lemon
juice, stirring constantly until
mixture boils. Pour hot mixture
over batter in pan; do not stir.

Bake 45 minutes. Cool 15
minutes; serve with whipped
topping.

Makes about 8 servings

German Chocolate Cake

1 (18¼-ounce) package
    German chocolate
    cake mix
1 cup water
3 eggs plus 1 egg yolk
½ cup vegetable oil
1 (14-ounce) can EAGLE®
    Brand Sweetened
    Condensed Milk (NOT
    evaporated milk)
3 tablespoons margarine or
    butter
⅓ cup chopped pecans
⅓ cup flaked coconut
1 teaspoon vanilla extract

Preheat oven to 350°F. Grease well and flour 13×9-inch baking pan.

In large mixer bowl, combine cake mix, water, *3 eggs,* oil and *¹/₃ cup* sweetened condensed milk. Beat on low speed until moistened, then beat on high speed 2 minutes. Pour into prepared pan.

Bake 40 to 45 minutes or until wooden toothpick inserted near center comes out clean. In small saucepan, combine remaining sweetened condensed milk, egg yolk and margarine. Over medium heat, cook and stir until thickened, about 6 minutes. Add pecans, coconut and vanilla; spread over warm cake.

Makes one 13×9-inch cake

Rainbow Sorbet Torte

**4 pints assorted flavors
    sorbet
1 package DUNCAN HINES®
    Moist Deluxe White
    Cake Mix
    Assorted fruit, for garnish**

1. Line bottom of 8-inch round cake pan with aluminum foil. Soften one pint of sorbet; spread evenly in pan. Return to freezer until firm. Run knife around edge of pan to loosen sorbet. Remove from pan; wrap in foil and return to freezer. Repeat for other flavors.

2. Preheat oven to 350°F. Grease and flour two 8-inch round cake pans. Prepare, bake and cool cake following package directions for No Cholesterol recipe.

3. To assemble torte, cut both cake layers in half horizontally. Place one cake layer on serving plate; top with one layer sorbet. Peel off foil; repeat layers. Wrap foil around plate and cake; return to freezer until ready to serve. To serve, garnish top with fruit.

Makes 10 to 12 servings

Rainbow Sorbet Torte

Mocha Fudge Cake

Mocha Fudge Cake

**1 package DUNCAN HINES®
    Moist Deluxe Butter
    Recipe Fudge Cake Mix
1 cup hot fudge ice cream
    topping
1 tablespoon FOLGERS®
    Instant Coffee
4 cups frozen non-dairy
    whipped topping, thawed
    and divided**

1. Preheat oven to 375°F. Grease
and flour two 9-inch round pans.

2. Prepare, bake and cool cake
following package directions.

3. For filling, combine hot fudge
topping and coffee crystals in
medium saucepan; heat until
coffee crystals are dissolved.
Cool. Fold 2 cups whipped
topping into fudge topping
mixture. Refrigerate 30 minutes.

4. Place one cake layer on
serving plate. Spread with 1 cup
filling. Top with second cake
layer. Add remaining 2 cups
whipped topping to remaining
filling. Frost top and sides of
cake with topping mixture.

Makes 12 to 16 servings

Tip: Garnish with chocolate
curls, coated coffee beans or
grated chocolate.

Harvey Wallbanger's Cake

**1 package DUNCAN HINES®
    Moist Deluxe Orange
    Supreme Cake Mix
3 eggs
³/₄ cup CITRUS HILL® Orange
    Juice
¹/₃ cup CRISCO® Oil or
    PURITAN® Oil
¹/₃ cup Galliano®
¹/₄ cup vodka
    Confectioners sugar**

1. Preheat oven to 350°F. Grease and flour 10-inch Bundt® pan.
2. Combine cake mix, eggs, orange juice, oil, Galliano® and vodka in large bowl. Beat at medium speed with electric mixer for 4 minutes; pour into pan. Bake 45 to 50 minutes or until wooden toothpick inserted in center comes out clean. Cool in pan 25 minutes. Invert onto serving plate. Cool completely. Dust with confectioners sugar.
Makes 12 to 16 servings
Tip: For a nonalcoholic cake, use 1/2 cup plus 1 tablespoon water in place of Galliano® and vodka.

Chocolate Cherry Cake

1 package DUNCAN HINES® Moist Deluxe Dark Dutch Fudge Cake Mix
1 package (8 ounces) cream cheese, softened
1/2 cup butter or margarine, softened
1/2 teaspoon almond extract
1 pound confectioners sugar (3 1/2 to 4 cups)
1 cup frozen dark sweet cherries, thawed, chopped and well drained

1. Preheat oven to 350°F. Grease and flour two 9-inch round cake pans.
2. Prepare, bake and cool cake following package directions. Place cream cheese, butter and almond extract in large bowl. Beat at medium speed of electric mixer until smooth. Gradually add sugar, mixing well after each addition. Measure 3/4 cup of cream cheese mixture; place in small bowl. Stir in cherries.
3. Place one cake layer on serving plate. Spread top with cherry mixture. Place other layer on top. Frost with plain cream cheese frosting. Refrigerate until ready to serve.
Makes 12 to 16 servings
Tip: You can use either fresh or canned dark sweet cherries.

Banana Split Refrigerator Cake

1 package DUNCAN HINES® Moist Deluxe Banana Supreme Cake Mix
1 envelope whipped topping mix
1 package (4-serving size) vanilla instant pudding and pie filling mix
1 1/2 cups milk
1 teaspoon vanilla extract
6 maraschino cherries, drained and halved
1 medium-size ripe banana, sliced
1/2 cup thinly sliced fresh pineapple pieces
1/4 cup coarsely chopped pecans or walnuts
1/2 cup hot fudge ice cream topping, warmed

1. Preheat oven to 350°F. Grease and flour 13×9×2-inch pan.
2. Prepare, bake and cool cake following package directions. Combine topping mix, pudding mix, milk and vanilla extract in large bowl. Beat at medium speed with electric mixer until stiff; spread over cooled cake. Place maraschino cherry halves, banana slices, pineapple pieces and chopped pecans randomly

Banana Split Refrigerator Cake

over pudding mixture; drizzle with fudge topping. Refrigerate until ready to serve. Cut into 3-inch squares.
Makes 12 servings
Tip: To prevent banana slices from darkening, slice into small amount diluted lemon juice. Drain thoroughly before placing on cake.

French Vanilla Brickle Cake

Cake
1 package DUNCAN HINES® Moist Deluxe French Vanilla Cake Mix
1 package (4-serving size) vanilla instant pudding and pie filling mix
4 eggs
1/2 cup sweetened condensed milk
1/2 cup butter or margarine, softened
1/2 cup almond brickle chips (reserve 2 teaspoons for garnish)
Glaze
1/2 cup confectioners sugar
1 tablespoon brown sugar
1 tablespoon milk

1. Preheat oven to 350°F. Grease generously and flour 10-inch Bundt® pan.
2. For Cake, combine cake mix, pudding mix, eggs, sweetened condensed milk and butter in large bowl. Beat at medium speed with electric mixer for 2 minutes. Fold in brickle chips; pour into pan. Bake 50 to 60 minutes or until wooden toothpick inserted in center comes out clean. Cool in pan 25 minutes. Invert onto serving plate; cool completely.
3. For Glaze, combine confectioners sugar and brown sugar in small bowl. Stir in milk until blended; drizzle over cake. Sprinkle with reserved 2 teaspoons almond brickle chips.
Makes 12 servings

Pecan Fudge Sheet Cake

Pecan Fudge Sheet Cake

**1 package DUNCAN HINES®
Moist Deluxe Devil's
Food Cake Mix
1/2 cup butter or margarine
1/4 cup plus 2 tablespoons
milk
1/4 cup unsweetened cocoa
1 pound confectioners sugar
(3 1/2 to 4 cups)
1 teaspoon vanilla extract
3/4 cup chopped pecans**

1. Preheat oven to 350°F. Grease
15 1/2×10 1/2×1-inch pan. Prepare
cake following package
directions; pour batter into pan.
Bake 20 to 25 minutes or until
wooden toothpick inserted in
center comes out clean.
2. For frosting, combine butter,
milk and cocoa in medium
saucepan. Stir over low heat
until butter is melted. Add
confectioners sugar and vanilla
extract, stirring until smooth.
Stir in pecans; pour over warm
cake. Cool completely.
Makes 20 servings

Tip: For best results, allow the
cake to cool undisturbed until
frosting is set, about 4 hours.

Cherry Dumplin' Cake

**2 (16-ounce) cans red tart
pitted cherries, well
drained
1 (14-ounce) can EAGLE®
Brand Sweetened
Condensed Milk (NOT
evaporated milk)
1 teaspoon almond extract
3/4 cup plus 2 tablespoons
cold margarine or butter
2 cups biscuit baking mix
1/2 cup firmly packed brown
sugar
1/2 cup chopped nuts**

Preheat oven to 325°F. Grease
9-inch square baking pan.
In medium bowl, combine
cherries, sweetened condensed
milk and extract. In large bowl,
cut *3/4 cup* margarine into *1 1/2
cups* biscuit mix until crumbly.
Stir in cherry mixture. Spread in
prepared pan.
In small bowl, combine
remaining *1/2 cup* biscuit mix
and sugar; cut in remaining
2 tablespoons margarine until
crumbly. Stir in nuts. Sprinkle
evenly over cherry mixture.
Bake 1 hour and 10 minutes or
until golden brown. Serve warm
with ice cream if desired.
Refrigerate leftovers.
Makes 6 to 8 servings
Microwave: In 2-quart round
microwave-safe baking dish,
prepare as above. Cook on 100%
power (high) 16 to 18 minutes.

Citrus Crown Cake

**1 package DUNCAN HINES®
Moist Deluxe Lemon
Supreme Cake Mix
1 jar (12 ounces) orange
marmalade
2/3 cup flaked coconut
1/4 cup butter or margarine,
melted**

1. Preheat oven to 350°F. Grease
generously and flour 10-inch
Bundt® pan.

2. Combine marmalade, coconut
and melted butter in small
mixing bowl; pour into pan.
3. Prepare cake following
package directions; pour batter
over marmalade mixture. Bake
50 to 55 minutes or until wooden
toothpick inserted in center
comes out clean. Cool in pan 10
minutes. Invert cake onto
serving plate. Cool completely.
Makes 12 servings
Tip: For best results, cut cake
with a serrated knife; clean
knife after each slice.

Peach Melba Upside Down Cake

**1 cup butter or margarine,
softened and divided
1 1/2 cups firmly packed brown
sugar
1 can (29 ounces) sliced
peaches in heavy syrup,
drained, with juice
reserved
1 cup fresh or frozen,
thawed raspberries
1 package DUNCAN HINES®
Moist Deluxe Lemon
Supreme Cake Mix
3 eggs**

1. Preheat oven to 375°F. Line
bottom of 13×9×2-inch baking
pan with aluminum foil.
2. Melt 1/2 cup butter in small
saucepan. Add brown sugar; stir
until dissolved. Spread in bottom
of pan. Arrange 1 peach slice
and 3 raspberries in pan as if for
12 individual servings.
3. Combine cake mix, 1 cup
peach juice, eggs and remaining
1/2 cup butter in large bowl; stir
until thoroughly combined. Pour
batter over fruit. Bake 35 to 40
minutes or until lightly
browned. Remove from oven;
invert onto serving tray. Remove
pan and foil; cool. Use fruit as
guide to cut into individual
servings.   *Makes 12 servings*
Tip: You can use fresh or frozen
blueberries in place of
raspberries.

Citrus Crown Cake

Fudge Marble Pound Cake

Fudge Marble Pound Cake

1 package DUNCAN HINES®
  Moist Deluxe Fudge
  Marble Cake Mix
1 package (4-serving size)
  vanilla instant pudding
  and pie filling mix
4 eggs
1 cup water
1/3 cup CRISCO® Oil or
  PURITAN® Oil

1. Preheat oven to 350°F. Grease and flour two 9×5×3-inch loaf pans.
2. Set aside cocoa packet. Combine cake mix, pudding mix, eggs, water and oil in large bowl. Beat at medium speed with electric mixer for 2 minutes. Measure 1 cup batter; place in small bowl. Stir in cocoa packet.
3. Spoon half the yellow batter in each loaf pan. Spoon half the chocolate batter on top of yellow batter. Run knife through batters to marble. Bake 45 to 50 minutes or until wooden toothpick inserted in center comes out clean. Cool in pan 5 minutes. Loosen cake from pan; invert onto wire rack. Cool completely. Cut loaves in 1/2-inch slices. *Makes 2 loaves*

Tip: To make fudge marble ice cream sandwiches, cut 1/2 gallon brick of fudge marble ice cream into 1/2-inch slices. Put ice cream between slices of pound cake.

Double Pistachio Cake Deluxe

1 package (2-layer size)
  white or yellow cake mix
1 package (4-serving size)
  JELL-O® Instant Pudding
  and Pie Filling, Pistachio
  Flavor
4 eggs
1 cup water
1/4 cup vegetable oil
1/4 cup chopped nuts
  Fluffy Pistachio Frosting
  (recipe follows)

Combine cake mix, pudding mix, eggs, water and oil in large bowl. Beat at low speed of electric mixer just to moisten, scraping sides of bowl often. Beat at medium speed 4 minutes. Stir in nuts. Pour into greased and floured 10-inch tube or fluted tube pan.

Bake at 350°F for 55 minutes or until cake tester inserted in center comes out clean and cake begins to pull away from sides of pan. (Do not underbake.) Cool in pan 15 minutes. Remove from pan; finish cooling on wire rack. Split cake into 3 layers. Fill and frost cake with Fluffy Pistachio Frosting. *Makes 12 servings*

Fluffy Pistachio Frosting

1 cup cold milk
1 package (4-serving size)
  JELL-O® Instant Pudding
  and Pie Filling, Pistachio
  Flavor
1/4 cup confectioners sugar
  (optional)
3 1/2 cups (8 ounces) COOL
  WHIP® Whipped Topping,
  thawed

Pour milk into large bowl. Add pudding mix and confectioners sugar. Beat with wire whisk until well blended, 1 to 2 minutes. Fold in whipped topping. Spread frosting on cake immediately.
Makes about 4 cups frosting
Note: Store frosted cake in refrigerator.

Prep time: 25 minutes
Baking time: 55 minutes

Chocolate Toffee Pecan Cake

Cake
1 package DUNCAN HINES®
  Moist Deluxe Devil's
  Food Cake Mix
1 package (4-serving size)
  chocolate instant
  pudding and pie
  filling mix
4 eggs
1 1/4 cups water
1/2 cup CRISCO® Oil or
  PURITAN® Oil
1 1/2 cups chopped pecans,
  divided
1 cup butterscotch flavored
  chips
1/2 cup almond brickle chips
Glaze
1 package (12 ounces) sweet
  or semi-sweet chocolate
  chips
1/4 cup plus 2 tablespoons
  butter or margarine

1. Preheat oven to 350°F. Grease and flour 10-inch Bundt® pan.
2. For Cake, combine cake mix, pudding mix, eggs, water, oil, 1 cup pecans, butterscotch and brickle chips in large bowl. Beat at medium speed with electric mixer for 2 minutes; pour into pan. Bake 55 to 60 minutes or until toothpick inserted in center comes out clean. Cool in pan 25 minutes; invert onto serving plate.
3. For Glaze, combine chocolate chips and butter in small saucepan. Heat over low heat until chips are melted; stir until smooth (glaze will be very thick). Spoon hot glaze over cooled cake. Garnish with remaining 1/2 cup pecans.
Makes 8 to 10 servings
Tip: You can prepare the glaze in the microwave oven. Place chips and butter in microwave-safe bowl and microwave at MEDIUM (50% power) for 1 1/2 minutes; stir. Microwave at MEDIUM an additional 1 1/2 minutes, or until chips are melted and smooth when stirred.

Hummingbird Cake

- **1 package DUNCAN HINES® Moist Deluxe Yellow Cake Mix**
- **1 package (4-serving size) vanilla instant pudding and pie filling mix**
- **½ cup CRISCO® Oil or PURITAN® Oil**
- **1 can (8 ounces) crushed pineapple, well drained (reserve juice)**
- **Reserved pineapple juice plus water to equal 1 cup**
- **4 eggs**
- **1 teaspoon cinnamon**
- **½ medium-size ripe banana, cut up**
- **½ cup finely chopped pecans**
- **¼ cup chopped maraschino cherries, well drained**
- **Confectioners sugar**

1. Preheat oven to 350°F. Grease and flour 10-inch Bundt® pan.

2. Combine cake mix, pudding mix, oil, pineapple, 1 cup juice and water mixture, eggs and cinnamon in large bowl. Beat at low speed with electric mixer until moistened. Mix at medium speed for 2 minutes. Stir in banana, pecans and cherries; pour into pan. Bake 50 to 60 minutes or until wooden toothpick inserted in center comes out clean. Cool in pan 25 minutes; invert onto serving plate. Sprinkle cake with confectioners sugar.

Makes 12 to 16 servings

Tip: Also great with Cream Cheese Glaze. For glaze, follow package directions on DUNCAN HINES® Cream Cheese Frosting label.

Chocolate Chip Crater Cake

- **2 cups all-purpose biscuit baking mix**
- **¼ cup granulated sugar**
- **⅔ cup milk**
- **1 egg**
- **1 teaspoon vanilla extract**
- **1 cup HERSHEY'S® Semi-Sweet Chocolate Chips**
- **Topping Mix (recipe follows)**

Preheat oven to 350°F. Grease 8-inch square baking pan.

In large mixer bowl, combine biscuit mix, granulated sugar, milk, egg and vanilla; beat on low speed until moistened. Increase speed to medium; beat 2 minutes until smooth. Pour half of batter into prepared pan; sprinkle chocolate chips over batter. Top with remaining batter, completely covering chips. Sprinkle Topping Mix evenly over batter.

Bake 25 to 30 minutes or until top springs back when touched lightly. Cool completely.

Makes about 9 servings

Topping Mix

- **¼ cup granulated sugar**
- **¼ cup packed dark brown sugar**
- **¼ cup all-purpose biscuit baking mix**
- **¼ cup butter or margarine, softened**
- **1 teaspoon ground cinnamon**

In small bowl, stir together all ingredients until well blended.

Milk Chocolate Cheesecake

- **1 package DUNCAN HINES® Moist Deluxe Fudge Marble Cake Mix, divided**
- **2 packages (8 ounces each) cream cheese, softened**
- **8 ounces milk chocolate, melted**
- **3 eggs**
- **⅔ cup whipping cream**
- **¼ cup plus 1 tablespoon butter or margarine, melted**
- **Whipped cream, for garnish**
- **Fresh strawberries, for garnish**

Chocolate Chip Crater Cake

1. Preheat oven to 350°F. Grease and flour 13×9×2-inch pan.

2. For filling, combine cocoa packet, ¼ cup dry cake mix, cream cheese and melted chocolate in large bowl. Beat at high speed with electric mixer for 2 minutes. Add eggs and cream. Beat 1 minute at high speed.

3. For crust, stir remaining dry cake mix and melted butter in medium bowl. Mixture will be crumbly. Sprinkle mixture into pan. Pour filling over crust mixture. Bake 30 to 35 minutes. Cool in pan. Refrigerate until chilled. Garnish each serving with whipped cream and strawberries.

Makes about 8 servings

Lattice Cherry Cheesecake

  1 (20 oz.) pkg. refrigerated sugar cookie dough
  2 (8 oz.) pkgs. PHILADELPHIA BRAND® Cream Cheese, softened
  1 cup sour cream
  ¾ cup sugar
  ¼ teaspoon almond extract
  3 eggs
  1 (21 oz.) can cherry pie filling

• Preheat oven to 350°F.

• Slice dough into ⅛-inch slices. Arrange slices, slightly overlapping, on bottom and sides of greased 9-inch springform pan. With lightly floured fingers, seal edges to form crust.

• Beat cream cheese, sour cream, sugar and extract in large mixing bowl at medium speed with electric mixer until well blended. Add eggs, one at a time, mixing well after each addition.

• Reserve ¼ cup batter; chill. Pour remaining batter over crust. Bake 1 hour and 10 minutes.

• Increase oven temperature to 450°F.

Lattice Cherry Cheesecake

• Spoon pie filling over cheesecake. Spoon reserved batter over pie filling in crisscross pattern to form lattice design.

• Bake 10 minutes. Loosen cake from rim of pan; cool before removing rim of pan.

Makes 10 to 12 servings

Prep time: 25 minutes plus chilling
Cooking time: 1 hour and 20 minutes

Variation: Substitute 13×9-inch baking pan for 9-inch springform pan. Prepare recipe as directed except for baking. Bake at 350°F, 40 minutes. Increase oven temperature to 450°F. Continue as directed.

Brownie Swirl Cheesecake

Brownie Swirl Cheesecake

**1 (8 oz.) pkg. brownie mix
2 (8 oz.) pkgs. PHILADELPHIA BRAND® Cream Cheese, softened
1/2 cup sugar
1 teaspoon vanilla
2 eggs
1 cup milk chocolate pieces, melted**

• Preheat oven to 350°F.
• Prepare basic brownie mix as directed on package. Pour batter evenly into greased 9-inch springform pan. Bake 15 minutes.
• Beat cream cheese, sugar and vanilla in large mixing bowl at medium speed with electric mixer until well blended.
• Add eggs, one at a time, mixing well after each addition. Pour over brownie layer.
• Spoon chocolate over cream cheese mixture. Cut through batter with knife several times for marble effect.
• Bake 35 minutes. Loosen cake from rim of pan; cool before removing rim of pan. Chill. Garnish with whipped cream and maraschino cherries, if desired.

Makes 10 to 12 servings

Prep time: 25 minutes plus chilling
Baking time: 35 minutes

Lemon Party Cheesecake

Lemon Party Cheesecake

**1 (18 1/4- or 18 1/2-ounce) package yellow cake mix*
4 eggs
1/4 cup vegetable oil
2 (8-ounce) packages cream cheese, softened
1 (14-ounce) can EAGLE® Brand Sweetened Condensed Milk (NOT evaporated milk)
1/4 to 1/3 cup REALEMON® Lemon Juice from Concentrate
2 teaspoons grated lemon rind, optional
1 teaspoon vanilla extract**

Preheat oven to 300°F. Reserve 1/2 cup dry cake mix. In large mixer bowl, combine remaining cake mix, 1 egg and oil; mix well (mixture will be crumbly). Press firmly on bottom and halfway up sides of greased 13×9-inch baking dish.
In same bowl, beat cheese until fluffy. Gradually beat in sweetened condensed milk until smooth. Add remaining 3 eggs and reserved 1/2 cup cake mix; on medium speed, beat 1 minute. Stir in remaining ingredients.

*If "pudding added" mix is used, decrease oil to 3 tablespoons.

Pour into prepared dish.
Bake 50 to 55 minutes or until center is set. Cool to room temperature. Chill. Cut into squares. Garnish as desired. Refrigerate leftovers.

Makes one 13×9-inch cheesecake

Marbled Cheesecake Bars

**2 cups finely crushed creme-filled chocolate sandwich cookies (about 24 cookies)
3 tablespoons margarine or butter, melted
3 (8-ounce) packages cream cheese, softened
1 (14-ounce) can EAGLE® Brand Sweetened Condensed Milk (NOT evaporated milk)
3 eggs
2 teaspoons vanilla extract
2 (1-ounce) squares unsweetened chocolate, melted**

Preheat oven to 300°F. Combine crumbs and margarine; press firmly on bottom of 13×9-inch baking pan.
In large mixer bowl, beat cheese until fluffy. Gradually beat in sweetened condensed milk until smooth. Add eggs and vanilla; mix well. Pour half the batter evenly over prepared crust. Stir melted chocolate into remaining batter; spoon over vanilla batter. With table knife or metal spatula, gently swirl through batters to marble.
Bake 45 to 50 minutes or until set. Cool. Chill. Cut into bars. Store covered in refrigerator.

Makes 24 to 36 bars

Prep time: 20 minutes
Baking time: 50 minutes

Pastry Chef Tarts

1 package (10 ounces) pie crust mix
1 egg, beaten
1 to 2 tablespoons cold water
1½ cups cold half and half or milk
1 package (4-serving size) JELL-O® Instant Pudding and Pie Filling, French Vanilla or Vanilla Flavor
Assorted berries or fruit*
Mint leaves (optional)

Preheat oven to 425°F. Combine pie crust mix with egg. Add just enough water to form dough. Form 2 to 3 tablespoons dough into a round. Press each round onto bottom and up sides of each 3- to 4-inch tart pan. (Use tart pans with removable bottoms, if possible.) Pierce pastry several times with fork. Place on baking sheet. Bake 10 minutes or until golden. Cool slightly. Remove tart shells from pans; cool completely on wire racks.

Pour half and half into small bowl. Add pudding mix. Beat with wire whisk until well blended, 1 to 2 minutes. Spoon into tart shells. Chill until ready to serve.

Arrange fruit on pudding. Garnish with mint leaves, if desired. *Makes 10 servings*

*We suggest any variety of berries, mandarin orange sections, melon balls, halved seedless grapes, sliced peaches, kiwifruit or plums.

Note: Individual graham cracker crumb tart shells may be substituted for baked tart shells.

Prep time: 20 minutes
Baking time: 10 minutes

Create-a-Crust Apple Pie

2 medium all-purpose apples, pared and sliced (about 2 cups)
1 tablespoon REALEMON® Lemon Juice from Concentrate
½ cup plus 2 tablespoons biscuit baking mix
1 (14-ounce) can EAGLE® Brand Sweetened Condensed Milk (NOT evaporated milk)
1½ cups water
3 eggs
¼ cup margarine or butter, softened
1½ teaspoons vanilla extract
½ teaspoon ground cinnamon
½ teaspoon ground nutmeg

Preheat oven to 350°F. In medium bowl, toss apples with REALEMON® brand, then *2 tablespoons* biscuit mix. Arrange on bottom of buttered 10-inch pie plate. In blender container, combine remaining ingredients. Blend on low speed 3 minutes. Let stand 5 minutes. Pour evenly over apples.

Bake 35 to 40 minutes or until golden brown around edge. Cool slightly; serve warm or chilled with vanilla ice cream. Refrigerate leftovers.

Makes one 10-inch pie

Brownie Pizza

1 package DUNCAN HINES® Brownies Plus Milk Chocolate Chunks Mix
1 egg
⅓ cup CRISCO® Oil or PURITAN® Oil
2 tablespoons water
Vanilla ice cream
Strawberry slices
Kiwi wedges
Pineapple chunks
Apricot halves
Chocolate syrup

1. Preheat oven to 350°F. Grease 13-inch round pizza pan.

2. Combine brownie mix, egg, oil and water in large bowl. Stir with spoon until well blended, about 50 strokes. Spread in pan. Bake 23 to 27 minutes. Cool completely.

3. Cut into wedges, top with scoops of ice cream, decorate with assorted fruit, then drizzle chocolate syrup over top.

Makes 12 servings

Tip: For convenience, purchase pre-cut fruit from the salad bar at your local grocery store.

Pastry Chef Tarts

Brownie Pizza

Hot Chocolate Pie

- 1 KEEBLER® Ready-Crust® Chocolate Flavored Pie Crust
- 1 egg yolk, slightly beaten
- ¾ cup granulated sugar
- ½ cup all-purpose flour
- 3 tablespoons unsweetened cocoa
- 1 teaspoon baking powder
- ¼ teaspoon salt
- ½ cup chopped nuts (optional)
- ¼ cup milk
- 2 tablespoons butter or margarine, melted
- ½ teaspoon vanilla
- ¼ cup packed brown sugar
- ½ cup cold water
- Whipping cream (optional)

Preheat oven to 350°F. Brush bottom and side of pie crust with egg yolk. Bake 5 minutes. Cool on wire rack.

In medium bowl, combine ½ cup of the granulated sugar, the flour, 1½ tablespoons of the cocoa, the baking powder and salt. Stir in nuts, milk, butter and vanilla. (If mixture seems too stiff, add a few more drops milk.) Spread mixture in pie crust. In small bowl, combine brown sugar, water, remaining ¼ cup granulated sugar and remaining 1½ tablespoons cocoa. Pour over top of pie.

Bake 30 to 35 minutes. Cool on wire rack. If desired, serve warm with whipped cream.

Makes 8 servings

Unbelievable Lemon Coconut Pie

- 1 (14-ounce) can EAGLE® Brand Sweetened Condensed Milk (NOT evaporated milk)
- 1 cup water
- ½ cup REALEMON® Lemon Juice from Concentrate
- ½ cup biscuit baking mix
- 3 eggs
- ¼ cup margarine or butter, softened
- 1½ teaspoons vanilla extract
- 1 (3½-ounce) can flaked coconut (1⅓ cups)

Preheat oven to 350°F. In blender container, combine all ingredients except coconut. Blend on low speed 3 minutes. Pour into greased *10-inch* pie plate; let stand 5 minutes. Sprinkle with coconut.

Bake 35 to 40 minutes or until knife inserted near edge comes out clean. Cool slightly; serve warm or cooled. Refrigerate leftovers.

Makes one 10-inch pie

Brownie Alaska

- 1 package DUNCAN HINES® Brownies Plus Double Fudge Mix
- ½ gallon brick strawberry ice cream
- 6 egg whites
- 2 cups marshmallow creme

1. Preheat oven to 350°F. Line 13×9×2-inch pan with aluminum foil.

2. Prepare, bake and cool brownie mix following package directions.

3. Invert brownie onto cookie sheet. Remove foil and cut brownie in half crosswise so each half measures 8½×6½ inches. Cut brick ice cream in half lengthwise. Place each half on brownie halves. Chill in freezer.

4. For meringue, preheat oven to 475°F. Beat egg whites until soft peaks form. Add marshmallow creme, ¼ cup at a time, beating well after each addition. Beat until stiff peaks form. Divide between two brownie halves.

Brownie Alaska

Spread over top and sides sealing edges completely. Bake 2 to 3 minutes or until meringue has browned. Serve immediately.

Makes 2 Brownie Alaskas,
8 to 10 servings each

Note: Recipe makes two Brownie Alaskas; one to serve and one to freeze for a quick dessert at a later time. To freeze, loosely wrap with aluminum foil.

Pumpkin Pie Crunch

- **1 package DUNCAN HINES®** **Moist Deluxe Yellow** **Cake Mix**
- **1 can (16 ounces) solid pack** **pumpkin**
- **1 can (12 ounces) evaporated** **milk**
- **3 eggs**
- **1½ cups sugar**
- **4 teaspoons pumpkin pie** **spice**
- **½ teaspoon salt**
- **1 cup chopped pecans**
- **1 cup butter or margarine,** **melted**
- **Whipped topping**

1. Preheat oven to 350°F. Grease bottom of 13×9×2-inch pan.

2. Combine pumpkin, evaporated milk, eggs, sugar, pumpkin pie spice and salt in large bowl. Pour into pan. Sprinkle dry cake mix evenly over pumpkin mixture; top with pecans. Drizzle with melted butter. Bake 50 to 55 minutes or until golden. Cool completely. Serve with whipped topping. Refrigerate leftovers.

Makes 16 to 20 servings

Pumpkin Pie Crunch

Quick and Easy Nutty Cheese Bars

Quick and Easy Nutty Cheese Bars

Base
   1 package DUNCAN HINES®
      Moist Deluxe Butter
      Recipe Golden Cake Mix
   ³/₄ cup chopped pecans or
      walnuts
   ³/₄ cup butter or margarine,
      melted
Topping
   2 packages (8 ounces each)
      cream cheese, softened
   1 cup firmly packed brown
      sugar
   ³/₄ cup chopped pecans or
      walnuts

1. Preheat oven to 350°F. Grease and flour 13×9×2-inch pan.

2. For Base, combine cake mix, ³/₄ cup pecans and melted butter in large bowl. Stir until well blended. Press mixture into bottom of pan.

3. For Topping, combine cream cheese and brown sugar in medium bowl. Stir with spoon until well mixed. Spread evenly over base. Sprinkle with ³/₄ cup pecans.

4. Bake 25 to 30 minutes or until edges are browned and cheese topping is set. Cool completely. Cut into 2¹/₄×2-inch bars. Refrigerate leftovers.

Makes 24 bars

Apple Streusel Squares

5 medium all-purpose apples, pared, cored and sliced (about 5 cups)
1 (14-ounce) can EAGLE® Brand Sweetened Condensed Milk (NOT evaporated milk)
1 teaspoon ground cinnamon
½ cup plus 2 tablespoons cold margarine or butter
1½ cups biscuit baking mix
½ cup firmly packed brown sugar
½ cup chopped nuts

Preheat oven to 325°F. In medium bowl, combine apples, sweetened condensed milk and cinnamon. In large bowl, cut *½ cup* margarine into *1 cup* biscuit mix until crumbly. Stir in apple mixture. Pour into ungreased 9-inch square baking pan.

In small bowl, combine remaining *½ cup* biscuit mix and sugar; cut in remaining *2 tablespoons* margarine until crumbly. Add nuts. Sprinkle evenly over apple mixture.

Bake 1 hour or until golden brown. Serve warm with ice cream or whipped topping if desired.

Makes 6 to 8 servings

Microwave: In 2-quart round microwave-safe baking dish, prepare as above. Cook on 100% power (high) 14 to 15 minutes, rotating dish after 7 minutes. Let stand 5 minutes.

Buttery Cranberry Cobbler

1 package DUNCAN HINES® Moist Deluxe Butter Recipe Golden Cake Mix, divided
1 cup quick-cooking oats, uncooked
¾ cup butter or margarine, softened and divided
2 eggs
⅓ cup water
1 can (16 ounces) whole berry cranberry sauce

1. Preheat oven to 375°F. Grease and flour 13×9×2-inch pan.

2. For topping, combine ½ cup dry cake mix, oats and ¼ cup butter in medium bowl with fork until crumbly. Set aside.

3. For base, place remaining dry cake mix in small bowl and cut in remaining ½ cup butter with fork until crumbly. Stir in eggs and water until mixture is moistened. Spread on bottom of pan.

4. Stir cranberry sauce until smooth. Spread over batter in pan. Sprinkle with topping. Bake 35 to 40 minutes or until wooden toothpick inserted in center comes out clean. Cool 10 minutes before serving.

Makes 10 to 12 servings

Apple Streusel Squares

Cherry Almond Brownie Squares

Cherry Almond Brownie Squares

- **1 (21.5- or 23.6-ounce) package fudge brownie mix**
- **1 (8-ounce) package cream cheese, softened**
- **1 (14-ounce) can EAGLE® Brand Sweetened Condensed Milk (NOT evaporated milk)**
- **1 egg**
- **1 teaspoon almond extract**
- **1 (21-ounce) can cherry pie filling, chilled**

Preheat oven to 350°F. Prepare brownie mix as package directs.

Spread into lightly greased 13×9-inch baking pan. Bake 20 minutes.

Meanwhile, in small mixer bowl, beat cheese until fluffy. Gradually beat in sweetened condensed milk, then egg and *1/2 teaspoon* almond extract. Pour evenly over brownie layer; bake 25 minutes longer or until set. Cool. Chill.

Stir remaining *1/2 teaspoon* almond extract into cherry pie filling. Serve with brownie squares. Refrigerate leftovers.

Makes 10 to 12 servings

Prep time: 20 minutes
Baking time: 45 minutes

Twin Angel Food Party Pies

- **1 package DUNCAN HINES® Angel Food Cake Mix**
- **2 packages (4-serving size) chocolate instant pudding and pie filling mix**
- **3 cups milk**
- **1/2 teaspoon almond extract**
- **1 container (16 ounces) frozen non-dairy whipped topping, thawed and divided**
- **1 can (21 ounces) cherry pie filling**

1. Preheat oven to 350°F. Prepare, bake and cool cake following package directions.

2. Cut cake in half horizontally with serrated knife. Place on serving plates with cut sides up. Cut around cake 1½ inches from outer edge, down ¾ inch and through to center. Gently pull out cut cake to leave a 1½-inch-wide rim. Fill center hole with removed cake. Repeat for second half.

3. For filling, combine both packages of pudding mix in large bowl. Prepare following package directions, using 3 cups milk and ½ teaspoon almond extract. Fold in 2 cups whipped topping.

4. Fill each cake with half the pudding mixture. Spoon half the cherry pie filling around outer edge of each cake. Garnish each cake with dollops of remaining 1 cup whipped topping. Refrigerate until ready to serve. To serve, cut filled cake as you would a pie.

Makes 12 to 16 servings

Tip: Try different flavor combinations of instant pudding and pie filling mix such as vanilla instant pudding mix and blueberry pie filling.

Twin Angel Food Party Pies

ESPECIALLY FOR KIDS

These fun-filled recipes will captivate the young—and young at heart! Creamy frostings and colorful jelly beans, licorice and gumdrops magically turn cupcakes into clowns, cookies into lollipops and a cake into a teddy bear. On the simpler side, there's a selection of yummy cookies and bars sure to please after-school appetites. Don't wait for a big event to treat someone special to one of these creations—they're great any time.

Clown Cupcakes

1 package DUNCAN HINES®
Moist Deluxe Yellow
Cake Mix
12 scoops vanilla ice cream
1 package (12 count) sugar
ice cream cones
1 container (7 ounces)
refrigerated aerosol
whipped cream
Assorted colored decors
Assorted candies for eyes,
nose and mouth

1. Preheat oven to 350°F. Place 2½-inch paper liners in 24 muffin cups.

2. Prepare, bake and cool cupcakes following package directions. To assemble each clown, remove paper from cupcake. Place top-side down on serving plate. Top with scoop of ice cream. Place cone on top of ice cream for hat. Spray whipped cream around bottom of cupcake for collar. Spray three small dots up front on cone. Sprinkle whipped cream with assorted colored decors. Use candies to make clown's face.

Makes 12 clown cupcakes

Note: This recipe makes 24 cupcakes: 12 to make into "clowns" and 12 to freeze for later use. Cupcakes will keep frozen in airtight container for up to 6 weeks.

Tip: For easier preparation, make the ice cream balls ahead of time. Scoop out balls of ice cream, place on baking sheet or in bowl and return to freezer to firm.

Mister Funny Face

1 package DUNCAN HINES®
Moist Deluxe White
Cake Mix
½ gallon vanilla ice cream
Whole pecans
Raisins
Red cinnamon candies
1 quart fresh strawberries,
halved *or* 2 packages
(10 ounces each) frozen
strawberry halves,
thawed

1. Preheat oven to 350°F. Place 2½-inch paper liners in 24 muffin cups.

2. Prepare, bake and cool cupcakes following package directions.

3. To serve, remove paper liners. Place each cupcake upside down on dessert plate. Place one scoop ice cream on top. Decorate ice cream as face, using whole pecans for ears, raisins for eyes and red cinnamon candies for mouth. Spoon strawberries around bottom of cupcake. Place one strawberry half on top of ice cream as hat.

Makes 24 cupcakes

Clown Cupcakes

Clockwise from top left: Pineapple Carrot Raisin Muffins, Crunch Top Blueberry Muffins, Taffy Apple Muffins

Crunch Top Blueberry Muffins

Crunch Topping (recipe follows)
2 cups all-purpose flour
²/₃ cup sugar
1 tablespoon baking powder
½ teaspoon salt
½ teaspoon ground nutmeg
1½ cups blueberries*
¾ cup milk
½ cup butter or margarine, melted
2 eggs, beaten

Preheat oven to 400°F. Grease or paper-line 6 (4-inch) muffin cups. Prepare Crunch Topping; set aside.

In large bowl, combine flour, sugar, baking powder, salt and nutmeg. Add 1 tablespoon of the flour mixture to the blueberries,

tossing to coat. In small bowl, combine milk, butter and eggs until blended. Stir into flour mixture just until moistened. Fold in blueberries. Spoon evenly into muffin cups. Sprinkle Crunch Topping over tops.

Bake 30 to 35 minutes or until wooden toothpick inserted in center comes out clean. Remove from pan. Cool on wire rack.

Makes 6 giant muffins

*If you are using frozen blueberries, do not thaw. Baking time may need to be increased by up to 10 minutes.

CRUNCH TOPPING: In medium bowl, combine ½ cup uncooked rolled oats, ½ cup all-purpose flour, ¼ cup packed brown sugar and 1 teaspoon ground cinnamon. With fork, blend in ¼ cup softened butter or margarine until mixture is crumbly.

Taffy Apple Muffins

2 cups all-purpose flour
½ cup granulated sugar
1 tablespoon baking powder
½ teaspoon salt
¼ teaspoon ground nutmeg
½ cup milk
¼ cup butter or margarine, melted
2 eggs
1 teaspoon vanilla
1 cup chopped apple
½ cup honey
½ cup packed dark brown sugar
¾ cup finely chopped walnuts

Preheat oven to 400°F. Grease 36 miniature muffin cups. In large bowl, combine flour, granulated sugar, baking powder, salt and nutmeg. In small bowl, combine milk, butter, eggs and vanilla until blended. Stir into flour mixture just until moistened. Fold in apple. Spoon into muffin cups. Bake 10 to 12 minutes or until lightly browned and wooden toothpick inserted in center comes out clean. Remove from pan.

Meanwhile, in small saucepan, heat honey and brown sugar over medium-high heat to a boil; stir to dissolve sugar. Dip warm muffins into hot glaze, then into nuts. Spear with popsicle sticks or wooden skewers, if desired.

Makes 36 miniature muffins

Pineapple Carrot Raisin Muffins

- 2 cups all-purpose flour
- 1 cup sugar
- 2 teaspoons baking powder
- ½ teaspoon ground cinnamon
- ¼ teaspoon ground ginger
- ½ cup shredded DOLE® Carrots
- ½ cup DOLE® Raisins
- ½ cup chopped walnuts
- 1 can (8 ounces) DOLE® Crushed Pineapple in Juice
- 2 eggs
- 1 teaspoon vanilla
- ½ cup margarine, melted

Preheat oven to 375°F. In large bowl, combine flour, sugar, baking powder and spices. Stir in carrots, raisins and nuts. In small bowl, combine undrained pineapple, eggs and vanilla. Add liquid mixture to flour mixture; stir just until moistened. Batter will be lumpy; do not overmix. Stir in margarine. Spoon batter evenly into 12 greased 2¾-inch muffin cups. Bake 20 to 25 minutes or until golden brown. Remove to wire rack to cool.

Makes 12 muffins

Easter Basket Cupcakes

- 1 package DUNCAN HINES® Moist Deluxe Yellow Cake Mix
- 3 tablespoons plus 1½ teaspoons water
- 6 drops green food coloring
- 1½ cups shredded coconut
- 1 container (16 ounces) DUNCAN HINES® Vanilla Frosting
- ½ pound assorted colors jelly beans
- 24 assorted colors pipe cleaners

1. Preheat oven to 350°F. Place 2½-inch paper liners in 24 muffin cups.

2. Prepare, bake and cool cupcakes following package directions.

3. Combine water and green food coloring in large container with tight fitting lid. Add coconut. Shake until coconut is evenly tinted green. Frost cupcakes with vanilla frosting; sprinkle coconut over frosting. Press 3 jelly beans into coconut on each cupcake. Bend pipe cleaners to form handles. Push into cupcakes. *Makes 24 cupcakes*

Tip: You can make fruit baskets by placing fruit slices on top of frosting in place of coconut and jelly beans.

Easter Basket Cupcakes

Fudge 'n' Banana Cupcakes

**1 package DUNCAN HINES®
  Moist Deluxe Devil's
  Food Cake Mix
3 large eggs
½ cup CRISCO® Oil or
  PURITAN® Oil
1⅓ cups water
½ cup (1 stick) butter or
  margarine
2 ounces (2 squares)
  unsweetened chocolate
1 pound confectioners sugar
½ cup half-and-half
1 teaspoon vanilla extract
4 medium bananas
2 tablespoons lemon juice**

1. Preheat oven to 350°F. Line 24 muffin cups with paper baking cups.

2. Combine dry cake mix, eggs, oil and water in large mixer bowl. Mix, bake and cool cupcakes as directed on package.

3. For frosting*, melt butter and chocolate in heavy saucepan over low heat. Remove from heat. Add confectioners sugar alternately with half-and-half, mixing until smooth after each addition. Beat in vanilla extract. Add more confectioners sugar to thicken or half-and-half to thin as needed.

4. Using small paring knife, cut cone-shaped piece from top center of each cupcake; remove. Dot top of each cone with frosting. Frost top of each cupcake spreading frosting down into cone-shaped hole. Slice bananas and dip in lemon juice. Stand three banana slices in each hole. Set cone-shaped pieces, pointed-side-up, on banana slices.

Makes 24 cupcakes

*Or use 1 can DUNCAN HINES® Dark Dutch Fudge or Chocolate Frosting.

Football Cake

**1 package DUNCAN HINES®
  Moist Deluxe Devil's
  Food Cake Mix
Decorator Frosting
  ¾ cup confectioners sugar
  2 tablespoons CRISCO®
    Shortening
  1 tablespoon cold water
  1 tablespoon non-dairy
    creamer
  ¼ teaspoon vanilla extract
  Dash salt
1 container (16 ounces)
  DUNCAN HINES®
  Chocolate Frosting**

1. Preheat oven to 350°F. Grease and flour 10-inch round cake pan. Prepare cake following package directions. Bake 45 to 55 minutes or until wooden toothpick inserted in center comes out clean.

2. For decorator frosting, combine confectioners sugar, shortening, water, non-dairy creamer, vanilla extract and salt in small bowl. Beat at medium speed with electric mixer for 2 minutes. Beat at high speed for 3 minutes. Add more confectioners sugar to thicken or water to thin frosting as needed.

3. Cut cake and remove 2-inch slice from center. Arrange cake as shown. Spread chocolate frosting on sides and top of cake. Place basketweave tip in pastry bag. Fill with decorator frosting. Make white frosting laces on football.

Makes 12 to 16 servings

Tip: If a 10-inch round pan is not available, make 2 football cakes by following package directions for baking with two 9-inch round cake pans.

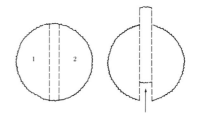

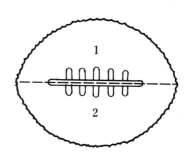

Fudge 'n' Banana Cupcakes

Football Cake

Merry-Go-Round Cake

1 package (6-serving size)
    JELL-O® Instant Pudding
    and Pie Filling, Vanilla
    Flavor
1 package (2-layer size)
    yellow cake mix
4 eggs
1 cup water
¼ cup vegetable oil
⅓ cup BAKER'S® Semi-Sweet
    Real Chocolate Chips,
    melted
⅔ cup cold milk
    Sprinkles (optional)
    Paper carousel roof
    (directions follow)
3 plastic straws
6 animal crackers

Preheat oven to 350°F. Reserve ⅓ cup pudding mix. Combine cake mix, remaining pudding mix, eggs, water and oil in large bowl. Beat at low speed of electri mixer just to moisten, scr ping sides of bowl often. Beat at medium speed 4 minutes. Pour ½ of the batter into greased and floured 10-inch fluted tu e pan. Mix chocolate into remaining batter. Spoon over batter in pan; cut through with spatula in zigzag pattern to marbleize. Bake 50 minutes or until cake tester inserted in center comes out clean. Cool in pan 15 minutes. Remove cake from pan; finish cooling on wire rack.

Beat reserved pudding mix and milk in small bowl until smooth. Spoon over top of cake to glaze. Garnish with sprinkles, if desired.

Cut 10- to 12-inch circle from colored paper; scallop edges, if desired. Make 1 slit to center (Diagram 1). Overlap cut edges together to form carousel roof; secure with tape (Diagram 2). Cut straws in half; arrange on cake with animal crackers. Top with roof.   *Makes 12 servings*

Prep time: 30 minutes
Baking time: 50 minutes

Merry-Go-Round Cake

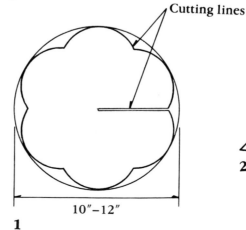

Cutting lines

10″–12″

1

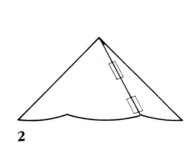

2

Teddy Bear Cake

**1 package DUNCAN HINES®
Moist Deluxe Cake Mix
(any flavor)
1 can (16 ounces) chocolate
syrup
1¹/₃ cups JIF® Creamy Peanut
Butter
3 tablespoons light corn
syrup
2 cups confectioners sugar
¹/₂ cup CRISCO® Shortening
2 tablespoons water
¹/₄ teaspoon vanilla extract
Licorice strings
Gumdrops**

1. Preheat oven to 350°F. Grease
and flour one 10×2-inch round
layer pan and 5 muffin cups.

2. Prepare cake mix following
package directions. Fill muffin
cups one-half full with batter.
Pour remaining batter into
round pan.

3. Bake 12 to 15 minutes for
cupcakes and 50 to 55 minutes
for round cake or until wooden
toothpicks inserted in centers
come out clean. Cool in pans 15
minutes. Invert onto wire racks;
cool completely.

4. For chocolate-peanut frosting,
combine chocolate syrup, peanut
butter and corn syrup. For white
frosting, combine confectioners
sugar, shortening, water and
vanilla extract in small bowl.
Beat until frosting is smooth and
of spreading consistency.

5. Spread chocolate frosting on
cooled round cake and two
cupcakes for ears. Position ears
at top of cake. Place remaining
cupcakes on lower portion for
snout (see photo). Spread white
frosting on snout, ear and eye
areas. Use licorice and gumdrops
for face.

Makes 12 to 16 servings

Teddy Bear Cake

Butterfly Cake

**1 package DUNCAN HINES®
Moist Deluxe Yellow or
Lemon Supreme
Cake Mix
2 containers (16 ounces)
DUNCAN HINES® Vanilla
or Cream Cheese
Frosting
Red food coloring
Red licorice laces
Pastel candy wafers**

1. Preheat oven to 350°F. Grease
and flour two 9-inch round cake
pans.

2. Prepare, bake and cool cake
following package directions. Fill

and frost with vanilla frosting as
for 2 layer cake. Refrigerate cake
1 hour for easier handling. Place
remaining frosting in small
bowl. Add a few drops red food
coloring to tint frosting pink.

3. To assemble, cut cake in half.
Place on serving plate with
round sides touching and with
cut sides out. Outline with pink
frosting using decorator's tube
(see Note). Arrange 2 licorice
laces for feelers. Decorate with
candy wafers for spots.

Makes 12 to 16 servings

Note: If decorator's tube is not
available, place tinted frosting in
small airtight plastic bag. Seal
top and cut off a tiny bottom
corner to use as tip.

Carousel Cake

Carousel Cake

- **1 package DUNCAN HINES®
  Moist Deluxe Cake Mix
  (any flavor)**
- **1 container (16 ounces)
  DUNCAN HINES® Vanilla
  or Cream Cheese
  Frosting
  Assorted garnishes such
  as chopped nuts,
  toasted coconut, mini
  chocolate chips, peanut
  butter chips, jelly beans,
  slivered almonds,
  chocolate decors or
  colored decors**

1. Preheat oven to 350°F. Grease
and flour two 9-inch round cake
pans.
2. Prepare, bake and cool cake
following package directions.
3. Frost cake with vanilla
frosting. Score top of cake into
8 equal wedges. Top each wedge
with a different garnish of your
choice.

Makes 12 to 16 servings

Mitt Cut-Up Cake

- **1 package (2-layer size)
  yellow cake mix**
- **1 cup cold milk**
- **1 package (4-serving size)
  JELL-O® Instant Pudding
  and Pie Filling,
  Chocolate or Chocolate
  Fudge Flavor**
- **3½ cups (8 ounces) COOL
  WHIP® Whipped Topping,
  thawed
  Chocolate sprinkles
  String licorice**

Preheat oven to 325°F. Prepare
cake mix as directed on package.
Pour 2 cups of the batter into
greased and floured 1-quart
ovenproof bowl; pour remaining
batter into greased and floured
9-inch round cake pan. Bake 50
minutes or until cake tester
inserted in centers comes out
clean. Cool 15 minutes. Remove
from pan and bowl; finish
cooling on wire racks. Cut cakes

as shown in Diagram 1.
Pour milk into medium bowl.
Add pudding mix. Beat with
wire whisk until well blended,
1 to 2 minutes. Fold in 2½ cups
of the whipped topping.
Spread pudding mixture over
sides and top of 9-inch layer. Use
remaining 1 cup whipped
topping to cover bowl-shaped
cake; place over 9-inch layer.
Decorate cake with chocolate
sprinkles and licorice to
resemble mitt and ball (Diagram
2). Chill cake until ready to
serve.   *Makes 12 servings*

Prep time: 30 minutes
Baking time: 50 minutes

Cutting line

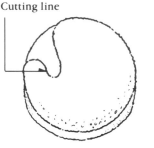

1

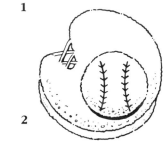

2

Back-to-School Pencil Cake

- **1 package DUNCAN HINES®
  Moist Deluxe Cake Mix
  (any flavor)**
- **5 cups sifted confectioners
  sugar**
- **¾ cup CRISCO® Shortening**
- **⅓ cup non-dairy powdered
  creamer**
- **½ cup water**
- **2 teaspoons vanilla extract**
- **½ teaspoon salt
  Food coloring (red and
  yellow)
  Chocolate jimmies**

1. Preheat oven to 350°F. Grease and flour 13×9×2-inch pan.

2. Prepare, bake and cool cake as directed on package.

3. For decorator frosting, combine confectioners sugar, shortening, non-dairy powdered creamer, water, vanilla extract and salt in large bowl. Beat at medium speed with electric mixer for 3 minutes. Beat at high speed for 5 minutes. Add more confectioners sugar to thicken or more water to thin frosting as needed. Measure small amount of frosting and tint pink with red food coloring. Color remaining frosting with yellow food coloring.

4. Cut cooled cake and arrange as shown. Spread pink frosting on cake for eraser at one end and for wood at other end. Spread yellow frosting over remaining cake. Decorate with chocolate jimmies for pencil tip and eraser band.

Makes 12 to 16 servings

Back-to-School Pencil Cake

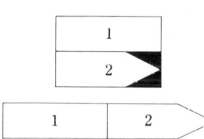

Peanut Butter and Jelly Cheesecake

1 cup graham cracker crumbs
3 tablespoons sugar
3 tablespoons PARKAY® Margarine, melted
2 (8 oz.) pkgs. PHILADELPHIA BRAND® Cream Cheese, softened
1 cup sugar
½ cup peanut butter
3 tablespoons flour
4 eggs
½ cup milk
½ cup KRAFT® Grape Jelly

• Preheat oven to 350°F.

• Stir together crumbs, 3 tablespoons sugar and margarine in small bowl. Press onto bottom of 9-inch springform pan. Bake 10 minutes.

• Beat cream cheese, 1 cup sugar, peanut butter and flour in large mixing bowl at medium speed with electric mixer until well blended.

• Add eggs, one at a time, mixing well after each addition. Blend in milk; pour over crust.

• Bake 55 minutes. Loosen cake from rim of pan; cool before removing rim of pan.

• Stir jelly until smooth; spread over cheesecake. Chill.

Makes 10 to 12 servings

Prep time: 30 minutes plus chilling
Cooking time: 55 minutes

Variation: Substitute 1 cup old fashioned or quick oats, uncooked, ¼ cup chopped peanuts and 3 tablespoons packed brown sugar for graham cracker crumbs and sugar in crust.

Hopscotch Cake

1 package DUNCAN HINES® Moist Deluxe Yellow Cake Mix
3 large eggs
⅓ cup CRISCO® Oil or PURITAN® Oil
1¼ cups water
1 package (6 ounces) butterscotch-flavored pieces (1 cup)
3 tablespoons butter or margarine
3½ cups confectioners sugar
4 to 5 tablespoons milk
Candy-coated chocolate pieces
8 licorice sticks

1. Preheat oven to 350°F. Grease and flour 13×9×2-inch pan.

2. Combine dry cake mix, eggs, oil and water in large mixer bowl. Mix, bake and cool cake as directed on package.

3. Combine butterscotch pieces and butter in small saucepan. Melt over low heat, stirring constantly. Combine butterscotch mixture and confectioners sugar in bowl. Add milk gradually, beating until mixture is of spreading consistency. Spread on cooled cake. Separate candy-coated chocolate pieces according to color. Arrange candy pieces into numbers on cake using one color for each number. Decorate with licorice sticks to make hopscotch pattern.

Makes 20 to 24 servings

Ice Cream Cone Cakes

**1 package DUNCAN HINES®
    Moist Deluxe Cake Mix
    (any flavor)
1 package (6 ounces) semi-
    sweet chocolate chips
5 cups confectioners sugar
3/4 cup CRISCO® Shortening
1/3 cup non-dairy powdered
    creamer
1/2 cup water
2 teaspoons vanilla extract
1/2 teaspoon salt
    Red maraschino cherries
        with stems
    Assorted decors
    Candy gumdrops
    Chocolate jimmies**

1. Preheat oven to 350°F. Grease and flour one 8-inch round baking pan and one 8-inch square baking pan.

2. For cake, prepare mix as directed on package. Pour 2 cups batter into round pan and 3 cups batter into square pan. Spread evenly.

3. Bake 30 to 35 minutes or until wooden toothpick inserted in center comes out clean. Cool in pans 15 minutes. Invert onto wire racks; cool completely.

4. For frosting, melt chocolate chips in saucepan over low heat; set aside. Combine confectioners sugar, shortening, non-dairy powdered creamer, water, vanilla extract and salt in large mixing bowl. Beat at medium speed with electric mixer for 3 minutes. Beat at high speed for 5 minutes. Add more confectioners sugar to thicken or water to thin frosting as needed. Divide frosting in half. Blend melted chocolate into one half.

5. Cut cooled cake and arrange as shown. Spread some of the chocolate frosting on cone parts. Decorate cones with remaining chocolate frosting, using decorator bag and writing tip (see photo). Spread white frosting on ice cream parts of cakes; decorate with cherries, assorted decors and gumdrops. Sprinkle chocolate jimmies over cones.

Makes 12 to 16 servings

Ice Cream Cone Cakes

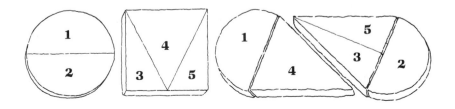

Peanut Butter Chips and Jelly Bars

1½ cups all-purpose flour
½ cup sugar
¾ teaspoon baking powder
½ cup butter or margarine
1 egg, beaten
¾ cup grape jelly
1⅔ cups (10-ounce package) REESE'S® Peanut Butter Chips, divided

Preheat oven to 375°F. Grease 9-inch square baking pan.

In large bowl, stir together flour, sugar and baking powder; cut in butter with pastry blender or fork to resemble coarse crumbs. Add egg; blend well. Reserve half of mixture; press remaining mixture onto bottom of prepared pan. Spread jelly evenly over crust. Sprinkle with 1 cup peanut butter chips. Stir together remaining crumb mixture with remaining ⅔ cup chips; sprinkle over top.

Bake 25 to 30 minutes or until lightly browned. Cool completely in pan on wire rack; cut into bars.

Makes about 1½ dozen bars

Monkey Bars

1 cup (2 sticks) butter, softened
½ cup firmly packed brown sugar
½ cup granulated sugar
2 eggs
1 tablespoon water
1 teaspoon vanilla extract
1¼ cups all-purpose flour
½ teaspoon baking soda
One 11½-oz. pkg. (2 cups) NESTLÉ® Toll House® Milk Chocolate Morsels
2½ cups whole-grain wheat flake cereal, divided
1 cup peanuts, finely chopped
1 cup raisins

Preheat oven to 350°F. Grease 13×9-inch baking pan. In large mixer bowl, beat butter, brown sugar and granulated sugar until creamy. Beat in eggs, water and vanilla extract. Gradually beat in flour and baking soda. Stir in milk chocolate morsels, 2 cups cereal, peanuts and raisins. Spread in prepared pan. Sprinkle with remaining ½ cup cereal.

Bake 30 to 35 minutes until golden brown. Cool completely. Cut into 2×1-inch bars.

Makes about 5 dozen bars

Granola Apple Cookies

1 cup firmly packed brown sugar
¾ cup margarine or butter, softened
1 egg
¾ cup MOTT'S® Natural Apple Sauce
1 teaspoon vanilla
3 cups granola with dates and raisins
1½ cups all-purpose flour
1 teaspoon baking powder
½ teaspoon baking soda
1 teaspoon cinnamon
½ teaspoon allspice
½ teaspoon salt
1 cup coconut
1 cup unsalted sunflower nuts

In large bowl, combine brown sugar, margarine, egg, apple sauce and vanilla; beat well. Stir in remaining ingredients; mix well. Refrigerate 1 to 2 hours for ease in handling.

Preheat oven to 375°F. Grease cookie sheets. Drop dough by teaspoonfuls 2 inches apart onto prepared cookie sheets. Bake 11 to 13 minutes or until edges are light golden brown. Immediately remove from cookie sheets. Store cookies in airtight container to retain their soft, chewy texture.

Makes about 5 dozen cookies

Variation: For larger cookies, press ¼ cup dough onto greased cookie sheet. Bake at 375°F for 13 to 15 minutes.

Top to bottom: Granola Apple Cookies, Granola Apple Bars

Granola Apple Bars

2 cups granola with dates and raisins
½ cup all-purpose flour
½ teaspoon baking powder
½ teaspoon baking soda
1 cup MOTT'S® Cinnamon Apple Sauce
1 teaspoon vanilla
1 egg, beaten
½ cup sunflower nuts
½ cup coconut

Preheat oven to 350°F. Grease 8- or 9-inch square pan. In large bowl, combine all ingredients; mix well. Pour into prepared pan. Bake 25 to 35 minutes or until wooden toothpick inserted in center comes out clean. Cool. Cut into bars.

Makes about 20 bars

Rocky Road Bars

Base
  2/3 cup BUTTER FLAVOR
      CRISCO®
  4 squares (1 ounce each)
      unsweetened chocolate
  2 cups granulated sugar
  4 eggs
  1 teaspoon vanilla
  1¼ cups all-purpose flour
  1 teaspoon baking powder
  1 teaspoon salt
Topping
  ¼ cup BUTTER FLAVOR
      CRISCO®
  1 square (1 ounce)
      unsweetened chocolate
  ⅓ cup evaporated milk
  ½ cup granulated sugar
  1¾ cups powdered sugar
  ½ teaspoon vanilla
  1 cup miniature
      marshmallows
  ⅓ cup JIF® Creamy Peanut
      Butter

1. Preheat oven to 350°F. Grease 13×9×2-inch pan with BUTTER FLAVOR CRISCO®.
2. For Base, combine BUTTER FLAVOR CRISCO® and chocolate in large microwave-safe bowl. Microwave at 50% (MEDIUM); stir after 1 minute. Repeat until smooth (or melt on rangetop in large saucepan on very low heat). Stir in granulated sugar. Add eggs, one at a time, stirring quickly into hot mixture. Stir in vanilla. Combine flour, baking powder and salt. Stir gradually into chocolate mixture. Spread in prepared pan. Bake 30 minutes or until set.
3. For Topping, start preparation 5 minutes before base is finished baking. Combine BUTTER FLAVOR CRISCO® and chocolate in medium microwave-safe bowl. Microwave at 50% (MEDIUM); stir after 1 minute. Repeat until smooth (or melt on rangetop in medium saucepan on very low heat). Add evaporated milk and granulated sugar. Beat at low speed of electric mixer until well blended. Add powdered sugar and vanilla; beat until blended.

Lemon Cut-Out Cookies

4. Sprinkle marshmallows over hot baked base. Pour chocolate topping over marshmallows. Drop JIF® Creamy Peanut Butter by teaspoonfuls on top of hot chocolate mixture. Swirl together using tip of knife. Cover pan immediately with foil. Cool in pan on cooling rack. Cut into 2×1½-inch bars.
      Makes about 36 bars
Note: If topping becomes too firm to pour, microwave on low to reheat.

Gorp Cookies

  2 eggs
  ½ cup vegetable oil
  ½ cup honey
  ½ teaspoon salt
  ½ teaspoon ground cinnamon
  2 cups rolled oats, uncooked
  1 cup SUN-MAID® Raisins or
      Golden Raisins
  ¼ cup chopped dried apricots
  ½ cup chopped DIAMOND®
      Walnuts
  ½ cup real semisweet
      chocolate pieces *or*
      carob chips
  ⅓ cup nonfat dry milk
      powder
  ⅓ cup toasted wheat germ

Preheat oven to 300°F. In large bowl, beat eggs, oil, honey, salt and cinnamon with wooden spoon. Stir in oats, dried fruits, walnuts, chocolate pieces, milk powder and wheat germ. Drop dough by rounded teaspoons about 2 inches apart onto ungreased cookie sheets.
Bake 15 to 18 minutes or until edges of cookies are firm. Remove to wire rack to cool.
      Makes about 3 dozen cookies

Lemon Cut-Out Cookies

  2¾ cups unsifted flour
  1 teaspoon baking powder
  ½ teaspoon baking soda
  ¼ teaspoon salt
  ½ cup margarine or butter,
      softened
  1½ cups sugar
  1 egg
  ⅓ cup REALEMON® Lemon
      Juice from Concentrate
      Lemon Icing, optional

Stir together flour, baking powder, baking soda and salt; set aside. In large mixer bowl, beat margarine and sugar until fluffy; beat in egg. Gradually add dry ingredients alternately with REALEMON® brand; mix well (dough will be soft). Chill overnight in refrigerator or 2 hours in freezer.

Preheat oven to 375°F. On well-floured surface, roll out one-third of dough to ⅛-inch thickness; cut with floured cookie cutters. Place 1 inch apart on greased cookie sheets; bake 8 to 10 minutes. Cool. Repeat with remaining dough. Ice and decorate as desired.
      Makes 4 to 5 dozen cookies
LEMON ICING: Mix 1¼ cups confectioners' sugar and 2 tablespoons REALEMON® brand until smooth. Add food coloring if desired.
      Makes about ½ cup icing

Oatmeal Scotch Chippers

1¼ cups BUTTER FLAVOR CRISCO®
1½ cups firmly packed brown sugar
1 cup granulated sugar
3 eggs
1¼ cups JIF® Extra Crunchy Peanut Butter
4½ cups old fashioned oats (not instant or quick), uncooked
2 teaspoons baking soda
1 cup semi-sweet chocolate chips
1 cup butterscotch-flavored chips
1 cup chopped walnuts

1. Preheat oven to 350°F. Combine BUTTER FLAVOR CRISCO®, brown sugar and granulated sugar in large bowl. Beat at medium speed of electric mixer until well blended. Beat in eggs. Add JIF® Extra Crunchy Peanut Butter; beat until blended.

2. Combine oats and baking soda; stir into creamed mixture with spoon. Stir in chocolate chips, butterscotch chips and nuts until blended.

3. Drop rounded teaspoonfuls of dough 2 inches apart onto ungreased cookie sheet.

4. Bake 10 to 11 minutes, or until lightly browned. Cool 2 minutes on cookie sheet. Remove to cooling rack.

Makes about 6 dozen cookies

Jumbo Double Chocolate Chip Cookies

1¼ cups unsalted butter, softened
¾ cup granulated sugar
⅔ cup packed brown sugar
½ teaspoon salt
2½ eggs*
3 drops red food coloring
3 cups sifted all-purpose flour
¾ cup unsweetened cocoa
½ teaspoon baking soda
2 packages (12 ounces each) semisweet chocolate chips
1 tablespoon shortening

Preheat oven to 375°F. In large bowl, beat butter, sugars, and salt until light and fluffy. Add eggs, 1 at a time, beating well after each addition. Beat in food coloring. In medium bowl, combine flour, cocoa and baking soda. Gradually fold flour mixture into butter mixture; fold in 3¼ cups (about 20 ounces) of the chips. Drop dough by ¾ cupfuls onto greased cookie sheets, leaving as much space as possible between cookies. (About 3 cookies will fit on each cookie sheet.) Flatten dough with dampened hands to make 4½-inch circles.

Bake 12 to 14 minutes or until centers feel medium-firm. (Do not overbake; centers will firm up when cool and cookies will be moist and chewy.) Let cookies cool 5 minutes before carefully removing from cookie sheets to wire racks; cool completely.

In small saucepan over low heat, melt remaining ¾ cup (about 4 ounces) chips and shortening; stir to blend. To decorate cookies, spoon chocolate mixture into pastry bag fitted with small plain tip. Pipe chocolate onto cookies to make face and zigzag border. Let stand until chocolate is set.

Makes nine 5½-inch cookies
*To measure ½ egg, lightly beat 1 egg in glass measuring cup; remove half for use in recipe.

Oatmeal Scotch Chippers

Top to bottom: Oatmeal Carmelita Bars, Chewy Fingers

Oatmeal Carmelita Bars

³/₄ cup BUTTER FLAVOR
  CRISCO®, melted
1¹/₂ cups quick oats (not
  instant or old fashioned),
  uncooked
³/₄ cup firmly packed brown
  sugar
¹/₂ cup all-purpose flour
¹/₂ cup whole wheat flour
¹/₂ teaspoon baking soda
¹/₄ teaspoon cinnamon
1¹/₃ cups milk chocolate chips
¹/₂ cup chopped walnuts
  1 jar (12.5 ounces) *or* ³/₄ cup
  caramel ice cream
  topping
  3 tablespoons all-purpose
  flour

1. Preheat oven to 350°F. Grease bottom and sides of 9×9×2-inch pan with BUTTER FLAVOR CRISCO®.
2. Combine BUTTER FLAVOR CRISCO®, oats, brown sugar, ¹/₂ cup all-purpose flour, whole wheat flour, baking soda and cinnamon in large bowl. Mix at low speed of electric mixer until crumbs form. Reserve ¹/₂ cup for topping. Press remaining crumbs into pan.
3. Bake 10 minutes. Sprinkle chocolate chips and nuts over crust.
4. Combine caramel topping and 3 tablespoons all-purpose flour. Stir until well blended. Drizzle over chocolate chips and nuts. Sprinkle reserved crumbs over caramel topping.
5. Return to oven. Bake for 20 to 25 minutes, or until golden brown. Run spatula around edge of pan before cooling. Cool completely in pan on wire rack. Cut into 1¹/₂×1¹/₂-inch squares.
Makes 3 dozen squares

Chewy Fingers

1¹/₄ cups BUTTER FLAVOR
  CRISCO®
³/₄ cup firmly packed brown
  sugar
³/₄ cup granulated sugar
  3 tablespoons maple syrup
  1 egg
  1 teaspoon vanilla
1³/₄ cups all-purpose flour
  1 teaspoon baking soda
  1 teaspoon salt
  3 cups quick oats (not
  instant or old fashioned),
  uncooked
³/₄ cup semi-sweet chocolate
  chips
  2 candy bars (2.1 ounces
  each) Butterfinger®, cut
  into ¹/₄-inch pieces

1. Preheat oven to 375°F. Grease cookie sheet with BUTTER FLAVOR CRISCO®.
2. Combine BUTTER FLAVOR CRISCO®, brown sugar, granulated sugar, maple syrup, egg and vanilla in large bowl. Beat at medium speed of electric mixer until well blended.
3. Combine flour, baking soda and salt; mix into creamed mixture at low speed until just blended. Stir in oats, 1 cup at a time, with spoon. Stir in chocolate chips and candy pieces.
4. Form dough into 1-inch balls. Place 2 inches apart on cookie sheet.
5. Bake 7 minutes for chewy cookies, 9 minutes for crisper cookies. Cool 2 minutes on cookie sheet. Remove to cooling rack.
Makes about 6¹/₂ dozen cookies

Pizzazz-Packed Giant Peanut Butter Cookies

  1 cup quick oats (not instant
  or old fashioned),
  uncooked
¹/₂ cup BUTTER FLAVOR
  CRISCO®
  1 cup JIF® Creamy Peanut
  Butter
¹/₂ cup firmly packed brown
  sugar
¹/₂ cup granulated sugar
  2 teaspoons orange juice
  1 teaspoon vanilla
  1 egg
³/₄ cup all-purpose flour
  1 tablespoon grated orange
  peel
¹/₂ teaspoon baking soda
¹/₂ teaspoon salt
  1 cup peanut butter chips

1. Preheat oven to 300°F. Spread oats on ungreased cookie sheet. Bake 5 minutes or until toasted, stirring occasionally. Cool to room temperature.
2. Heat oven to 375°F. Grease cookie sheet with BUTTER FLAVOR CRISCO®.
3. Combine BUTTER FLAVOR CRISCO®, JIF® Creamy Peanut Butter, brown sugar, granulated sugar, orange juice and vanilla in large bowl. Beat at medium speed of electric mixer until well blended. Beat in egg.
4. Combine flour, orange peel, baking soda and salt; mix into creamed mixture at low speed until just blended. Stir in peanut butter chips and oats with spoon.
5. Drop ¹/₄ cupfuls of dough 3 inches apart onto cookie sheet. Flatten slightly with greased glass.
6. Bake 10 to 12 minutes, or until lightly browned. Cool 2 minutes on cookie sheet. Remove to cooling rack.
Makes about 14 jumbo cookies

Buttery Butterscotch Cutouts

**3 cups all-purpose flour
1 cup butterscotch chips, melted
½ cup granulated sugar
½ cup firmly packed brown sugar
1 cup LAND O LAKES® Butter, softened
1 egg
2 tablespoons milk
2 teaspoons vanilla
Powdered sugar for sprinkling**

In large mixer bowl, combine flour, melted butterscotch chips, granulated sugar, brown sugar, butter, egg, milk and vanilla. Beat at low speed, scraping bowl often, until well mixed, 1 to 2 minutes. Divide dough into halves. Wrap in waxed paper; refrigerate until firm, 1 to 2 hours.

Preheat oven to 375°F. Roll out dough on well-floured surface to ⅛-inch thickness. Cut out with 2½-inch cookie cutter. Place 1 inch apart on ungreased cookie sheets. Bake for 5 to 8 minutes, or until edges are lightly browned. Remove immediately; cool completely. Dust cookies with powdered sugar or decorate as desired.

Makes about 4 dozen cookies

Party Peanut Butter Cookies

**1½ cups all-purpose flour
½ cup sugar
½ teaspoon baking soda
¾ cup JIF® Creamy Peanut Butter, divided
½ cup BUTTER FLAVOR CRISCO®
¼ cup light corn syrup
1 teaspoon vanilla**

1. Combine flour, sugar and baking soda in medium bowl. Cut in ½ cup of the JIF®

Creamy Peanut Butter and BUTTER FLAVOR CRISCO® until mixture resembles coarse meal. Stir in corn syrup and vanilla until blended.

2. Form dough into 2-inch roll; wrap in waxed paper. Refrigerate 1 hour.

3. Preheat oven to 350°F. Cut dough into ¼-inch slices. Place ½ of the slices 2 inches apart on ungreased cookie sheet. Spread ½ teaspoon JIF® Creamy Peanut Butter on each slice; top with remaining slices. Seal edges with fork.

4. Bake 10 minutes, or until lightly browned. Cool completely on cookie sheet.

Makes about 2 dozen cookies

Buttery Butterscotch Cutouts

Peanut Butter Cremes

**¾ cup BUTTER FLAVOR CRISCO®
1 cup JIF® Creamy Peanut Butter
1 cup firmly packed dark brown sugar
1 cup marshmallow creme
1 egg
2 teaspoons vanilla
1¾ cups all-purpose flour
1 teaspoon baking powder
1 teaspoon salt**

1. Preheat oven to 350°F. Combine BUTTER FLAVOR CRISCO®, JIF® Creamy Peanut Butter, brown sugar and marshmallow creme in large

bowl. Beat at medium speed of electric mixer until well blended. Beat in egg and vanilla.

2. Combine flour, baking powder and salt; mix into creamed mixture at low speed until just blended.

3. Drop rounded tablespoonfuls of dough 2 inches apart onto ungreased cookie sheet.

4. Bake 11 minutes, or until lightly browned. Cool 2 minutes on cookie sheet. Remove to cooling rack.

Makes about 4 dozen cookies

Lollipop Sugar Cookies

Lollipop Sugar Cookies

⅔ cup **BUTTER FLAVOR CRISCO®**
¾ **cup sugar**
1 **tablespoon plus**
    1 **teaspoon milk**
1 **teaspoon vanilla**
1 **egg**
2 **cups all-purpose flour**
1½ **teaspoons baking powder**
¼ **teaspoon salt**
24 to 30 **flat ice cream sticks**
    Assorted decorations
    (baking chips, raisins,
    red hots, snipped dried
    fruit, flake coconut, nuts,
    colored sugar)

1. Combine BUTTER FLAVOR CRISCO®, sugar, milk and vanilla in large bowl. Beat at medium speed of electric mixer until well blended. Beat in egg.

2. Combine flour, baking powder and salt; mix into creamed mixture at low speed until just blended. Cover and refrigerate for several hours or overnight.

3. Preheat oven to 375°F.

4. Form dough into 1½-inch balls. Push ice cream stick into center of each ball. Place balls 3 inches apart on ungreased cookie sheet. Flatten balls to ½-inch thickness with large, smooth, greased and floured spatula. Decorate as desired. Press decorations into dough.*

5. Bake 8 to 10 minutes or until set. Cool 2 minutes on cookie sheet. Remove to cooling rack.

Makes about 2 dozen cookies

*Cookies can also be painted before baking. Mix 1 egg yolk and ¼ teaspoon water. Divide into 3 small cups. Add 2 to 3 drops food color to each. Stir. Use clean watercolor brushes to paint designs on cookies.

Chocolate Kiss Thumbprint

½ **cup BUTTER FLAVOR CRISCO®**
½ **cup sugar**
1 **tablespoon milk**
½ **teaspoon vanilla**
1 **egg, separated**
1 **square (1 ounce)**
    unsweetened chocolate,
    melted and cooled
1 **cup all-purpose flour**
¼ **teaspoon salt**
¾ **cup chopped nuts**
30 **milk chocolate kisses,**
    unwrapped

1. Preheat oven to 350°F. Grease cookie sheet with BUTTER FLAVOR CRISCO®.

2. Combine BUTTER FLAVOR CRISCO®, sugar, milk, vanilla and egg yolk. Beat at medium speed of electric mixer until well blended. Add melted chocolate; mix well.

3. Combine flour and salt. Add to chocolate mixture; mix until blended. Form dough into 1-inch balls.

4. Beat egg white slightly with fork. Coat balls with egg white; roll in chopped nuts. Place 2 inches apart on cookie sheet. Press thumb gently in center of each cookie.

5. Bake 7 minutes. Remove from oven; place chocolate kiss in each thumbprint. Return to oven for one more minute. Remove to cooling rack.

Makes about 2½ dozen cookies

Preparation time: 30 minutes
Bake time: 8 minutes

Cookies in a Crust

Cookies in a Crust

1 KEEBLER® Ready-Crust®
    Butter Flavored Pie Crust
2 eggs
1/3 cup all-purpose flour
1/3 cup granulated sugar
1/3 cup packed brown sugar
1/2 cup butter or margarine,
    melted, cooled
1 package (6 ounces)
    semisweet chocolate
    chips
2/3 cup chopped walnuts
    Whipped cream (optional)

Preheat oven to 325°F. In large
bowl, beat eggs until foamy. Add
flour and sugars; blend
thoroughly. Mix in melted butter.
Stir in chips and walnuts; pour
into pie crust. Bake 1 hour or
until golden brown. Cool on wire
rack. If desired, garnish with
whipped cream.

Makes 8 servings

Snickerdoodles

1 cup BUTTER FLAVOR
    CRISCO®
2 cups sugar, divided
2 eggs
2 tablespoons milk
1 teaspoon vanilla
2 3/4 cups all-purpose flour
2 teaspoons cream of tartar
1 teaspoon baking soda
3/4 teaspoon salt
2 teaspoons cinnamon

1. Preheat oven to 400°F.
Combine BUTTER FLAVOR
CRISCO®, 1 1/2 cups sugar, eggs,
milk and vanilla in large bowl.
Beat at medium speed of electric
mixer until well blended.
2. Combine flour, cream of tartar,
baking soda and salt. Mix into
creamed mixture. Shape dough
into 1-inch balls.
3. Combine remaining 1/2 cup
sugar and cinnamon in small
bowl. Roll balls of dough in
mixture. (*Hint:* Sugar mixture
can be put in reclosable plastic
bag. Put 2 to 3 dough balls at a
time in bag. Shake to sugar-coat
dough.) Place 2 inches apart on
ungreased cookie sheet.

4. Bake 7 to 8 minutes. Remove
to wire rack.
    Makes about 6 dozen cookies
Colored Sugar Variation: Add
2 teaspoons cinnamon to flour
mixture in Step #2. Combine
3 tablespoons colored sugar and
3 tablespoons granulated sugar
for coating instead of cinnamon
and sugar mixture.

Preparation time: 30 minutes
Bake time: 7 to 8 minutes

Cocoa Snickerdoodles

1 cup butter or margarine,
    softened
3/4 cup packed brown sugar
3/4 cup plus 2 tablespoons
    granulated sugar
2 eggs
2 cups uncooked rolled oats
1 1/2 cups all-purpose flour
1/4 cup plus 2 tablespoons
    unsweetened cocoa
1 teaspoon baking soda
2 tablespoons ground
    cinnamon

Preheat oven to 375°F. Lightly
grease cookie sheets or line with
parchment paper.
Beat butter, brown sugar and the
3/4 cup granulated sugar in large
bowl until light and fluffy. Add
eggs; mix well. Combine oats,
flour, the 1/4 cup cocoa and the
baking soda in medium bowl.
Stir into butter mixture until
blended. Mix the 2 tablespoons
granulated sugar, the cinnamon
and the 2 tablespoons cocoa in
small bowl. Drop dough by
rounded teaspoonfuls into
cinnamon mixture; toss to coat.
Place 2 inches apart on prepared
cookie sheets.
Bake 8 to 10 minutes or until
firm in center. Do not overbake.
Remove to wire racks to cool.
    Makes about 4 1/2 dozen cookies

Banana Oatmeal Cookies with Banana Frosting

Cookie
 ¾ cup **BUTTER FLAVOR CRISCO®**
 1 cup firmly packed brown sugar
 1 egg
 1 cup mashed ripe bananas (2 to 3 medium)
 1½ cups all-purpose flour
 1 teaspoon salt
 1 teaspoon cinnamon
 ½ teaspoon baking soda
 ¼ teaspoon nutmeg
 1¾ cups quick oats (not instant or old fashioned), uncooked
 ½ cup coarsely chopped walnuts

Banana Frosting
 2 tablespoons **BUTTER FLAVOR CRISCO®**
 ¼ cup mashed ripe banana
 1 teaspoon lemon juice
 2 cups powdered sugar
 Finely chopped walnuts (optional)

1. Preheat oven to 350°F. Grease cookie sheet with BUTTER FLAVOR CRISCO®.

2. For Cookie, combine BUTTER FLAVOR CRISCO® and brown sugar in large bowl. Beat at medium speed of electric mixer until well blended. Beat in egg. Add mashed bananas. Beat until blended.

3. Combine flour, salt, cinnamon, baking soda and nutmeg; mix into creamed mixture at low speed until blended. Stir in oats and nuts with spoon.

4. Drop 2 level measuring tablespoonfuls of dough into a mound 2 inches apart onto cookie sheet. Repeat with remaining dough.

5. Bake 15 to 17 minutes or until set. Cool 1 minute on cookie sheet. Cool completely on wire rack.

6. For Frosting, combine BUTTER FLAVOR CRISCO®, banana and lemon juice in medium bowl. Beat at medium speed of electric mixer until well blended. Add powdered sugar 1 cup at a time. Beat at low speed after each addition until blended. Frost cooled cookies. Sprinkle with nuts.

Makes about 5 dozen cookies

Hermits

 ¾ cup **BUTTER FLAVOR CRISCO®**
 1½ cups firmly packed brown sugar
 2 tablespoons milk
 3 eggs
 2½ cups all-purpose flour
 1 teaspoon salt
 1 teaspoon cinnamon
 ¾ teaspoon baking soda
 ¼ teaspoon nutmeg
 ⅛ teaspoon ground cloves
 1 cup raisins
 ¾ cup chopped walnuts
 Powdered sugar

1. Preheat oven to 400°F. Combine BUTTER FLAVOR CRISCO®, brown sugar and milk in large bowl. Beat at medium speed of electric mixer until well blended. Add eggs one at a time, beating well after each addition.

2. Combine flour, salt, cinnamon, baking soda, nutmeg and cloves; mix into creamed mixture at low speed just until blended. Stir in raisins and nuts.

3. Drop level tablespoonfuls of dough 2 inches apart onto ungreased cookie sheet.

4. Bake 7 to 8 minutes or until set. Remove immediately to cooling rack. Sift powdered sugar over cooled cookies.

Makes about 5 dozen cookies

Golden Snacking Granola

 2 cups rolled oats, uncooked
 1½ cups coarsely chopped nuts
 1 (3½-ounce) can flaked coconut (1⅓ cups)
 ½ cup sunflower meats
 ½ cup wheat germ
 2 tablespoons sesame seeds
 1 teaspoon ground cinnamon
 1 teaspoon salt
 1 (14-ounce) can EAGLE® Brand Sweetened Condensed Milk (NOT evaporated milk)
 ¼ cup vegetable oil
 1 cup raisins
 1 cup banana chips, optional

Preheat oven to 300°F. In large bowl, combine all ingredients except raisins and banana chips; mix well. Spread evenly in aluminum-foil-lined 15×10-inch jellyroll pan or baking sheet. Bake 55 to 60 minutes, stirring every 15 minutes. Remove from oven; stir in raisins and banana chips if desired. Cool. Store tightly covered at room temperature.

Makes about 2½ quarts

Golden Snacking Granola

Crunchy Chocolate Chipsters

- ½ **cup BUTTER FLAVOR CRISCO®**
- ½ **cup firmly packed brown sugar**
- ½ **cup granulated sugar**
- 2 **tablespoons milk**
- 1 **egg**
- 1 **teaspoon vanilla**
- 1¼ **cups all-purpose flour**
- ½ **teaspoon baking soda**
- ¼ **teaspoon salt**
- 2 **cups crisp rice cereal**
- 1 **cup semi-sweet miniature chocolate chips**

1. Preheat oven to 350°F. Grease cookie sheet with BUTTER FLAVOR CRISCO®.

2. Combine BUTTER FLAVOR CRISCO®, brown sugar, granulated sugar and milk in large bowl. Beat at medium speed of electric mixer until well blended. Beat in egg and vanilla.

3. Combine flour, baking soda and salt; mix into creamed mixture at low speed until blended. Stir in rice cereal and chocolate chips. Drop level measuring tablespoonfuls of dough 2 inches apart onto cookie sheet.

4. Bake 9 minutes, or until set. Remove immediately to cooling rack.

Makes about 4 dozen cookies

Gaiety Pastel Cookies

- 1½ **cups (3 sticks) PARKAY® Margarine, softened**
- 1 **cup sugar**
- 1 **package (4-serving size) JELL-O® Brand Gelatin, any flavor***
- 1 **egg**
- 1 **teaspoon vanilla**
- 3½ **cups all-purpose flour**
- 1 **teaspoon CALUMET® Baking Powder**
- **Additional JELL-O® Brand Gelatin, any flavor***

Preheat oven to 400°F. Beat margarine at medium speed of electric mixer until light and fluffy. Gradually beat in sugar and 1 package of the gelatin. Mix in egg and vanilla. Stir in flour and baking powder until well blended.

Force dough through cookie press onto greased cookie sheets. Sprinkle with additional gelatin. Decorate, if desired. Bake 13 minutes for medium cookies (about 2-inch diameter) or 8 minutes for small cookies (about 1-inch diameter) or until golden brown around edges. Remove; cool on racks. Store in loosely covered container.

Makes about 5 dozen medium cookies or 10 dozen small cookies

*For best results, use same flavor gelatin to flavor cookies and for garnish.

Prep time: 40 minutes
Baking time: 40 minutes

Oatmeal-Chocolate Raisin Cookies

- 1 **cup BUTTER FLAVOR CRISCO®**
- ¾ **cup firmly packed dark brown sugar**
- ¾ **cup granulated sugar**
- 2 **eggs**
- 2 **tablespoons milk**
- 2 **teaspoons vanilla**
- 2 **cups all-purpose flour**
- 1 **teaspoon baking powder**
- 1 **teaspoon baking soda**
- 1 **teaspoon salt**
- 2 **cups quick oats (not instant or old fashioned), uncooked**
- 2 **cups chocolate-covered raisins**
- 1 **cup coarsely chopped pecans**

1. Preheat oven to 350°F. Grease cookie sheet with BUTTER FLAVOR CRISCO®.

2. Combine BUTTER FLAVOR CRISCO®, brown sugar, granulated sugar, eggs, milk and vanilla in large bowl. Beat at medium speed of electric mixer until well blended.

3. Combine flour, baking powder, baking soda and salt; mix into creamed mixture at low speed until just blended. Stir in oats, raisins and nuts with spoon.

4. Drop rounded teaspoonfuls of dough 2 inches apart onto cookie sheet.

5. Bake 10 to 12 minutes, or until set. Remove immediately to cooling rack.

Makes about 6 dozen cookies

Granola & Chocolate Chip Cookies

- ½ **cup BUTTER FLAVOR CRISCO®**
- ½ **cup firmly packed brown sugar**
- ¼ **cup granulated sugar**
- 1 **egg**
- 2 **tablespoons milk**
- ½ **teaspoon vanilla**
- 1¼ **cups all-purpose flour**
- ½ **teaspoon baking soda**
- ½ **teaspoon cinnamon**
- ¼ **teaspoon salt**
- 2 **cups granola cereal**
- 1 **cup semi-sweet chocolate chips**

1. Preheat oven to 350°F. Grease cookie sheet with BUTTER FLAVOR CRISCO®.

2. Combine BUTTER FLAVOR CRISCO®, brown sugar, granulated sugar, egg, milk and vanilla in large bowl. Beat at medium speed of electric mixer until well blended.

3. Combine flour, baking soda, cinnamon and salt; mix into creamed mixture at low speed until just blended. Stir in granola and chocolate chips with spoon. Drop dough by rounded tablespoonfuls 2 inches apart onto cookie sheet.

4. Bake 10 to 12 minutes, or until lightly browned but soft in center. Cool 3 minutes on cookie sheet. Remove to cooling rack.

Makes about 4 dozen cookies

Cherry Oatmeal Cookies

1¼ cups flour
½ teaspoon ground cinnamon
¼ teaspoon salt
¼ teaspoon baking soda
**½ cup butter or margarine,
  softened**
**1 cup packed dark brown
  sugar**
1 egg
½ teaspoon vanilla
¼ cup milk
1 teaspoon vinegar
**1 cup quick-cooking oats,
  uncooked**
**½ cup red maraschino
  cherries, chopped**
**Red maraschino cherry
  halves, if desired**

Preheat oven to 375°F. In small bowl, combine flour, cinnamon, salt and baking soda; set aside. In large mixer bowl, beat butter and brown sugar until creamy. Add egg and vanilla; beat until fluffy. Combine milk and vinegar; add to creamed mixture, beating until blended. Beat in flour mixture until blended. Stir in oats; mix well. Gently fold in chopped cherries.

Drop teaspoonfuls of dough 2 inches apart onto ungreased cookie sheets. Garnish with additional cherry halves, if desired. Bake 10 to 12 minutes or until lightly browned around edges. Cool on wire racks.

Makes about 3 dozen cookies

Favorite recipe from **National Cherry Foundation**

Ice Cream Cookie Sandwich

**2 pints chocolate chip ice
  cream, softened**
**1 package DUNCAN HINES®
  Moist Deluxe Dark Dutch
  Fudge Cake Mix**
**½ cup butter or margarine,
  softened**

1. Line bottom of one 9-inch round cake pan with aluminum foil. Spread ice cream in pan; return to freezer until firm. Run knife around edge of pan to loosen ice cream. Remove from pan; wrap in foil and return to freezer.

2. Preheat oven to 350°F. Line bottom of two 9-inch round cake pans with aluminum foil. Place cake mix in large bowl. Add butter; mix thoroughly until crumbs form. Place half the cake mix in each pan; press lightly.

Bake 15 minutes or until browned around edges; do not overbake. Cool 10 minutes; remove from pans. Remove foil from cookie layers; cool completely.

3. To assemble, place one cookie layer on serving plate. Top with ice cream. Peel off foil. Place second cookie layer on top. Wrap in foil and freeze 2 hours. To keep longer, store in airtight container. Let stand at room temperature 5 to 10 minutes before cutting.

Makes 10 to 12 servings

Ice Cream Cookie Sandwich

FESTIVE HOLIDAY BAKING

Festive gatherings call for plenty of festive foods and these lavish recipes will certainly be the showpiece of any holiday affair. Seasonal ingredients are used in fresh, new ways— Cranberry Orange Cheesecake Bars and Festive Eggnog Cake are just a couple temptations to make your holiday entertaining extra special. Celebrate the season by filling your home with the warmth and good cheer of old-fashioned baking.

Nut-Filled Christmas Wreath

2 tablespoons warm water (105° to 115°F)
1 package active dry yeast
3 tablespoons sugar
2 eggs
¼ cup butter or margarine, melted, cooled
3 tablespoons milk
¾ teaspoon salt
½ teaspoon ground cardamom
2½ to 3 cups all-purpose flour
Cherry-Nut Filling (recipe follows)
Almond Icing (recipe follows)

In large bowl, combine water, yeast and 1 tablespoon of the sugar; stir to dissolve yeast. Let stand until bubbly, about 5 minutes. Add remaining 2 tablespoons sugar, the eggs, butter, milk, salt and cardamom; mix well. Stir in 1½ cups of the flour until smooth. Stir in enough of the remaining flour to make dough easy to handle. Turn out onto lightly floured surface. Knead 10 minutes or until dough is smooth and elastic, adding as much remaining flour as needed to prevent sticking. Shape dough into ball. Place in large, lightly greased bowl; turn dough once to grease surface. Cover with waxed paper; let rise in warm place (80° to 85°F) until doubled, about 1 hour. Meanwhile, prepare Cherry-Nut Filling. Punch dough down. Roll out dough on floured surface into 24×9-inch rectangle. Sprinkle Cherry-Nut Filling over dough to within 1 inch from edges. Roll up dough, jelly-roll style, beginning on 24-inch side; pinch seam to seal. Using sharp knife, cut roll in half lengthwise; turn each half cut-side up. Carefully twist halves together, keeping cut sides up to expose filling. Place dough on greased cookie sheet; shape into a ring. Pinch ends together to seal. Cover; let stand in warm place until almost doubled, about 45 minutes.

Preheat oven to 375°F. Bake 20 minutes or until evenly browned. Remove bread from cookie sheet to wire rack; cool slightly. Prepare Almond Icing; drizzle over warm coffee cake. Serve warm or at room temperature.
Makes 1 coffee cake

CHERRY-NUT FILLING: In medium bowl, combine ¾ cup chopped nuts (pecans, walnuts, almonds or hazelnuts), ¼ cup *each* all-purpose flour, chopped candied red cherries, chopped candied green cherries and softened butter or margarine, 2 tablespoons brown sugar and ½ teaspoon almond extract; mix well.

ALMOND ICING: In small bowl, combine 1 cup sifted powdered sugar, 1 to 2 tablespoons milk and ¼ teaspoon almond extract; blend until smooth.

Clockwise from top left: Apple-Cranberry Muffins (page 272), Nut-Filled Christmas Wreath, Wholesome Wheat Bread (page 272)

Wholesome Wheat Bread

5¹/₂ to 6 cups whole wheat flour
2 packages active dry yeast
1 teaspoon salt
1 teaspoon ground cinnamon
1 cup KARO® Dark Corn Syrup
1 cup water
¹/₂ cup HELLMANN'S® or BEST FOODS® Real Mayonnaise
2 eggs

In large mixer bowl, combine 2 cups of the flour, the yeast, salt and cinnamon. In medium saucepan, combine corn syrup, water and real mayonnaise; heat mixture over medium heat, stirring occasionally, until very warm (120° to 130°F). Pour hot mixture into flour mixture; beat at medium speed 2 minutes. Reduce speed to low; beat in 2 more cups of the flour and the eggs until well mixed. Beat at medium speed 2 minutes. By hand, stir in enough of the remaining flour to make dough easy to handle.

Turn out onto lightly floured surface. Knead 10 minutes or until dough is smooth and elastic, adding as much remaining flour as needed to prevent sticking. Shape dough into ball. Place in large, greased bowl; turn dough once to grease surface. Cover with towel; let rise in warm place (80° to 85°F) until doubled, about 1 hour.

Punch dough down; divide in half. Cover; let rest 10 minutes. Shape each half into 8×4-inch oval. Place on large greased and floured baking sheet. Cut 3 slashes, ¹/₄ inch deep, in top of each loaf. Cover; let rise in warm place until doubled, about 1¹/₂ hours.

Preheat oven to 350°F. Bake 30 to 40 minutes or until loaves are browned and sound hollow when tapped. Immediately remove from baking sheet to wire racks to cool.   *Makes 2 loaves*

Glazed Fruit Crescents

Glazed Fruit Crescents

1 (9-ounce) package NONE SUCH® Condensed Mincemeat, crumbled
¹/₄ cup orange juice
2 tablespoons finely chopped nuts
³/₄ teaspoon grated orange rind
2 (8-ounce) packages refrigerated crescent rolls
²/₃ cup confectioners' sugar
4 teaspoons orange-flavored liqueur *or* orange juice
Additional grated orange rind, optional

Preheat oven to 375°F. In small saucepan, combine mincemeat and orange juice. Over medium heat, bring to a boil; cook and stir 1 minute. Add nuts and *¹/₂ teaspoon* orange rind. Separate and flatten dough into 16 triangles. Spoon 1 tablespoon mincemeat mixture on shortest side of each triangle. Starting at shortest side, roll up. Place point-side down on ungreased baking sheets.

Bake 12 to 15 minutes or until golden. Meanwhile, combine sugar, liqueur and remaining *¹/₄ teaspoon* orange rind; mix until smooth. Spoon over hot rolls; garnish with additional rind if desired. Serve warm.
          Makes 16 rolls

Tip: To use NONE SUCH® Ready-to-Use Regular *or* Brandy & Rum Mincemeat instead of condensed mincemeat, omit orange juice. Combine 1¹/₃ cups ready-to-use mincemeat with nuts and rind. Omit cooking; proceed as above.

Apple-Cranberry Muffins

1³/₄ cups plus 2 tablespoons all-purpose flour
¹/₂ cup sugar
1¹/₂ teaspoons baking powder
¹/₂ teaspoon baking soda
¹/₂ teaspoon salt
1 egg
³/₄ cup milk
³/₄ cup sweetened applesauce
¹/₄ cup butter or margarine, melted
1 cup fresh cranberries, coarsely chopped
¹/₂ teaspoon ground cinnamon

Preheat oven to 400°F. In medium bowl, combine 1³/₄ cups of the flour, ¹/₄ cup of the sugar, the baking powder, baking soda and salt. In small bowl, combine egg, milk, applesauce and melted butter; mix well. Add egg mixture to flour mixture; stir just until moistened. Batter will be lumpy; do not overmix. In small bowl, toss cranberries with remaining 2 tablespoons flour; fold into batter. Spoon batter evenly into 12 greased 2³/₄-inch muffin cups.

In measuring cup, combine remaining ¹/₄ cup sugar and the cinnamon. Sprinkle over tops of muffins. Bake 20 to 25 minutes or until golden brown. Remove to wire rack to cool.
          Makes 1 dozen muffins

*Favorite recipe from **Western New York Apple Growers Association, Inc.***

Jarlsberg Party Swirl

1 loaf frozen bread dough
1 cup shredded Jarlsberg cheese
¼ cup chopped pitted ripe olives
¼ cup minced green pepper
¼ teaspoon chili powder
¼ teaspoon garlic salt
Melted butter or margarine

Place bread dough in greased shallow bowl. Cover; defrost and let rise until doubled according to package directions.

Preheat oven to 375°F. In small bowl combine cheese, olives, green pepper, chili powder and garlic salt. Blend well.

Divide dough into thirds. On lightly floured board, roll each into 15×3-inch rectangle. Brush with melted butter. Reserving ¼ cup cheese mixture for topping, sprinkle remaining cheese mixture evenly over dough rectangles. Roll up each rectangle jelly-roll fashion, starting from 15-inch side. Braid rolls together; pinch ends to seal and tuck under. Place braid on ungreased baking sheet.

Bake 25 minutes. Sprinkle reserved cheese mixture down center of bread; bake 5 minutes longer. Serve warm.

Makes 1 large loaf

*Favorite recipe from **Norseland Foods***

Cranberry Streusel Coffee Cake

Cranberry Streusel Coffee Cake

Cake Batter:
1½ cups flour
1½ teaspoons baking powder
½ teaspoon salt
6 tablespoons (¾ stick) unsalted butter, softened
¾ cup granulated sugar
2 teaspoons grated orange rind
2 eggs
½ cup milk
Streusel:
½ cup light brown sugar
¼ cup flour
½ teaspoon cinnamon
2 tablespoons butter, softened
½ cup chopped walnuts
Cranberry Filling:
1½ cups OCEAN SPRAY® Fresh or Frozen Cranberries
¼ cup granulated sugar
2 tablespoons orange juice

1. Preheat oven to 350°F. Grease and flour 8-inch square cake pan.
2. Cake Batter: Stir together flour, baking powder and salt in small bowl until well mixed.

Cream butter, granulated sugar and orange rind in large bowl. Add eggs, one at a time, beating well after each addition. Stir in flour mixture alternately with milk, beginning and ending with flour; set aside.

3. Streusel: Combine all streusel ingredients in small bowl. Mix together with fork until crumbly; set aside.

4. Cranberry Filling: Place all ingredients in small saucepan. Cook over medium heat, stirring constantly, until berries start to pop. Remove from heat; cool to room temperature.

5. Spread half of the coffee cake batter over bottom of prepared pan. Sprinkle with half of the streusel mixture; spoon on half the cranberry filling. Cover with remaining batter; top batter with remaining filling and sprinkle with remaining streusel.

6. Bake 50 to 60 minutes or until wooden toothpick inserted in center comes out clean. Cool on wire rack. Serve warm or at room temperature.

Makes one 8-inch coffee cake

Colonial Cranberry Breads with Nutmeg-Rum Glaze

4 cups all-purpose flour
1 cup granulated sugar
1 cup firmly packed light brown sugar
2 teaspoons baking soda
2 teaspoons cream of tartar
1 teaspoon ground cinnamon
1 teaspoon ground allspice
½ teaspoon freshly grated nutmeg
½ teaspoon salt
Large pinch freshly ground black pepper
1½ cups freshly squeezed orange juice, seeds removed
6 tablespoons unsalted butter, melted
2 eggs
4 cups OCEAN SPRAY® Fresh or Frozen Cranberries, rinsed, drained and picked over
1½ cups pecans or walnuts
2 tablespoons grated orange zest
Nutmeg-Rum Glaze (recipe follows)

Place rack in center of oven; preheat oven to 350°F. Butter and flour six 5¾×3¼×2-inch loaf pans. In large mixing bowl, sift together flour, granulated sugar, brown sugar, baking soda, cream of tartar, cinnamon, allspice, nutmeg, salt and black pepper.

In medium mixing bowl, whisk together orange juice, butter and eggs until blended; set aside. Place cranberries, nuts and orange zest in food processor; pulse several times, just until cranberries are coarsely chopped (do not overprocess).

Make well in center of dry ingredients; pour in liquid mixture. Stir very lightly with large rubber spatula, just until mixture is moistened but not thoroughly mixed. Gently fold in cranberry mixture just until blended. Spoon batter into

prepared pans, filling about ⅔ full. Tap each pan on countertop to remove air bubbles; gently smooth tops of batter.

Place filled pans on baking sheet, spacing slightly apart. Bake 50 to 60 minutes or until loaves are golden and wooden toothpick inserted in center comes out clean (do not overbake). Remove from oven; carefully invert loaves onto wire rack set over large sheet of waxed paper. Carefully turn loaves right side up; cool until warm. Using teaspoon, drizzle loaves with Nutmeg-Rum Glaze. Cool completely.

Makes 6 small loaves

Nutmeg-Rum Glaze

2 cups sifted confectioners' sugar
2 tablespoons milk
2 tablespoons dark rum, brandy or apple cider
½ teaspoon pure vanilla extract
1 teaspoon freshly grated nutmeg

In medium mixing bowl, combine confectioners' sugar, milk, rum, vanilla and nutmeg. Add a little more rum or sugar so that glaze can be drizzled onto loaves in thin lines.

Kugelhopf

1 package (16 ounces) hot roll mix
⅓ cup warm water (105° to 115°F)
⅔ cup milk
½ cup butter or margarine, softened
½ cup granulated sugar
2 teaspoons grated orange peel
1 teaspoon grated lemon peel
½ teaspoon mace
2 eggs
1 cup DIAMOND® Walnuts
Powdered sugar, for garnish

In small bowl, dissolve yeast from hot roll mix in warm water. In small saucepan, scald milk over low heat; set aside to cool to lukewarm (105° to 115°F). In large bowl, cream butter, granulated sugar, peels and mace. Beat in eggs one at a time. Add milk, yeast and flour from mix; beat until smooth. Cover; let rise in warm place (85°F) until doubled, about 30 minutes. Stir dough down. Finely chop ¼ cup of the walnuts; sprinkle into well-buttered 10-inch fluted tube pan. Coarsely chop remaining ¾ cup walnuts and stir into dough. Spoon into pan. Cover; let rise in warm place until doubled, about 30 minutes.

Preheat oven to 375°F. Bake 35 minutes or until lightly browned. Cool in pan 5 to 10 minutes. Loosen edges; invert onto serving plate. Dust with powdered sugar.

Makes 1 large kugelhopf

Skillet Walnut Pumpkin Bread

Cornmeal
⅓ cup butter or margarine, softened
1 cup sugar
2 eggs, slightly beaten
1 cup canned pumpkin
¾ cup milk
1 cup all-purpose flour
¾ cup cornmeal
1 teaspoon ground allspice
1 teaspoon baking soda
½ teaspoon baking powder
1 cup chopped DIAMOND® Walnuts
DIAMOND® Walnut halves, for garnish

Preheat oven to 375°F. Grease 9-inch cast-iron skillet. Dust with cornmeal; set aside.

In large bowl, beat butter, sugar and eggs. Add pumpkin and milk; mix to blend thoroughly. In medium bowl, combine flour, the ¾ cup cornmeal, allspice, baking soda and baking powder. Add to pumpkin mixture, stirring just until blended. Stir in chopped walnuts. Pour into prepared skillet. Garnish center with walnut halves.

Bake 45 minutes or until wooden toothpick inserted in center comes out clean. Serve warm.

Makes 6 to 8 servings

Note: Substitute a deep 9-inch round or square baking pan if cast-iron skillet is unavailable.

Dutch St. Nicolas Cookies

¾ cup butter or margarine, softened
½ cup packed brown sugar
2 tablespoons milk
1½ teaspoons ground cinnamon
¼ teaspoon ground nutmeg
¼ teaspoon ground ginger
¼ teaspoon ground cloves
2 cups sifted all-purpose flour
1½ teaspoons baking powder
½ teaspoon salt
½ cup toasted chopped almonds
¼ cup coarsely chopped citron

In large bowl, cream butter, brown sugar, milk and spices. In small bowl, combine flour, baking powder and salt. Add flour mixture to creamed mixture; blend well. Stir in almonds and citron. Knead dough slightly to make ball. Cover; refrigerate until firm.

Preheat oven to 375°F. Roll out dough ¼ inch thick on lightly floured surface. Cut out with cookie cutters. Place 2 inches apart on greased cookie sheets. Bake 7 to 10 minutes or until lightly browned. Remove to wire racks to cool.

Makes about 3½ dozen cookies

Favorite recipe from Almond Board of California

Fruited Shortbread Cookies

2½ cups unsifted flour
1 teaspoon baking soda
1 teaspoon cream of tartar
1 cup margarine or butter, softened
1½ cups confectioners' sugar
1 egg
1 (9-ounce) package NONE SUCH® Condensed Mincemeat, crumbled
1 teaspoon vanilla extract
Lemon Frosting, optional
Candied cherries or nuts, optional

Preheat oven to 375°F. Stir together flour, baking soda and cream of tartar; set aside. In large mixer bowl, beat margarine and sugar until fluffy. Add egg; mix well. Stir in mincemeat and vanilla. Add flour mixture; mix well (dough will be stiff). Roll into 1¼-inch balls. Place on ungreased cookie sheets; flatten slightly.

Bake 10 to 12 minutes or until lightly browned. Cool. Frost with Lemon Frosting and garnish with candied cherries or nuts if desired.

Makes about 3 dozen cookies

LEMON FROSTING: In small mixer bowl, combine 2 cups confectioners' sugar, 2 tablespoons softened margarine or butter, 2 tablespoons water and ½ teaspoon grated lemon rind until well blended.

Makes about ⅔ cup frosting

Fruited Shortbread Cookies

Star Christmas Tree Cookies

Star Christmas Tree Cookies

Cookies
    1 package DUNCAN HINES®
        Moist Deluxe Yellow or
        Devil's Food Cake Mix
    ½ cup CRISCO® Shortening
    ⅓ cup butter or margarine,
        softened
    2 egg yolks
    1 teaspoon vanilla extract
    1 tablespoon water
Frosting
    1 container (16 ounces)
        DUNCAN HINES® Vanilla
        Frosting
    Green food coloring
    Red and green sugar
        crystals, for garnish
    Assorted colored candies
        and decors, for garnish

1. Preheat oven to 375°F.

2. For Cookies, combine shortening, butter, egg yolks and vanilla extract. Blend in cake mix gradually. Add 1 teaspoonful water at a time until dough is of rolling consistency. Divide dough into 4 balls. Flatten one ball with hand; roll to ⅛-inch thickness on lightly floured surface. Cut with graduated sized star cookie cutters. Repeat using remaining dough. Bake large cookies together on ungreased cookie sheet 6 to 8 minutes or until edges are light golden brown. Cool cookies 1 minute; remove from cookie sheet. Repeat with smaller cookies, testing for doneness at minimum bake time.

3. For Frosting, tint vanilla frosting with green food coloring. Frost cookies and stack, beginning with largest cookies on bottom and ending with smallest cookies on top. Rotate cookies when stacking to alternate corners. Decorate as desired with colored sugar and assorted candies and decors.
    Makes 2 to 3 dozen cookies

Tip: If assorted star cutters are not available, use your favorite cutters. Stack cookies into large "tree" or into smaller trees using 3 to 5 cookies per tree.

Double-Dipped Hazelnut Crisps

3/4 **cup semisweet chocolate chips**
1 1/4 **cups all-purpose flour**
3/4 **cup powdered sugar**
2/3 **cup whole hazelnuts, toasted, hulled and pulverized***
1/4 **teaspoon instant espresso coffee powder**
   Dash salt
1/2 **cup butter or margarine, softened**
2 **teaspoons vanilla**
4 **squares (1 ounce each) bittersweet or semisweet chocolate**
4 **ounces white chocolate**
2 **teaspoons shortening, divided**

Preheat oven to 350°F. Lightly grease cookie sheets or line with parchment paper.

Melt chocolate chips in top of double boiler over hot, not boiling, water. Remove from heat, cool. Blend flour, sugar, hazelnuts, coffee powder and salt in large bowl. Blend in butter, melted chocolate and vanilla until dough is stiff but smooth. (If dough is too soft to handle, cover and refrigerate until firm.) Roll out dough, one fourth at a time, 1/8 inch thick on lightly floured surface. Cut out with 2-inch scalloped round cutters. Place 2 inches apart on prepared cookie sheets.

Bake 8 minutes or until not quite firm. (Cookies should not brown. They will puff up during baking and then fall again.) Remove to wire racks to cool.

Place bittersweet and white chocolates into separate small bowls. Add 1 teaspoon shortening to each bowl. Place bowls over hot water; stir until chocolate is melted and smooth. Dip cookies, one at a time, halfway into bittersweet chocolate. Place on waxed paper; refrigerate until chocolate is set. Dip other halves of cookies into white chocolate; refrigerate until set. Store cookies in airtight container in cool place. (If cookies are frozen, chocolate may discolor.)

Makes about 4 dozen cookies

*To pulverize hazelnuts, place in food processor or blender. Process until thoroughly ground with a dry, not pasty, texture.

Pecan Florentines

3/4 **cup pecan halves, pulverized***
1/2 **cup all-purpose flour**
1/3 **cup packed brown sugar**
1/4 **cup light corn syrup**
1/4 **cup butter or margarine**
2 **tablespoons milk**
1/3 **cup semisweet chocolate chips**

Preheat oven to 350°F. Line cookie sheets with foil; lightly grease foil.

Combine pecans and flour in small bowl. Combine brown sugar, corn syrup, butter and milk in medium saucepan. Stir over medium heat until mixture comes to a boil. Remove from heat; stir in flour mixture. Drop batter by teaspoonfuls about 3 inches apart onto prepared cookie sheets.

Bake 10 to 12 minutes or until lacy and golden brown. (Cookies are soft when hot, but become crispy as they cool.) Cool completely on foil.

Place chocolate chips in small heavy-duty plastic bag; close securely. Set bag in bowl of hot water until chips are melted, being careful not to let any water into bag. (Knead bag lightly to check that chips are completely melted.) Pat bag dry. With scissors, snip off small corner from one side of bag. Squeeze melted chocolate over cookies to decorate. Let stand until chocolate is set. Peel foil off cookies.

Makes about 3 dozen cookies

*To pulverize pecans, place in food processor or blender. Process until thoroughly ground with a dry, not pasty, texture.

Left to right: Double-Dipped Hazelnut Crisps, Pecan Florentines

Chocolate Raspberry Linzer Cookies

2⅓ cups all-purpose flour
1 teaspoon baking powder
½ teaspoon salt
½ teaspoon cinnamon
1 cup granulated sugar
¾ cup (1½ sticks) butter, softened
2 eggs
½ teaspoon almond extract
One 12-oz. pkg. (2 cups) NESTLÉ® Toll House® Semi-Sweet Chocolate Morsels
6 tablespoons raspberry jam or preserves
Confectioners' sugar

In small bowl, combine flour, baking powder, salt and cinnamon; set aside. In large mixer bowl, beat granulated sugar and butter until creamy. Beat in eggs and almond extract. Gradually beat in flour mixture. Divide dough in half. Wrap in plastic wrap; refrigerate until firm.

Preheat oven to 350°F. On lightly floured board, roll half of dough ⅛ inch thick. Cut with 2½-inch fluted round cookie cutter. Repeat with remaining dough. Cut 1-inch round centers from half of unbaked cookies. Place cookies on ungreased cookie sheets. Reroll dough trimmings.

Bake 8 to 10 minutes. Let stand on cookie sheets 2 minutes. Remove from cookie sheets; cool completely.

Melt semi-sweet chocolate morsels. Spread 1 measuring teaspoonful chocolate on flat side of each whole cookie. Top with ½ measuring teaspoonful raspberry jam. Sprinkle confectioners' sugar on cookies with center holes; place sugar-side up on top of chocolate-jam cookies to form sandwiches.

Makes about 3 dozen cookies

Chocolate Mint Pinwheels

One 10-oz. pkg. (1½ cups) NESTLÉ® Toll House® Mint Flavored Semi-Sweet Chocolate Morsels, divided
¾ cup (1½ sticks) butter, softened
⅓ cup sugar
½ teaspoon salt
1 egg
1 teaspoon vanilla extract
2¼ cups all-purpose flour

Melt ½ cup mint chocolate morsels; cool to room temperature. Set aside. In large mixer bowl, beat butter, sugar and salt until creamy. Beat in egg and vanilla extract (mixture may appear curdled). Gradually beat in flour. Place 1 cup dough in bowl; blend in melted chocolate. Shape each dough into a ball; flatten and wrap with plastic wrap. Refrigerate about 1½ hours.

Preheat oven to 375°F. Between sheets of waxed paper, roll each ball of dough into a 13×9-inch rectangle. Remove top layers of waxed paper. Invert chocolate dough onto plain dough. Peel off waxed paper. Starting at 13-inch side, roll up jelly-roll style. Cut into ¼-inch-thick slices. Place slices on ungreased cookie sheets. Bake 7 to 10 minutes. Let stand on cookie sheets 2 minutes. Remove from cookie sheets; cool completely.

Melt remaining 1 cup mint chocolate morsels. Spread slightly rounded ½ teaspoonful chocolate on flat side of each cookie. Refrigerate to set chocolate.

Makes about 3½ dozen cookies

New Wave Chocolate Spritz Cookies

One 6-oz. pkg. (1 cup) NESTLÉ® Toll House® Semi-Sweet Chocolate Morsels
1 cup (2 sticks) butter, softened
⅔ cup sugar
1 teaspoon vanilla extract
2 eggs
2½ cups all-purpose flour
One 4-oz. jar cinnamon candies

Melt semi-sweet chocolate morsels; set aside. In large mixer bowl, beat butter, sugar and vanilla extract until creamy. Beat in eggs. Stir in melted chocolate. Gradually beat in flour. Cover dough; refrigerate until firm.

Preheat oven to 400°F. Place dough in cookie press. Using star tip, press cookie dough into 2-inch circles onto ungreased cookie sheets. Decorate with candies. Bake 5 minutes or just until set. Let stand on cookie sheets 2 minutes. Remove from cookie sheets; cool.

Makes about 7½ dozen cookies

Snowball Cookies

2 cups all-purpose flour
2 cups finely chopped pecans
1 cup LAND O LAKES® Sweet Cream Butter, softened
¼ cup granulated sugar
1 teaspoon vanilla
Powdered sugar

Preheat oven to 325°F. In large bowl, combine all ingredients *except* powdered sugar; beat until well mixed. Shape teaspoonfuls of dough into 1-inch balls. Place 2 inches apart on ungreased cookie sheets.

Bake 18 to 22 minutes or until very lightly browned. Remove to wire racks to cool slightly. Roll cookies in powdered sugar while still warm and again when cool.

Makes about 3 dozen cookies

*Clockwise from top right: Chocolate Mint Pinwheels, Chocolate Raspberry Linzer Cookies,
New Wave Chocolate Spritz Cookies*

"Buttery" Drop Cookies

"Buttery" Drop Cookies

½ cup **BUTTER FLAVOR CRISCO®**
¾ cup **sugar**
1 tablespoon **milk**
1 **egg**
½ teaspoon **vanilla**
1¼ cups **all-purpose flour**
¼ teaspoon **salt**
¼ teaspoon **baking powder**

1. Preheat oven to 375°F. Grease cookie sheet with BUTTER FLAVOR CRISCO®.
2. Combine BUTTER FLAVOR CRISCO®, sugar and milk in medium bowl. Beat at medium speed of electric mixer until well blended. Beat in egg and vanilla. Beat until blended.
3. Combine flour, salt and baking powder; mix into creamed mixture at low speed until just blended.
4. Drop dough by level measuring tablespoonfuls 2 inches apart onto cookie sheet.
5. Bake 7 to 9 minutes or until set. Cool 2 minutes on cookie sheet. Remove to cooling rack.

Makes about 3 dozen cookies

Note: For larger cookies, drop 2 level measuring tablespoonfuls of dough into a mound for each cookie. Place 3 inches apart on greased cookie sheet. Bake at 375°F for 11 to 13 minutes, or until set. Cool 2 minutes on cookie sheet. Remove to cooling rack.

Variations for "Buttery" Drop Cookies

Frosted "Buttery" Drop: Bake and cool larger "Buttery" Drop Cookies. Frost cooled cookies as wreaths or ornaments for the holiday season.

Creamy Vanilla Frosting: See page 66 for recipe.

Chocolate Dipped: See page 66 for recipe.

Chocolate Nut: See page 66 for recipe.

Raspberry-Coconut: Bake small "Buttery" Drop Cookies. Spread ½ to 1 teaspoonful raspberry jam on each hot cookie. Sprinkle with flake coconut.

Chocolate Sandwich Cookies: Bake small "Buttery" Drop Cookies. Spread Chocolate Frosting on bottom of half of the cookies. Top with remaining cookies. Gently press together.

Chocolate Frosting: See page 66 for recipe.

Makes about 2 cups frosting

Ricotta Crescents

2½ cups all-purpose flour
1 teaspoon salt
¾ cup (1½ sticks) unsalted butter, softened
1 cup POLLY-O® Ricotta Cheese
1 cup sugar, divided
1½ teaspoons grated orange peel
2 tablespoons ground cinnamon
¾ cup raspberry or apricot jam

In small bowl, combine flour and salt. In large bowl with electric mixer at medium speed, beat butter and ricotta until well blended. Beat in ½ cup sugar and orange peel, scraping sides of bowl with rubber spatula. With mixer on low speed, beat in flour mixture until dough forms. Wrap dough in plastic wrap; refrigerate 2 hours or overnight.

Preheat oven to 375°F. Line 2 large cookie sheets with foil; grease foil. In small bowl, combine remaining ½ cup sugar and cinnamon. Sprinkle pastry board or countertop with 1 tablespoon of the cinnamon-sugar. Divide dough into 6 pieces; shape each piece into ball.

With rolling pin, roll out 1 ball of dough into 8-inch circle, turning over several times to coat well with cinnamon-sugar. With knife, cut into 8 wedges. Spoon ½ teaspoon jam on wide end of each wedge. Starting at wide ends, tightly roll up wedges; pinch ends to seal. Place on prepared cookie sheets, curving ends slightly to form crescent. Repeat with remaining dough.

Bake 15 to 20 minutes or until golden brown. Immediately transfer to wire racks to cool.

Makes about 50 cookies

Fruit Burst Cookies

1 cup margarine or butter, softened
¼ cup sugar
1 teaspoon almond extract
2 cups all-purpose flour
½ teaspoon salt
1 cup finely chopped nuts
SMUCKER'S® Simply Fruit

Preheat oven to 400°F. Cream margarine and sugar in large bowl until light and fluffy. Blend in almond extract. Combine flour and salt; add to margarine mixture and blend well. Shape level tablespoons of dough into balls; roll in nuts. Place 2 inches apart on ungreased cookie sheets; flatten slightly. Indent centers; fill with fruit spread.

Bake 10 to 12 minutes or just until lightly browned. Cool on wire racks.

Makes about 2½ dozen cookies

Fruit Burst Cookies

Chocolate Kahlúa® Bears

¼ cup KAHLÚA®
2 squares (1 ounce each) unsweetened chocolate
⅔ cup shortening
1⅔ cups sugar
2 eggs
2 teaspoons vanilla
2 cups sifted all-purpose flour
2 teaspoons baking powder
¾ teaspoon salt
½ teaspoon ground cinnamon
Chocolate Icing (recipe follows)

Add enough water to KAHLÚA® in measuring cup to make ⅓ cup liquid. In small saucepan over low heat, melt chocolate; cool. In large bowl, beat shortening, sugar, eggs and vanilla until light and fluffy. Stir in chocolate. In small bowl combine flour, baking powder, salt and cinnamon. Add dry ingredients to egg mixture alternately with ⅓ cup liquid. Cover; refrigerate until firm.

Preheat oven to 350°F. Roll out dough, one fourth at a time, about ¼ inch thick on well-floured surface. Cut out with bear-shaped or other cookie cutters. Place 2 inches apart on ungreased cookie sheets.

Bake 8 to 10 minutes. Remove to wire racks to cool. Spread Chocolate Icing in thin, even layer on cookies. Let stand until set; decorate as desired.

Makes about 2½ dozen cookies

CHOCOLATE ICING: In medium saucepan, combine 6 squares (1 ounce each) semisweet chocolate, ⅓ cup butter or margarine, ¼ cup KAHLÚA® and 1 tablespoon light corn syrup. Cook over low heat until chocolate melts, stirring to blend. Add ¾ cup sifted powdered sugar; beat until smooth. If necessary, beat in additional KAHLÚA® to make icing of spreading consistency.

Mint-Chocolate Truffle Squares

Crust:
1½ cups all-purpose flour
¾ cup (1½ sticks) butter, softened
½ cup granulated sugar
2 tablespoons NESTLÉ® Cocoa

Topping:
One 10-oz. pkg. (1½ cups) NESTLÉ® Toll House® Mint Flavored Semi-Sweet Chocolate Morsels
½ cup (1 stick) butter
4 eggs
¼ cup granulated sugar
2 tablespoons all-purpose flour
1 teaspoon vanilla extract
Confectioners' sugar

Crust: Preheat oven to 350°F. In small mixer bowl, beat flour, butter, granulated sugar and cocoa until soft dough forms; spread into bottom of ungreased 13×9-inch baking pan. Bake 8 to 9 minutes or until barely set.

Topping: Melt mint chocolate morsels and butter, stirring until smooth; set aside. In small mixer bowl, beat eggs and granulated sugar until light and fluffy, about 3 minutes. At low speed, beat in flour, vanilla extract and melted chocolate mixture. Pour over Crust.

Bake 18 minutes or *just* until wooden toothpick inserted into center comes out clean. (Topping may puff and crack, but will flatten as it cools.) Cool completely. Sprinkle with confectioners' sugar. Cut into 1½-inch squares.

Makes 4 dozen squares

Jammy Fantasia

Crust
1½ cups all-purpose flour
1½ cups quick oats (not instant), uncooked
½ cup firmly packed brown sugar
½ teaspoon baking soda
¾ cup BUTTER FLAVOR CRISCO®
2 tablespoons water
1 cup apricot or raspberry preserves

Drizzle (optional)
¾ cup confectioners' sugar
1 tablespoon plus ½ teaspoon milk
¼ teaspoon vanilla

Preheat oven to 375°F. For Crust, combine flour, oats, brown sugar and baking soda. Cut in BUTTER FLAVOR CRISCO® until coarse crumbs form. Reserve 1¾ cups of mixture; set aside. Drizzle water over remaining crumbs; toss to mix. Press firmly into ungreased 13×9×2-inch baking pan. Spread preserves over crust. Sprinkle with reserved crumbs; pat gently.

Bake 25 to 30 minutes. Cool in pan. For Drizzle, combine confectioners' sugar, milk and vanilla; stir well. Drizzle over top of cookies. Cut into festive triangles or 2×1½-inch bars.

Makes 36 bars

Prep time: 25 minutes
Bake time: 25 to 30 minutes

Cranberry Orange Ricotta Cheese Brownies

Filling
1 cup ricotta cheese
3 tablespoons whole-berry cranberry sauce
¼ cup sugar
1 egg
2 tablespoons cornstarch
¼ to ½ teaspoon grated orange peel
4 drops red food color (optional)

Brownie
½ cup butter or margarine, melted
¾ cup sugar
1 teaspoon vanilla extract
2 eggs
¾ cup all-purpose flour
½ cup HERSHEY'S® Cocoa
½ teaspoon baking powder
½ teaspoon salt

Preheat oven to 350°F. Grease 9-inch square baking pan.

To prepare Filling, in small mixer bowl, beat ricotta cheese, cranberry sauce, sugar, egg and cornstarch until smooth. Stir in orange peel and food color, if desired.

To prepare Brownie, in small bowl, stir together melted butter, sugar and vanilla; add eggs, beating well. Stir together flour, cocoa, baking powder and salt; add to butter mixture, mixing thoroughly. Spread half of chocolate batter in prepared pan. Spread cheese mixture over top. Drop remaining chocolate batter by teaspoonfuls onto cheese mixture.

Bake 40 to 45 minutes or until wooden toothpick inserted in center comes out clean. Cool completely. Cut into squares. Refrigerate leftovers.

Makes about 16 brownies

Cranberry Orange Ricotta Cheese Brownies

Pumpkin Jingle Bars

Pumpkin Jingle Bars

    ¾ cup MIRACLE WHIP® Salad
        Dressing
    1 (two layer) spice cake mix
    1 (16 oz.) can pumpkin
    3 eggs
        Vanilla frosting
        Red and green gum drops,
        sliced

One Bowl Method:
• Mix first four ingredients at medium speed of electric mixer until well blended.
• Pour into greased 15½×10½×1-inch jelly roll pan. Bake at 350°F, 18 to 20 minutes or until edges pull away from sides of pan. Cool.
• Decorate with frosting and gum drops. Cut into bars.

Makes about 3 dozen

Prep time: 5 minutes
Cooking time: 20 minutes

Almond & Fruit Meringue Bars

    3 cups sifted all-purpose
        flour
    ¾ cup granulated sugar
    ½ teaspoon salt
    1 cup butter or margarine,
        cold
    2 eggs, separated
    ¼ cup water
    ⅛ teaspoon cream of tartar
    ¾ cup sifted powdered sugar
    1 teaspoon vanilla
    ¼ teaspoon ground cinnamon
    3 tablespoons finely
        chopped candied fruits
    ¾ cup toasted chopped
        almonds

Preheat oven to 350°F. In large bowl, combine flour, granulated sugar and salt. Cut in butter until mixture resembles coarse crumbs. In small bowl, beat egg yolks lightly with water; sprinkle over flour mixture, tossing to moisten evenly. Shape dough into ball. If dough is too soft to handle, cover and refrigerate until firm.

In small mixer bowl, beat egg whites with cream of tartar at high speed until soft peaks form. Gradually beat in powdered sugar until whites are glossy and stand in stiff peaks. Gently fold vanilla, cinnamon and candied fruits into meringue; set aside.

Divide dough in half. Roll out each half into 12×8-inch rectangle on lightly floured surface. Spread half the meringue mixture over each rectangle; sprinkle with almonds. Cut each rectangle into sixteen 4×1½-inch bars. Place on ungreased cookie sheets. Bake 15 to 18 minutes or until lightly browned. Remove to wire racks to cool.   *Makes 32 bars*

*Favorite recipe from **Almond Board of California***

Holiday Chocolate Chip Squares

2¼ cups all-purpose flour
1¼ teaspoons baking powder
¼ teaspoon salt
1 cup (2 sticks) butter, softened
1¼ cups sugar
1 egg
1 teaspoon vanilla extract
One 12-oz. pkg. (2 cups) NESTLÉ® Toll House® Semi-Sweet Chocolate Morsels
1 cup nuts, chopped
3 (6-oz.) jars (30) maraschino cherries, drained and patted dry
8 small candy spearmint leaves, cut into quarters lengthwise and halved

Preheat oven to 350°F. Grease 13×9-inch baking pan. In small bowl, combine flour, baking powder and salt; set aside.

In large mixer bowl, beat butter and sugar until creamy. Beat in egg and vanilla extract. Gradually blend in flour mixture. Stir in semi-sweet chocolate morsels and nuts.

Spread in prepared pan. Press 30 maraschino cherries into dough, spacing them to form 6 rows, 5 cherries per row. Place 2 spearmint leaves at base of each cherry; press into dough.

Bake 25 to 30 minutes. Cool completely. Cut into 2-inch squares.   *Makes 30 squares*

Frosted Maraschino Brownies

24 red maraschino cherries
1 package (23.6 ounces) brownie mix
2 cups powdered sugar
½ cup plus 1 tablespoon butter or margarine, softened
3 tablespoons milk
2 tablespoons instant vanilla pudding mix
1 ounce sweet baking chocolate

Drain cherries, reserving juice for another use. Blot cherries with paper toweling; set aside. Prepare and bake brownie mix according to package directions in 13×9×2-inch pan; cool completely in pan on wire rack.

In medium bowl, beat sugar, ½ cup of the butter, the milk and pudding mix until smooth. Cover; refrigerate until slightly thickened. Spread frosting over cooled, uncut brownies in pan. Arrange cherries in rows over frosting.

In small saucepan over low heat, melt chocolate and remaining 1 tablespoon butter; stir to blend. Cool slightly. Drizzle chocolate mixture over brownies. When chocolate is set, cut into bars.
          Makes about 2 dozen brownies

*Favorite recipe from **National Cherry Foundation***

Applesauce Fruitcake Bars

1 (14-ounce) can EAGLE® Brand Sweetened Condensed Milk (NOT evaporated milk)
2 eggs
¼ cup margarine or butter, melted
2 teaspoons vanilla extract
3 cups biscuit baking mix
1 (15-ounce) jar applesauce
1 cup chopped dates
1 (6-ounce) container green candied cherries, chopped
1 (6-ounce) container red candied cherries, chopped
1 cup chopped nuts
1 cup raisins
Confectioners' sugar

Preheat oven to 325°F. In large mixer bowl, beat sweetened condensed milk, eggs, margarine and vanilla. Stir in remaining ingredients except confectioners' sugar; mix well. Spread evenly into well-greased and floured 15×10 inch baking pan.

Bake 35 to 40 minutes or until wooden toothpick inserted in center comes out clean. Cool. Sprinkle confectioners' sugar over top. Cut into bars. Store tightly covered at room temperature.
          Makes 36 to 48 bars

Applesauce Fruitcake Bars

Bavarian Cookie Wreaths

3½ cups unsifted all-purpose flour
1 cup sugar, divided
3 teaspoons grated orange peel, divided
¼ teaspoon salt
1⅓ cups butter or margarine
¼ cup Florida orange juice
⅓ cup finely chopped blanched almonds
1 egg white beaten with 1 teaspoon water
Holiday Icing (recipe follows), optional
Red cinnamon candies

Preheat oven to 400°F. In large bowl, mix flour, ¾ cup sugar, 2 teaspoons grated orange peel and salt. Using pastry blender or 2 knives, cut in butter until coarse crumbs form. Add orange juice; stir until mixture holds together. Knead a few times; press into ball.

Shape dough into ¾-inch balls; lightly roll each on floured board into 6-inch-long strip. Twist 2 strips together to make rope. Pinch ends of rope together to make wreath; place on lightly greased cookie sheet.

In shallow dish, mix almonds with remaining ¼ cup sugar and 1 teaspoon orange peel. Brush top of wreaths with egg white mixture; sprinkle with almond-sugar mixture.

Bake 8 to 10 minutes or until lightly browned. Remove to wire racks; cool completely. Fill pastry bag fitted with small leaf tip with Holiday Icing. Decorate wreaths with icing leaves and candies.

Makes about 5 dozen cookies

Holiday Icing

1 cup confectioners' sugar
2 tablespoons butter or margarine, softened
1 to 2 teaspoons milk
Few drops green food color

In small bowl, mix confectioners' sugar, butter, 1 teaspoon milk and few drops green food color. Add more milk if necessary to make frosting thick, but spreadable.

*Favorite recipe from **Florida Department of Citrus***

Date-Filled Cookies

Cookies
3½ cups all-purpose flour
1 teaspoon baking powder
½ teaspoon baking soda
½ teaspoon salt
1 cup sugar
⅓ cup CRISCO® Oil
3 eggs
1 tablespoon lemon juice
1 teaspoon grated lemon peel
1 teaspoon vanilla
Filling
1 package (8 ounces) pitted dates, cut up
¼ cup water
2 tablespoons lemon juice
Dash ground cinnamon

For Cookies, combine flour, baking powder, baking soda and salt in medium bowl. Combine sugar, CRISCO® Oil, eggs, lemon juice, lemon peel and vanilla in large bowl; mix well. Stir in flour mixture. Cover and refrigerate at least 2 hours.

Meanwhile, for Filling, combine dates, water, lemon juice and cinnamon in small saucepan. Cook on medium heat, stirring constantly, until thick. Cool.

Preheat oven to 350°F. Grease cookie sheet lightly. Place dough on lightly floured surface; divide dough in half. Roll each half to ⅛-inch thickness. Cut into 3-inch rounds. Place 1 teaspoon date mixture on center of each round; fold in half over date mixture. Press edges lightly with fork to seal. Place 2 inches apart on cookie sheet. Bake 10 to 12 minutes or until light brown. Cool on wire rack.

Makes about 3 dozen cookies

Old-Fashioned Harvest Cookies

¾ cup BUTTER FLAVOR CRISCO®
1 cup firmly packed dark brown sugar
1 egg
¾ cup canned solid packed pumpkin (not pumpkin pie filling)
2 tablespoons molasses
1½ cups all-purpose flour
1 teaspoon nutmeg
½ teaspoon baking powder
½ teaspoon baking soda
¼ teaspoon salt
¼ teaspoon cinnamon
2½ cups quick oats (not instant or old fashioned), uncooked
1½ cups finely chopped dates
½ cup chopped walnuts

1. Preheat oven to 350°F. Grease cookie sheet with BUTTER FLAVOR CRISCO®.

2. Combine BUTTER FLAVOR CRISCO® and brown sugar in large bowl; beat at medium speed of electric mixer until well blended. Beat in egg, pumpkin and molasses.

3. Combine flour, nutmeg, baking powder, baking soda, salt and cinnamon. Mix into creamed mixture at low speed until just blended. Stir in, one at a time, oats, dates and nuts with spoon.

4. Drop rounded tablespoonfuls of dough 2 inches apart onto cookie sheet.

5. Bake 10 to 12 minutes or until bottoms are lightly browned. Cool 2 minutes on cookie sheet. Remove to cooling rack.

Makes about 4 dozen cookies

Pecan Date Bars

Crust
    1 package DUNCAN HINES®
      Moist Deluxe White
      Cake Mix
  ⅓ cup butter or margarine
  1 egg
Topping
    1 package (8 ounces)
      chopped dates
  1¼ cups chopped pecans
    1 cup water
  ½ teaspoon vanilla extract
    Confectioners sugar

1. Preheat oven to 350°F. Grease and flour 13×9×2-inch pan.

2. For Crust, cut butter into cake mix with pastry blender or 2 knives until mixture is crumbly. Add egg; stir well (mixture will be crumbly). Pat mixture into bottom of pan.

3. For Topping, combine dates, pecans and water in medium saucepan; bring to a boil. Reduce heat and simmer until mixture thickens, stirring constantly. Remove from heat; stir in vanilla extract. Spread date mixture evenly over crust. Bake 25 to 30 minutes. Cool completely. Dust with confectioners sugar.

Makes about 32 bars

Tip: Pecan Date Bars are moist and store well in airtight containers. Dust bars with confectioners sugar to freshen before serving.

Pecan Date Bars

Christmas Tree Cake

Christmas Tree Cake

1 package DUNCAN HINES®
  Moist Deluxe Cake Mix
  (any flavor)
5 cups confectioners sugar
³/₄ cup CRISCO® Shortening
¹/₂ cup water
¹/₃ cup non-dairy creamer
2 teaspoons vanilla extract
¹/₂ teaspoon salt
1 tablespoon green food
  coloring
  Peppermint candies
  Pretzel rods
  Large gumdrops

1. Preheat oven to 350°F. Grease and flour 13×9×2-inch pan. Prepare, bake and cool cake following package directions.

2. For decorator frosting, combine confectioners sugar, shortening, water, non-dairy creamer, vanilla extract and salt in large bowl. Beat at medium speed with electric mixer for 3 minutes. Beat at high speed for 5 minutes. Add more confectioners sugar to thicken or more water to thin as needed. Reserve 1 cup frosting. Tint remaining frosting with green food coloring.

3. Cut cooled cake and arrange as shown. Spread green frosting over cake. Decorate tree with reserved white frosting and peppermint candies. Make tree trunk of pretzel rods. Roll out large gumdrop and cut with star cookie cutter. Top tree with gumdrop star.

Makes 16 to 20 servings

Tip: To make the garland, pipe frosting using a pastry bag fitted with a star tip, or use red rope licorice.

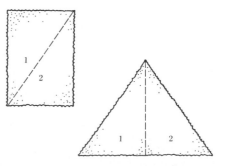

Pumpkin Streusel Cake

Streusel
  ¹/₃ cup butter or margarine
  1 cup firmly packed brown
    sugar
  2 teaspoons ground
    cinnamon
  1 cup chopped nuts
Cake
  1 package DUNCAN HINES®
    Moist Deluxe Yellow
    Cake Mix
  1 can (16 ounces) solid pack
    pumpkin
  3 eggs
  ¹/₄ cup butter or margarine,
    softened

1. Preheat oven to 350°F.

2. For Streusel, cut ¹/₃ cup butter into brown sugar and cinnamon using pastry blender or 2 knives. Stir in chopped nuts. Set aside.

3. For Cake, combine cake mix, pumpkin, eggs and ¹/₄ cup butter in large bowl. Beat at medium speed with electric mixer for 2 minutes. Spread half of batter into 13×9×2-inch pan. Sprinkle half of streusel over batter. Spread remaining batter over streusel. Sprinkle top with remaining streusel. Bake 40 to 45 minutes or until wooden toothpick inserted in center comes out clean.

Makes 16 to 20 servings

Tip: Serve warm as a coffeecake or cool as a dessert topped with whipped topping.

Glazed Cranberry Mini-Cakes

1/4 **cup butter or margarine, softened**
1/4 **cup packed light brown sugar**
1/4 **cup granulated sugar**
1 **egg**
1 **teaspoon vanilla extract**
1 **cup all-purpose flour**
1/2 **teaspoon baking powder**
1/4 **teaspoon baking soda**
1/4 **teaspoon salt**
1 **cup coarsely chopped fresh cranberries**
1/2 **cup coarsely chopped walnuts**
1/3 **cup HERSHEY'S® Vanilla Milk Chips**
   Vanilla Chip Glaze (recipe follows)

Preheat oven to 350°F. Lightly grease or paper-line 36 small muffin cups (1¾ inches in diameter).

In small mixer bowl, beat butter, brown sugar, granulated sugar, egg and vanilla extract until light and fluffy. Stir together flour, baking powder, baking soda and salt; gradually mix into butter mixture. Stir in cranberries, walnuts and vanilla milk chips. Fill muffin cups ¾ full with batter.

Bake 12 to 14 minutes or until wooden toothpick inserted in center comes out clean. Cool in pans on wire racks 5 minutes; invert onto racks. Cool completely on wire racks.

Prepare Vanilla Chip Glaze; dip rounded portion of each cake into glaze or spread glaze on top. Place on waxed-paper-covered tray; refrigerate 10 minutes to set glaze.

Makes about 3 dozen mini-cakes

VANILLA CHIP GLAZE: In small microwave-safe bowl, place 1 cup HERSHEY'S® Vanilla Milk Chips; sprinkle 2 tablespoons vegetable oil over chips. Microwave at HIGH (100%) 30 seconds; stir. If necessary, microwave at HIGH additional 30 seconds or just until chips are melted when stirred.

Rich Walnut Fruitcake

3 **cups SUN-MAID® Raisins, chopped**
2 **cups coarsely chopped mixed candied fruits and peels**
1 **cup candied cherries, halved**
1 **cup SUN-MAID® Zante Currants**
1/2 **cup bourbon or orange juice**
1 **cup butter or margarine, softened**
1 **cup packed brown sugar**
6 **eggs**
1/2 **ounce unsweetened chocolate, melted**
3 **cups DIAMOND® Walnuts, coarsely chopped**
2 **cups all-purpose flour**
1 **teaspoon ground cinnamon**
1 **teaspoon ground nutmeg**
1 **teaspoon ground cloves**
3/4 **teaspoon salt**
1/2 **teaspoon baking soda**
   Candied fruits, for garnish
   DIAMOND® Walnut halves, for garnish

In large bowl, combine fruits and bourbon; toss well to mix. Let stand, covered, 3 to 4 hours or overnight.

Preheat oven to 300°F. Grease well and flour 12-cup tube pan. In another large bowl, cream butter. Beat in brown sugar until fluffy. Beat in eggs, one at a time, until well blended. Stir in melted chocolate. (Mixture will appear slightly curdled.) Combine butter mixture, fruits and walnuts. In medium bowl, sift flour with spices, salt and baking soda. Stir into fruit mixture until well blended. Spoon batter into prepared pan.

Bake 2 hours and 20 minutes or until center springs back when lightly touched. Cool completely, then remove from pan; wrap in foil and store in a cool, dry place. Before serving, decorate with candied fruits and walnut halves.   *Makes one large cake*

Glazed Cranberry Mini-Cakes

Festive Eggnog Cake

Cake
- 1⅓ cups granulated sugar
- ½ cup LAND O LAKES® Butter, softened
- 2 eggs
- 2½ cups all-purpose flour
- ½ cup chopped blanched almonds
- 1¼ cups milk
- 1 tablespoon baking powder
- 1 teaspoon nutmeg
- ½ teaspoon rum extract

Glaze
- 1 cup powdered sugar
- 2 tablespoons LAND O LAKES® Butter, softened
- 4 to 5 teaspoons milk
- ¼ teaspoon rum extract
  Whole almonds
  Candied cherries

Preheat oven to 350°F. Grease and flour 10-inch fluted tube pan.

For Cake, in large mixer bowl combine granulated sugar and butter. Beat at medium speed, scraping bowl often, until well mixed (2 to 3 minutes). Add eggs; continue beating until light and fluffy (3 to 5 minutes). Add remaining cake ingredients. Reduce to low speed; continue beating, scraping bowl often, until well mixed (2 to 3 minutes). Pour into prepared pan.

Bake 45 to 55 minutes or until wooden toothpick inserted near center comes out clean. Cool in pan 10 minutes. Loosen edge; remove from pan and cool completely.

For Glaze, in small bowl combine all ingredients until smooth. Drizzle over cake; garnish with whole almonds and candied cherry halves. Store tightly covered.

Makes 16 servings

Nut and Pumpkin Poundcake

- 1¾ cups all-purpose flour
- ½ cup pecans, finely chopped or ground
- 1½ teaspoons ground cinnamon
- 1 teaspoon baking soda
- ½ teaspoon salt
- ½ teaspoon ground mace
- ¼ teaspoon ground nutmeg
- 1 cup butter, softened
- ¾ cup granulated sugar
- ½ cup packed light brown sugar
- 3 eggs
- 1 cup LIBBY'S® Solid Pack Pumpkin
  Marzipan Bow

Preheat oven to 325°F. Grease and flour 9×5-inch loaf pan.

In medium bowl, combine flour, pecans, cinnamon, baking soda, salt, mace, and nutmeg; set aside. In large mixer bowl, cream butter, granulated sugar and brown sugar. Add eggs; beat until light and fluffy. Mix in pumpkin and dry ingredients; beat well. Pour batter into prepared pan.

Bake 1 hour and 15 minutes or until wooden toothpick inserted in center of cake comes out clean. Cool in pan 10 minutes; turn onto wire rack to cool completely.

Makes 1 large loaf

MARZIPAN BOW: On board lightly dusted with powdered sugar, roll out one 7-ounce package marzipan or almond paste into rectangle 4 inches wide, 20 inches long, and ¹/₁₆ inch thick. Cut into four ½-inch-wide strips. Arrange two strips over cooled bread to create tied package effect. Create ribbon bow ends by cutting two 5-inch lengths. Attach at point where marzipan ribbons cross; press to hold. Make bow by creating two ribbon loops; pinch center. Add bow where ribbons cross; press to hold.

Special Honeyed Fruit Cake

Cake
- 1 package DUNCAN HINES® Moist Deluxe Butter Recipe Golden Cake Mix
- 6 egg whites
- ⅔ cup water
- ½ cup margarine, melted
- 1 tablespoon molasses
- 1 cup chopped nuts
- ½ cup raisins

Syrup
- ¼ cup CITRUS HILL® Orange Juice
- ¼ cup honey
- ¼ cup granulated sugar
  Juice and grated peel from 1 lemon
- ¼ teaspoon ground cinnamon

Glaze
- ¾ cup confectioners sugar
- 2 tablespoons skim milk
- ½ teaspoon brandy
  Candied cherry halves
  Pecan halves

1. Preheat oven to 375°F. Grease and flour 10-inch Bundt® pan.

2. For Cake, combine cake mix, egg whites, water, margarine and molasses in large bowl. Beat at medium speed with electric mixer for 2 minutes. Fold in nuts and raisins. Pour into pan. Bake 35 to 40 minutes or until wooden toothpick inserted in center comes out clean. Cool cake 10 minutes. Invert onto serving plate; return cake to pan. Poke holes in cake 1-inch apart with a skewer or meat fork.

3. For Syrup, combine all syrup ingredients in small saucepan over medium heat. Simmer 10 minutes, stirring occasionally. Pour hot syrup evenly over cake in pan. Cool cake completely before inverting onto serving plate.

4. For Glaze, combine confectioners sugar, milk and brandy in small bowl. Beat until smooth. Drizzle over cooled cake. Garnish with candied cherries and pecans.

Makes 12 to 16 servings

Special Honeyed Fruit Cake

Jubilee Chocolate Cake

¾ teaspoon baking soda
1 cup buttermilk or sour
**   milk***
1½ cups cake flour or 1¼ cups
**   all-purpose flour**
1½ cups sugar, divided
½ cup HERSHEY'S® Cocoa
½ teaspoon salt
½ cup vegetable oil
2 eggs, separated
½ teaspoon vanilla extract
**   Vanilla ice cream**
**   Flaming Cherry Sauce**
**   (recipe follows)**

Preheat oven to 350°F. Grease and flour 13×9×2-inch baking pan.

Stir baking soda into buttermilk until dissolved; set aside. In large mixer bowl, stir together flour, 1 cup sugar, cocoa and salt. Add oil, buttermilk mixture, egg yolks and vanilla; beat until smooth.

In small mixer bowl, beat egg whites until soft peaks form; gradually add remaining ½ cup sugar, beating until stiff peaks form. Gently fold egg whites into chocolate batter. Pour batter into prepared pan.

Bake 30 to 35 minutes or until cake springs back when touched lightly in center. Cool in pan. Cut into squares; top each

Jubilee Chocolate Cake

square with scoop of ice cream and serving of Flaming Cherry Sauce.

Makes 10 to 12 servings

To sour milk: Use 1 tablespoon white vinegar plus milk to equal 1 cup.

Flaming Cherry Sauce

1 can (16 or 17 ounces)
**   pitted dark or light sweet**
**   cherries, drained**
**   (reserve ¾ cup liquid)**
1½ tablespoons sugar
1 tablespoon cornstarch
**   Dash salt**
½ teaspoon grated orange
**   peel**
¼ cup cherry-flavored liqueur
**   or brandy**

In saucepan or chafing dish, stir together reserved cherry liquid, sugar, cornstarch and salt. Cook over medium heat, stirring constantly, until mixture boils, about 1 minute. Add cherries and orange peel; heat sauce thoroughly.

In small saucepan, over low heat, gently heat liqueur; pour over cherry mixture. Carefully ignite with long match. Stir gently; serve as directed. (Repeat procedure for sufficient amount of sauce for entire cake.)

Makes 4 to 6 servings

Holiday Stripe Cake

1 package DUNCAN HINES®
**   Moist Deluxe White**
**   Cake Mix**
1 package (3 ounces) black
**   cherry flavored gelatin**
1 package (3 ounces) lime
**   flavored gelatin**
2 cups boiling water, divided
1 container (8 ounces) frozen
**   whipped topping, thawed**
**   and divided**
**   Red and green gumdrops**

1. Preheat oven to 350°F. Grease and flour two 8- or 9-inch round cake pans. Prepare, bake and cool cake following package directions.

2. Place cake layers top-sides up in two clean round cake pans. Punch holes in cake with fork in concentric circles.

3. Add 1 cup boiling water to each flavor gelatin in separate bowls; stir until dissolved. Pour black cherry gelatin slowly over first cake layer. Pour lime gelatin slowly over second cake layer. Refrigerate 3 hours or until gelatin is set.

3. Dip one cake pan in warm water 10 seconds. Invert cake layer onto serving plate. Spread 1 cup whipped topping on cake. Unmold second layer and carefully place on first layer. Frost top and sides with remaining whipped topping. Garnish with gumdrops. Refrigerate until ready to serve.
Makes 12 servings

Tip: Use your favorite flavor of red gelatin instead of black cherry.

Almond Chocolate Torte

2½ cups BLUE DIAMOND®
**   Blanched Whole**
**   Almonds, lightly toasted**
9 squares (1 ounce each)
**   semisweet chocolate**
¼ cup butter or margarine
6 eggs, beaten
¾ cup sugar
2 tablespoons all-purpose
**   flour**
¼ cup brandy
**   Fudge Glaze**
**   (recipe follows)**
**   Easy Raspberry Sauce**
**   (recipe follows)**

Preheat oven to 350°F. In food processor or blender, process 1 cup of the almonds until finely ground. Generously grease 9-inch round cake pan; sprinkle with 2 tablespoons ground almonds.

In top of double boiler, melt chocolate and butter over simmering water, blending thoroughly; cool slightly. In large bowl, beat eggs and sugar. Gradually beat in chocolate mixture. Add flour, remaining ground almonds and brandy; mix well. Pour batter into prepared cake pan.

Bake 25 minutes or until wooden toothpick inserted into center comes out almost clean. Let cool in pan on wire rack 10 minutes. Loosen edge; remove from pan. Cool completely on wire rack.

Prepare Fudge Glaze. Place torte on wire rack over sheet of waxed paper. Pour Fudge Glaze over torte, spreading over top and side with spatula. Carefully transfer torte to serving plate; let glaze set.

Prepare Easy Raspberry Sauce; set aside. Arrange remaining 1½ cups whole almonds, points toward center, in circle around outer edge of torte. Working towards center, repeat circles, overlapping almonds slightly. To serve, pour small amount of Easy Raspberry Sauce on each serving plate; top with slice of torte.

Makes 10 to 12 servings

FUDGE GLAZE: In small saucepan, combine 6 tablespoons water and 3 tablespoons sugar. Simmer over low heat until sugar dissolves. Stir in 3 squares (1 ounce each) semisweet chocolate and 1 tablespoon brandy. Heat, stirring occasionally, until chocolate melts and glaze coats back of spoon.

EASY RASPBERRY SAUCE: In food processor or blender, puree 2 packages (10 ounces each) thawed frozen raspberries. Strain raspberry puree through a fine sieve to remove seeds. Stir in sugar to taste.

Mocha Almond Roll

Mocha Almond Roll

- ¾ cup cake flour
- 1 teaspoon baking powder
- ¼ teaspoon salt
- 3 eggs
- 1 cup granulated sugar
- ⅓ cup water
- 1½ teaspoons vanilla
- ½ teaspoon almond extract
  Powdered sugar
- 1 cup BLUE DIAMOND® Blanched Almond Paste
- 2¾ cups whipping cream
- 6 squares (1 ounce each) semisweet chocolate, chopped
- 3 tablespoons coffee-flavored liqueur
  Chocolate curls (optional)

Preheat oven to 375°F. Grease 15½×10½×1-inch jelly-roll pan; line with waxed paper and grease again.

In small bowl, combine flour, baking powder and salt. In large bowl, beat eggs until foamy. Gradually beat in granulated sugar. Beat in water, ½ teaspoon of the vanilla and the almond extract. Gradually beat in flour mixture until smooth. Pour batter into prepared pan.

Bake 12 to 15 minutes or until wooden toothpick inserted into center comes out clean. Immediately invert cake onto towel sprinkled with powdered sugar; remove waxed paper. While still warm, roll up cake and towel beginning at short end; cool completely.

Roll almond paste between 2 pieces of waxed paper into 15×10-inch rectangle. In small saucepan over low heat, stir ¾ cup of the cream and the chocolate until smooth. Remove from heat; stir occasionally until thickened. In medium bowl, beat remaining 2 cups whipping cream, ¾ cup powdered sugar, the liqueur and remaining 1 teaspoon vanilla until soft peaks form. Beat in ⅓ cup chocolate mixture until stiff peaks form.

Unroll cake; spread with remaining chocolate mixture. Place almond paste on top. Spread 1¼ cups whipped cream mixture over almond paste, leaving 1-inch border at 1 short end; roll up cake from opposite side. Frost cake with remaining whipped cream mixture; refrigerate. If desired, garnish with chocolate curls.

Makes 8 to 10 servings

Left to right: Walnut Holiday Cake, Cherry Pecan Pound Cake

Walnut Holiday Cake

- 2 tablespoons dark rum
- 4 single graham cracker squares
- 6 eggs, separated
- 1 teaspoon grated orange peel
- 2 cups powdered sugar
- ¼ teaspoon cream of tartar
- 3½ cups finely ground toasted California walnuts
- ¼ cup grated semisweet chocolate
- 6 squares (1 ounce each) semisweet chocolate
- 6 tablespoons butter or margarine
- 1 tablespoon honey
  California walnut halves for garnish

Preheat oven to 350°F. Grease 9-inch springform pan; line bottom with waxed paper and grease again.

In small bowl, pour rum over graham crackers. When crackers are softened, mash with fork. In large bowl, beat egg yolks at medium speed until lemon colored. Add orange peel and powdered sugar; beat at high speed until thick, about 3 minutes. Beat cracker mixture into yolk mixture. In large mixer bowl, beat egg whites with cream of tartar at high speed until stiff but not dry peaks form. Gently fold beaten whites, ground walnuts and grated chocolate into yolk mixture. Pour batter into prepared pan.

Bake 45 to 50 minutes or until wooden toothpick inserted into center comes out clean and small crack appears on surface. Let cool completely in pan on wire rack. Remove side of springform pan. Invert cake onto serving plate; remove bottom of pan and waxed paper. Place waxed-paper strips under cake to cover plate. In top of double boiler, melt chocolate squares and butter over simmering water; stir to blend. Stir in honey. Pour chocolate mixture over cake; let stand until slightly cool. Spread over top and side of cake. Remove paper strips. Garnish with walnut halves. When firm, cut into thin wedges.

Makes about 16 servings

*Favorite recipe from **Walnut Marketing Board***

Cherry Pecan Pound Cake

 1 cup butter or margarine, softened
 1 cup sugar
 4 eggs
 1 teaspoon vanilla
 1/2 teaspoon almond extract
 1/2 teaspoon salt
 1/8 teaspoon ground nutmeg or mace
 1 1/2 cups all-purpose flour
 1 jar (6 ounces) maraschino cherries, drained and chopped
 1/4 cup chopped pecans

Preheat oven to 325°F. Grease and flour 9×5×3-inch loaf pan.

In large bowl, beat butter and sugar until light and fluffy. Add eggs, vanilla, almond extract, salt and nutmeg; beat until thoroughly blended. Stir in flour, 1/2 cup at a time, mixing just until blended. Stir in cherries and pecans. Spread batter evenly in prepared pan.

Bake 60 to 70 minutes or until wooden toothpick inserted near center comes out clean. Let cool in pan on wire rack 10 minutes. Loosen edges; remove from pan. Cool completely on wire rack.

Makes 1 loaf

*Favorite recipe from **American Egg Board***

Chocolate Hazelnut Gateau

Cake:
One 12-oz. pkg. (2 cups) NESTLÉ® Toll House® Semi-Sweet Chocolate Morsels, divided
 3/4 **cup sugar**
 2/3 **cup (10 2/3 tablespoons) butter, softened**
 3 **eggs, separated**
 1 **teaspoon vanilla extract**
 1/2 **teaspoon salt**
 3/4 **cup all-purpose flour**
 1/4 **cup cold milk**
 2/3 **cup ground toasted hazelnuts *or* almonds**
Glaze:
 3 **tablespoons butter**
 2 **tablespoons light corn syrup**
 1 **tablespoon water**
 1 **cup NESTLÉ® Toll House® Semi-Sweet Chocolate Morsels, reserved from 12-oz. pkg.**

Cake: Preheat oven to 350°F. Grease 9×2-inch springform pan. Melt 1 cup semi-sweet chocolate morsels; set aside. In large mixer bowl, beat sugar and butter until creamy. Beat in melted chocolate, egg yolks, vanilla extract and salt. Gradually beat in flour and milk. Stir in hazelnuts.

In small mixer bowl, beat egg whites just until stiff peaks form; do not overbeat. Fold into chocolate batter. Spread into prepared pan.

Chocolate Hazelnut Gateau

Bake 25 to 30 minutes. Cool 10 minutes; remove from pan. Cool completely.

Glaze: In small saucepan, combine butter, corn syrup and water. Stirring constantly over low heat, *bring just to a boil;* remove from heat. Stir in remaining 1 cup semi-sweet chocolate morsels until smooth. Cool to room temperature. Pour Glaze over cake, covering top and side. *Makes 8 to 10 servings*

Orange Dream Cake

 3/4 **cup MIRACLE WHIP® Salad Dressing**
 1 **two-layer yellow cake mix**
 1 **envelope DREAM WHIP® Whipped Topping Mix**
 3/4 **cup orange juice**
 3 **eggs**
 2 **teaspoons grated orange peel**
 1 1/2 **cups powdered sugar**
 2 **tablespoons milk**
 1 **tablespoon multicolored sprinkles**

• Preheat oven to 350°F.

• Beat salad dressing, cake mix, whipped topping mix, juice, eggs and peel at medium speed with electric mixer for 2 minutes. Pour into greased and floured 10-inch fluted tube pan.

• Bake 35 to 40 minutes or until wooden toothpick inserted near center comes out clean. Let stand 10 minutes; remove from pan. Cool.

• Stir together powdered sugar and milk until smooth. Drizzle over cake. Decorate with sprinkles.

Makes 8 to 10 servings

Prep time: 10 minutes
Cooking time: 40 minutes

Pineapple-Cranberry Cake

1 can (20 ounces) DOLE®
    Crushed Pineapple in
    Syrup*
3 cups all-purpose flour
2 teaspoons baking soda
1 teaspoon ground cinnamon
1 teaspoon ground ginger
½ teaspoon salt
3 eggs
1½ cups sugar
¾ cup mayonnaise
4 cups fresh cranberries,
    chopped
1 cup DOLE® Raisins
1 cup chopped walnuts
1 tablespoon grated orange
    peel
    Pineapple Frosting (recipe
    follows)

Preheat oven to 350°F. Grease
and flour 13×9×2-inch pan.
Drain pineapple; reserve ½ cup
syrup.

In medium bowl, combine flour,
baking soda, spices and salt. In
large bowl, beat eggs, sugar,
mayonnaise, pineapple and
reserved ½ cup syrup. Gradually
add flour mixture, beating until
well mixed. Stir in cranberries,
raisins, walnuts and orange peel.
Pour batter into prepared pan.

Bake 50 to 55 minutes or until
wooden toothpick inserted into
center comes out clean. Let cool
completely in pan on wire rack.
Frost with Pineapple Frosting.
Cover; refrigerate cake to set
frosting. Store in refrigerator.
Makes about 12 servings

PINEAPPLE FROSTING: In
medium bowl, beat 1 package
(8 ounces) softened cream cheese
and ½ cup softened margarine.
Beat in 1 cup powdered sugar
and 1 teaspoon grated orange
peel until light and fluffy. Stir in
1 can (8 ounces) well-drained
DOLE® Crushed Pineapple in
Syrup.*

*Or use Pineapple packed in
Juice if desired.

Maple Pumpkin Cheesecake

Maple Pumpkin Cheesecake

1¼ cups graham cracker
    crumbs
¼ cup sugar
¼ cup margarine or butter,
    melted
3 (8-ounce) packages cream
    cheese, softened
1 (14-ounce) can EAGLE®
    Brand Sweetened
    Condensed Milk (NOT
    evaporated milk)
1 (16-ounce) can pumpkin
    (about 2 cups)
3 eggs
1 cup CARY'S®, VERMONT
    MAPLE ORCHARDS or
    MACDONALD'S Pure
    Maple Syrup
1½ teaspoons ground
    cinnamon
1 teaspoon ground nutmeg
½ teaspoon salt
    Maple Pecan Glaze

Preheat oven to 300°F. Combine
crumbs, sugar and margarine;
press firmly on bottom of 9-inch
springform pan or 13×9-inch
baking pan. In large mixer bowl,
beat cheese until fluffy.
Gradually beat in sweetened
condensed milk until smooth.
Add pumpkin, eggs, ¼ cup pure
maple syrup, cinnamon, nutmeg
and salt; mix well. Pour into
prepared pan.

Bake 1 hour and 15 minutes or
until edge springs back when
lightly touched (center will be
slightly soft). Cool. Chill. Top
with Maple Pecan Glaze.
Refrigerate leftovers.
Makes one 9-inch cheesecake

MAPLE PECAN GLAZE: In
saucepan, combine remaining
¾ cup pure maple syrup and
1 cup (½ pint) BORDEN® or
MEADOW GOLD® Whipping
Cream; bring to a boil. Boil
rapidly 15 to 20 minutes or until
thickened; stir occasionally. Add
½ cup chopped pecans.
Makes about 1¼ cups glaze

Prep time: 30 minutes
Baking time: 1 hour 15 minutes

Pumpkin Orange Cheesecake

1½ cups gingersnap cookie crumbs (about 32 cookies)
¼ cup margarine or butter, melted
3 (8-ounce) packages cream cheese, softened
1 (14-ounce) can EAGLE® Brand Sweetened Condensed Milk (NOT evaporated milk)
1 (16-ounce) can pumpkin (about 2 cups)
2 eggs
3 tablespoons orange-flavored liqueur *or* orange juice
1 teaspoon pumpkin pie spice
¼ teaspoon salt
Whipped topping or whipped cream

Pumpkin Orange Cheesecake

Preheat oven to 300°F. Combine crumbs and margarine. Press firmly on bottom and halfway up side of 9-inch springform pan. In large mixer bowl, beat cheese until fluffy. Gradually beat in sweetened condensed milk until smooth. Add remaining ingredients except whipped topping; mix well. Pour into prepared pan.

Bake 1 hour and 15 minutes or until edge springs back when lightly touched (center will be slightly soft). Cool to room temperature. Chill. Serve with whipped topping. Garnish as desired. Refrigerate leftovers.

Makes one 9-inch cheesecake

Prep time: 20 minutes
Baking time: 1 hour 15 minutes

Cranberry Orange Cheesecake Bars

1 package DUNCAN HINES® Bakery Style Cranberry Orange Nut with Crumb Topping Muffin Mix
¼ cup butter or margarine
1 package (8 ounces) cream cheese, softened
½ cup sugar
1 egg
3 tablespoons CITRUS HILL® Orange Juice
½ teaspoon vanilla extract

1. Preheat oven to 350°F. Grease an 8- or 9-inch square pan.

2. Rinse cranberries with cold water and drain.

3. Cut butter into muffin mix with pastry blender or 2 knives in medium bowl. Press into bottom of pan. Bake 15 minutes.

4. Blend cream cheese and sugar until smooth in large bowl. Add egg, orange juice and vanilla extract; beat well. Spread over baked crust. Sprinkle with cranberries. Sprinkle topping from packet over cranberries; return to oven. Bake 35 to 40 minutes for 8-inch pan (or 30 to 35 minutes for 9-inch pan) or until filling is set. Cool completely. Refrigerate until ready to serve.

Makes 12 to 16 servings

Egg Nog Cheesecake

1¼ cups vanilla wafer crumbs (about 36 wafers)
¼ cup sugar
¼ cup margarine or butter, melted
3 (8-ounce) packages cream cheese, softened
1 (14-ounce) can EAGLE® Brand Sweetened Condensed Milk (NOT evaporated milk)
3 eggs
¼ cup dark rum
1 teaspoon vanilla extract
½ teaspoon ground nutmeg
Rum Sauce

Preheat oven to 300°F. Combine crumbs, sugar and margarine; press firmly on bottom of 9-inch springform pan *or* 13×9-inch baking pan. In large mixer bowl, beat cheese until fluffy. Gradually beat in sweetened condensed milk until smooth. Add eggs; mix well. Stir in rum, vanilla and nutmeg. Pour into prepared pan.

Bake 40 to 50 minutes or until cake springs back when lightly touched. Cool. Chill. Serve with Rum Sauce. Refrigerate leftovers.

Makes one 9-inch cheesecake

RUM SAUCE: In small bowl, dissolve 1 tablespoon cornstarch in 1 cup water. In medium saucepan, melt 2 tablespoons margarine or butter. Stir in ⅓ cup firmly packed light brown sugar and cornstarch mixture. Bring to a boil, stirring constantly. Reduce heat; simmer 10 minutes. Remove from heat; add 2 tablespoons dark rum. Cool. Just before serving, stir in ½ cup chopped pecans.

Makes about 1¼ cups sauce

Double Chocolate Cheesecake

3 tablespoons butter, melted
¾ teaspoon mint extract, optional
1 cup chocolate wafer crumbs (about 20 wafers)
4 packages (8 oz. each) cream cheese, softened
6 squares (1 oz. each) semi-sweet chocolate, melted
1⅓ cups sugar
3 tablespoons flour
1 teaspoon vanilla
6 eggs
1 cup dairy sour cream
2 tablespoons sugar
½ teaspoon vanilla
Chocolate curls, optional

Preheat oven to 500°F. In small bowl, stir together butter and mint extract. Add crumbs; blend well. Press evenly on bottom and ½ inch up side of greased 9-inch springform pan. Set aside.

In large mixing bowl, beat cream cheese, chocolate, 1⅓ cups sugar, flour and 1 teaspoon vanilla at low speed until blended. Beat at high speed until smooth. Add eggs, one at a time, beating well after each addition. Pour into prepared pan. Bake 10 minutes. *Reduce oven temperature to 250°F*; continue baking an additional 50 to 60 minutes or until cake tester inserted near center comes out clean. Cool on wire rack 10 minutes. Leave oven on.

In small bowl, blend together sour cream, 2 tablespoons sugar and ½ teaspoon vanilla; spread evenly over cake. Bake an additional 5 minutes. Cool on wire rack 45 minutes to 1 hour. Refrigerate until firm, at least 8 hours or overnight. Garnish with chocolate curls, if desired. To serve, remove rim of pan and cut cheesecake into wedges.

Makes 12 servings

*Favorite recipe from **American Egg Board***

White Treasure Pecan Pie

One 10-oz. pkg. (1½ cups) NESTLÉ® Toll House® Treasures® Premier White Deluxe Baking Pieces, divided
3 eggs
½ cup light corn syrup
2 tablespoons (¼ stick) butter, melted
1 teaspoon vanilla extract
1½ cups pecans, chopped
One unbaked 9-inch pastry shell
½ cup pecan halves
Ice cream or whipped cream, optional

Preheat oven to 425°F. Melt over hot (not boiling) water, 1 cup Treasures® premier white deluxe baking pieces, stirring until smooth.

In large mixer bowl, beat eggs, corn syrup, melted butter and vanilla extract until smooth; blend in melted baking pieces. Stir in chopped pecans and remaining ½ cup Treasures premier white deluxe baking pieces. Pour filling into pie shell. Arrange pecan halves decoratively on top of filling.

Bake 15 minutes. *Turn oven control to 350°F.* Bake 30 minutes longer or until knife inserted halfway between edge and center comes out clean. Cool completely. Serve with ice cream or whipped cream.

Makes 6 to 8 servings

White Treasure Pecan Pie

Libby's® Famous Pumpkin Pie

2 eggs, lightly beaten
1³/₄ cups (16-ounce can)
    LIBBY'S® Solid-Pack
    Pumpkin
³/₄ cup sugar
¹/₂ teaspoon salt
1 teaspoon ground cinnamon
¹/₂ teaspoon ground ginger
¹/₄ teaspoon ground cloves
1¹/₂ cups (12-fluid-ounce can)
    ***undiluted* CARNATION®**
    Evaporated Milk
1 9-inch (4-cup volume)
    unbaked pie crust
    Praline Topping or Orange
    Cloud Topping
    (recipes follow)

Preheat oven to 425°F. In large mixing bowl, combine all ingredients in order given except pie crust and toppings. Pour into unbaked pie crust. Bake 15 minutes; *reduce oven temperature to 350°F.* Bake an additional 40 to 50 minutes, or until knife inserted near center comes out clean. Top cooled pie with either Praline Topping or Orange Cloud Topping, if desired.

Makes one 9-inch pie

Note: When using metal or foil pie pan, bake on preheated cookie sheet. When using glass or ceramic pie plate, do not use cookie sheet.

Praline Topping

1 *baked* 9-inch LIBBY'S®
    Famous Pumpkin Pie,
    cooled
1 cup pecan halves
¹/₂ cup packed light brown
    sugar
2 tablespoons half and half
2 teaspoons butter
¹/₂ teaspoon vanilla extract
¹/₄ teaspoon orange zest,
    finely chopped
1 egg white, stiffly beaten

Place pecans in medium bowl. Butter cookie sheet; set aside. In *small* saucepan, combine brown sugar and half and half. Bring to a boil over medium heat, stirring frequently. Add butter; continue to boil, stirring constantly, until temperature reaches 250°F on candy thermometer (hard ball stage).

Remove from heat; stir in vanilla and orange zest. Immediately pour hot mixture over pecans, tossing with two forks to coat nuts. Quickly spread on cookie sheet, pulling apart to separate. When completely cool, chop candied nuts into small pieces. Preheat oven to 350°F. Stir candied nuts into beaten egg white. Spoon nut mixture over cooled pie. Bake 10 to 15 minutes or until golden. Cool.

Makes topping for one 9-inch pumpkin pie

Orange Cloud Topping

1 *baked* 9-inch LIBBY'S®
    Famous Pumpkin Pie,
    cooled
1¹/₃ cups (7-ounce jar)
    marshmallow creme
2 tablespoons thawed
    orange juice concentrate
2 teaspoons orange zest,
    finely chopped
3 egg whites, room
    temperature
1 teaspoon cornstarch
¹/₈ teaspoon cream of tartar
3 tablespoons sugar
    Orange zest (optional)

Preheat oven to 350°F. In medium bowl, combine the marshmallow creme, orange juice concentrate and orange zest; set aside. In small mixer bowl, combine egg whites, cornstarch and cream of tartar; beat until thick and foamy. Beat in 3 tablespoons sugar, one tablespoon at a time, until meringue is stiff and shiny. Fold half of meringue into the marshmallow mixture; blend well. Fold in *remaining* meringue; blend gently. Spread over pie, sealing to edge of crust. Bake 12 to 15 minutes or until golden. Garnish with additional orange zest, if desired. Cool 15 minutes before serving. Pie cuts easily with moistened knife.

Makes topping for one 9-inch pumpkin pie

Apple Mince Pie

Apple Mince Pie

Pastry for 2-crust pie
1 jar NONE SUCH® Ready-to-
    Use Mincemeat (Regular
    ***or* Brandy & Rum)**
3 medium all-purpose
    apples, cored, pared and
    thinly sliced
3 tablespoons flour
2 tablespoons margarine or
    butter, melted
1 egg yolk plus
    2 tablespoons water,
    mixed

Place rack in lower half of oven; preheat oven to 425°F. Turn mincemeat into pastry lined 9 inch pie plate. In large bowl, toss apples with flour and margarine; spoon evenly over mincemeat. Cover with top crust; cut slits near center. Seal and flute. Brush egg mixture over crust. Bake 10 minutes. *Reduce oven temperature to 375°F*; bake 25 minutes longer or until golden. Cool. Garnish as desired.

Makes one 9-inch pie

Tip: 1 (9-ounce) package NONE SUCH® Condensed Mincemeat, reconstituted as package directs, can be substituted for NONE SUCH® Ready-to-Use Mincemeat.

Prep time: 30 minutes
Baking time: 35 minutes

Deep Dish Almond Pumpkin Pie

Crust
  Pastry for 9-inch Classic
  CRISCO® *Single* Crust
  prepared with BUTTER
  FLAVOR CRISCO®
  (page 166)
Almond Layer
  1 cup finely chopped
    almonds
  1/2 cup firmly packed brown
    sugar
  3 tablespoons butter or
    margarine, softened
  2 teaspoons all-purpose flour
  1/4 teaspoon almond extract
Pumpkin Filling
  1 1/4 cups granulated *brown*
    sugar
  1 package (3 ounces) cream
    cheese, softened
  2 eggs
  1 1/4 cups cooked or canned
    solid pack pumpkin (not
    pumpkin pie filling)
  1/2 cup evaporated milk
  1/3 cup dairy sour cream
  1 tablespoon molasses
  1 teaspoon cinnamon
  1/2 teaspoon nutmeg
  1/2 teaspoon salt
  1/4 teaspoon ginger
  1/8 teaspoon ground cloves
  1/2 teaspoon almond extract
Decorations
  Reserved pastry
  1 egg white, lightly beaten
  1 teaspoon water
  Whole almonds (optional)

1. Preheat oven to 425°F. For crust, reserve small amount of pastry for decorative cutouts for top of finished pie.

2. For Almond Layer, combine almonds, brown sugar, butter, flour and almond extract; toss with fork until well blended. Spoon into unbaked pie shell. Press firmly on bottom and partway up side of crust. Refrigerate.

3. For Pumpkin Filling, cream granulated brown sugar and cream cheese in large bowl. Beat in eggs, pumpkin, milk, sour cream and molasses at low speed of electric mixer. Add cinnamon, nutmeg, salt, ginger, cloves and almond extract; beat 1 minute. Spoon over almond layer.

4. Bake 15 minutes. *Reduce oven temperature to 350°F;* bake for 50 to 60 minutes. Cover edge of crust with foil, if necessary, to prevent overbrowning. Cool to room temperature.

5. *Increase oven temperature to 400°F.* Line baking sheet with foil.

6. For Decorations, roll out reserved pastry and cut out desired shapes. Place on baking sheet. Combine egg white and water; brush over pastry cutouts. Garnish each with an almond. Bake 5 to 7 minutes or until golden brown. Cool. Arrange on top of cooled pie.

Makes one 9-inch pie

Traditional Mince Pie

  Pastry for 2-crust pie
  1 jar NONE SUCH® Ready-to-
    Use Mincemeat (Regular
    or Brandy & Rum)
  1 egg yolk plus
    2 tablespoons water,
    optional

Place rack in lowest position in oven; preheat oven to 425°F. Turn mincemeat into pastry-lined 9-inch pie plate. Cover with top crust; cut slits near center. Seal and flute. For a more golden crust, mix egg yolk and water; brush over entire surface of pie.

Bake 30 minutes or until golden. Cool slightly. Garnish as desired. *Makes one 9-inch pie*

Tip: Prepare pastry for 9- or 10-inch 2-crust pie. In saucepan, combine 2 (9-ounce) packages NONE SUCH® Condensed Mincemeat, crumbled, and 3 cups water; bring to a boil. Cook and stir 1 minute. Cool. Turn into pastry-lined pie plate. Proceed as above.

Kiwifruit Meringue Pie

  5 (about 3 oz. *each*)
    California kiwifruit,
    peeled
  1 1/4 cups sugar, divided
  6 tablespoons cornstarch
  1 1/2 cups water
  1 tablespoon lime juice
  1 teaspoon grated lime peel
  4 eggs, separated
  2 tablespoons butter or
    margarine
  One baked 9-inch pie shell

Preheat oven to 375°F. In food processor or blender, puree 2 to 3 kiwifruit to equal 1/2 cup puree. Slice and quarter remaining kiwifruit; set aside.

Combine 1 cup sugar and cornstarch in 2-quart saucepan. Stir in water, kiwifruit puree, lime juice and peel. Cook and stir over medium-high heat until mixture thickens and comes to a full boil. Beat egg yolks in small bowl; blend in small amount of hot liquid. Add egg yolk mixture to hot mixture. Cook over low heat 2 minutes. Stir in butter; cool slightly. Stir in remaining kiwifruit. Pour into prepared pie shell.

Beat egg whites until frothy; gradually add remaining 1/4 cup sugar. Beat until whites hold stiff glossy peaks. Spread meringue on top of pie, sealing carefully to edge of pie shell to prevent shrinking and weeping. Bake 5 minutes or until meringue is lightly browned. Cool completely before serving.

Makes 6 to 8 servings

Favorite recipe from **California Kiwifruit Commission**

Deep Dish Almond Pumpkin Pie

Plum Pudding Pie

⅓ cup plus 2 tablespoons
  KAHLÚA®
½ cup golden raisins
½ cup chopped pitted dates
⅓ cup chopped candied
  cherries
½ cup chopped walnuts
⅓ cup dark corn syrup
½ teaspoon pumpkin pie
  spice
¼ cup butter or margarine,
  softened
¼ cup packed brown sugar
2 tablespoons all-purpose
  flour
¼ teaspoon salt
2 eggs, slightly beaten
1 (9-inch) unbaked pie shell
1 cup whipping cream
  Maraschino cherries
  (optional)

In medium bowl, combine ⅓ cup
of the KAHLÚA®, the raisins,
dates and cherries; mix well.
Cover; let stand 1 to 4 hours.

Preheat oven to 350°F. Stir
walnuts, corn syrup and spice
into fruit mixture. In large bowl,
cream butter, brown sugar, flour
and salt. Stir in eggs. Add fruit
mixture; blend well. Pour into
unbaked pie shell.

Bake 35 minutes or until filling
is firm and crust is golden. Cool
completely on wire rack.

When ready to serve, in small
bowl, beat whipping cream with
remaining 2 tablespoons
KAHLÚA® just until soft peaks
form. Spoon cream into pastry
bag fitted with large star tip and
pipe decoratively on top. If
desired, garnish pie with
maraschino cherries.

Makes 8 servings

Top to bottom: Plum Pudding Pie, Pumpkin & Cream Cheese Tart

Pumpkin & Cream Cheese Tart

Pie crust mix for single 9-inch crust
4 packages (3 ounces each) cream cheese, softened
³/₄ cup packed brown sugar
2 eggs
1 teaspoon ground cinnamon
¼ teaspoon ground nutmeg
1 teaspoon grated orange peel
1 can (16 ounces) solid pack pumpkin
1 can (16 ounces) OCEAN SPRAY® Whole Berry Cranberry Sauce
Glazed Orange Slices (recipe follows)

Preheat oven to 425°F. Prepare pie crust mix according to package directions. Press dough onto bottom and 1½ inches up side of ungreased 9-inch springform pan; set aside.

In large bowl, beat cream cheese and brown sugar until light and fluffy. Beat in eggs, 1 at a time. Stir in cinnamon, nutmeg, orange peel and pumpkin until smooth and well blended. Pour into pastry-lined pan; spread evenly.

Place in 425°F oven; *immediately reduce oven temperature to 350°F.* Bake 35 minutes or until center is almost set. Cool completely in pan on wire rack. Spread whole berry cranberry sauce on top. Arrange Glazed Orange Slices in an overlapping ring on top of the cranberry sauce. Refrigerate until serving time. Remove side of springform pan before serving.

Makes 10 to 12 servings

GLAZED ORANGE SLICES: In medium skillet, combine 1 cup granulated sugar and ¼ cup water. Bring to a boil over medium heat; boil 1 minute. Add 12 thin orange slices. Cook over low heat, turning frequently, 5 minutes or until slices are almost translucent.

Spirited Egg Nog Custard Pie

1 (9-inch) unbaked pastry shell
1 (14-ounce) can EAGLE® Brand Sweetened Condensed Milk (NOT evaporated milk)
1¹/₃ cups warm water
2 tablespoons light rum
1 tablespoon brandy
1 teaspoon vanilla extract
½ teaspoon ground nutmeg
3 eggs, well beaten

Preheat oven to 425°F. Bake pastry shell 8 minutes; remove from oven. In large bowl, combine all ingredients except eggs and pastry shell; mix well. Stir in eggs. Pour into pastry shell.

Bake 10 minutes. *Reduce oven temperature to 325°F;* continue baking 25 to 30 minutes or until knife inserted near center comes out clean. Cool. Chill if desired. Refrigerate leftovers.

Makes one 9-inch pie

Pumpkin Egg Nog Pie

1 (9-inch) unbaked pastry shell
1 (16-ounce) can pumpkin (about 2 cups)
1½ cups BORDEN® or MEADOW GOLD® Egg Nog
2 eggs
½ cup sugar
½ teaspoon ground cinnamon
½ teaspoon salt
¼ teaspoon ground cloves
¼ teaspoon ground ginger

Preheat oven to 425°F. In large mixer bowl, combine all ingredients except pastry shell; mix well. Pour into pastry shell.

Bake 15 minutes. *Reduce oven temperature to 350°F;* bake 40 to 45 minutes longer or until knife inserted near edge comes out clean. Cool. Refrigerate leftovers.

Makes one 9-inch pie

Creamy Eggnog Dessert

Crust
1 package DUNCAN HINES® Moist Deluxe Swiss Chocolate Cake Mix
½ cup butter or margarine, melted
½ cup chopped pecans
Filling
1 package (8 ounces) cream cheese, softened
1 cup sugar
1 container (12 ounces) frozen whipped topping, thawed and divided
2 packages (4-serving size each) French vanilla instant pudding and pie filling mix
3 cups cold milk
¼ teaspoon rum extract
¼ teaspoon ground nutmeg

1. Preheat oven to 350°F.

2. For Crust, combine cake mix, butter and pecans. Reserve ½ cup mixture. Press remaining mixture into bottom of 13×9×2-inch pan. Bake 15 to 20 minutes or until surface is firm. Cool. Toast reserved ½ cup mixture on cookie sheet at 350°F for 3 to 4 minutes, stirring once. Cool completely. Break lumps with fork to make small crumbs.

3. For Filling, beat cream cheese and sugar until smooth in large bowl. Stir in 1 cup whipped topping; spread over cooled crust. Refrigerate. Combine pudding mix and milk in small bowl; beat 1 minute. Add rum extract and nutmeg; spread over cream cheese layer. Spread remaining whipped topping over pudding layer. Sprinkle with reserved toasted mixture. Refrigerate at least 2 hours.

Makes 12 to 16 servings

Linzertorte

- 6 ounces unblanched almonds
- 1 cup butter or margarine, cold
- ½ cup granulated sugar
- 3 egg yolks, slightly beaten
- 1 teaspoon vanilla
  Grated peel of 1 lemon
- 1 teaspoon ground cinnamon
- ¼ teaspoon ground cloves
  Pinch salt
- 1 cup all-purpose flour
- 1 cup raspberry jam
  Powdered sugar

Preheat oven to 350°F. In food processor or blender, process almonds until finely ground; set aside. In large bowl, beat butter until soft and fluffy. Gradually beat in granulated sugar. Add egg yolks and vanilla; blend well. Stir in lemon peel, spices, salt and almonds; mix well. Stir in flour. Wrap one quarter of the dough; refrigerate.

Pat remaining dough evenly onto bottom and 1 inch up side of ungreased 9-inch springform pan. (Crust will be fairly thick.) Spread raspberry jam evenly onto bottom of crust. Roll out chilled dough ½ inch thick on lightly floured surface. Cut into 6 strips, ½ to ¾ inch wide. Arrange strips in diamond-shaped lattice pattern over top of jam.

Bake 45 to 50 minutes or until lightly browned. Cool in pan on wire rack 5 minutes; remove side of pan. Cool completely. Sprinkle with powdered sugar.

Makes 8 servings

Linzertorte

Nutcracker Sweets

Base
- ⅓ cup BUTTER FLAVOR CRISCO®
- ½ cup JIF® Creamy Peanut Butter
- 1½ cups firmly packed brown sugar
- 2 eggs
- 1½ cups all-purpose flour
- 1½ teaspoons baking powder
- ½ teaspoon salt
- ¼ cup milk
- 1 teaspoon vanilla

Frosting and Drizzle
- ¼ cup BUTTER FLAVOR CRISCO®
- ⅔ cup JIF® Creamy Peanut Butter
- 4 cups (1 pound) confectioners' sugar
- ½ cup milk
- ½ cup semi-sweet chocolate pieces

Preheat oven to 350°F. Grease 15×10×1-inch baking pan.

For Base, cream BUTTER FLAVOR CRISCO® and JIF® Creamy Peanut Butter in large bowl at medium speed of electric mixer. Blend in brown sugar. Beat in eggs, one at a time, beating until creamy. Combine flour, baking powder and salt in small bowl; set aside. Combine milk and vanilla in measuring cup. Add dry ingredients and milk mixture alternately to creamed mixture. Mix at low speed of mixer, scraping sides of bowl frequently. Beat until blended. Spread batter into prepared pan. Bake 18 to 20 minutes. Cool.

For Frosting, cream BUTTER FLAVOR CRISCO® and JIF® Creamy Peanut Butter in large bowl at medium speed of electric mixer. Add sugar and milk; beat until fluffy. Spread on cooled cookie base. For Drizzle, melt chocolate pieces on *very* low heat in small saucepan. Drizzle chocolate from end of spoon back and forth over frosting. Cut into 2-inch squares. Refrigerate 15 to 20 minutes until chocolate is firm. *Makes 3 dozen squares*

ACKNOWLEDGMENTS

The publishers would like to thank the companies and organizations listed below
for the use of their recipes in this book.

Almond Board of California
American Dairy Association
American Egg Board
Amstar Sugar Corporation
Arm & Hammer Division, Church &
   Dwight Co., Inc.
Armour Food Company
Best Foods, CPC International
Blue Diamond Growers
Borden Kitchens, Borden, Inc.
California Apricot Advisory Board
California Cling Peach Advisory Board
California Kiwifruit Commission
California Tree Fruit Agreement
Carnation Company
Checkerboard Kitchens, Ralston Purina
   Company
Diamond Walnut Growers, Inc.
Dole Food Company
Fleischmann's® Yeast, Specialty Brands, Inc.
Florida Department of Citrus
Hershey Chocolate U.S.A.
The HVR Company
Keebler Company
Kellogg Company
Kerr Corporation
Kraft General Foods, Inc.
Land O'Lakes, Inc.
Lawry's Foods, Inc.

Leaf Incorporated
Maidstone Wine & Spirits, Inc. (Kahlúa)
McIlhenny Company
Mott's U.S.A., a division of Cadbury
   Beverages Inc.
Nabisco Foods Company
National Cherry Foundation
National Pecan Marketing Council
Nestlé Chocolate and Confection Company
Norseland Foods, Inc.
The North American Blueberry Council
Ocean Spray Cranberries, Inc.
Oklahoma Peanut Commission
Oregon Washington California Pear Bureau
Pet Incorporated
Pollio Dairy Products Corporation
The Proctor & Gamble Company, Inc.
The Quaker Oats Company
Sargento Cheese Company, Inc.
The J. M. Smucker Company
Sunkist Growers, Inc.
Sun-Maid Growers of California
Thomas J. Lipton Company
USA Rice Council
Walnut Marketing Board
Washington Apple Commission
Western New York Apple Growers
   Association, Inc.
Wisconsin Milk Marketing Board

PHOTO CREDITS

The publishers would like to thank the companies and organizations listed below
for the use of their photographs in this book.

American Egg Board
Armour Food Company
Best Foods, CPC International
Blue Diamond Growers
Borden Kitchens, Borden, Inc.
California Apricot Advisory Board
California Kiwifruit Commission
California Tree Fruit Agreement
Carnation Company
Checkerboard Kitchens, Ralston Purina
   Company
Dole Food Company
Hershey Chocolate U.S.A.
The HVR Company
Keebler Company

Kellogg Company
Kerr Corporation
Kraft General Foods, Inc.
Land O'Lakes, Inc.
Lawry's Foods, Inc.
Leaf Incorporated
Mott's U.S.A., a division of Cadbury
   Beverages Inc.
Nabisco Foods Company
National Pecan Marketing Council
Nestlé Chocolate and Confection Company
Ocean Spray Cranberries, Inc.
The Proctor & Gamble Company, Inc.
The J. M. Smucker Company
Wisconsin Milk Marketing Board

INDEX

METRIC CONVERSION CHART

VOLUME MEASUREMENT (dry)

⅛ teaspoon = .5 mL
¼ teaspoon = 1 mL
½ teaspoon = 2 mL
¾ teaspoon = 4 mL
1 teaspoon = 5 mL
1 tablespoon = 15 mL
2 tablespoons = 25 mL
¼ cup = 50 mL
⅓ cup = 75 mL
⅔ cup = 150 mL
¾ cup = 175 mL
1 cup = 250 mL
2 cups = 1 pint = 500 mL
3 cups = 750 mL
4 cups = 1 quart = 1 L

VOLUME MEASUREMENT (fluid)

1 fluid ounce (2 tablespoons) = 30 mL
4 fluid ounces (½ cup) = 125 mL
8 fluid ounces (1 cup) = 250 mL
12 fluid ounces (1½ cups) = 375 mL
16 fluid ounces (2 cups) = 500 mL

WEIGHT (MASS)

½ ounce = 15 g
1 ounce = 30 g
3 ounces = 85 g
3.75 ounces = 100 g
4 ounces = 115 g
8 ounces = 225 g
12 ounces = 340 g
16 ounces = 1 pound = 450 g

DIMENSION

$\frac{1}{16}$ inch = 2 mm
⅛ inch = 3 mm
¼ inch = 6 mm
½ inch = 1.5 cm
¾ inch = 2 cm
1 inch = 2.5 cm

OVEN TEMPERATURES

250°F = 120°C
275°F = 140°C
300°F = 150°C
325°F = 160°C
350°F = 180°C
375°F = 190°C
400°F = 200°C
425°F = 220°C
450°F = 230°C

BAKING PAN SIZES

Utensil	Size in Inches/Quarts	Metric Volume	Size in Centimeters
Baking or	8 × 8 × 2	2 L	20 × 20 × 5
Cake pan	9 × 9 × 2	2.5 L	22 × 22 × 5
(square or	12 × 8 × 2	3 L	30 × 20 × 5
rectangular)	13 × 9 × 2	3.5 L	33 × 23 × 5
Loaf Pan	8 × 4 × 3	1.5 L	20 × 10 × 7
	9 × 5 × 3	2 L	23 × 13 × 7
Round Layer	8 × 1½	1.2 L	20 × 4
Cake Pan	9 × 1½	1.5 L	23 × 4
Pie Plate	8 × 1¼	750 mL	20 × 3
	9 × 1¼	1 L	23 × 3
Baking Dish	1 quart	1 L	
or Casserole	1½ quart	1.5 L	
	2 quart	2 L	